MAN
of the
WORLD

MAN
of the
WORLD

Herbert Bayard Swope:
A Charmed Life
of Pulitzer Prizes, Poker and Politics

Alfred Allan Lewis

THE BOBBS-MERRILL COMPANY, INC.
Indianapolis · New York

For permission to reprint, acknowledgment is made to the following:

The *Nation,* for William P. Beasell's letter to the editor.

Saturday Review, for the Robert E. Sherwood poem.

The Viking Press, Inc., for two letters from *The Letters of Alexander Woollcott,* edited by Beatrice Kaufman and Joseph Hennessey. Copyright 1944 by Beatrice Kaufman and Joseph Hennessey, © renewed 1972 by Joseph Hennessey.

The Viking Press, Inc., for four poems from *The Portable Dorothy Parker.* Copyright 1926, 1954 by Dorothy Parker.

Harper & Row Publishers, Inc., for a rhyme by Franklin P. Adams on p. 26 of *The End of the World: A Post-Mortem,* edited by James W. Barrett. Copyright 1931 by Harper & Row Publishers, Inc.

The Saturday Evening Post, for "Symphony in Brass" by Stanley Walker. Copyright 1938 by the Curtis Publishing Company.

Atheneum Publishers, for excerpts from *Myself Among Others* by Ruth Gordon. Copyright 1970, 1971 by Atheneum Publishers.

Published by The Bobbs-Merrill Company, Inc.
Indianapolis   New York

Designed by Gail Herzog Conwell
Manufactured in the United States of America

First printing

Library of Congress Cataloging in Publication Data
Lewis, Alfred Allan.
    Man of the world.

    Bibliography: p.
    Includes index.
    1. Swope, Herbert Bayard, 1882–1958.   2. Journalists
—United States—Biography.   I. Title.
PN4874.S796L4   070.5'0924 [B]   76-45577
ISBN 0-672-51858-9

To
Margaret Hayes Swope
But for whom and all that

ACKNOWLEDGMENTS

To mention all of the people with whom I spoke and corresponded about the Swopes would take still another volume. To them all, I extend my deepest gratitude. Collectively, they quite literally gave me hundreds of hours of their valuable time. I beg their forgiveness for not mentioning every one of them by name but listing only those who lent some special and very personal observations:

Dr. Alvan L. Barach, Lyda Barclay, Mrs. David Bergman, Jerry Berns, Dr. Harlan Bickerman, Bayard Brandt, Jane Swope Brandt, Abe Burrows, Rose Carlebach, Samuel Barrymore Colt, Marc Connelly, Robert Considine, Kay Cowdin, Mrs. Russel Crouse, Mrs. Howard Cullman, Howard and Lucinda Ballard Dietz, Mrs. Nelson Doubleday, Ruth Dubonnet, Drew Dudley, Francis Dunne, Morris L. Ernst, Douglas and Mary Lee Fairbanks, Jr., James A. Farley, George Field, Mae Fielding, Liz Fitzpatrick, Father George B. Ford, Martin Gabel, Kathleen Gilmore, Monroe Goldwater, Sheilah Graham, Mrs. Harold Guinzberg, William Harbach, W. Averell Harriman, Radie Harris, William Randolph Hearst, Jr., Joseph P. Hennessey, Dorothy Hirshon, Marcella Markham Kingdon, Steve and Betty Comden Kyle, Ring Lardner, Jr., Anita Loos, Clare Boothe Luce, Bert Morgan, Robert Moses, Charles Munn, Michael Pearman, Mrs. Kenneth Powell, Terry Lewis Robinson, Clyde Roche, Irving and Anne Kaufman Schneider, Professor Paul Seabury, Irene Selznick, Liza Shaw, Toots Shor, Arthur and Joan Alexander Stanton, Marti Stevens, Mrs. William Rhinelander Stewart, Ralph Strain, Jule Styne, Frank Sullivan, Herbert Bayard Swope, Jr., Margaret Hayes Swope, Tracy Swope, Howard Teichman, Alfred Gwynne Vanderbilt, Robert F. and Phyllis Cerf Wagner, Carrie Waterbury, Mrs. John N. Wheeler, John Hay Whitney, and William Wolfston.

I was most fortunate in having had access to Swope's voluminous files of correspondence, his scrapbooks, and his desk diaries—all dating back to before World War I and terminating only at his death. The private correspondence of Margaret Powell Swope was also placed at my disposal. Without the generosity of Herbert Bayard Swope, Jr., in making this invaluable material available, the book would not have been possible.

The back issues of the New York *World, New York Times,* New York *Journal American,* St. Louis *Post-Dispatch,* the *Nation, New Yorker,* and *Time* were also sources of information that were of immeasurable help.

CONTENTS

INTRODUCTION

There are those who are great men for all times. The nature of their achievements is seemingly eternal and colors our lives for generations after their deaths. There are also the ones who are great only within their own times: in a sense, this type is a measure of his time. His achievements become remarkable when viewed within a given era and a special place. The latter is also marked by the quality of the people he knew and the style in which he lived. He is one of the celebrities who give to an age its special glamour—the definitive shape, excitement, and tone that provide the substance of nostalgia.

Such a man was Herbert Bayard Swope.

Go to any library. Select at random the biography or autobiography of an important person who landed on the New York City shores at some point during the first half of the twentieth century. Run your finger down the index. You will almost surely come to the listing: Swope, Herbert Bayard.

His fame was so widely broadcast that people all over the world knew the name. They might not have been precisely aware of who he was or what he had accomplished, but they knew the name. He was the epitome of the phrase "legend in his own lifetime." Characters in plays and novels were thinly disguised portraits of him. He gave rise to a stream of puns:

"Where there's life, there's Swope."

"Do not Swope until Swopen to."

"Swope springs eternal."

"The glory of the Swopen word."

"Man cannot live on Swope alone."

He was described as "the most charming extrovert in the Western world." In some promotion copy published in 1925, the *New Yorker* magazine promised that, among other things, it would answer the question "Is there a Herbert Bayard Swope?" Almost a quarter of a century later it had progressed from question of existence to question of essence: it published a piece by E. J. Kahn, Jr., titled "What Is Herbert Bayard Swope?"

Swope started his newspaper career as a reporter. It was soon generally agreed that he was the best reporter in town. In 1917 he won the first Pulitzer Prize ever awarded in journalism for his perceptive reportage in a series of articles collectively titled *Inside the German Empire*. That was the first time the word "inside" was ever used in the title of a book dealing with the internal affairs of a country. It was not long before there was a plethora of "Insides."

As executive editor of the New York *World,* he turned a slumping newspaper into the liveliest daily in town. He left a legacy of journalistic style that lingers on to this day. He invented the Op Ed (opposite editorial) page—and its name—as a forum for airing the journalistic biases of a series of distinguished commentators. It is currently a prominent feature in the *New York Times* among many other papers across the country. Before Briton Haddon co-founded *Time* magazine with Henry Luce, he took a job on the *World* expressly to take notes on the workings of the paper and its editor. The best of the language known as "Timese" can be traced directly back to the Swope style. When Harold Ross started the *New Yorker,* he publicly stated that one of his goals was to capture in a weekly the quality found daily in the *World*. This adds up to quite an impressive journalistic heritage for one man to have left behind. And that was only part of the extraordinary "world" of Swope.

Swope was one of the greatest conversationalists of his time. There were those who carped that sometimes he tended to be a monologist, but even they had to agree that listening to him was a fascinating experience. He was the quintessential dispenser of facts, trivia, and the opinions of his crowd, and that crowd included just about everybody worth knowing.

Supreme Court Justice Felix Frankfurter called Swope the "creator of statesmen." That included elder statesmen. Depending on where one sat in the grandstands, it appeared either that the public image of Bernard M. Baruch was shaped by Swope or that Baruch was the father figure who enabled Swope to live in the magnificent fashion in which he did by helping him in the stock market. The relationship was probably based on an amalgam of both elements.

In the '20s, '30s, and '40s, he and his equally remarkable wife, Margaret, were the most famous and very probably the best host and hostess on the Eastern seaboard. In their New York apartment and at weekend parties in their home, first at Great Neck and later at Sands Point, Long Island, the guests ranged from Noel Coward and Ethel Barrymore, through assorted Vanderbilts and Harrimans, to Winston Churchill and Albert Einstein. The two shifts of servants were part of social folklore. It was said that one could get anything from a hamburger to pheasant under glass at any hour of the day or night.

What follows is the story of the remarkable Swopes—Herbert Bayard and his wife, Maggie—who created a life-style, at work or at play, in the years between the two World Wars, that can never be duplicated.

a filing clerk in a law office and was the sole support of her two younger brothers and her adorable, often exasperating, always beguiling mother.

She could not really afford Sherry's, but she had to be there. It was her school. She leaned over the balcony, carefully observing the fashionable crowd, making mental notes on how they ate and dressed and walked and spoke. Her critical intuition was so keen that, despite her youthful inexperience, she was already able to appreciate who really belonged and to dismiss the parvenu.

It was not merely the patrons who interested her; she memorized the place—linen, crystal, silver, china, table settings, flowers, wall hangings—instinctively disregarding that which was not genuinely tasteful and beautiful. She gladly sacrificed her own lunch and dinner to make up the price of admittance. The late-afternoon repast was served complete with little cucumber and watercress sandwiches, sumptuous pastries, and the ice cream for which the establishment was famous. The "snack" was more than sufficient to satisfy her slight appetite for food, while the rest fed a more profound hunger.

She was realist enough to know that none of these things would ever be of use in her modest Far Rockaway home; it was not a question of snobbish place-dropping, nor was she a phony, with airs above her station. This need was something else; and she could not, for the life of her, define it. She only knew that it was there, and that she rather liked it. She was as pragmatic in her way as Mr. William James, and would always prefer what was there to what was missing.

That afternoon, her pretty young companion was an actress opulently endowed after the fashion of that period. She was excitedly prattling on about an audition she was to have with Florenz Ziegfeld, who was then preparing the second edition of his *Follies*.

Her friend suddenly asked why Margaret did not come along and also audition. Without removing her attention from the activity below her, Margaret asked dryly: "With my bust and derrière? Is Ziegfeld going to glorify the American boy this year?"

Suddenly she gasped. A tall, striking young man had just entered the room. He had a shock of glorious red hair, piercing blue eyes, the ramrod-erect carriage of a military man. Heads were turning; greetings engulfed him. Everything about him commanded attention, from his patrician profile and athlete's physique to the elegance of his attire, complete with spotless spats, gleaming shoes, perfectly cut suit, immaculate chamois gloves, and Malacca cane. Margaret cried, "Who is he?"

Her friend glanced down. "Herbie Swope." She paused for a moment, and then, for some reason, added his full name, as if it were a title. "Herbert Bayard [pronounced By-yard] Swope."

"Do you know him?"

"Slightly. Jack Barrymore introduced us. They used to room together."

Margaret leaped up, pulling her friend to her feet. "Come on. You've got to introduce us."

"Why? He's just an out-of-work reporter."

"Silly ass! He's the man I'm going to marry!"

Although Herbert Bayard Swope was considered the quintessential New Yorker for over a half-century, he actually was born in St. Louis, Missouri, on January 5, 1882. He later described his birthplace as "a sort of nice fat lady."

He was the youngest of the four children of Isaac and Ida Swope. They were a solid middle-class family of German-Jewish ancestry who had prospered in the new world. At the time of Herbert's birth, his father was already fifty-one years old, separated from his youngest child by nearly two generations.

His mother was only thirty-four at the time of his birth, but her life was already being lived vicariously through her two daughters, Golda and Dolly (née Julia), who were, respectively, fifteen and seventeen years Herbert's senior. Previously she had implanted the tired Teutonic strictures into the very being of her elder son, the ten-year-old Gerard—obedience, sobriety, diligence, industry, and punctuality—but for her youngest child, she had only words.

Isaac Swope was such a taciturn man that he was known as "Silent" Swope. He was in the watchmaking business and did not relish any sound louder than a hushed, monotonous ticktock, ticktock. His youngest child's loquaciousness and exuberant outbursts at mealtimes continually resulted in the boy's expulsion from the table.

The Swope uncles owned one of the most prosperous shoe emporiums in the city. They made their deliveries in horse-drawn wagons that were constructed in the shape of a shoe. Herbert loved to hitch rides on these unique conveyances and explore the whole city. He adored the rough drivers who smelled of tobacco and the stables and who, more often than not, turned the reins over to him while they took a break for a pitcher of beer.

There were often detours to the race track at the St. Louis Fair

Grounds, so that the drivers could place some bets. Soon the boy was shouting, "I'll take a quarter of that!"

For all his malingering, Swope's intelligence and scholastic gifts were never seriously doubted. An early ambition to study law at Harvard was given proper consideration. Neither family nor educators thought it beyond his capacities.

Had there been nothing in their basic natures to explain the difference between the two Swope brothers, the effect on the family of the depression of 1893 would have been sufficient.

Suddenly the money was gone, and Gerard was still a year away from his degree at Massachusetts Institute of Technology. That degree came first in the list of priorities; the family would simply have to make sacrifices to allow the older son to complete his education, and Herbert's plans for his future were sacrificed. Not only was he to be sent to a public high school; he could also forget any dream of a college education.

"Silent" Swope had become a poor relation to his brother and sisters, and it was unbearable. He withdrew into a personal depression from which he was never again to emerge. The management of the high-spirited youngest child was left entirely to his mother, and she relied on her older son for help. The result was a series of long and pompous letters lecturing Herbert on behavior, with the writer holding himself up as a model of deportment.

From the youth's point of view, Gerard's lectures were totally unfair and showed a complete lack of understanding of his situation. It was all very well for his brother to go on endlessly about cultivating the solid bourgeois virtues of thrift and modesty. These qualities had not failed Gerard: all that he had ever wanted from his parents, he had received; all of his plans and ambitions had been realized.

In fact, it was obvious that there was no understanding to be found anywhere in his family, and Herbert wanted it desperately. He turned to those who accepted him without question. The carnies and race-track touts thought the kid was a card, a tall-tale teller who could talk faster and funnier than any dude twice his age; and they accepted him as one of their own. When he needed a meal, a drink, a bet, a girl, they helped him to find them. With more adolescent romantic bravura than genuine debauch, he boasted at seventeen: "My ambition is to eat all the food in town, drink all the liquor in town, and sleep with all the women in town."

Isaac Swope, who had long since relinquished his role as head of the family to his older son, died in 1899. Without any thought for the welfare and needs of her youngest offspring, Ida Swope immediately returned to Berlin to spend the next quarter-century living with her daughters, who had both married Germans, and their families. When she did come back to this country, it was that neglected child who took her in for the rest of her life.

His father's estate had come to slightly over seven thousand dollars, and Swope thought he might use his share of it to get started at Harvard. But his loneliness was so overwhelming that he gave up all thought of Harvard and used his legacy to follow his mother to Germany. But in spite of a fluency in the language that enabled him to enroll for courses at the University of Berlin, he was simply too American to live for long in any country other than the United States. He was also too much Herbert Bayard Swope, and it was not long before his sisters' terribly correct families were lifting their eyebrows, wishing woefully that the young man were anyplace but there.

Within the year, Herbert was back in St. Louis and back among companions who accepted him for what he was. He took a job as cashier at the race track, a position that pleased him as much as it alarmed his family and their friends.

Emergency messages went out to every connection in St. Louis: "Get that boy off the race track!"—while the boy was having the time of his life. He flourished in the atmosphere of the place: the seediness, the violence, the high spirits, the free-wheeling, easy come–easy go atmosphere, the rhythmic beat of the hoofs against the counterpoint of the roaring crowd—it was his kind of music. The concert halls of Berlin could not hold a candle to the fast, catchy magic of this American ragtime.

Life was a gamble, high stakes, winner take all; and, if you lost, so what?—there was always tomorrow and another crack at the brass ring. Money was a game and not a god. How that notion rocked the starched, thrifty German-American community in which he had grown up! They might have closed their minds and locked their doors to him, but he was still one of them. Something had to be done.

Henry Ittleson, who was later to make a great fortune as the founder of Commercial Investment Trust (CIT), was married to one of Dolly Swope's best friends. As manager of the St. Louis branch of the May Company, he had access to the newspapers through the large amount of advertising that was placed through him. He sent Herbert to see Florence D. White, who was the city editor of the St. Louis *Post-Dispatch*.

The *Post-Dispatch* was the logical choice for Ittleson. In a sense, it was aligned to the closely knit community of the Swopes and their friends. The publisher and owner was an Austro-Hungarian Jew named Joseph Pulitzer. He had emigrated to this country as a mercenary hired by an American agent to serve in the union army during the Civil War. After the armistice, he moved west to St. Louis. He thought that his chances for making his way in the United States would be better there because of the large German-speaking population. He became both a naturalized citizen and a reporter on the German-language daily, the *Westliche Post*. Within five years he owned the paper. Within another five, he owned the English-language *Post-Dispatch* and had married into the family of Jefferson Davis, former president of the Confederacy. The Yankees might have brought him to America, but the South annexed him through marriage.

Pulitzer was a gambler, a man with an eye on the main chance, and a great journalist. In short, he was the perfect hero for young Swope. There was even a slight physical resemblance between the two. When Swope later became executive editor of Pulitzer's New York *World,* the similarities combined to give rise to some outlandish speculation. A rumor circulated alleging that Swope was Pulitzer's illegitimate son. After all, the gossipers reasoned, how could an obscure immigrant couple have created such a unique creature as Herbert Bayard Swope? They failed to take into account that the same couple had produced the equally unique if totally different Gerard Swope, who was to become president of General Electric.

As a reporter, Swope did five things brilliantly: 1. He could get a story. 2. He could write it very quickly. 3. He could make it extremely readable. 4. He could give monumental significance to the most insignificant event. 5. He never spared the words.

Once very early in his career he was dashing off a rather lengthy story when an editor approached and asked what page he was on. When Swope answered that he was on the eleventh, the editor said: "Well, sonny, you just number the next page three, and you can go on from there."

When Swope was hired for the *Post-Dispatch,* it was the beginning of a long association with both the Pulitzer papers and Florence D. White (a man, despite his name), although it would have been difficult to predict it at the time. The young man obviously had the makings of a good newspaperman, but he was a cocky teenager with little control over his youthful egocentricity. Swope later admitted that he had been a hellion and that he had sorely tried White's patience. He said bemusedly, "If I had been my editor in those days, I wouldn't have lasted out the week."

One can well imagine how incensed the old hands were by this young pup who could talk as good a story as he wrote, who was always sure of his facts, and who took it on himself to correct any mistakes they might make by rattling off statistics with an aggravating speed and a dazzling accuracy.

During his brief tenure on the paper, he was suspended three times, twice for fighting in the city room. The third suspension came from playing football under an assumed name for St. Louis University in a game against Christian Brothers College. In those days it was common practice for colleges to hire outside help. It was no more corrupt than the contemporary practice of offering athletic scholarships with huge allowance and living-expense clauses to young athletes who are not expected to perform in the classroom but whose performances on the playing field can be enormously lucrative to the school in terms of gate receipts and television contracts.

Swope, a natural athlete, was offered ten dollars but received only three. There was nothing he could do about it, no court in which to appeal dishonest practices in illegal deals, and Swope was understandably furious. But playing a little football on the side hardly justified suspension from the paper. Many reporters indulged in moonlighting to stretch their incomes. The real reason for his punishment was that the team he had helped to defeat happened to be Editor White's alma mater. Swope exclaimed: "Damn! Had I known then what I learned about how St. Louis pays, I should have played for the Christian Brothers. With a name like that, they've got to know the first commandment of the New Testament: Thou shalt not cheat a sporting man."

He was earning eight dollars a week, which gave him cause to do a little gloating to Gerard. With a first-rate education and a brilliant record at MIT, his brother had started at Western Electric in Chicago at a salary of only six dollars a week. One can envision the righteous young engineer banking three of the six. The only bank that would see four of Herbert's eight would be at the black jack table.

The budding journalist, in the chips, immediately began to emulate his cronies at the track. When a sport gets his hands on some extra cash, the first thing he does is invest it in sprucing up, the theory being that a dapper front inspires confidence. At seventeen Swope became the first and only reporter in St. Louis to wear a pair of spotless pearl-gray spats.

His spell of high life was short-lived. White finally let him go because he was seeking far too many stories at the race track. Where else could a young man in spats pass as part of the crowd?

Not long after Herbert was fired, Western Electric transferred Gerard to St. Louis, and he brought his new bride back to live in the family home. The young woman was the daughter of a wealthy banker. Gerard had met her at Jane Addams's Hull House, where a young man could manage to make the acquaintance of an incipient Lady Bountiful while turning a good deed.

The city was too small to contain both Herbert and his spatless, spotless brother. He quickly took himself off to replace Gerard in Chicago, where he found a job as a copy reader on the Chicago *Tribune*. When an opening came up for a reporter on the far less important daily *Inter-Ocean,* he took it.

At the turn of the century, Chicago was a great newspaper town, with a collection of reporters who wrote the most colorful and readable copy in the country. They were fearless, hard-drinking, two-fisted womanizers, and Swope felt at home immediately.

Swope's Chicago was obviously a vastly different city from the one that his brother knew. Gerard had devoted his spare time to worthy social projects like Hull House. Herbert's social projects never took him out of the less than two-square-mile district known as the Loop, except, of course, in pursuit of a story. Gerard probably never entered the area except in pursuit of business.

The Loop was ablaze with brightly lit theaters, restaurants, and bars. It had a night life more brazen than any that the young man had ever known, with brawls, bets, booze, and babes all easy to find. Given his zest for life, his youth, and his stamina, Swope could be profligate in the pleasure he took in all of it.

Within a year of his arrival in Chicago, Swope was sought out by a scout for the New York *Herald*. Simply to state the fact that he had been offered and had signed a contract was not in keeping with the Swope style. He had to make a story of it, even if it cast him in a less favorable light than the truth did.

"I took this flathead from the *Herald* off on a toot and got him thoroughly soused. The next morning, he had a hangover as big as Lake Michigan. But he also had a new reporter. He regretted the former, but it's my opinion that he was fairly well satisfied with the latter."

The *Herald* was a morning paper, and Swope's duties did not begin until about two in the afternoon. Swope was always able to write faster and often better than his colleagues. He soon realized that he could complete what was expected of him in about one-eighth of the time allocated to the task. As his adventures in exploring New York's gaudy high and low lives started to last until closer and closer to sunrise, his appearances in the newspaper office started to get closer and closer to sunset. The editor, Leo Redding, complained, and the young reporter replied cockily: "Leo, admit it. Whenever I come in, I'm still worth more than any two other men you've got on your staff."

Swope found the perfect playmate for his early morning carousing in the actor John Barrymore. Deciding to join forces, they took a furnished flat in the Times Square area. The new lights of Broadway did not cause either of them to lose any sleep, because they were seldom home before they were turned off. If one or the other did chance to be at home during the hours when the streets were still aglow, it was a safe bet that he was not alone—and if in bed, engaged in an activity a bit more athletic than sleep.

There were great similarities between the two young men. They were exactly the same age. Both had striking physical appearances and commanding, ebullient personalities. They were extremely attractive to and attracted by women. Both were newspapermen—Barrymore was employed as an illustrator on the *Evening Journal*. Each had responded to familial restraints with rebellion. In Barrymore's case, he had resolved, in defiance of three generations of theatrical tradition, to become a painter. His brother Lionel was appearing with his uncle John Drew in an epic titled *The Mummy and the Humming Bird*. His twenty-two-year-old sister Ethel had become an overnight star just one year before in Clyde Fitch's *Captain Jinks of the Horse Marines*. When she had taken the play to London to repeat her triumph, a feisty young stage-door Johnny named Winston Churchill had proposed marriage and had been firmly turned down.

That year, Ethel was back in New York starring in something called *A Country Mouse* and proving she wasn't one by daring to appear in men's trousers in the curtain raiser, *Carrots*. She first met Swope when John took him around to meet her after a performance. The young beauty looked him over from the vantage point of her two years' seniority. She said: "He can't be a friend of yours, Jack. He's not drunk, and he isn't asking for a handout." She looked a little closer. "Or is he?"

The profound difference between the friends lay in their choice of addictive vices. For Barrymore it was alcohol, and it both ruined his extraordinary talent and shortened his life. The distinguished part of his career, which included being the greatest Hamlet of his generation, ended years before his death at the age of sixty.

Swope was a gambling man. Playing cards and the horses is a far more acceptable social vice than drinking. Alcoholics are generally shunned, but the big bettors are romantic, extremely likable rogues who give a great deal of vicarious pleasure to those too timid to do anything but stand by and watch.

By 1903 the New York whirl was temporarily over for both of the young men. Swope was spending more time (and making more money) in the poker and pool parlors than in the city room, and the *Herald* was forced to let him go. He took a job as an advance road press agent for the theatrical producers Klaw and Erlanger.

At the same time, Barrymore decided not to fight destiny and opted for an acting career. He was in Chicago appearing in *Magda,* a somber Germanic epic by Hermann Sudermann. There was nothing somber about his reunion with Swope when his pal blew into the Windy City in advance of a rather turgid adaptation of Dickens's *A Tale of Two Cities*.

The new press agent happily introduced the new actor to all of the haunts that he had discovered during his tenure on the *Inter-Ocean*. It was their last fling together. They drifted apart in the years that followed. The newspaperman's base remained New York City, while the actor went off to Hollywood to become one of the most successful romantic stars in films.

The two men would occasionally meet in later years, when they happened to be in the same city at the same time. In the '30s, two reunions were engineered by Swope's son. Young Herbert had heard dozens of stories about the actor's escapades and longed to meet him. When he read in a gossip column that Barrymore was "drying out" at the New York Hospital, he urged his father to take him along on a visit. He later recalled:

> The visit was emotional, laughing, nostalgic. Pop was going out for the evening, so he was clad in dinner jacket with a black homburg and vicuna coat and white silk scarf. Barrymore and Pop together, reminiscing, caused the hospital room to fill with such active memories that one could sense the presence of beautiful women, the smell of fine cooking, the click of a roulette wheel, the adventures of two young and handsome rogues about town in a much more romantic era. I felt like an anachronism.
>
> After all the boasting about past escapades, Barrymore asked my father to bring him up to date on the news of New York during the years he'd been wasting in Hollywood. One piece of gossip brought forth the sharp Barrymore wit. Some time before, Bennett Cerf had married the actress Sylvia Sidney in a secret ceremony on a Carib-

bean island. Pop described the arrival of Miss Sidney: "She had on a blonde wig, dark glasses, and a large hat with a veil." Barrymore took a huge puff on his cigarette, raised his left eyebrow up to his hairline, and said: "Hmm . . . otherwise nude, I presume."

The second meeting was sadder. Barrymore had returned to Broadway in a trite little comedy called *My Dear Children,* which was a hit only because of the Barrymore presence. We went to supper at Twenty-One, after the show, with the actor; the young woman he'd married, Elaine Barrie; and her mother and stepfather, Mr. and Mrs. Jacobs. Barrymore had a bad cold, and his nose would drip ever so slightly. Elaine or her mother, busily talking to my father, would lean over and tell Barrymore to blow his nose, like a small child. I felt embarrassment and shock, for he had been my boyhood hero. He was not drinking, as I recall—perhaps some wine or beer. Suddenly he turned to me and told me, in detail, how he planned to do *Macbeth* entirely in its Scottish form—settings, costumes, language. He said: "Imagine how strong, how tough, those Scots were. They went around in icy winter, clad in kilts." His voice rose to the same pitch that had hypnotized audiences and critics on both sides of the Atlantic. "Why, their balls must have been made of *iron!*"

Swope, Sr., saw Barrymore for the last time during one of the illnesses that led to his death in 1942. The prematurely aged actor grasped the hand of his still vigorous friend. "Herb, it was a great party, wasn't it?"

With tears in his eyes, Swope patted the dying man's shoulder. "One of the greatest, Jack. I wouldn't have missed it for anything."

"But you, you wily old fox, you knew when to go home."

Swope looked away for a moment. He murmured: "Did I? I wonder." Then he looked back and smiled enigmatically. "You're going to beat the rap, flathead. You'll see."

Theatrical drum-beating was not for Swope; he was a newspaperman. He returned to New York and took a job as reporter on the *Morning Telegraph.* It was a paper with a large section devoted to news of the turf. If there was any truth to the allegation that the track was Swope's greatest love, he should have been very happy there. He was not. For all its inadequacies, the *Herald* was a paper committed to the real news of the day, and so was Swope. He started to badger Leo Redding, making large promises to mend his ways, and finally persuaded him to reinstate him in his old job.

Despite his promises, Swope continued to make the rounds of the fashionable cafés, with frequent stops at the gambling houses, mixing with equal ease among the swells and the sports. He was the first to know whenever anything interesting was happening to those who made the news in the city. This made him doubly valuable to the *Herald,* a paper that devoted much of its space to the activities of the very people who considered Swope the only reporter around worthy of being called "friend."

He began to carry a very elegant walking stick, prompted at first more by physical necessity than by any desire to appear the fashion plate— during this period, Swope received a bullet just above his knee that he would carry for the rest of his life. He sometimes referred to it as a Heidelberg dueling scar that slipped, but finally admitted to his wife: "My dear, it was a case of not getting my leg through the window fast enough to satisfy a rather irate husband who arrived home much earlier than expected."

She nodded and observed dryly: "It's a good thing you're an athlete. One step slower, and you'd never have been able to sit down again."

When the British Rear Admiral Prince Louis of Battenberg visited New York City, it was only natural that the *Herald* should send its best society reporter to follow him around. The Prince went slumming late one evening in Chinatown, where he visited an infamous establishment known as "Nigger Mike" Salter's. The place was attractive to the uptown carriage trade for two reasons: it had a reputation for being a favorite haunt of opium smugglers and white slavers (although there was no record of any society belle ever having been transported by either vice), and it offered the best ragtime in town. One of the singing waiters was a soulful-eyed Russian immigrant named Israel Baline. When the Prince tipped Izzy a dime, those eyes widened in awe and he muttered, "I'm going to frame it." The incident was dutifully reported in the *Herald* the next morning.

Within the next few years, there were interesting name switches involving both Baline and Battenberg. Israel Baline established himself as a successful songwriter. A man of great social ambition, he took his first step "up" by renouncing his perfectly good Russian-Jewish name to align himself with his lofty German co-religionists. Thenceforth, he bore the same last name as the capital of their homeland—he became Irving Berlin.

For Prince Louis, who was related by marriage to the British royal family, the German sound of his name was a source of embarrassment.

Even though the royal family actually carried more German than English blood in its blue veins, when hostilities broke out between England and Germany in 1914 it was considered politic for the king to disguise all relationship to his cousins along the Rhine (including the Kaiser), and Prince Louis of Battenberg, born in Gratz, became Louis Mountbatten, the Marquis of Milford Haven.

The night of the expedition to Nigger Mike's and the events of the following morning were dutifully chronicled by Alexander Woollcott in his biography of Irving Berlin: "Thus, it befell that the next day Irving Berlin made his first appearance in the public prints. The reporter who thus exploited him was a ruddy and impressive lad named Swope."

By 1907 Swope was once again bored by the mediocrity of the *Herald*. All of his good resolves had been forgotten. At the end of that year, the paper and he parted company—this time for good.

Swope was then twenty-five years old, and he began to take stock of his future. He knew that the only newspaper that really suited his style was Pulitzer's New York *World*. He asked for a job, but there were no openings at the time. He would wait. He took a sporting risk and decided to keep himself available by living off his earnings as a gambler. It was during this period that Margaret Honeyman Powell entered and changed his life.

TWO

Maggie Powell knew at first glance that she was going to marry Herbert Swope, and that he would have little to say in the matter beyond the appropriate question at the appropriate moment. However, it did not take her very much longer to realize that it was not going to be easy or, more to the point, that there was nothing in Herbert's life about which he had little to say. But she was not deterred for a second.

Maggie's mother, Jane Black Powell, known as Mimi, was born in Edinburgh. Mimi's father was an elder in the Scotch Presbyterian Church, but Maggie had inherited none of the traditional Scottish qualities of thrift and prudence. There was as little in her antecedents as there was in Swope's to suggest the human beings that they both eventually became. On almost every level they were two people very largely created by and for each other.

Maggie was born on April 3, 1889, in Far Rockaway, New York. Her mother was a lovable and mild-mannered woman whose daughter completely dominated her life almost from the moment she entered the world. Her father, James Scott Powell, was a secretive man possessed of a wayward charm that completely entranced his daughter. He was employed as a conductor on the Long Island Railroad, but there is at least one indication that he was a man of greater culture than his position in life would signify. His firstborn was named for her maternal grandmother, Margaret Honeyman. But he thoroughly detested his mother-in-law and refused to call his daughter by that name. Margaret is derived from the Greek word *margarités,* which means pearl, so from the beginning he called the child Pearl—his Pearl of great value. It was a name that she also permitted her closest friends to use.

The child bore a close physical resemblance to her father. They both looked slightly like American Indians, and Powell claimed to have some Indian blood. True or not, it was a notion that appealed to his daughter. She always sided with the redskins of this world and was not likely to root for a cowboy or anybody else simply because he was considered a good guy.

The first few years of Margaret's life revolved around her father. She would not have her dinner until he came home with the little present he bought her each day. When he took to coming home less and less frequently, she continued to wait, thinking he would be forced to come home soon, for he would not let his child go without food. It was a naïve belief that seldom was rewarded by his appearance.

By the time she had reached her eleventh year, the girl knew that her beloved father was a definite alcoholic. When her mother said that he was too ill to come down in the morning, she understood without further comment that he was sleeping off the previous night's binge. He was a fastidious man despite his addiction and hated things like window shades that were not drawn to the same level in all windows. On those mornings that she awaited his first appearance, the child went around the house leveling shades, fluffing cushions, placing objects at the angles she knew were most pleasing to him. Everything had to be perfect by the time he came down; then he would be in a good mood, and he might return without delay that evening with her present, and they would be happy, and he would know that he didn't need drink or anything else so long as he had her. It seldom worked.

Powell would go out again as soon as he'd slept off the last binge. Then he was gone forever, and his daughter was left with the conviction that if she loved somebody, she had to keep him with her, to hold on possessively with all of her strength, or she would lose him. "Out of sight, out of mind." She would say that years later, tossing off the cliché a little too lightly.

James Powell died during the same year that his youngest child, Bruce, was born, and Mimi was utterly helpless. There was no money. She had an infant son and an older one, Kenneth, still in grade school. She did not know where to turn. Margaret cradled her forlorn mother in her arms and, rocking her gently to and fro, murmured soothingly: "Don't worry, Mimi, darling. We'll manage. I'll see to that. I'll get a job. I'm going to take care of the boys and you."

She did not have to go far in her search for employment. In those days, Far Rockaway was a middle-class resort within easy commuting distance of the city. The Powells made some extra money by renting their house for the summer and moving in with Mimi's relatives, the Blacks. Their tenant was a rising young attorney named James N. Rosenberg. His practice was expanding rapidly, and he hired Margaret as a file clerk. She had neither the training nor the experience to qualify for more lofty employment and considered herself lucky to have gotten the job.

For the young attorneys in the office, her diminutive beauty was enhanced by the modesty and reserve with which she conducted herself. They made the typical masculine error of confusing her lack of interest in them with old-fashioned virtue. When Margaret did become interested in a man, there was nothing old-fashioned about the way she made her feelings known to him.

Swope was fascinated by her from the very beginning. He had never known a girl quite like her. The females of his acquaintance fell into one of two categories: good girls or good sports.

The good girls were the sort he could safely introduce to his brother Gerard, but, aside from that, he had very little use for them. He had to respect them too much to enjoy them.

The good sports were the sort whom he hurried across the street should Gerard be approaching from the opposite direction. But they were fun. They enjoyed making the rounds with him and being a part of his normal life.

Pearl Powell was both a good sport and a good girl. He nicknamed her Pug because she was like an adorable puppy clinging to him, always underfoot, never letting him get away. The milk train was often her means of transportation at the end of an evening with Swope. She would arrive at Far Rockaway just before dawn, to find a weary Mimi waiting up for her. Then she would grab a few hours of sleep and be off again to clock in at the office by nine.

Her daughter's new life was too much for Mimi to bear silently. This gambler was changing Pearl's way of living. She had to speak her mind, and one morning when Pearl walked in a few steps ahead of the rising sun, she confronted her in the kitchen and insisted she change her ways. Pearl was ruining her reputation, her health; causing her mother too much anxiety. "And for what?" she cried. "For that bum! He doesn't even have a steady job. He couldn't marry you if he wanted to. And I don't think he does or ever will."

Pearl picked up a kitchen knife and weighed it menacingly in her hand. "I love you very much, Mimi. I swear—I'll always take care of you. But I'd rather see you dead than risk losing him."

Their eyes held for a moment, and then they fell weeping into each other's arms. Pearl had made her choice, right or wrong, at the risk of everything she held dear. She wanted Swope and would hang on until she got him. She could live without him, but she would only be existing, marking time as she fulfilled her obligations. He was adventure, the color and pulse of her being.

Their evenings fluctuated with his luck. When he was riding a winning streak, they would start off with dinner at Rector's or Delmonico's. After dinner, they would be off to the theater. The variety was limitless, with more than forty legitimate theaters and nearly two hundred new productions each season, not to mention the six first-rate vaudeville houses with new bills weekly. One night they went to see *Tillie's Nightmare,* in which Marie Dressler became the toast of the town singing "Heaven Will Protect the Working Girl." Pearl prayed that she was right.

When things were not going well for Swope, it would be the places where he had charge accounts, like Churchill's or Browne's Chop House on Broadway. He was one of the founding members of the White Squadron, a group of fast and furious talkers who met weekly at Browne's for food and conversation. At one of the first meetings, Swope introduced and proposed for membership a fast-talking young vaudevillian turned songwriter. He predicted: "This kid's going places. You wait and see."

They did not have to wait long. The kid's name was George M. Cohan. Within two years, he was writing and starring in a musical titled

George Washington Jr. One of the songs he wrote and introduced in it was "You're a Grand Old Rag." The audience did not take kindly to the title. Swope was among the first to come backstage on opening night and suggest that he change "rag" to "flag." The composer agreed and speedily sold over a million copies of sheet music.

Browne's functioned as Swope's private post office. In those days of his changing fortunes, he switched hotels too often to keep one as a permanent address. He was usually one step ahead of a furious manager waving an unpaid bill. Under the circumstances, the hotels were not likely to be very good about forwarding his mail.

Churchill's also had its advantage for him. There was generally a good poker game going on in the back room. To find some action, all Swope had to do was change tables after dinner.

When things were really grim, there was always a hash house in the disreputable, gaudy district called the Tenderloin. It was a blatant strip of pool halls, saloons, and whorehouses that stretched west of Eighth Avenue toward a residential section known as Hell's Kitchen. The Tenderloin was not noted for the honesty of its poker games, nor was it populated with what might be described as good losers. Swope was neither a timid winner nor one to suffer cheats patiently. A free-for-all was sometimes the climax of the night's festivities.

Although Pearl rarely fought with Swope in those early days, she was not at all averse to a good fight with anybody else. As he waded into the fray, he would hand her his pince-nez and walking stick. She would carefully put away the glasses and would have cheerfully used the cane to club anybody who might be proving too much for him to handle alone. It did not prove necessary.

Pearl was not always the little helpmate. When sufficiently provoked, she could and did wield that stick against her lover. The two had a date for the opening of the *Ziegfeld Follies of 1910*. She was to pick up the tickets and then meet him for something to eat at the Knickerbocker Hotel, across Times Square from the theater. She was particularly keen on seeing the show because of a new girl named Fanny Brice, whom Ziggie described as "the vamp from the Lower East Side."

Swope did not turn up at the hotel until after eleven. Knowing Pearl, he was not surprised to find that she was still waiting. He bent over to explain that a winning streak in a crap game had detained him. Expecting her customary approbation, he started to tell her about it. "I was so hot—"

At that moment, his temperature was considerably reduced by a cold shower of shredded tickets being poured over his head. As he picked the pieces out of his hair, she smiled sweetly and said: "Shall we order?"

Swope sat down with as much dignity as he could muster. "I think I've lost my appetite."

"That's funny. I'm starving." Beckoning to the maître d', she ordered every expensive dish and, as Swope later described it, "proceeded to eat herself even."

The next day he used his winnings to buy her a handsome diamond ring. She asked: "Does this mean we're engaged?"

It was one of the few times in his life when he was speechless. He had only thought of the ring in terms of a peace offering. "Uh . . . uh . . . let's call it a long-term investment. I wouldn't want to rush you into anything."

She kissed him and said: "Herbert, you're so impetuous. You just sweep a girl right off her feet."

He really did regard the ring as a long-term investment. It was in and out of hock with every turn in his fortunes. She never questioned his need for it, nor did she ever doubt that it would eventually be returned to her. She loved the excitement of living on the turn of a card, on a lucky roll at the crap table.

The notorious gambler Arnold Rothstein was a close friend of Swope during the first two decades of this century. It was a friendship that Pearl never completely understood. Undoubtedly, Rothstein was responsible for getting Swope into many of the big games. There were grounds to suspect that he might have helped the young journalist when his luck was running low. He was certainly a source of hot tips at the track.

It was a relationship that opened Swope to criticism no matter how he handled it. In the beginning, he was accused of opportunism, of getting close to a shady character in order to have a source of inside stories as well as for reasons of personal gain. Later, when Rothstein became involved in almost every form of illegality, Swope was forced to drop him. By then he was the executive editor of an important newspaper and could not maintain a friendship with somebody who asked for the wrong kind of favors in regard to the manner in which the press handled his criminal activities. The very same people who initially accused him of opportunism for associating with Rothstein then accused him of opportunism for dropping him.

The truth was that there was something at work that was deeper than the profit motive. Swope saw in Rothstein a kind of alter ego. They both came from and were in rebellion against a solid middle-class family background. They had a similar fascination with Broadway high life and hobnobbing with the swells. The two were addicted to gambling and kept an eye on the main chance. When they first became close, Swope was out of work, and there is no doubt that Rothstein's life as a professional gambler offered an alluring alternative to regular employment.

More and more, Rothstein became Swope's dark mirror image. Swope could look and see much of himself in that reflection. He soon realized that it was the negative part of himself that was staring back at him, the part he disliked and feared the most. It was his weakness rather than his strength, his indolence rather than his industry, his opportunism rather than his ambition, his shrewdness rather than his intelligence. Still, there was something perversely attractive about the portrait, and it took all of his strength to turn away from Rothstein and make a new start at his career. He derived some of this strength from his deepening involvement with Pearl. The "love of a good woman" who was also a good sport was no negligible factor in the reshaping of his life.

One indication of the depth of Pearl's feeling for Swope: in August 1909 she accepted his invitation to accompany him to Saratoga for the racing season. It was the sort of thing that no respectable girl would dare to do, but under her lover's careful tutelage she was rapidly becoming a daring modern. She was not hypocrite enough to allow a reputation for chastity to outweigh their need for each other.

She asked: "By the way, who's going to be my chaperone?"

"Arnold Rothstein."

She nodded gravely. "Thanks. My mother will be so relieved. Do you think white slavery is preferable to black slavery?"

He shrugged. "I'm an abolitionist."

There was to be another great attraction at Saratoga in addition to the races: Rothstein's marriage to a beautiful showgirl named Carolyn Green. Pearl's comment on that: "Going along on somebody else's honeymoon has always been one of my greatest ambitions."

Carolyn Rothstein and Pearl became friends. When she was criticized for maintaining a relationship with "that sort of woman," Pearl retorted: "She's more of a lady than most of the ladies I know."

In 1909 Swope received a message from Sherman W. Morse, the city editor of the New York *World,* who had been on the *Herald* with him and knew he could be a first-rate reporter when forced to work at the top of his form. Morse offered him a job paying seven dollars a week plus space rates.

Swope hesitated for a moment. The basic pay was one dollar less than he had received on his first newspaper job with the *Post-Dispatch*. He could make many times that amount in one evening at cards.

But he could lose it just as easily.

He needed the stability of a career, because he was thinking of settling down—or was he? Was he actually capable of settling down? That was a gamble, too, and an exciting one. He was putting his money on himself without hedging the bet. He was optimistic enough to think the odds were in his favor.

Besides, he thought, there would be time for cards and horses; there always had been before. Reading his mind, Morse warned him: "This time, the newspaper's going to have to be more than an avocation. There'll be no more hanging around the track and gambling halls on the pretext of looking for stories. You'll take the assignments I give you, and you'll do your best with them."

Swope was silent for a moment, and then he nodded. "Agreed. I'll take the job."

THE WORLD

THREE

"This is Swope. Swope of the *World*."

That was how he started his telephone conversations, and the telephone was a necessary appendage to his existence. One of his physician friends observed that if ever an operation were performed on Swope's ear, the surgeon would undoubtedly find a telephone embedded in it. Arthur Krock later said that Swope made the telephone as necessary an accessory to a gentleman's evening apparel as cuff links.

By the start of 1911, Swope had become one of the *World*'s leading reporters. On March 13 of that year Clarence Darrow and Carl Meyer arbitrated a strike at the clothing manufacturing firm of Hart, Schaffner, and Marx in Chicago. Sidney Hillman represented the employees, and the contract that was hammered out led to his organizing the Amalgamated Clothing Workers of America three years later. For the first time, the rights of employer, employee, and union were defined.

The year before this landmark decision, there was a strike in New York City of the ladies' shirtwaist makers, known in labor history as "the uprising of the 20,000." The settlement granted the workers a fifty-two-hour week (formerly they had worked an eighty-four-hour week) and an increase in wages. It did not, however, provide for a closed shop, nor did it eliminate the horrendous conditions of the sweatshop factory.

Swope had followed both events closely. On Saturday afternoon, March 25, 1911, while the more affluent citizens of New York City were devoting themselves to the quiet pleasures of home, family, and leisure, a calamitous fire broke out in the Triangle Shirtwaist Company, a non-union sweatshop in a building just east of Washington Square. The disaster was not unrelated to what had happened in Chicago less than two weeks before, and Swope was among the first to make the connection. Realizing that the working class would demand some display of concern from the civic government, he broke in on a press conference being held by the District Attorney, Charles S. Whitman. As the conventional release was being handed out, the Swope voice boomed: "That will be enough, boys. The Triangle building's on fire, and I think the D.A. ought to be there."

He gathered them together, and, amid the wail of police sirens (a sound that always quickened the Swope pulse), he led them uptown to the scene of the disaster. The Swope interest in a story was always proprietary.

Within a half-hour, he had them all back in the District Attorney's office. Addressing the other reporters, he said: "I think this is what the D.A. should say for the morning papers."

Whitman realized that he was incapable of finding the words that would mollify the public, so he allowed Swope to dictate the statement that was carried in the District Attorney's name by all of the papers. So impressive were the words that the reporter then and later put into Whitman's mouth that they eventually carried the man to the Governor's mansion.

The March 26 Sunday edition of the *World* carried this two-line banner headline across the top of the front page just under the masthead:

154 KILLED IN SKYSCRAPER FACTORY FIRE: SCORES BURN, OTHERS LEAP TO DEATH

Beneath it were two large photographs. One showed the exterior of the building, still very much intact, and the other its interior wreckage and debris. The entire page was given over to Swope and his reportage of the fire, in which he underscored the fact that there was only one fire escape to service the entire ten-story building and that seven hundred workers, mostly girls, were trapped inside, with no means of exit.

The rest of the papers also carried the fire story on their front pages. In response to public demand, regulations governing safety measures against fire in public buildings were strengthened and enforced. Equally far-reaching were the changes the tragedy helped initiate in child labor laws and the impetus it gave to greater unionization of the ladies' garment workers and the elimination of the sweatshop.

A good fire is always news, and the Triangle Shirtwaist blaze would assuredly not have gone unnoticed even without Swope, but it is doubtful that the highly competitive press of the period would have followed up quite so avidly had he kept the story to himself and not shared the statement that he had improvised for Whitman.

Not yet in his thirtieth year, Swope of the *World* had definitely "arrived" in New York City. No longer did he have to hustle into places, blustering at all and sundry: "What's new? What's new!" (In Swope's stentorian tone, it was an exclamation as well as a question.) If anything really was new, people sought him out to tell him about it. There was a certain cachet in being able to boast: "I gave the story to Swope."

As husband material Swope was still of questionable quality. But Margaret hung on, knowing what was best for both of them, and finally prevailed. The wedding was set for January 10, 1912, in Baltimore, Maryland. The city was selected for its distance from family and its proximity to H. L. Mencken, whom Swope wanted to act as his best man. He thought that Mencken had the most controversial mind he had ever encountered. To the objective observer this might have seemed an odd qualification for participating in a wedding, but Swope couldn't resist controversy even in love. Neither could Margaret. Her perfect marriage was like her perfect meals—all the better for a little spice.

The ceremony was only one in a series of Swope's Baltimore visits with Mencken. On an earlier occasion, the touring company of a Nora Bayes musical was in town, and the future groom and best man invited six of the chorus girls from the show—aptly titled *The Jolly Bachelors*—to accompany them to the most notorious whorehouse in the city. The madam and some of her charges were inhospitable enough to set upon their new visitors with such violence that many others present were obliged to flee in varying states of disarray and dishabille, for the paddy wagon could be heard rattling around the corner. The two newspapermen virtuously took the police officers to task for allowing such shocking goings-on in their fair city. As they walked away, Swope was heard muttering: "Next thing you know, even the Bay will be polluted. Pity the poor crabs." Mencken nodded solemnly. "And all those sailors, too."

The bride took up residence in Swope's apartment at 530 West 113th Street and proceeded to adapt her habits to the needs of her new husband. She became a night person and remained one for the rest of her life, because she could not fall asleep until he was safely home, and that would not be until the early hours of the morning. It was probably just as well; she would not have been able to stay asleep once he had come bounding into the bedroom with his characteristic exuberance, longing to tell her all that had happened while they had been apart. She would prepare breakfast while he regaled her with such colorful accounts of his day that even the most trivial incident seemed enthralling.

When he left for work in the early afternoon, she was still half-asleep, but she would reach out and grab hold of his coat, clinging tightly and pleading: "Don't leave me! Don't leave me alone!"

The old fears had not been entirely cast off. If he left, would he return? He would disengage himself, calming her, telling her not to be foolish, reasoning that if he did as she requested, he would lose his job. Later, when she knew that he was hers forever, she would tell this story as an amusing anecdote. "A friend once asked: 'What would you have done if he'd said, "To hell with the job; I'm staying with you"?'

"I replied: 'Why, I'd have left him, of course.' "

That was the era of the great floating palaces, when the rich and mighty could sail the Atlantic in unsurpassed luxury, their every wish a command to the ever-attentive crew. The British White Star Line led the field with the most superbly appointed of these mammoth steamers. In April 1912 it launched the *Titanic* on its maiden voyage from Southampton to New York. It was the largest ship afloat and sailed with a full complement of 2,224 passengers and crew; the company boasted in every publicity release that it had at last built an unsinkable ship. At 2:00 A.M. on April 15, 1912, the unsinkable *Titanic,* cruising at full speed, hit an iceberg in the North Atlantic. Within a matter of hours it lay at the bottom of the ocean.

Word reached New York City at a time when reporters on the morning papers had already closed up shop to go home, and those on the evening papers had not yet come on duty. The predawn news belonged to the man who was up to get it. The rumor was that the survivors would be landed at Halifax, Nova Scotia. Without even waiting for the assignment, Swope was on the first train, leaving before the rest of the New York reporters, who were still dousing sleep with black coffee and hastily hustling into trousers.

A cable ship finally arrived, carrying the bodies of some three hundred victims. The figure was as deceptive as the visible tip of that fatal iceberg. By the time all hands were accounted for, it was discovered that over fifteen hundred had perished.

The authorities cordoned off the pier on which the corpses were being unloaded. While the other reporters were milling around in the local pubs wondering what to do next, Swope cornered the commander of the port. After some fast and furious talking, he was given access to the dock at all hours of the day and night.

The short, pudgy man from the *New York Times,* Alexander

Woollcott, was among the noisiest of those who protested this favoritism. When the angry shouts died down, his fellow journalists decided that it was impossible to beat Swope, so they might just as well join him. They would all need cable facilities to send back their stories, and they drafted him to see that this was arranged in all of their names.

Word reached Halifax that the *Carpathia* was heading for the port of New York City at full steam, carrying a cargo of seven hundred survivors and over twelve hundred of the dead. While Swope was racing back to New York, the United States Senate and President Taft, respectively, nominated Senator William B. Smith and Secretary of Commerce Charles B. Nagel to represent them in an investigation of the tragedy.

The first thing that Swope discovered upon arriving in New York was that the *Carpathia* was going to be early and would likely dock before the train carrying the investigating party arrived from Washington. Swope had the train from the capital flagged down in New Jersey, with a message instructing the party to proceed posthaste from Pennsylvania Station to the pier.

Not trusting the distinguished gentlemen to be able to fend for themselves, he was waiting at the station with a fleet of carriages and a police escort to rush them across town to the dock. With Swope in the first car shouting "Faster! Faster!" they went at such a hair-raising clip that many of the passengers were certain they were going to be the victims of a second tragedy.

Swope's reportage of the entire *Titanic* story was an example of the colorful journalism of the period at its best, but Swope considered the Becker case the biggest story of his career. Coming so soon after the *Titanic* story, this saga was enough to cause the acerbic Woollcott to retire from the front pages forever. The *New York Times* man had a nervous breakdown, which he later attributed to aggravation over Swope's continual scooping at every turn. "I said then that I would never again be a daily reporter," Woollcott told Swope's son years later.

Police Lieutenant Charles Becker was in charge of the "strong arm squad" which had been organized within the department especially to handle gambling and other forms of vice in the Broadway and Tenderloin districts. It proved such a lucrative job for a corrupt cop that in less than twelve months he had managed to bank over one hundred thousand dollars. It was an example of prodigious thrift, considering that his take-home pay was only twenty-five hundred dollars a year.

Swope was not the first to put the finger on Becker. He was under constant investigation by the more virtuous members of the establishment and the press. But he always had eluded prosecution through affiliation with an influential band of crooked politicians, crooked policemen, and honest crooks. Swope coined a name for this group— "the system"—and it has passed into the language.

Herman Rosenthal was the proprietor of a small-time gambling house. He had been operating quite successfully, and free from police harassment, thanks to the graft he doled out to Becker and his confrères. At first he didn't mind paying up. It was part of the game, a kitty for cops. But the lieutenant was a very greedy man; the more protection money he received, the more he wanted. Rosenthal became so incensed at this breach of the crooks' code that he decided to tell his story to the grand jury. From that day on, Rosenthal was a marked man.

It was at this point that Swope entered the picture. Rosenthal was having some difficulty convincing the rest of the press of the veracity of his story. Swope was familiar enough with the gamblers' world to know that he was telling the truth. He listened carefully, got a signed statement, and began to publish Rosenthal's account exclusively in the *World*. The reporter decided that a clincher was necessary to add authenticity to the series. He wanted an official statement from the District Attorney that he would act on Rosenthal's evidence.

Charles Whitman was still in that office, and Swope went to see him. He came away with the document he had been seeking. As in the Triangle fire pronouncement, the District Attorney's words had a distinctly Swopean flavor.

> I have had Rosenthal's charges under investigation for some time. I have no sympathy for Rosenthal the gambler, but I have real use for Rosenthal, who, abused by the police, proposes to aid decency and lawfulness by revealing conditions that are startling. This man will have a chance to tell his story to the grand jury.

The cadences can be compared with Swope's own statement after the death of Arnold Rothstein:

> Make no mistake as to my attitude. I have no paean of praise to sing for him, but, on the other hand, I can see injustices that have been done by having every crime on the calendar charged to his account.

Early on the morning of July 16, 1912, the day he was to appear before the Grand Jury, Rosenthal was having a late supper with some friends at the Metropole on West 43rd Street near Broadway. The doorman brought a message that a man wanted to see him outside on some urgent business. As he stepped through the front door, the gambler was gunned down by four hired assassins who went by the savory underground names of Gyp the Blood, Lefty Louie, Whitey Lewis, and Dago Frank. Although the area was filled with policemen, one of them standing no more than fifteen yards from the victim, the hoods managed to get away in a waiting car.

At the time of the shooting, Swope was prowling through the vicinity, making his usual nocturnal rounds in search of the kind of action that makes news. He heard about the slaying and was at the West 47th Street police precinct within a matter of minutes. What he discovered there galvanized him into action.

The police were doing their damnedest to lose the license plate number of the getaway car. They had even jailed the witness who had taken it down. Swope brushed past the protesting desk sergeant and put through a call to the District Attorney's home. When he reported what was happening, a reluctant Whitman stammered: "What do you think I should do?"

Swope's answer was an order: "Get into your clothes and get down to the police station as fast as you can."

Becker also hurried to the station that morning, but he was too late. Whitman had arrived ahead of him. He could not prevent a tracer from going out with the number of the getaway car.

The next day the *World* ran Swope's story, including Rosenthal's statement to him. The reporter called it his "death warrant." The killers, hiding out in the Catskills, were soon located. They were arrested, tried, and sent to the electric chair on the twenty-fifth anniversary of the invention of that singular piece of furniture.

Becker had used intermediaries to contact the assassins. They could not testify who actually had hired them, because they did not know his identity. Becker was still not officially implicated.

The story would have died there had it not been for Swope. He knew the truth and would not be satisfied until it was admitted. He was relentless in pursuing the story in the pages of the *World*. Word reached Swope that there was a "contract" out on him, but he still would not give up. And his courage paid off. There were demands for investigations into Becker's affairs. Becker's superiors tried in vain to ignore the public outcry, for the trail of corruption led to very high places in New York City officialdom.

At first, Whitman was equivocal. He knew that if he continued on the Becker case, he could expect no help from his superiors. Indeed, they might well throw up every kind of obstacle, and even go so far as to hinder his career. Swope played on his vanity and ambition, arguing persuasively that, far from hurting his career, this investigation could be the start of a brilliant future in politics. He succeeded in persuading the District Attorney to turn up the heat full blast.

It was not long before two small-time gamblers, Bald Jack Rose and Bridgie Weber, came forth with offers to turn state's evidence to avoid prosecution. For the first time Becker was actually implicated, because the duo admitted that they had acted as his go-betweens in hiring Rosenthal's killers. Naturally, Swope got a copy of Rose's confession and scooped the town by printing it in full. Rose quoted Becker's reaction to viewing the corpse at the station house on the night of the murder. The language was colorful enough for Swope to have invented it, and perhaps he did do a little embellishing. It was an era in which reporters wanted hoods to sound like hoods and not like dropouts from Harvard Business School, an era when the language of newspapers had to be as evocative as pictures in television news clips are today. Becker was alleged to have said: "It was a pleasant sight for me to look and see that squealing Jew there, and if it hadn't been for Whitman, I would have reached down and cut out his tongue and hung it up somewhere as a warning to future squealers."

Rose and Weber were soon joined by two other gangsters who had been in on the conspiracy, Sam Schepps and Harry Vallon. Whitman had enough evidence to arrest Becker and charge him with first-degree murder.

On October 27, 1912, Swope completely took over the Metropolitan Section of the Sunday *World* with a pungent narrative as exciting as any lurid detective melodrama of the period. It was titled "Slain by the System." Like a book, it was divided into chapters. It began with this introduction:

> "Herman Rosenthal has squealed again."
>
> Through the pallid underworld the sibilant whisper ran. It was heard in East Side dens; it rang in the opium houses in Chinatown; it crept up to the semipretentious stud and crap games of the Fourteenth Street region, and it reached into the more select circles of uptown gambling, where business is always good and graft is always high.
>
> Rosenthal had squealed once too often.
>
> This time, his action was a direct affront to the "System." He had

publicly defied it. He had set it, through its lieutenant, at naught. He had publicly thrown down the gauntlet, and it was snatched up, to be returned in the form of four bullets crashing through his head while he stood in the heart of the city under a blaze of lights that enabled bystanders to follow every move of the four assassins who, their job having been done, and well done, swarmed aboard the gray automobile that had brought them to their work, and fled, secure, as they thought, from successful pursuit because they were acting under the sheltering hand of Police Lieutenant Charles Becker, who had issued the order to Jack Rose:

"I want Herman Rosenthal croaked!"

The story, and Swope's central position in it, has continued to fascinate newspapermen for over half a century. John Wheeler, later to become president of the North American Newspaper Alliance, was a young reporter on the *Herald* at the time of the murder. Forty years later, he still recalled every detail of the case and wrote about it for national syndication.

There were two sensational trials, and Swope was all over the case and had the rest of the reporters in town tincanning after him. This chronicler knows, for he was working for the *Herald* at the time. The first time around, the jury disagreed, and at the next trial, the former police lieutenant was convicted and sentenced to the electric chair.

It was generally agreed that if Swope had not routed Whitman out of bed, the number of the murder car would have been covered up. With the newspaperman advising him, Whitman finally got the conviction. As a result of this sensational trial, [Whitman] was elected Governor of New York.

Mayor Gaynor did not dare run for reelection. Police Commissioner Waldo was fired. Becker's last appeal for clemency was turned down by Governor Whitman. By the time the former lieutenant was electrocuted, Swope had won renown as a reporter who could make and break politicians.

When Louis B. Snyder, associate professor of history at the College of the City of New York, and Richard B. Morris, professor of history at Columbia University, published *A Treasury of Great Reporting* in 1949, they still considered Swope's handling of the story classic. In their introduction to the reprint of Swope's account they said, "It was one of the great crime stories of all time."

FOUR

During the first years of their marriage, Margaret Swope watched her husband with some apprehension. They were a very popular young couple, they were madly in love, and they were having a baby. He had every reason to be one of the happiest men in town—but he wasn't. Why wasn't he? As she saw it, one of the problems was that he was working too hard, spending too much time away from her. She could make him happy if he would let her, but she was losing her hold on him, and there was nothing she could do about it. Her pregnancy truly confined, for, according to the customs of the period, she was to be glimpsed as seldom as possible outside of her home and certainly never to make the rounds of the Broadway spots that Swope frequented. She later observed: "They treated an expectant mother as if she were carrying typhoid instead of a baby. She was kept under lock and key. It took a war for them to admit that pregnancy might be communicated, but it wasn't contagious."

Margaret decided that the solution was to make their home more attractive to Swope. The first step she took was to move them into larger quarters on Morningside Drive, a tree-lined residential street that wound around the western border of Columbia University, with a striking vista of Harlem, still one of the city's more substantial neighborhoods, opening beneath it. Using all of her innate flair and taste, and spending far more than they could afford, she created a setting for her husband, a place in which he could entertain his friends much more comfortably than in any restaurant.

There was a second motive for the move. She was worried about her family and had started formulating a plan to have them with her. She recognized her family's need to be looked after, and she recognized Swope's need for a family that would adore him. Rather than wait for the birth of a child, who might or might not fulfill that need, she moved her mother and brothers in with them. It was not long before her family became his family. It was a responsibility he discharged without question for the rest of their lives.

In the presidential race of 1912, Woodrow Wilson ran against the incumbent Republican President William Howard Taft and the new Progressive party's candidate, former President Theodore Roosevelt. Had the Republicans united behind either man, they would have won.

33

The combined Taft-Roosevelt vote was 7,604,518, while Wilson was a minority winner with 6,293,454, or 41.9 percent of the popular vote.

People still argue whether Roosevelt or Wilson was the greater president. The question never existed in Swope's mind. From the beginning, Wilson was his man, and his depression lifted as soon as he was assigned to cover Wilson's campaign.

Wilson once described himself in these words: "I am a vague, conjectural personality, more made up of opinions and academic prepossessions than of human traits and red corpuscles." In essence, Wilson was the opposite to whom Swope could be very much attracted. In Wilson he had found the father figure so necessary to him, the man who would replace Gerard in that role for the next few years. His reaction to Wilson was straightforward and predictable. He later said, "I was in love with him."

Wilson also found much that was admirable in the dashing young reporter. He had the color and flamboyance to which gray men are often attracted. The president-elect was a man who had difficulty calling anyone by his first name, but he did manage a "Bayard" for Swope. He said that he thought Swope had one of the toughest and quickest minds he had ever encountered. This was a valuable asset to a slow and pedagogical man thrust into a powerful office during a period when quick decisions were demanded of him, and he often made use of Swope.

When Wilson's advisers told him that it would be politically wise to appoint a young New York Democrat to a Washington post—provided that he could find one who had no ties to the Tammany machine—he asked Swope to suggest somebody. The reporter came up with an aristocratic young New York State assemblyman who had both an excellent image and an untarnished record. His name was Franklin Delano Roosevelt, and on Swope's recommendation, Wilson appointed him Assistant Secretary of the Navy.

The two young men were essentially alike. They could be teammates or friendly antagonists in any of the games they both adored—they viewed things from the same vantage. For example, they could both intellectually understand but never emotionally commit themselves to Wilson's belief: "A presidential campaign may easily degenerate into a mere personal contest and so lose its real dignity. There is no indispensable man."

They both adored personal contests and very much believed in indispensable men, who, for Swope, ranged from his brother through Wilson to Al Smith and Bernard Baruch. For Roosevelt, the indispensable man was consistently Roosevelt.

Wilson's first inaugural address elicited a profound commitment from Swope. The special qualities of greatness in that speech have been compared to those in the addresses of Jefferson, Lincoln, Roosevelt, and Kennedy. At one point Wilson said:

> At last a vision has been vouchsafed us of our life as a whole. We see the bad with the good, the debased and decadent with the sound and vital. With this vision, we approach our new affairs. Our duty is to cleanse, to reconsider, to restore, to correct the evils without impairing the good, to purify and humanize every process of our human life without weakening or sentimentalizing it. . . . This is not a day of triumph; it is a day of dedication. Here, muster not the forces of party but the forces of humanity. Men's hearts wait upon us: men's lives hang in the balance; men's hopes call upon us to say what we will do. Who shall live up to the great trust? Who dares fail to try? I summon all honest men, all patriotic, all forward-looking men to my side. God helping, I will not fail them, if they will but counsel and sustain me!

Swope heard and answered that summons. He was never again the same. Professionally, he could not completely forsake the slime of New York City's underside; that was where the local news was, and reporting it was his business. But it was no longer the most important thing in his career. Although he would never be above using some of the old exuberant news-gathering devices, in his own fashion he would hold fast to that larger vision for the rest of his life.

A good story was a good story to Swope, in any context. He was a superb raconteur. The 1912 campaign provided one of his favorite yarns, and he never tired of telling it. His friends relished it and were not above repeating it in all manner of accents, from the patrician New English of Henry Cabot Lodge to the New Yorkese of Alfred E. Smith, each trying vainly to make a creditable imitation of the inimitable Swope. The story concerned an evening spent with the Democratic gubernatorial candidate William Sulzer, a Tammany hack with delusions of grandeur. The original Swope account was as follows:

> Stretching out his long legs, and letting go a wad of tobacco juice, he [Sulzer] said: "Swope, I've been following your career for some time. I told Mr. Pewlitzer what a likely fellow you are." I said: "Thank you very much, Bill. What do you want?" Smiling a little

self-consciously, he then told me that he was going to close his campaign that night among his friends, the Jews up on Second Avenue in, I think, the Seventh Assembly District, and he would like to have me see how highly he was thought of by those who properly appreciated him.

So that night I went up, along with Ed Hill of the *Sun,* and Frank O'Malley, the *Sun*'s star; also Dill of the *Herald,* and others. We sat in front of the pulpit in a synagogue that was literally packed with Bill's neighbors.

Bill appeared on the rostrum, and there was a wild shout of joy. He raised his hand to still the tumult and, after shooting a large and juicy mouthful (which just missed the Ark of the Covenant), looking exactly like Henry Clay, with the forelock, and posturing like him, began in his sepulchral tone and accentuated slowness of speech in this way: "My friends, and I call you my friends advisedly, historians say that the Jews are an ungrateful people. William Sulzer denies this." He always spoke of himself in the third person. That enabled him to be more self-laudatory than if he used I. "Mark you, and mark you well, when William Sulzer was Chairman of the House Committee on Foreign Affairs, he drafted and had passed a resolution of protest to the Tsar of all the Roosians anent the Kishinev massacre. And from that day to this, the Roosians never dared have another massacre."

The crowd went wild. They cheered and yelled and wept. Again he raised his hand, and again let go another projectile in the form of more tobacco juice—this time just missing the press bench—and went on: "Because of that, there are fifteen million Jews on their knees every night thanking their God for William Sulzer."

I leaned forward from my seat and said, in a stage whisper: "Bill, the Jews don't kneel when they pray." In his anxiety to make his point, he swallowed part of his cud. With a voice, hoarse and ecstatic, trained to yell, he said: "My learned young friend, Mr. Herbert Bayard Swope, of the New York *World*"—at which point I tried to cut in, saying, "Thanks for the ad, Bill," which he ignored—"says the Jews don't kneel when they pray. They may not kneel for others, but they kneel for William Sulzer."

At that, the crowd went completely delirious. They screamed: "We do, Bill, we do."

Sulzer was subsequently elected Governor of New York State and was later impeached. The impeachment proceedings were conducted by the majority leader of the State Assembly, Aaron Jefferson Levy, a Jew who obviously did not kneel for Sulzer.

The Sulzer story continued to be told by Swope and his cronies for almost thirty years. It finally took one of the tellers, and a Supreme Court Justice, to give it a topper and lay it to rest. When the politician died in 1941, Felix Frankfurter wired Swope: "I hope they will kneel when they pray for Billy Sulzer."

In the spring of 1914, most of the people in America would not have believed it possible that the major European powers would be at war with each other by the autumn. Even the few who did see the possibility thought it was a conflict that would never involve the United States. It was a family affair. The King of England was an uncle of the Kaiser of Germany, and the Czar of Russia was the King's cousin. The best thing to do in any family squabble was to mind one's own business, and America's business had nothing to do with kings, emperors, and czars.

The United States had always been transportation happy. Henry Ford brought out his first Model T, the "Tin Lizzie," in 1908. By 1914 he was manufacturing 250,000 a year. The automobile was becoming ubiquitous, and its novelty was wearing thin. No longer did the streets ring with the jeer "Get a horse!"

The country was setting its sights on the sky. The Wright brothers had made their first successful flight in 1903, but it was not until 1909 that the government patent office finally accepted their machine. The flying fever was spreading, and the New York *World* decided to capitalize on it with promotional contests offering big prizes to those early daredevil pilots. Glenn Curtiss collected the first prize of $10,000 for the breathtaking feat of having flown all the way from Albany to New York City with only two stops.

In 1914 Lord Northcliffe's London *Daily Mail* got into the act by offering $50,000 to the first pilot to negotiate a flight between North America and the British Isles. There was to be a seventy-two-hour time limit on the trip, but there was no restriction on the number of stops the plane could make.

At Hammondsport, New York, Glenn Curtiss was building a plane that would be used to compete for the *Mail* money. He was planning to christen it the *America,* and it truly became an Anglo-American venture when a British naval officer, Lieutenant John Porte, was brought over to pilot the ship.

Swope convinced Ralph Pulitzer and his managing editor, Charles M. Lincoln, that the *World* deserved an exclusive stake in the historic adventure. After all, they had provided the lead with the first flight contests. He was sent to Hammondsport with orders to obtain the American rights to Lieutenant Porte's story, which he would ghost-write for the pilot.

The idea was not original with the *World*. Reporters from papers all over the country had already converged on the small town on the shores of Lake Keuka, one of the famous Finger Lakes of New York State. They doubted that any would succeed in his purpose, because Porte was so phlegmatic with the press that they did not think even the great Swope could break through. Their doubts, along with their hopes, ended when the pilot appeared in the dining room for breakfast the morning after Swope's arrival. Porte's British reserve had relaxed enough for him to be overheard telling the headwaiter: "Mr. Swope says he will be down right away. He wants you to have his breakfast ready: orange juice, two poached eggs with crisp toast, a rasher of bacon, and piping hot coffee."

In view of the kind of solicitous concern that Porte was showing to Swope's desires, one could only wonder who indeed was going to be the ghost. The pilot fulfilled another of Swope's desires when he allowed him to come along on one of the test flights. Swope's enthusiasm was so great that he even suggested making the flight with Porte. To Margaret's vast relief, both the *Daily Mail* and the *World* vetoed the idea.

The flight was scheduled to depart from Newfoundland, to make one stop in the Azores, another in Portugal, and then to go on to Great Britain. Forbidden to make the flight, Swope decided to proceed to the Azores and be on hand when Porte arrived there. Actually, he secretly planned to fly the next leg of the journey to the Iberian coast.

Swope booked passage on the Austrian ship *Franz Josef*, scheduled to depart from New York City on July 4, 1914. Austria was a landlocked country. Only through its annexation of the Serbian states Bosnia-Herzegovina (now part of Yugoslavia) did it gain access to the Adriatic Sea. On June 28, 1914, exactly one week before Swope was to depart, the Austrian Archduke Francis Ferdinand was assassinated by a Serbian revolutionary at Sarajevo in Bosnia. Any retaliation by Austria would threaten a fragile peace, because Russia was committed to protect the Serbs.

Swope was more excited than ever about the trip. The Azores would bring him two thousand miles closer to Europe, and Europe was where the important news was in the making. Margaret loathed traveling, but in view of her husband's agitation, she suspected that this might be the start of a long separation, so she left Mimi in charge of the family and accompanied him.

The *Franz Josef* was overcrowded with Austrian nationals returning to their homeland. What had seemed remote in New York was suddenly very close on that ship. The imminence of war filled all thoughts and conversations. The closer they got to the Azores, the more certain Swope became that, somehow, he would have to make his way to Germany. He had to know how the coming events would affect his family there. And of course there was also the story, the big story, of life inside the German Empire during a war. But first, he had to finish the Porte story.

The Swopes disembarked at Horta, the largest town on the island of Fayal in the Azores. Fayal was a small island in the middle of the Atlantic that miraculously managed to be untouched by sea breezes. A cooling dip in the ocean was out of the question because of the proliferation of jellyfish. It was hot, humid, buggy—and the most uncomfortable place that either had ever known.

The accommodations made Margaret recall Rockaway Beach as a veritable paradise. She vowed never again to visit any place where César Ritz had not preceded her. In later years she expanded that view to include Addison Mizner.

The kindest thing that the Swopes could manage to say about the plumbing was that it had a life of its own. Their consumption of mouthwash was prodigious. They not only gargled with it, they also flushed with it.

Porte's agent, an American naval pilot named John Lansing Callan, had proceeded to Ponta Delgada, a town on one of the other islands, and was making preparations for the plane to land there. To make matters worse, word had leaked out, and reporters from other papers were following the pilot around and filing stories on all of his activities.

Swope wired his managing editor, Charles M. Lincoln, that he had to find a way to reach Callan and to get him and the supplies over to Horta. Lincoln responded that there was an American cruiser on a tour of duty in the Azores. That was all that was necessary to galvanize Swope, and his next wire read:

CONGRATULATIONS ON CRUISER STOP WILL HAVE NAVY DEPARTMENT
INSTRUCT OFFICERS I AM HERE FOR PORTE AND TO COOPERATE WITH
ME

The number of newsmen in Ponta Delgada was greater than even Swope had anticipated. Still more alarming was word of another group that would be waiting for them in Portugal. He did not intend to hop out of that plane into the arms of his competitors, so he secretly changed the second stop from Portugal to Vigo in Spain. He returned to Horta and cabled Lincoln:

> CALLAN AND I AGREE HORTA BEST POINT FOR PORTE'S FIRST AND ONLY LANDING STOP WIRE PORTE FOR APPROVAL STOP CALLAN WILL COME HERE WITH SUPPLIES FROM PONTA STOP IF PLAN ADOPTED KEEP QUIET LETTING OTHER PAPERS FIGURE ON PONTA STOP HORTA THREE HOURS NEARER TO AMERICA THAN PONTA AND JUST AS NEAR VIGO

For good measure, he also wired Porte:

> CALLAN HERE AFTER TOURING ISLANDS STOP BOTH ADVISE MAKING HORTA FIRST AND ONLY PORT AS YOU ORIGINALLY PLANNED USING PONTA FOR EMERGENCY STOP WATER AND WEATHER HERE MOST FAVORABLE MACHINE SHOPS GOOD DISREGARD CALLAN'S LETTER TO ST JOHNS [NEWFOUNDLAND] STOP CABLE ME IMMEDIATE REPLY AND CALLAN WILL RETURN HERE WITH ALL SUPPLIES

He signed the message "Callanswope."

The delays continued in America, and Swope began to bombard Lincoln with requests to abandon the project and set sail for Europe. He almost got his way on July 11, when Lincoln wired:

> FLIGHT IMPROBABLE BEFORE SEPTEMBER STOP WHEN COULD YOU SAIL FOR EUROPE

Swope elatedly began to make plans, but the following day brought another message forcing him to change them.

> MATTER MORE PROMISING FLIGHT NOW POSSIBLE BETWEEN FIFTH AND SEVENTH AUGUST STAY FOR PRESENT AND COMPLETE AR-RANGEMENTS

Austria was openly making plans to invade Serbia, while Serbia countered with threats to call in her allies, the Russians. Swope was afraid it would all be over before he got there and was agitating to leave immediately, but the next two weeks only brought a series of frustrating cables from Lincoln:

> STILL EXPERIMENTING TO GET BOAT TO LIFT LOAD FROM WATER NO SUCCESS YET

NEW BOTTOM FOR BOAT APPARENTLY SUCCESSFUL AUGUST FIRST
DEFINITELY SET FOR SHIPMENT FROM NEW YORK

PORTE HOPES TO LEAVE BY AUGUST TENTH

DUBIOUS AGAIN STOP NEW BOTTOM FAILURE

On July 23 Austria-Hungary sent an ultimatum with ten demands to Serbia. Swope could not stand the thought of remaining in the Azores for another moment. He wired Lincoln:

BEST PLAN IS TO GO TO EUROPE IMMEDIATELY RETURNING HERE IF
FLIGHT TAKES PLACE IN SEPTEMBER STOP DO YOU APPROVE STOP RUSH
REPLY WITH DETAILS

Under pressure from Great Britain and Russia, Serbia accepted all but two of Austria's demands on July 25.

On July 26 British Foreign Minister Sir Edward Grey suggested that a conference of England, Germany, France, and Italy be called to settle the Austro-Serbian dispute, and the proposal was rejected by Germany. Swope wired Lincoln:

BY GOING PONTA OR MADEIRA GET EUROPEAN CONNECTION IN ABOUT
TEN DAYS STOP CABLE APPROVAL STOP CALLAN HERE WE WILL
ARRANGE FOR POSSIBLE OCTOBER FLIGHT

On July 28 Austria declared war on Serbia, and Lincoln cabled:

ALL CLEAR LOOKS LIKE WAR EUROPE

The Swopes departed for Marseilles that evening. Herbert spent most of the journey in the radio cabin watching the dispatches as they provided a daily chronicle of Europe's descent into war.

July 29: In high-level meetings, Germany decides to declare war on Russia and France, hoping for British neutrality.

July 31: Russia and Germany both order a general mobilization.

August 1: Germany and Russia declare war.

August 2: Germany invades France.

August 3: Germany invades Belgium. England, guarantor of that country's sovereignty, is forced to declare war on Germany.

On the next day, the ship stopped at Lisbon. The restless Swope disembarked with his wife. He could not afford to waste another moment. The outbreak of war had canceled all plans for a transatlantic flight, and Swope felt free to roam the Continent for as long as his newspaper would permit.

Lincoln had ordered him to go to Paris, but instead he opted for England. The *World* had a very good news bureau in London under the direction of James M. Tuohy, and he could be sure that his dispatches would be transmitted with maximum efficiency. Beyond that, Swope's major means of gathering news was via conversation, and his French was not up to the game.

From the moment he arrived in London, Swope began to send a barrage of requests that he be permitted to cover the war in Germany for the *World*. He knew that if he got the German assignment, he would be moving around, visiting the front. He would have little or no time for Margaret; it would be best and safest for her if she went home. She totally agreed with him on a rational level, but emotionally she found it increasingly difficult to be away from him.

"You are the most unceasingly satisfying human in the world," she would tell him later, although she would rarely admit that to anybody else and would often take the public position that one of her major jobs in their marriage was to cut him down to size. When he went on too long on one subject or another, she would deftly apply a verbal stiletto. Friends were amazed when Margaret first started to speak up. She had always been such a docile, adoring wife. She explained: "Night after night, I'd sit there and listen to Herbert and his pals go on and on and on. Finally, something dawned on me. I realized that most of it was a crock of shit, so I told them so."

Swope retorted: "The two largest mistakes of my life were (1) I taught you how to think, and (2) I taught you how to speak."

He offered her an alternative to going home. If he got the German assignment, she could remain in Berlin with his mother. She replied: "I'll go home."

Along with Ochs of the *New York Times,* Ralph Pulitzer was trying desperately to bolster American sympathy for the Germans. Like Swope, the publishers had been brought up in homes that extolled the virtues of all things Germanic. It took a great deal of both time and evidence to make New York City's two major newspapers recant on their predisposition toward Germany. Next to the United States, turn-of-the-century Germany had offered the greatest amount of freedom and opportunity to the ancestral people of the publishers. A marked anti-Semitism was not among the Kaiser's faults, and memories of the

Dreyfus affair were still vivid enough to make a pro-French feeling difficult to engender in these men.

The insights that Swope had into the German character in 1914 were prophetic and influenced the position later taken by Woodrow Wilson. Swope saw the necessity of a peace with honor for Germany. Had the French permitted that in 1918, there surely would never have been a Hitler. He also predicted that Germany would never be totally victorious and that she would never be totally defeated, even by an unconditional surrender. History has borne him out. After two such unconditional surrenders and partition, she has emerged as not one but two economically powerful nations, the wealthiest in Western Europe and the second richest in Eastern Europe.

FIVE

Swope's European stories were carried in the Pulitzers' St. Louis *Post-Dispatch* and in newspapers all over the country that subscribed to the World News Syndicate. His national prominence grew with each piece that was printed.

Swope had been back in New York less than a month when he was offered the job of city editor of the *World*. It was to be the most challenging job of his career and a great opportunity for him, but he had misgivings even after accepting. He had never been very good at delegating authority; he liked working alone, doing things in his own way at his own pace.

As the new editor, Swope galvanized the city room. Suddenly reporters were alert, charged by the currents of energy that emanated from his desk. No matter how trivial an assignment might be, Swope had a way of making it seem of vital importance to the paper. He once assigned a run-of-the-mill story to a very good reporter. The man looked dubious, so Swope launched into an account of the events as if he had been on the scene and were doing the writing. He gave it shading, color, a richness of detail. The reporter nodded excitedly, exclaiming, "I got you, boss!"

The man raced back to his desk and started to roll a piece of paper into his typewriter. "What do you think you're doing?" asked Swope.

"I'm writing the story."

Swope became apoplectic: "Flathead! You haven't even gone out on the assignment!"

"Don't have to. You told me all I need to know."

"Without checking up on it, how do you know I was telling the truth? God damn it! Don't take anybody's word for anything. Not even mine. Now, get the hell out of here!"

The reporter started to go. He turned and said, "You know, boss, if it didn't happen the way you just told it—it should have."

Swope drove himself so hard that he became physically ill. His doctor ordered a complete rest. Partly to recuperate, partly because he was crazy about all sporting events, and mostly because he was longing to be a reporter again, he took Margaret on a trip to Cuba to cover the fight between the first black heavyweight champion, Jack Johnson, and "the great white hope," Jess Willard. Johnson was aging and out of shape; Willard was young, unrelenting, and merciless. He was redeeming the "honor" of his race by inflicting the cruelest punishment on Johnson that one fighter could inflict on another.

Swope's story evoked it all: the color of the sport; the sultriness of the locale; the savagery of the contest; the racial implications; the taunting derision of the maddened crowd; the hopelessness of the old man. Charles Lincoln called it "a classic of sports writing."

Upon returning from Cuba, Swope found that in his absence there had been a great deal of tampering with policies that he had initiated. A power struggle was developing, and he held the least important position of the men vying for control.

There was a controversy with Lincoln over one of his reporters, and Swope shot a sharp wire off to Pulitzer, who was visiting in St. Louis. Scrawled across the top of the office copy in his own hand was the word "personal."

> I resent, as city editor, the use being made of Justice, who has been a member of my staff for two months. Although I have had frequent conferences with Lincoln in the week since my return, he gave no explanation of Justice's absence from work, beyond saying that he was temporarily detached. This lack of confidence placed me in an embarrassing position in which I learned from an outsider where Justice was. Am I to assume that I was not to be trusted? Swope.

An edgy truce was negotiated, but Swope was becoming increasingly disenchanted with being an editor. Gang wars in New York City could not match the excitement of the big war in Europe, which he longed to return to as a correspondent. Although Pulitzer kept promising that he would send Swope back, he was very slow in acting on that promise.

It was not until the beginning of the summer of 1916 that Ralph Pulitzer reluctantly decided to make good his pledge to Swope. The gesture was not inspired by any spirit of fair play toward the editor he was beginning to call his friend. The United States government was still hoping to remain neutral, but the war in Europe was definitely the number-one story in the whole world. A natural sympathy plus a more relaxed attitude toward censorship combined to attract all of the best correspondents to covering the story from the Allied side. The little that was coming out of Germany was so heavily biased toward the Kaiser that it was almost unprintable. His Imperial Majesty preferred that his government deal only with newsmen who painted a favorable picture of him. The *World*'s regular correspondent in Berlin was Karl von Wiegand. The name itself was sufficient indication of where his sympathies lay.

Pulitzer knew that the Germans trusted Swope because of his fairness to them in 1914. He was obviously the only man on the staff who would be able to go to Germany and send back anything resembling balanced reportage. If this should not prove feasible, he could still interview the important people in the regime, dig out the facts, and then return to write a series of articles.

Margaret did not want him to go alone. If he was going to get his head blown off, she wanted to be there to catch it. He argued: "Soldiers are going off to war without their wives every day."

She replied: "That's their problem. I'm going with you."

"You hate traveling."

"That's my problem. I'm still going."

She was adamant. He would have to find a way to take her with him. It was not going to be easy. He was certain that the paper would not react favorably to the idea of taking a wife along on an assignment to a country at war.

In a meeting with Charles Lincoln, Swope pointed out that he might run into some problems in getting what they wanted. The Germans had convenient memories and might choose to forget his work in 1914. Conditions had changed, and they were very suspicious of journalists whom they could not control. Lincoln replied: "If you have any difficulties, you can always pretend you're there in the role of loving son and brother who has not seen his family in over two years."

Swope seized the opportunity. He cried: "Bully idea! In that case, you must see that it's vital to us for me to take Margaret along. She's never met my mother, and we can say I want to introduce them."

In Berlin, the journalist had a powerful ally in James W. Gerard, who was then the United States ambassador to Germany. The diplomat was an old friend and had received instructions from President Wilson to extend every courtesy of the embassy to his young friend from the New York *World*.

It appears extremely likely that Swope was on a special mission for the president, as he had been called to a private meeting at the White House just before he embarked for Europe; later found among his papers was a yellowing *World* envelope across which he had scrawled "private notes for Wilson." It was crammed with handwritten notes in his unmistakable, almost indecipherable scrawl. These notes, destined first for the president's eyes, would later be incorporated into Swope's series of articles on the German experience.

Swope made practical use of his favored position with the ambassador. The other foreign correspondents spent half their time bemoaning the fact that what little news did get through the German censorship office was so heavily edited that it was of almost no use from a reportorial point of view; the other half they spent in *gemütlich* beer halls, downing enough to forget the frustrating nature of their careers in Berlin.

The only American dispatches with which the Germans dared not tamper were those sent in the diplomatic pouches. And after Swope had a friendly chat with Ambassador Gerard, the Pulitzer papers began to receive his uncensored reports through the good offices of the embassy. The other journalists cried "foul play!"—which could be translated as "sour grapes."

During his two months in Germany, Swope was ubiquitous—whether in the capital city or on the front lines, he was on the scene. He was almost killed when a battle with Allied artillery broke out while he was inspecting the German front along the Somme River. He was the only American correspondent in Berlin to be given interviews by both the German Chancellor and the Minister for Foreign Affairs. Even more significant than that, he was able to get the reports of these interviews back to the United States, where they were printed as written. The usual procedure was for a high-ranking German official to give an interview in which he would be engagingly frank, knowing full well that the government would be able to censor what it did not want transmitted. In a prison camp in Cambrai, Swope found two British pilots who, in violation of all of the articles of war concerning treatment of prisoners, were scheduled for court-martial. He saved their lives by persuading Ambassador Gerard to intervene on their behalf.

Gerard was leaving for home in September, and Swope wanted to be aboard the ship with him. It would not only enable him to get some exclusive stories from the ambassador, but it would also get him home in time to campaign for the reelection of Wilson. The more he observed in Germany, the more certain he became that Wilson was the man best equipped to direct American policy during a foreign war in which the country's neutrality was becoming increasingly difficult to maintain. His adored president was going to need all of the help that he could get. In 1912 Wilson had been only a minority winner, and in the intervening four years his popularity had not noticeably increased. There was simply no appealing warmth to the man: he was all intellect and integrity. The energy with which he promoted domestic social reform and dealt with delicate foreign relations puzzled an electorate that felt more comfortable with a chief executive who spoke of high ideals than with one who acted upon them.

The Swopes left Berlin with Gerard to sail for home on the Danish ship, the *Frederick VIII*. Swope's private papers were not songs of praise to his German hosts; they included the astute evaluations and notes that he had made solely for the president. He was afraid that they might all be confiscated at the border, so he took the precaution of having the ambassador carry them to Copenhagen in the diplomatic pouch.

Margaret had spent a disquieting two months in the formidable bosom of the German Swopes. She later described her position as exactly analogous to Swope's: "a neutral risking life and limb on the front lines." She continually said how glad she was to be going home—until the very last moment before boarding, when she suddenly dug in on the pier and refused to get on the ship. Swope demanded an explanation: "What on earth has provoked this outrageous display of orneriness?"

She nodded toward the *Frederick VIII,* which was festooned with lettering in several languages declaring its neutrality, like icing on a plain cake. "Before I get on that Danish pastry, I want the captain to promise he'll turn back if I change my mind in the middle of the ocean."

"Of all the unreasonable . . . you know you hated Berlin!"

"Strange as it seems—I prefer your German relatives to German U-boats."

Without another word he picked her up and tossed her over his shoulder like a seaman's duffel bag, while she shrieked a stream of epithets that were impressive even by dockside standards.

Passing the astonished ship's officers, Swope pointed to the fanny doubled over his arm and said firmly: "Drunk, you know. Hopeless case. Bane of my existence."

He locked her in their cabin and released her only after the ship had set sail. As they strolled along the promenade deck, he said, "Don't you realize that a crossing should be a pleasure? There are games, entertainments, amusing people."

She glanced around at the motley assortment of adventurers and refugees fleeing the war. "Do me a favor, Herbie," she said. "Lock me up in the cabin again."

Back in New York, Swope's energies were awesome. He was actively campaigning for Wilson's reelection, serving as city editor of the *World,* giving his views to all manner of groups on what was happening in Germany, sounding the call for American preparedness to enter the war, as well as making his nightly rounds of the city in search of local news. He also signed a contract with the Century Publishing Company to bring out his series on Germany in book form. All that remained was to write the articles and do it quickly, while they were still topical.

He had his German notes; he had the talent; he had the desire; he had the stamina. Time was the only thing that was in short supply. He assigned a young reporter named Lewis Gannett to help with the pieces. One of Gannett's major qualifications for the job was that he could take dictation on the typewriter. From 3:00 A.M. to 8:00 A.M. Swope dictated and Gannett typed.

It was not unusual for Swope to arrive in white tie and tails after a night on the town. The younger man might be nodding over his typewriter, but after a day of work and a night on the town, the energetic editor was ready to go. In machine gun–like staccato, Swope rattled off the stories, already perfectly phrased in his mind, so that they were ready to go to the presses as soon as the typist removed them from his machine.

Gannett went on to become a distinguished literary critic. He later described Swope as "the yellingest editor in newspaper history."

Election night of 1916 was a fateful evening in Swope's life. In his own way, he helped to elect a president after everybody else was ready to concede defeat. He also met a man who was destined to become his most intimate friend, beginning a relationship that was to alter both of them in many ways through all the years that followed.

The race between Wilson and Charles Evans Hughes was a very close one. Until late on election night it was a dead heat, with California holding the deciding electoral votes. The first returns from the southern part of the state swung so decisively toward Hughes that by midnight his son was introducing him to the press as "the president-elect of the United States." The Hughes family was not alone in feeling this way. Newspapers all across the country, including the *New York Times,* were proclaiming "Hughes and Fairbanks Elected."

At the strongly pro-Wilson *World,* even Lincoln was ready to concede the race. Swope begged him to wait. As a result of Swope's efforts, the paper's ambiguous headline was "Hughes Elected in Close Contest?"

Swope knew that there was still a chance. The northern part of California was then the more heavily populated portion of the state, and voters there were still going to the polls. He raced over to the Democratic party headquarters at the Hotel Belmont.

Most of the party workers and political freeloaders had gone home, certain that there would be no celebration that night. The floor was strewn with the ticker tape that had brought the bad news from all over the country. The ballroom was a devastated area, a wasteland of empty bottles and chairs, as if hastily vacated in a race to get out lest losing prove a fatal disease. Only the diehards remained, gathered in knots in different parts of the vast room, mourning the loss of power, vultures picking among the bones for some overlooked morsel of influence.

Swope raced past them as if they were not there, and burst into a small dining room off the far end of the ballroom, where the men he felt should have known better were even glummer than the flunkies and hacks in the ballroom. In their shirtsleeves, with features obscured by the gray smoke of a political backroom, the almighties of the party sat wondering how they had managed to bring off the nearly impossible—having an incumbent president defeated in his bid for a second term.

Those present were Vance McCormick, chairman of the Democratic National Committee; William G. McAdoo, President Wilson's son-in-law; Thomas Chadbourne, an attorney adept enough to represent the interests of labor and management simultaneously; and two trustees of City College who were both very heavy contributors to the party, William McCombs and Bernard M. Baruch. The atmosphere of a wake was pervasive. They had obviously quit, and they barely looked up when Swope bustled into the room. This infuriated him; resisting the impulse to overturn the table and physically shake them out of their lethargy, he contented himself with an ear-splitting roar.

"You fellows are a lot of damn quitters!"

Startled expressions spread across the faces of the distinguished assembly. They weren't used to being addressed in that fashion—not by somebody with less money than they had. At last, Swope thought, they were showing some signs of life, and he continued in a more reasonable tone, saying that California belonged to the Democrats unless they let the opposition "steal" it.

McCormick was sure that the reporter would not have said that unless he had gotten wind of some foul play on the West Coast. He wired his people in California to be alert to any attempts at skulduggery. He received an answer that there had indeed been some attempts at cheating, but, thanks to the warning, they would be able to scotch them. If the opposition tried again, they'd better bring their coffins with them.

Swope further advised his party leaders to spend some money immediately to get the rest of the vote out in northern California and to ensure a fair count of the ballots. McCormick glanced at Baruch, who, amused by the young man's exuberant optimism, shrugged assent. Despite his avowed belief that Wilson did not have a chance, Baruch was already into the campaign for $50,000. What were a few more dollars at that point?

Baruch took his leave, smiling speculatively at the dynamic redhead. The next morning, Mrs. McAdoo awakened her father with the news that the *New York Times* had altered its position and now declared the election "unsettled." President Wilson replied, "You tell that to the marines."

A little later, Baruch was awakened by Henry Morgenthau, Sr. "Bernie, we're in!"

The future elder statesman recalled the animated editor. He was the only one who had never lost his faith. Interesting young man—he would have to keep an eye on him.

It was not official that Wilson actually had won until Friday of that week. The president was not surprised when he was later told what had transpired at the Hotel Belmont. He had always known that Bayard (as he called him) was one of the few gentlemen of the press upon whom he could rely. It was not long before Swope was recognized as Wilson's unofficial spokesman to the nation. Journalists everywhere would read his columns to find out what the president was actually thinking about a given issue.

SIX

Early in January of 1917, the Century Company published Swope's series of articles on Germany in book form. *Inside the German Empire* was an instantaneous success. The reviews ranged from the *New York Times*'s "invaluable" to the *Literary Digest*'s "highly interesting." The New York *World* took justifiable pride in the work of its city editor, stating, "There is nothing just like it."

His fame grew, bringing demands for his services as a public speaker. It was not simply for ego gratification that he made room in a busy schedule for all of these engagements. He believed that it was his duty to alert the American people to the dangers inherent in Germany's martial temperament and its growing antagonism toward the United States. There was another factor that influenced Swope in his decision to turn orator. Wilson needed a spokesman, and his was a most persuasive voice to turn loose on the lecture platform, to let echo through the banquet hall.

The special nature of Swope's relationship to the president was not lost on the rest of the press. The New York *Tribune*'s scantily cloaked reference to Swope read, "A *World* correspondent who has assumed recently to speak with understanding of the intentions of the administration. . . ." The Boston *Transcript* was calling Swope "the White House transmitter of orthodox opinion." In one issue of the *North American Review,* he was called "the missing link between the White House and the *World*"; another described him as "the tentatively authorized spokesman for the administration through the *World*."

Swope's public-speaking form left an indelible impression upon all those privileged to hear him. Years after his death, his secretary, Kathleen Gilmore, could still recall it vividly. "He was fantastic. He never read from a paper. When Herbert gave a speech, he needed no more than a three-by-five index card with some key words printed on it. Usually, he didn't even look at that."

His son said, "It was uncanny. He never lowered his eyes from his audience. And everybody listening felt as if he was speaking to them alone."

The late Walter Lippmann put it this way: "One didn't necessarily agree with what Herbert Swope said. But one could not help admiring the style with which he said it."

In early 1917 his speaking engagements ran the gamut from John D. Rockefeller's Bible Class at the Fifth Avenue Baptist Church, through the New York Chapter of the American Institute of Banking, to the annual dinner of the Sports Writers' Association. With minor variations designed for the specific audience, the major theme was always the same: Germany would not long respect American neutrality, and it would be in the country's best interests to prepare for war.

Reporting on the Sports Writers' dinner, the sporting sheet the *Morning Telegraph* noted that the sobriety of his speech was in no way diminished by his sartorial sumptuousness.

> Herbert Swope, city editor of the New York *World,* failed in his attempt to shame those present with his evening clothes, and then turning around, he squared himself with an account of the great interest taken by the fighting armies of Europe in sports. Swope has just recently returned from Europe [Actually, four months had passed since his return from Europe.] and he said he found the soldiers had come to look on war as a sport, the greatest ever devised. . . . Incidentally, Swope said in his opinion the war would last for two years yet, providing things continued in a normal manner in the German Empire.

His estimate of the length of the war was off by only two months, but he had not taken into account the dispatch with which America was to enter into hostilities.

Swope the social figure was also very much a part of the scene in New York City. At dinners in honor of the Serbian emissary, on committees to invite the Japanese mission to New York, and as one of the leading celebrators of Ambassador Gerard's return from his post in Germany, Swope was among those conspicuously cited in the entire press, not merely in his own paper. His name began to appear on lists that seldom mentioned any newsmen at all below the level of publisher.

When Mr. and Mrs. William Randolph Hearst gave a Valentine's Eve theater party at the great hit of the day, *The Century Girl,* which starred Elsie Janis, Leon Errol, and Hazel Dawn, among the guests there and at supper afterward were the Herbert Bayard Swopes, along with the Seward Webbs, the Angier Biddle Dukes, Hamilton Fish, and William Rhinelander Stewart.

When Mr. and Mrs. Swope gave a supper party at the Ritz Carlton, the Hearsts were *not* among the guests, who included Lord Northcliffe,

Herbert Bayard Swope in Halifax,
Nova Scotia, in 1912, to cover the
Titanic story.

(*Below*) At tennis, 1912.

With Maggie Swope on the
way to the Azores, July 1914.

HBS and his bride Maggie in Bermuda
in 1912.

(*Below*) With aviator John Lansing Callan
aboard the S.S. *Roma,* between the Azores
and Lisbon, August 1914.

HBS *(seated, on left)* and the other Peace Conference correspondents grouped around
Colonel Edward M. House at the American Peace Headquarters, the Hotel Crillon,
Paris, in May 1919.

Herbert and Maggie Swope on the *Ile de France*, 1922.

(*Below, left*) The debonair reporter on vacation in Bermuda. (*Right*) With Judge (later New York Mayor) John O'Brien in 1924.

Harold Talbott, Mrs. Talbott (Peggy Thayer), and HBS in the early 1920s.

Laurette Taylor inscribed this photo: "To Herbert Swope, 'the fourth dimension,' from 'the first.' "

Jane and Herbert, Jr. (Ottie), on the beach at Great Neck, about 1927.

(*Above*) Laurence Stallings—marine, critic, playwright.

(*Above right*) Joshua Cosden and Maggie at Palm Beach in the early 1920s.

(*Right*) Rear Admiral Richard E. Byrd.

Bruce Powell, Maggie's brother, in 1922.

Governor Alfred E. Smith and Swope at Saratoga in 1927.

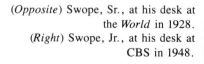
(*Left to right*) Edwin M. Post, Mrs.
Alexander Laughlin (Miss Mellon),
(*seated*) Mrs. William Randolph
Hearst, Prince Christopher of Greece,
Mrs. Post, and HBS at the 1928
Beaux Arts Ball.

(*Opposite*) Swope, Sr., at his desk at
the *World* in 1928.
(*Right*) Swope, Jr., at his desk at
CBS in 1948.

Mimi Powell in Palm Beach in 1926.

(*Left to right*) Swope, Bernard Baruch, and Condé Nast at the Louis-Nova fight, September 29, 1939.

Swope, Alfred E. Smith, and FDR at the famous "old potato" reconciliation, arranged by Swope, on November 5, 1932.

HBS at Saratoga Race Course in 1929.

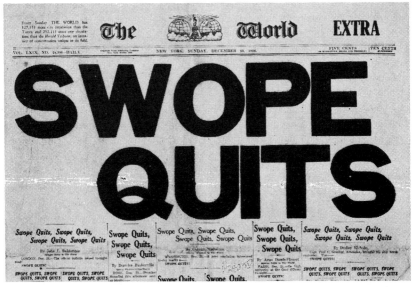

Special edition of the New York *World* brought out by his staff on the day of Swope's resignation, December 23, 1928.

Ambassador and Mrs. Elkus, Ambassador and Mrs. Gerard, Mr. and Mrs. August Belmont, and the Marquis de Polignac.

Swope's feelings about Hearst were equivocal. He considered him one of the outstanding publishers of his day, but also overly susceptible to flattery. He had nothing but disdain for the manner in which Hearst allowed himself to be manipulated by the German propagandists, who unctuously paid court to him with lavish praise like "newspaper king." At the same time, he did not think it an entirely unmerited title: Swope later rated Hearst one of the four greatest newspaper publishers of his time, along with Adolph S. Ochs of the *New York Times,* the senior Pulitzer, and Lord Northcliffe of the London *Daily Mail.*

Swope had reached only the age of thirty-five, but he was already evincing all of the traits that would distinguish him for the rest of his life, traits which of themselves were pleasing and admirable but which collectively would one day limit what rightfully should have been his limitless horizon. With Swope in mind, Bernard Baruch observed with some degree of acuity, "It is often not in a man's best interests to be too popular."

He was a commanding figure at any gathering; he was never reticent about sounding off on any subject that was close to him, and doing so in a manner enthralling enough to hold the attention of all within earshot. By contrast, Hearst was essentially a shy and retiring man, which was indeed strange in a man celebrated for his hospitality. However, it must be recounted that most of his entertaining was done to amuse either his wife, Millicent, or his mistress, Marion Davies. He would rather have been alone than surrounded by the masses of social and theatrical celebrities upon whom the women doted. He had little in common with these publicity seekers, for his was real power, while theirs was only an evanescent fame that often existed largely at his pleasure.

A duality would always color the relationship between the publisher and the editor. For Hearst, the younger man was a disquieting figure, because he resisted pat characterization. For Swope, the tycoon was disquieting for precisely the opposite reason. Hearst's public personality was one almost of ingenuousness. He preferred this apparent pat characterization, feeling that it gave him an edge on people to have them indulging in broad generalizations about him rather than delving into his extremely complex personality. Let them call him a pro-German pacifist this year and a warmonger imperialist the next; it allowed him to play his game secretly.

On April 2, 1917, President Wilson went before a special joint session of Congress to ask that a state of war be declared between the United States and Germany, urging in ringing tones that "the world must be made safe for democracy." The resolution was passed by a vote of 82 to 6 in the Senate and 373 to 50 in the House of Representatives.

On April 3, Swope was invited to dinner at the home of Mr. and Mrs. August Belmont. He had known Mrs. Belmont since he first arrived in New York, when, as Eleanor Robson, she had been the toast of Broadway in the hit that was to serve her for years, *Merely, Mary Ann*. In 1910 Miss Robson married the great financier who, among other accomplishments, built the New York subways. She retired from the stage at the height of a brilliant career, thus giving rise to dozens of subsequent Broadway and Hollywood plots about the star who married the millionaire and lived happily ever after.

That April evening, Mrs. Belmont had invited Swope especially to have him make a speech for her other guests, the most influential members of the Metropolitan Opera Association, an organization in which she was beginning to take an interest (she was later to found the Metropolitan Opera Guild). His subject was the place of German music in an American opera company's repertory during the war. Swope's unpopular position was that art had nothing to do with politics. He failed to persuade his listeners, and German music was banned from the opera house for the duration.

On April 5, Swope lunched with William Randolph Hearst at the Manhattan Club. At that very moment war was being declared, and the Hearst press was forced to change attitudes in mid-week. Their April first Sunday editions still clung tenaciously to the notion that peace was possible. The president's speech that Monday made a hash of that, and by Thursday Hearst was busily trying to mend executive fences and retain his commanding position as a gatherer and disseminator of news. One prime way to do this was to capture Wilson's favorite newsman for his staff. An attractive offer was made and rejected. In the years that followed, the two were often to come close to working together without ever being able to overcome the obstacle of their incompatible individuality.

On April 6, President Wilson signed the official congressional declaration. A state of war existed between Germany and the United States. Strangely enough, it would take several months before a similar state existed between the Americans and the other major Central Power. It was not until December 7 (an ominous date in this country's martial history) that war was declared against the Austro-Hungarian Empire.

Swope wanted desperately to be a part of the war effort. His first idea was to return to Europe as a front-line correspondent. Ralph Pulitzer, Florence White, and Charles Lincoln collectively vetoed that proposal. Good foreign correspondents were not difficult to procure. Every good journalist in the country was longing to go overseas. But a reporter who had the ear of the president during wartime was an irreplaceable asset to any paper. The only voyage they wanted Swope to make was the one to Washington.

To hell with them, he thought. I'll go into the service. I'm still young and healthy. Margaret Swope's comment on that idea is unprintable.

There were still too many men in their twenties not yet in uniform for the army to bother with a nearly middle-aged man encumbered with enormous familial responsibilities.

It was the first time he ever regretted the obligations that he had assumed with matrimony. Those Powells! From then on, he would periodically shout, complain, sputter, and fume, but, curse his fate though he might, nobody ever took him too seriously on that subject.

Once he was going through his catalogue of personal harassments, including lack of privacy in his own home, for the benefit of Alexander Woollcott. The waspish theater critic lifted one eyebrow skeptically and said, "Privacy in the Swope ménage is about as likely as privacy on a subway at rush hour."

Swope ranted on about always having Ken or Bruce or Mimi underfoot, about never even being permitted the luxury every stray cat has of being left to himself when feeling ill. He wailed: "Perhaps they should all go away—set up housekeeping for themselves."

Woollcott replied, "There's nothing wrong with you, Swope, except that you seem to have a little trouble moving your Powells."

Swope glared for a moment and then threw back his head and broke into that astonishing silent laugh of his. He, who could be so vocal in all other matters, never uttered a risible sound. The only indication that he was laughing was the way his mouth turned up, his teeth bared and his body shook.

Once George S. Kaufman and Moss Hart sat directly behind him at the opening of a new comedy. Hart asked, "Is Swope laughing? I don't hear him."

"Sure he is," Kaufman reassured him. "Look at his back. It's shaking. With Swope, that's laughter."

"It could be a twitch."

Kaufman shook his head: "I don't think so. The Swopes are too elegant to twitch in public."

At that point, Margaret turned around and hissed, "Would you two assholes shut the hell up!"

In June 1917 Swope won the first Pulitzer Prize ever awarded in journalism for his series on Germany. It was given for "the best example of a reporter's work during the year, the test being strict accuracy, terseness, the accomplishment of some public good commanding public attention and respect."

The remarkable reportorial achievement of the series was that the book remained valid even after America went to war with Germany and despite the fact that the tone was measured and objective rather than propagandistic and hostile toward the enemy nation.

SEVEN

"The *World* is publishing the most important dispatches coming out of Washington. With unequaled sources of information, Herbert Bayard Swope is giving the *World*'s readers the best presentation of the developments of the war from the national capital. Mr. Swope is an international authority, and the value of his work is not approached by that of any other writer in Washington."

The paragraph was part of a series of institutional advertisements that the *World* began to run at the start of 1918. It appeared on a full page under the headline: THE WORLD LEADS IN NEWS OF THE WAR.

Swope had set up headquarters at the Seward Park Hotel and was serving as his newspaper's special correspondent in Washington, D.C. If he couldn't go overseas, he was going to do the next best thing, and that was to be close to the source of war news at home. The battlefront thing still rankled. Swope's paragraph in the ad was extremely laudatory, but the galling point was that it was not the leading item. The lead justifiably belonged to Lincoln Eyre, who was following the exploits of the American troops in France.

Swope had impressed Bernard M. Baruch on that memorable election night of 1916. Early in 1918, Baruch was made head of the War Industries Board. The board's function was to coordinate the supply of raw materials with the demands of industry. It evaluated industrial priorities in terms of the war effort and determined which companies got what and the order in which they got it, thereby proving invaluable in converting a peacetime economy into an efficient war machine.

Baruch later wrote of his colleagues: "Few administrators in Washington were ever more fortunate than I in their associates. They were the most remarkable group I have ever known. The credit for the record and reputation of WIB belongs to them."

He recalled how Swope joined that "remarkable group."

"One day Swope had come to me to get a story on the lagging production of French 75-mm guns. He backed me against a lamppost and poured questions at me. I don't think I ever gave him what he hoped to get, but I was impressed with his knowledge and with his tenacious, inquiring mind. I asked him to join me."

Swope accepted, although it meant going off salary at the *World*. His colleagues on the War Industries Board were different from the men he hitherto had known. Previously he had been associated with men in society, in the arts, and in journalism, where style and wit were a man's passport to position. That was not sufficient with this group, nor did wealth alone interest them. Power was the prime mover. Everything that these industrialists accomplished was an exercise in the manipulation of power.

Swope's special province was public relations. Knowing how easily words could be misinterpreted by the press, Baruch sought to protect his staff by ordering that all public statements be cleared with the journalist before being released.

Swope was true to Baruch's designation for him—"flying executive"—but his duties did not end there. Swope's intuitive grasp of almost every kind of problem made him invaluable in the most unlikely situations. After one meeting a construction-supply manufacturer who had never met or even heard of him before mused aloud: "What kind of fellow is this—who can walk into a meeting on how to make bricks cheaply or cut down on the size of nails, and grasp things so quickly?"

On another occasion, the president requested that Baruch make a conspectus of all war activities in the government. Baruch replied that he would do so, and then he called upon Swope with a most germane question. "Herb, what's a conspectus? I've just agreed to make one for the president."

Swope answered immediately that it was a general review or digest. Once Baruch was clear on what it was, he put Dean Edwin F. Gay of Harvard in charge of preparing it. In addition to knowing how to gather the best available talents in their respective fields, Baruch knew how to utilize them to his own and occasionally their best advantage.

The board was an example of this special Baruch genius. At full strength, it comprised 750 men, including Swope's brother Gerard, and represented an unprecedented cross section of American power and prestige. The impressiveness wound all the way down to the stenographer, Billy Rose, future theatrical impresario and millionaire. Like Swope, Rose knew how to manipulate those in power. Unlike him, he seldom did it for altruistic reasons.

After the war ended, President Wilson paid special tribute to the members of the WIB:

> These men turned aside from every private interest of their own, devoted the whole of their trained capacity to the tasks that supplied the sinews of the whole great undertaking. Their patriotism, the unselfishness, the thorough-going devotion and distinguished capacity that marked their toilsome labors, month after month, made them fit mates and comrades for the men in the trenches and on the sea.

Swope could only ask, "Were we *that* good?" The personal doubts persisted. He wondered whether his contribution could truly measure up to that of the man under fire. For years after, he tended to dismiss his role in the war. In fact, he seldom spoke of any of his accomplishments. His anecdotes were marvelous because he was so seldom the central figure in them. They almost never began with a tiresome "I."

A Swope observer, who was not particularly a friend, once put it this way: "Herb Swope can talk louder, longer, and faster than anybody I know. The one thing that makes it bearable is that he hardly ever talks about Swope."

He was that rarest of anomalies, a modest egotist.

For the two decades following the end of the war, Baruch hosted a yearly reunion of his War Industries Board staff. There would come a time during each of these evenings when Swope would be called upon to tell the host's favorite story on himself. It became as much a set piece among their friends as his Billy Sulzer saga.

He reminded them of the meetings Baruch and he had periodically had with the president during 1918. After one of them, they were all sitting around enjoying a social visit. Wilson told them about a book he'd just finished reading that held that all human beings were reincarnations of animals. They began to give designations to various members of the administration. There were foxes, tigers, lions, and even a mouse, but the proper species for Baruch eluded the president. Swope would continue:

> Turning to Baruch, he said that he was at a loss to find his prototype, especially when Baruch was deep in thought, or in disagreement with the one he was listening to, when he had the habit of scrounching down in his chair and piercing his companions through with a look. I said that, at the War Industries Board, we said that when Baruch assumed that attitude he was like a snake in the grass (in the pleasanter sense), ready to strike at the first sign of weakness. Then I added that this was not especially true, that I thought Baruch's real prototype was the elephant—the Asiatic elephant, which has five toes, as against his African brother, which has only three, it being agreed that Baruch would have all the toes that nature permitted. The Baruch elephant, representing the embodiment of all animal wisdom, would be walking along a narrow path and come to a deep river, across which was thrown a flimsy bamboo bridge. First the elephant would try it with his trunk, then with his right foreleg, then with his left, and, backing up to it, repeat the process with his hindlegs. Having completed his inspection, the elephant, turning to his followers, would announce: "This bridge is perfectly safe and will carry my weight—but I guess I'll let some other sucker cross first."

One can only speculate on how many of that distinguished assemblage, Swope included, had the furtive feeling that at one point or another they might have played the sucker, and wondered further what species of animal that made them.

EIGHT

The war was over. That meant only one thing to Margaret Swope—the resumption of her life with Herbert. The reunion was a joyous one, for he did adore her and the families: his, hers, and theirs. But a problem cropped up that was to plague him for the rest of his life: her extravagance was prodigious. Margaret created the kind of home and atmosphere that he undoubtedly loved, for he himself was a true lover of comfort, but she spared no expense. There was a permanent staff of three servants, with extra help employed for parties. Margaret was the upholsterers' delight, for her credo apparently was "when in doubt, recover." There had been no recession in this life-style, despite the fact that he had been off his salary for the five months devoted to the War Industries Board—off salary but not off the job, for he had continued to direct the Washington bureau of the *World*. His wealthy colleagues on the board had given up their positions to become what were later known as dollar-a-year men. There was something in Swope that would not permit him to do less. Her reckless spending and his pride meshed to form a legend of immense wealth that lasted their lifetimes and continued to haunt their children long after their deaths. As Bennett Cerf, who actually was one, observed: "Herb wasn't really a millionaire. He lived too well."

During his absence, Margaret had simply let the bills mount up. Her attitude toward debts was always rather cavalier. She knew that if she ignored them long enough, Swope would eventually step in and take care of them. But at that point, his savings were exhausted, and there was no way that he could immediately replenish them.

A problem was simultaneously developing in his professional life that threatened to overshadow all others. Charles M. Lincoln, the same managing editor of the *World* who had been one of Swope's early supporters, was beginning to resent him. Ralph Pulitzer attempted to accommodate both and ended by satisfying neither. Swope, the Pulitzer prize–winning analyst of German affairs, was being given paltry assignments that any hack reporter could have covered. The instructions came from his editor, while his publisher hinted vaguely at better things to come.

The biggest story of the day was the coming European peace conference. Swope wanted to cover it, but Lincoln was doing his best to make certain that he wouldn't be considered for the job.

Pulitzer and Lincoln, who had no experience in international affairs, were going over, primarily to be a part of the excitement. With the help of Lincoln Eyre and James M. Tuohy, the *World* men in Paris and London respectively, plus Louis Seibold, who was acting as general utility man, the coverage could be more than adequate. There would be no need for the only man on the paper who actually had been in Germany since the beginning of the war and whose reportage had done so much to shape American attitudes toward that country at the critical time when the United States was about to declare war.

Swope went over Lincoln's head to Ralph Pulitzer and got the European assignment by threatening to leave the paper and cover the story for another publication. The next problem was securing accommodations on the *Orizaba,* the overcrowded ship allocated to the press.

It was to depart at 3:00 P.M., December 1, and it was not until 11:00 A.M. that Swope received word that there would be space for him aboard. He had four hours in which to pack, put all of his affairs in order, and make the three-quarters-of-an-hour journey to Hoboken, New Jersey, the port of embarkation.

The most painful part of his departure was the scene with Margaret. He tried to explain that he was going for both of them. It was the greatest assignment of his career, and by accepting he could regain the ground lost during the war, thus reestablishing his reputation. Once that was accomplished, they need never be separated again, for he would be able to have any position he chose in the city.

The only thing that she heard was that he was leaving her again. The only thing that mattered was that they still would not be living together, after not having been truly together for almost a year. She didn't give a damn about his future or anything else, beyond wanting him to be with her, to be hers alone.

Among the reasons he had for going to Europe, there was one that remained unexpressed. The only word that Gerard and he had received from the German branch of the family was that his mother, Ida, had been very ill. He thought that, once over there, he might be able to find a way of getting to see her or, at the very least, getting help to her should it prove necessary.

The newspapers claimed that there were approximately three hundred journalists on the *Orizaba.* By Swope's account, which was probably more accurate, there were only fifty-three working reporters. The rest of the passengers were editors, publishers, and a motley assortment who somehow had managed to wangle spurious credentials in order to make the voyage.

It was clear that the new men were going to have a difficult time competing with the seasoned correspondents who had been on European assignments since the beginning of the war and, in some cases, before that. To combat the superiority gained from experience, they organized themselves into what they designated the United States Press Delegation to the Peace Conference. The premise was that in unity there was at least an approximation of strength.

Swope was selected to head the delegation by an almost unanimous vote. There were many valid reasons for this, the primary one being that, through the personal relationships that had ripened during his stay in Washington, he had access to all of the key figures representing the United States. Another considerable factor was his known fairness and generosity.

His colleagues were to be well satisfied with their choice. When France and England attempted to censor what news could be transmitted by the journalists, Swope went directly to Wilson and got the concessions that made their jobs possible. When the newsmen were informed that no provision had been made for them to accompany the president on a state visit to Belgium, they complained to Swope, who went straight to the top. A press car was added to Wilson's train. When Arthur Krock wanted an exclusive interview with Baruch, it was Swope who arranged it, despite the fact that Baruch was considered his own personal preserve and was supposedly off-limits to the others.

He treated his competitors as his personal charges and was always ready to help in any situation. Even Charles Lincoln had good reason not to regret Swope's position as head of the delegation, although he had taken it as a personal affront when the vote was first announced. Lincoln became ill not long after arriving in France, and it was Swope who pulled the necessary strings to get him admitted to the American Hospital in Neuilly, despite a desperate shortage of beds. When Damon Runyon came down with influenza in Paris and could find no better physician than the house man at the YMCA, Swope stepped in and brought the president's own physician, Admiral Cary Grayson, to prescribe for him.

In a letter dated Sunday night, December 8, five hours out of Brest, Swope wrote to Margaret:

My beautiful darling—

    It is just a week since I saw you. The memory of your kiss and the tears that went with it are still fresh in my thoughts—and ever will be. I have missed you frightfully.

He described his election and life on the ship, concluding the passage with:

There have been no unpleasantnesses in the *World* group except that Lincoln, inside of him, got sore at my election. He told R.P. privately that he resented the fact that I seemed to pay no attention to his authority. But I'm going to smooth him down—might as well be pleasant while we're together on the job.

Christmas Day found the press corps going to London to witness Wilson's official reception at Buckingham Palace. It was the result of Swope's first intercession on their behalf, for originally they had not been scheduled to accompany the president.

While sitting up all night on the boat train from Paris, Swope dashed off a fourteen-page handwritten letter to Margaret. In addition to giving a description of his daily activities, he betrayed many of his anxieties on both a personal and a professional level.

    . . . How are the accounts going? Is the *World* check coming regularly? Do write me a long letter, for I'm hungering for *home* details. Don't skimp your answers, but come through fully. I haven't heard from you since I arrived, except through David [Bagley].

    And now as for me. I'm writing this on the train to Boulogne en route to London. The British government is taking a party of American newsmen over to witness Wilson's reception there. . . .

He did not mention that he was responsible for the trip. All his letters to her were marked by a reticence about his accomplishments and an insecurity about the quality of his work. He simply mentioned that he was going "because it's a chance to add a solid English background to my equipment . . . ."

The trip to London was an exhilarating change, and it did "add a solid English background" to his "equipment." In addition to the official receptions, Lord Northcliffe, who admired him, procured invitations for him to attend a full round of "upper crust" functions. So many noble names like Southampton, Monmouth, and Reading were on the guest list at one memorable dinner party that Swope later described it as "looking more like an American railroad timetable than a list of notables."

His birthday, January 5, found him back in Paris and feeling lonelier than ever. He wrote and complained to Margaret of the dreariness of that day:

> I know few people here, and I'm satisfied that this should be so, for I am not happy in this atmosphere. There is something lacking from the old-time air of Paris. War has left its impression indelibly upon the city. It lacks the old nonchalance; it has become self-absorbed and selfish.

Although he had some qualms, he broached the subject of her joining him. He had received three letters from her by this time, but was ever eager for more. His preoccupation with both the pleasures and disappointments of his role as head of her family was apparently continuing to absorb much of his time away from work:

> Ralph and Lincoln are returning this week, going before the peace sessions really open. I am to be left in charge to do the bigger part of the work. No one knows how long the situation will continue. If it promises to be protracted, I'd like very much to have you come over. Do you think it can be done? I wouldn't like you to leave things unsettled at home where your influence is *vital*, especially at this point. On my return from London, I found your dear letter awaiting me, written on the twelfth of December. It made me happy, and I read and reread it with avidity. Do write me more home details—I hunger for them all.

Swope wrote a story on January 6 about British-American unity on the establishment of the League of Nations. In a rather gratuitous addendum, he noted:

> Bernard Baruch, who will arrive here next week, will take charge of America's economic interests and act as chief adviser on questions of raw supplies for the world, having been sent for by the President to handle these matters.

It was at about this point that Swope's letters to Margaret grew less frequent—but no less sincere in their reaffirmations of his love. Baruch's presence was only part of the reason. More compelling was Swope's deepening involvement as a committed observer of events in which the smallest compromise could have overwhelming repercussions in the ensuing years.

Although a dedicated liberal on the question of any nation's right to determine its own political constitution, he was among the first American correspondents to see the dangers inherent in an unchecked Bolshevist victory in Russia and the greater danger of a peace treaty that did not take into account the affairs of that vast country. His criticism extended to the lack of action by the president he usually considered sacrosanct. On January 7 he wrote, in a prescient dispatch:

> All the world is sitting on the crater of a Bolshevist volcano. Only statesmen of the farthest vision and of the widest operations can prevent an eruption which will engulf the present system and wipe out the existing principles of democracy resting upon the freedom of the individual protected by laws of property rights and national sovereignty. . . .

After describing some of the attractions that Russia was holding out to the downtrodden, he inserted a reproving comment on the "Micawberlike" attitude of the peace conference leaders:

> A curious ostrichlike policy is being maintained by most leaders of public opinion on the question of a social uprising, evidence of which is seen on all sides, but which seemingly is to be checked by the mere denial of its existence. Nor is the President himself free from criticism of ignoring the situation. He preaches a vast political reform and is succeeding in substantiating his words by his practice, but he is silent on the bigger social questions which are, after all, the taproots of world politics. . . .

Swope was equally apprehensive about those abroad who would resort to force as a solution:

> They are shortsighted persons who believe that force is the only method of dealing with the condition and who would send armies into Russia upon the assumption that they would form a basis for reconstruction, not realizing that the very armies themselves form the most fruitful soil in which to plant the seeds of protest. . . .

Clemenceau was opposed to freedom of the press. He wanted the public to know only so much as the leaders thought they should know and attempted to prevail upon the other nations to adopt a "gag rule." Working with Arthur Krock (then editor of the Louisville *Courier-Journal*) and J. E. Nevan (of the Press Association), Swope rallied the American, British, and a segment of the French press to take a position demanding free access to the Peace Conference, which was to commence on January 19 in the Great Clock Hall of the Quai d'Orsay Palace. They applied concerted pressure on the heads of their respective governments. Swope described the results as: "Recession by the conference from news suppression and the adoption of a formula whereby the public is to gain information of matters in solution instead of being compelled to await their crystallization."

He described the "gag rule" that had elicited this successful press protest, and its consequences:

> The rule responsible for these activities—which would hide the deliberations of a body charged with the greatest purpose in the history of the world—was designed to obscure the record of compromises of the various delegates to the conference because of the delicate governmental balances in the continental countries. Since this is contrary to the principles of America and Britain, and the fate of particular continental politicians is not material when weighed against the information due to the peoples who sacrificed their blood and treasure to win the war, the press correspondents of the two English-speaking nations, and particularly the Americans, resolved to stand against it to the last.
>
> It is one of the finest demonstrations ever seen of the thoroughly patriotic spirit of the American press and a close reflection of the nation's ideals and principles.

By the time the Peace Conference actually got under way, Woodrow Wilson had become committed to the idea that the only solution to the Russian problem was a political one and that it had to be based upon some sort of limited recognition. The British were prepared to go along with him. In spite of French opposition, it was necessary to keep channels open for possible accord with Lenin, and Wilson decided to send William C. Bullitt, a young special assistant in the State Department, on a secret and unofficial mission to meet Lenin and see what accommodations were possible. Bullitt was very much under the influence of the brilliant and radical editor Lincoln Steffens, and suggested that he be invited to accompany him. Wilson agreed. Steffens was a writer of international repute who, although not himself a Communist, was well known for his Bolshevist sympathies, and the president thought that it would be a gesture of good faith if the only journalist to cover the mission was one predisposed toward the leftist regime.

When Steffens returned to Paris twenty-two days later, he was dazed by the euphoric experience. He told in his autobiography of meeting Bernard Baruch in Jo Davidson's studio, where the sculptor was working on a head of the statesman: " 'So you've been over to Russia?' Bernard Baruch said. I answered very literally. 'I have been over into the future, and it works!' "

Steffens knew a good line when he coined it, and he started repeating it in a more polished version within a few days. He was sitting around at the Crillon with Swope, Arthur Krock, and John Wheeler. They asked for his impressions of the trip, and he replied, "I've seen the future, and it works." He launched into praise for the Communist accomplishment, ending with a contrast with degenerate Paris. He said, "Why, they don't even have any prostitutes on the streets."

Swope cried: "Good God, Stef—what did you do?"

Had the offers Lenin transmitted through Bullitt been accepted and honored by both sides, they might have changed the shape and substance of modern Europe. They went far beyond anything that Wilson would have dreamed of requesting. In exchange for recognition, Russia pledged to pay its war debts, give economic concessions to the West, withdraw the Soviet armies from Siberia, the Urals, the Balkan states, Archangel, White Russia, and the Ukraine.

Having viewed the Russian situation from the same point of view as Steffens, young William Bullitt had no doubt that Lenin was sincere. He resigned from the American delegation in protest against the lack of enthusiasm for the proposals he brought back. He later testified before Congress that the League of Nations would be a useless enterprise, immeasurably helping those who ultimately vetoed American participation.

Although Swope deplored Bullitt's stand on the League in 1919, he did agree that the Russian offers should have received greater consideration. He remained an ardent advocate of the League and continued to believe that, had we joined it and backed our convictions with our strength, the prospects for world peace would have been improved. Soon after Steffens and Bullitt returned to Paris, Swope wrote with enormous insight:

> More and more clearly does it appear as the days of the Peace Conference near their close that the final treaty to be signed will be merely an incident in the world disorders and not an end.

Unsatisfied ambitions and unrealized hopes are poor foundations upon which to build a permanent peace structure, and the structure itself is the political type of architecture, remote from the new problems of a social nature confronting the world and to which the conference has addressed itself but little, if at all.

The wrath that is being stored up will show itself for many years to come, and its manifestation can be met only with force. It is a realization of this condition that has made France insist upon and receive from Great Britain and America something more tangible in the way of assurances of protection than is afforded in the League of Nations.

France is to gain this security, but what about the other nations which are more in need of defense? With them, unless the League of Nations achieves success that is doubtful at the beginning, it will be as always has been the case—a survival of the fittest—and the edifice so carefully constructed by precept will fail in use.

There are today questions of a pressing nature which the conference cannot settle, and it requires no gift of prophecy to say that they will continue to plague future generations for years to come.

Swope's persistence in his beliefs prompted a joshing letter from Franklin D. Roosevelt, upon the newsman's return to the United States.

Highly Esteemed Stranger,
It is good to know that you have returned to the land where democracy is still safe, and I trust you have discarded your Paris accent, English clothes, and Lisbon habits. I really want to look you over and see for myself whether you are still the same good old Swope or have taken on the manners and customs of a Billy Bullitt.*

Word from Margaret was so irregular that the lack of response to his letters almost seemed calculated. On January 26, he was complaining that he had not heard a word for over a month and that he longed for "the touch of your warm red lips and the feel of your arms holding me to your beautiful body."

His friend Billy Fleischmann brought over two letters from Margaret on February 2. One filled him with joy, for it was an expression of love and fondness and concern. It was typical of Margaret that she also had to send the deflator.

---

*Roosevelt later appointed Bullitt the first American ambassador to the Soviet Union.

In the second letter, she unjustly chastised him for not giving a damn about her or the family. She accused him of having gone to Europe just to have a good time, while she was left home, saddled with all of the responsibilities. He immediately took up pencil and foolscap to dash off a fourteen-page reply explaining how unfair he felt she was being to him and how utterly miserable and depressed he'd been made by her letter. He said that he would rather not hear from her at all than get mail like that, and then he paradoxically begged her to write every other day, no matter how mundane or abrasive her messages might be. He ended by saying:

> Sometimes I feel like chucking the whole thing and going back. But what then? It would be playing straight into the hands of the opposition. No, the only thing to do is to do the job just as well as I can and give it all I've got. Then, I can look for other and better things; then, I can love you more, for love must be built on one's own self-respect as well as the respect of the other. Don't, don't make it hard.

By February, she managed to write again in a better frame of mind. He responded immediately by cable:

> LETTER TWENTY-FIRST MADE ME HAPPY BECAUSE CHEERY TONE STOP
> AM WELL BUT HOMESICK PLEASE WRITE DAILY LOVE HERBERT
> EYRE

The worst thing about the revelatory correspondence that they were to carry out by wire was that all messages had to be sent and received by Lincoln Eyre. He knew all and said nothing. Swope was always grateful for his discretion and kindness.

In Swope's letter of March 19, there was again the familiar reproach to her for not writing. He also mentioned that

> The biggest lecture bureau in America offered me $6,000 *guarantee* with a split above that sum for ten weeks on the circuit this summer. I have practically turned it down, because I decline to be away from you this summer. Tell White about this and ask him his opinion. Incidentally, you can tell him, and keep it in mind to remind me, that I plan to take a *long* vacation this summer—first because I had *none* last year and for five months relieved the paper of my salary [while on the WIB, a period during which he had continued to send dispatches without being paid for them] and second because I've been over here for *three* months with a single day off.

As it developed, he did not spend the summer with her, but not because of the lecture tour. His ambivalence at the time may have been caused by a desire to have her approve of the lecture tour. More likely, he wanted the message carried to the paper. He was obviously intent upon pushing the editors for some sort of decision, flexing his muscles to show that he did not really need the *World,* for he continued:

> Also tell him that a friend of mine* has a bid in for the *Herald* and that I wish he would immediately write me his appraisal of the *net cash* worth of the *Herald, Evening Telegram,* and *Paris Herald.* [The *World* might well have been included in this list were it not for the fact that by the terms of the senior Pulitzer's will, it could not be sold.] Tell him you're delivering the message for me to get it to him promptly, and I want him to answer immediately care of Hotel Meurice, rue de Rivoli. Have him give his reasons for his figures and add that I asked you to ask him if he has any news for me regarding me, R.P., and C.M.L. [Pulitzer and Lincoln]; say that you don't know what I mean but I said he'd understand, as I had written him about an incident on the voyage over. F.W. [White] likes secrets—you know how to keep one better than anybody else, so pretend you're not in on this, though of course you are, as you are on all I know and everything I do.

---

   *More about this later.

In February, President Wilson returned to the United States to place the plans for the formation of the League of Nations before the American Congress. On the twenty-seventh of that month, Swope wrote about European astonishment at the violence of Republican attacks on the Democratic president and on the League, which he had done more to formulate than any other man at the Peace Conference.

In Wilson's absence, his chief aide, Colonel Edward M. House, was left in charge of the negotiations. Evidently, House was shaken by what was happening in Congress. He allowed attacks on the president to go unanswered. He made concessions that the Europeans, sensitive to their advantage, demanded, concessions that Wilson would never have permitted no matter how strong the opposition he faced at home.

Wilson returned in March to a *fait accompli*—a revised and weakened charter had been agreed upon by all parties, including the American mission. His problems at home made it impossible for him to repudiate the actions of his own people in Paris without creating still greater dissension, and he was forced to acquiesce.

The president broke with House privately, for he could make no public gesture that would not be open to misinterpretation. He told the colonel that nothing in life for which you did not have to fight was worthwhile. House replied fatuously, "Anglo-Saxon law is built on compromise."

Wilson was too weary to continue the dispute. He simply sighed and dismissed the man he had until then trusted so completely. He later told Mrs. Wilson, "House has given away everything I had won before we left Paris. He has compromised on every side."

There was no open indication of the breach between the president and the man who had been his closest adviser. Although Swope secretly felt that House's ego was such that an appeal to his vanity would cause him to place self-opinion above the American position, he was not above using that same vanity to gain his own ends. Swope later admitted that it was through House that he got a copy of the revised League of Nations covenant, which the *World* printed on April 3, in advance of any other paper on either side of the Atlantic.

On the same day that Swope's scoop appeared, Wilson became ill with what was publicly described as influenza. Swope learned confidentially from Admiral Grayson that it was a stroke. The reporter suppressed the information, aware of the potentially disastrous consequences of such news both back home and in Paris, where the other powers would take it as a signal to push through still more of their shortsighted and nationalistic demands. The story never broke in the press. The true nature of the president's illness remained a secret until long after the conference had ended.

Margaret's lackadaisical correspondence began to reflect a deepening depression. Swope received a letter from Florence White telling him that his mother-in-law had been down to see him, because Margaret suspected that Swope was staying away just to have a lark, and that she was extremely worried by her daughter's melancholy unhappiness.

Swope was so upset that he sat down in Baruch's suite and wrote a thirty-four-page letter on Ritz stationery, to be delivered to Margaret by the Attorney General of the United States, who was leaving the next day for home. By the time he finished, it was two in the morning, and Baruch had long since retired for the night. The audacity of Swope's behavior seems somewhat startling but apparently offended neither his host nor the cabinet member who was being used as a messenger boy.

There was an exuberance, an infectious enthusiasm about Swope that disarmed even the most staid critics, provided they had an inner largeness of spirit beneath the surface hauteur. Sir Harold Nicolson, who was then attached to the British delegation, called Swope "the star turn in the American journalistic world." He then commented with some candor on the differences between them. "He bursts with boost. He is very vulgar. He is a nice man. My liking for the Americans is becoming a vice. I like the scholarly sort, such as Coolidge, Seymour, Day, and Allen Dulles. I also have a weakness for the noisy sort such as Swope, because he is so unlike me. I feel like a mouse much impressed by a jaguar."

In his letter Swope revealed the reason he had asked Margaret to question White about the *Herald*.

> It may not be out of the way for me to say that Baruch is thinking seriously of buying the *Herald* and has asked me to go with him. I think I shall if he gets it. I am really fond him, and he of me. He believes in me, and I think I might go a long way with him beside me.

The April 10 edition of the Paris *Herald* had reprinted, with his permission, a summary of Swope's reportage on the changes in the League covenant. In the introduction, the paper stated: "Mr. Herbert Bayard Swope, the special correspondent of the New York *World*, has scored the biggest journalistic success of the conference by obtaining an analytic synopsis of the new document."

Though all this was true, the *Herald*'s generosity to Swope in publishing the note may have been inspired partially by Baruch's interest in acquiring the paper, because there was no reason not to lift his story, change a few words, and give him no credit at all. The deal may have fallen through because of price and terms, or the whole thing may have been no more than a caprice on the part of Baruch. There was no further mention of it in the correspondence of either Swope or Baruch. It was not the last time that Baruch was to raise Swope's hopes with the illusory promise of his own newspaper.

Without Swope's knowing it, two forces that would affect his entire future were coming into operation. The first was his faith in Baruch, which was so often to be misplaced; the second was the incredible web Margaret was weaving to bind him to her side forever, to keep him there no matter what professional enticement might come along to separate them. There were those who later said Swope could have been one of the most important men in the country were it not for the two people he loved most in the world.

A few weeks later the *World*'s headline read:

SIGHING IN RELIEF, ALLIES PRONOUNCE DOOM OF GERMANY

It was a dispatch by Herbert Bayard Swope, datelined May 7.

What followed was a remarkably good example of the journalistic style of the period, filled with well-observed and telling details about the participants, as well as small melodramatic flourishes and changes in tense that heightened the narrative. The piece was remarkable on a couple of other counts. Although the Germans were sitting with their backs to the press section, Swope's descriptions of them were done from a frontal point of view, which leads to the most remarkable fact of all: *Swope was not officially present at the meeting.*

Only nine tickets had been allotted to the entire American press corps. Straws were drawn for them, and Swope was among the losers. It was agreed that the winners would brief the others immediately after the ceremonies, in order that all might have detailed stories of the event to send back to their papers.

At the post-session briefing, Swope kept interrupting to correct those describing the events. Charles Selden, of the *New York Times,* exploded: "Swope, can't you keep your damned mouth shut for five minutes? How the hell would you know what went on? You weren't even there."

Swope's eyes twinkled mischievously. "Who says I wasn't?"

Swope's sartorial elegance was something his colleagues took for granted, when they weren't making jokes about it. However, it was only at that moment that they took note of his special grandeur that day: spats, striped trousers, cutaway coat, waistcoat, wing-tipped collar, gray silk cravat with a softly iridescent pearl stickpin, and a top hat that one of them described as looking so natural on him that he might have been born in it.

Swope's friend General Harry H. Bandholtz was the chief of military police for the AEF. Appreciating a good joke that would harm nobody, he lent the reporter his limousine so that he could crash the ceremonies. When Swope emerged from the car, looking more like the popular image of a diplomat than most of the genuine articles did, nobody questioned his right to a seat among the distinguished guests of the delegates.

He had enjoyed a far better view of the proceedings than any of the other reporters, and he gleefully shared his observations with them at the briefing. Selden was livid and returned directly to the American press headquarters, where he posted the following notice:

> Members of the organization of American correspondents attached to
> the peace conference who resent the action of Mr. Swope in violating
> the rules for attendance at the Versailles meeting and who think that
> Mr. Swope should not continue to be a member of the organization's
> committee may indicate their feelings by signing this paper.

He affixed his own signature to the humorless posting and waited.
When Swope saw the petition, he gaily signed his own name in a bright
red crayon directly under Selden's signature. The contrast between the
flamboyant red scrawl and the careful Palmer penmanship told the story.
Nobody else signed, and Swope was ceremoniously presented with the
document. He kept it as a souvenir of one of the few light moments of his
stay.

By mid-May, Swope was more concerned than ever about the state of
his wife's health. Her mother, Mimi, feared that Pearl might have been
having a nervous breakdown. For his own peace of mind, Swope could
not bring himself to believe that her illness was a physically incapacitat-
ing one. He wrote:

> This letter goes to you by the hand of Billy Fleischmann, who is
> returning on the *Leviathan*. When he sees you, he will have a plan to
> lay before you which I wish you to act upon as you please and as you
> think best. It concerns your coming over here to meet me and to return
> when I do. If things permit of your coming I shall be happy beyond
> words to have you here.

The letter is lost, but she obviously agreed to come over, for he began
to make plans for both of them to visit his mother, whom he had not seen
since 1916. Ida Swope was in bad health and in dreadful financial straits.
The German branch of the Swope family had invested all of their money
in Romanian and Hungarian state bonds, both of which were worthless.
Gerard was nowhere in sight, and Swope felt that it was his personal
duty to look after her.

At the last moment, Margaret wired that the doctor did not think it
advisable for her to make the trip. He wired back as soon as he got her
message:

> JUNE 11 WHY DOES THE DOCTOR OPPOSE YOUR TRIP WIRE BACK
> IMMEDIATELY WHAT HE SAYS IN DETAIL STOP WHAT SHIP LEAVES ON
> THE EIGHTEENTH IS BILLY RETURNING THEN STOP CABLE ME PLANS

YOUVE IN MIND STOP OUTLOOK HERE IS END WILL COME ABOUT
TWENTIETH IN WHICH CASE ID LEAVE END OF MONTH STOP IM EAGER
TO HAVE YOU COME BUT ONLY IF YOURE PERFECTLY WELL AND CAN
GO ON TRANSPORT TENDEREST LOVE HERBERT

EYRE

His next wire, dated June 18, found him concerned about her, his mother, and his insurance premiums in fairly equal measure.

BITTERLY DISAPPOINTED YOUR UNCOMING STOP WHAT MADE IT IM-
POSSIBLE STOP EXPECT FINISH HERE IN WEEK THEN MOTHER THEN
HOME AND YOU FOR WHOM IM LONGING STOP HAVE YOU ARRANGED
NOTES AND ALL INSURANCE PREMIUMS TENDERLY HERBERT

EYRE

Baruch was leaving for home on the president's ship, on the day after the signing of the treaty. Swope wrote a letter in cablese to Margaret, which Baruch had agreed to deliver to her along with a present. He told her that only the act of writing up the ceremonies prevented him from departing with Baruch. Within a few words, he contradicted himself by saying that he would be extending his stay to see his mother.

THAT IS A DUTY AND ONE I AM SURE WILL HAVE YOUR HEARTIEST
APPROVAL STOP THERE ARE NOT MANY MORE CHANCES LEFT AND SHE
FEELS THAT VERY DEEPLY STOP

It was more of his reach-and-withdrawal tactics. He would be with her if he could, but he couldn't, so he wouldn't. One must also doubt that he really believed that anything that kept him from her would have had her "heartiest approval." He quickly changed the subject to a more agreeable one by describing at great length the presents that he was sending her.

A BLUE AND WHITE ENAMELED CIGARETTE BOX AND A SMALLER BOX
TO HOLD POWDER AND PUFF STOP IT IS SET WITH SAPPHIRES AND
COMES FROM CARTIERS STOP IT IS VERY BEAUTIFUL STOP I HAD TO
CHOOSE AMONG SEVERAL THINGS THAT INCLUDED A BRACELET A PIN
AND A WHITE AND GOLD ENAMELED VANITY BOX STOP I SELECTED
THIS FOR YOU BECAUSE IT WAS DISTINCTLY PARIS AND BECAUSE I
THOUGHT IT WOULD PLEASE YOU STOP IF IT DOESNT YOU ARE AT
LIBERTY TO TAKE IT TO CARTIER AND EXCHANGE IT STOP FOR YOUR

INFORMATION IT COST 4750 FRANCS STOP MY IDEA IS FOR YOU PRO-
VIDED YOU KEEP THEM TO TAKE THEM TO CARTIER AND HAVE THEM
ENGRAVE ON THE STONES AND ALSO HAVE CHAINS ATTACHED TO
THEM SO THAT YOU CAN CARRY THEM ON YOUR WRIST STOP BUT YOU
MUST BE CAREFUL TO KEEP THEM FROM KNOCKING TOGETHER BE-
CAUSE OTHERWISE THEYLL SCRATCH STOP CARTIER HIMSELF SAID TO
ATTACH CHAINS AND ENGRAVE THEM WOULD NOT COST MORE THAN
300 FRANCS SO TELL THEM THAT AT THE NEW YORK OFFICE AND SAY
THAT THE ARRANGEMENT WAS MADE BY BARUCH PERSONALLY WHO
ALSO RESERVED THE RIGHT TO EXCHANGE STOP YOU CAN DO JUST AS
YOU WISH BUT I THINK YOULL LIKE THEM STOP POSSIBLY THE
SMALLER BOX COULD BE FIXED WITH A PARTITION FOR A REGULAR
VANITY CASE BUT I THINK IT WILL DO IF YOU HAVE A MIRROR
INSERTED AND PUT IN A GOLD POWDER PUFF AND POSSIBLY A LIP-
STICK IF YOU CARRY ONE STOP AT ANY RATE IT GOES WITH ALL MY
LOVE AS WELL AS HIS [Baruch's] ADMIRATION AND AFFECTION STOP
HE SEEMS GENUINELY FOND OF YOU AND HE IS SURELY A WARM
FRIEND OF MINE STOP FOR THAT ALONE I KNOW YOULL LIKE HIM

An interesting study in contrasts between the egotistical Baruch, "reserving the right to exchange" the gifts, and the Pulitzer Prize-winning Swope, so insecure about his own taste as to agree. Perhaps Baruch chose even more expensive gifts to bring to Maggie in Herbert's name, even advancing the money. But change them he did, as Swope wrote in a postscript:

> There's been a change of plans. B.M. doesn't much care for the things selected for you, so he's taking a shot at it himself. It's in the lap of the gods—I don't know what he'll bring, but I'm sure it will be something beautiful.

What the gifts actually were remains a mystery. Margaret's reaction to the idea that her husband had permitted another man to choose presents for her was understandable rage. It colored her meeting with Baruch.

When the two met in New York, Margaret immediately began to complain about her financial problems. She concluded by asking for a loan of two hundred dollars. It provoked what sounded like the beginning of a very long lecture on the virtues of economy and thrift. She interrupted: "Look, I know you're used to having people hang on your every word. But before you go on, tell me whether you're going to give me the two hundred dollars. If you're not, skip the two-bit lecture, and I'll be on my way."

Swope did not return immediately after doing the piece on the signing of the peace treaty. He lingered in Paris through the beginning of July, making arrangements to meet his mother.

In a wire, Margaret begged him to return immediately, again claiming ill health. He replied:

CABLE REQUESTING RETURN ARRIVED JUST AS LEAVING TO SEE MOTHER STOP DELAYED HERE BY TIME REQUIRED ARRANGE PASSPORTS STOP AWAITING FURTHER WORDS SO CABLE IMMEDIATELY REAL MEANING MESSAGE STOP IF HEALTH IN QUESTION WILL DROP EVERYTHING FOR YOU BUT OTHERWISE FEEL DEEP DUTY NOT LOSE CHANCE SEE MOTHER FOR MAYBE LAST TIME STOP REPLY IM- MEDIATELY URGENT RATE THROUGH OFFICE TO PARIS WHICH WILL FORWARD TENDEREST LOVE HERBERT

EYRE

She did not reply immediately. She did not reply at all, and he wired again after waiting for four days.

MOTHER EN ROUTE TO MEET ME FOR TWO DAYS AFTER WHICH IM SAILING TO YOU STOP EARNESTLY HOPE PLANS MEET YOUR APPROVAL AS BEING RIGHT STOP TENDEREST LOVE HERBERT

The plan did not meet with her approval, and that night she wired an alarming description of her condition. He answered the next day:

RETURNING PARIS IMMEDIATELY TAKING FIRST BOAT TO YOU BE BRAVE

On the twenty-third, he was back in Paris and heard again from her. What she said was most bewildering, for now that he had altered his plans for her, she had taken a miraculous turn for the better and was planning to go away with the family for a summer holiday. He cabled:

RETURN ACCOMMODATIONS VERY DIFFICULT EITHER ON TRANSPORT OR PASSENGER BOAT BUT EXPECT BOOKING IN A FEW DAYS BRINGING ME HOME ABOUT BEGINNING MONTH STOP IF DOCTOR THINKS TRIP BENEFICIAL GO BUT CANT UNDERSTAND HOW YOU CAN MAKE THIS BUT COULDNT COME ABROAD STOP WHATEVER YOU DO WILL BE RIGHT BUT WOULD BE DEEPLY DISAPPOINTED IF YOU NOT HOME ON ARRIVAL STOP WAIT AND WE WILL GO AWAY TOGETHER TENDEREST LOVE HERB

She altered her plans, and he again altered his. Ida was on her way to Coblenz to meet him, and his next message, relayed through Eyre, read:

> FROM COBLENZ STOP IN COBLENZ TO MEET MOTHER STOP BOOKING TO
> AMERICA VERY DIFFICULT BUT HAVE PROMISE OF PASSAGE ON FIFTH
> STOP BE BRAVE AND DONT WORRY TENDERLY HERBERT

He was still in Paris on August seventh, promising to leave on the thirteenth on the *Kaiserin Augustin Victoria*. It was the fastest booking he could obtain, and he begged her to explain that to White and Lincoln. He was beginning to worry about what was transpiring at the office, for, after a description of his moving reunion with his mother, he added:

> I am worried about the attitude people at home are assuming about my work. I'd like to have your judgment on it. I KNOW I've worked hard and intelligently and effectively, so I am not *really* concerned about the outcome, but Cosgrave* writes that he expected so much more that he's disappointed. You know I never think too highly of my own performance, but I do think in this case he's unjust, don't you?

He had been gone for nine months. Part of the delay in his return was caused by a genuine desire to see the job through, part by a sense of filial duty, part by enjoyment of the place he had made for himself in Europe, and part by a desire to postpone the inevitable clash with Lincoln. He knew that the two of them could no longer function on the same paper. If Lincoln won, it would be the end of the most exciting role of his life—that of Swope of the *World*.

Pulitzer had maintained an enigmatic silence about the conflict. Swope's two greatest champions, Cosgrave and White, were both displeased with his procrastination and disappointed by his performance. His conflicting fears and emotions neither reduced his resiliency nor prevented him from sending a final wire on the eleventh, which may have sounded rather imperious under the circumstances, but was still profoundly Swopian.

> SAILING THIRTEENTH KAISERIN AUGUSTA FROM BREST STOP HAVE
> ALEX ATTEND TO EXPEDITE AND GET TRUCK FOR BAGGAGE FROM
> WORLD CIRCULATION DEPARTMENT STOP YEARNING TO SEE YOU
> TENDERLY HERB

---

*John O'Hara Cosgrave, editor of the Sunday *World*.

NINE

Paradox became the prevailing characteristic of America as well as of the rest of the world during the postwar years. Within one year, Congress enlightenedly emancipated women and puritanically prohibited alcohol. Wilson's greatest hope for world peace, the League of Nations, was denied American participation in the same year that the president won the Nobel Peace Prize.

Even to men as astute as Swope, the future of the world looked wonderfully promising in the decade immediately preceding the Wall Street crash of '29. They deluded themselves into believing that the world had finally recognized the futility of war, and so they turned their attention to the perfection of peace, to setting an example of justice at home that would inspire those abroad.

In America, it was a period of prosperity, of new freedoms, of good times that seemed as if they would never end. There was a New York scene, a nascent literary establishment that, though more a demi-culture than a profound one, was strong enough to last with modifications, to this day. Substitute ERA for women's votes, pot for bootleg hooch, Elaine's saloon for the Algonquin, Sagaponack for Great Neck, *New York* magazine for the *New Yorker,* and the parallels hold. Then as now, there were serious writers and artists, but, then as now, it was the literary personalities that one heard about and envied and celebrated. They were larger than life and only slightly smaller than fiction. These were the staples of the popular press, and of all that press, there was no paper so popular, in the best sense of the word, as the New York *World,* as re-created by Herbert Bayard Swope. That halcyon decade of the twenties brought Swope, in his prime, to the time of his life.

It did not seem that this would be the case when he first arrived back from Europe. Ralph Pulitzer continued to vacillate, and Lincoln seemed more solidly entrenched at the paper than ever. Swope's public welcome had been a warm one. He was too well known and popular to be ignored, and the *World* had sent a reporter to interview him on the dock, but privately, he knew that he was in for a battle for his life.

Swope had a vision of the kind of paper that the *World* should be, and Maggie encouraged him to fight for it, not only for himself but for her. If he had the *World,* he would stay put, and she would have him. "Stop worrying about how good Ralph thinks you are, and start showing him how good *you* think you are."

Swope decided to take Pulitzer at his word when he offered him a position as his "special assistant." He started by making small suggestions that gradually increased in scope. Lincoln's irritation grew in direct proportion. Cosgrave, who disliked Lincoln, encouraged Swope to attempt an office insurrection. At this point, a series of events coalesced in a manner very favorable to Swope.

Several problems were converging upon Ralph Pulitzer at the same time. White was complaining about decreased circulation and dwindling profits, while he and his brothers continued to take money out of the paper without putting anything back into it. Frank Cobb, the extraordinary editor of the editorial page, dated back to Pulitzer's father's day and persisted in an attitude that was at once paternal and patronizing. Lincoln's complaints about Pulitzer's new assistant multiplied daily, although he agreed with Cosgrave that Swope was making some marvelously innovative suggestions. Pulitzer wanted a buffer between his problems and himself, somebody who could share the responsibilities he could not face alone and who could assume the blame should anything go wrong.

Most of all, Pulitzer knew that he needed somebody dynamic enough to take command and imaginative enough to breathe some new life into the *World*. It would be foolish to remove Cosgrave or White, both of whom were doing an excellent job, from their respective positions. Lincoln did not have the imagination. He thought that there was nothing wrong that a little money could not fix. He was a plodding victim of habit. Cobb was excellent: liberal, courageous, often forward-looking, but his health was beginning to fail, and the editorial page was all the responsibility he wanted.

Swope was the logical choice. When he was approached with the offer, he replied that he could only accept if given complete authority to make all the changes that he felt were mandatory. Pulitzer agreed on the condition that Swope did not spend the paper out of existence.

A new title had to be concocted, one that immediately placed him above Lincoln, who was the managing editor, and made him answerable only to the publisher. Swope and Pulitzer hit upon "executive editor." There had never been an executive editor before, on the *World* or any other paper. It conjured up authority without defining it, and seemed to say that the man who bore the title spoke directly for the publisher.

There was a daily news council at the *World*, which all heads of departments were expected to attend. In it, the stories, features, and editorials—the composition and make-up of the next edition—were discussed. Swope had attended these meetings, first as city editor and later as assistant to the publisher. He was discreetly absent on the day Pulitzer announced his new position.

Cobb immediately protested. Nobody was going to tell him what went on the editorial page. Having already discussed this with Swope, Pulitzer was able to say that the new executive editor understood that the page was completely Cobb's baby. It was not that easy to placate Lincoln, who realized rightly that his own position had been vastly diminished, that Swope could use him as little better than a copy boy, should he choose. Pulitzer remained firm, and Lincoln had no alternative but to resign. Soon afterward, he went to work for the New York *Herald,* where there was no Swope and the atmosphere was comparatively restful.

Swope had won. It was a time for celebrating. Margaret knew that if he had his way he would be out with the boys whooping it up every night. He was not about to have his way. If there was any whooping to be done, he would do it at home. Celebrations were indeed called for, and Margaret decided to give a series of parties.

There may have been parties that were more lavish and imaginative, but there were never any parties that were more fun than the parties of the '20s, and if any hostess could be called their progenitor, it was Margaret Swope. At the Swopes', you could find everybody from August Belmont to the new young fellow on the *Times,* George S. Kaufman; from the Comtesse de Polignac to Fanny Brice. To the musical accompaniment of a promising pianist named Gershwin, Margaret mixed, mingled, and juggled with a dexterity that would have put a prestidigitator to shame. What was later vulgarized as Café Society started spontaneously as Chez Swope.

Extra servants were brought in to serve drinks and dinner. Among them was a pretty young woman named Mae Fielding, who arrived to act as waitress one evening. Guests were still arriving when the time came for the servants to depart. They were mostly theater people who had come directly from the shows in which they were appearing. Mae said that the newcomers must be hungry, and that the help ought to stay to do some sandwiches for them.

The cook looked at her wearily. "You want to give them sandwiches. There's the bread, and there's the cold cuts. You make them." The other waitresses added that she could also serve them, and the staff went, leaving her alone.

Mae carefully cut the crust off the bread, made the sandwiches and served them. Margaret and she looked at each other. It was a partnership made in heaven, and Mae not only served the sandwiches, but she stayed on for over forty years. She later said, "It suited me just fine. They were night people, and I was a night person."

There was later a legend that the Swopes had two staffs of servants, night and day. This was not strictly true. But they had Mae Fielding, who, like her employers, slept until after noon and stayed up until after four in the morning. Any kind of food could be ordered by a card player at any hour of the morning, and Mae, with one or two lackeys, was almost always there to prepare and bring it. She was so devoted to Herbert that she would only reluctantly let anybody else look after him. This gave rise to another legend that was often repeated in the gossip columns. It was said that Swope had a female valet. The story delighted Mae, and she was not above adding little touches to fuel it, whenever anybody was around who might repeat it.

While Margaret arranged for playing hard, Swope started working hard. What he realized most acutely about the *World* was that it did not have the resources to compete as a news source with a paper like the *New York Times*. Splendidly gifted with rationales, he decided that if he could not publish all the news that was fit to print, he would publish all the news that was fit to read. He once explained the secret of his success with the amalgam of modesty and flippancy that was so characteristic of him: "I take one story each day and bang the hell out of it."

Of course, he did much more than that. He re-created the failing paper in his own robust image. He served as executive editor from 1920 through 1928. So enduring was his accomplishment that almost a half-century later, in 1973, two books came out, both carrying reprints of articles and features from Swope's *World: The Best in the World,* edited with introductions by John K. Hutchens and George Oppenheimer (and dedicated to Swope), and *The World and the 20's (The Best From New York's Legendary Newspaper)*, by James Boylan.

In his introduction, Mr. Hutchens said: "The *World* was an extension of Swope's personality as newspapers have not often been since the heyday of personal journalism."

Boylan observed in his introduction that Swope had "those indispensable antennae that can catch the sounds of an age. The *World* tended to reflect the broad range of Swope's interests and enthusiasms."

If Swope could not have Cobb's jealously guarded editorial page, he would take the page opposite the editorials and turn it into the most lively and readable page in any newspaper in the country. The Op Ed page, as

Swope called it, previously had been devoted to a miscellanea of community-service notices, ranging from society press releases to obituaries. Swope's success can be reckoned from Mr. Oppenheimer's observations:

> Maybe it is my imagination or just a cliché from the vocabulary of an elder citizen, but it seems to me that there are not as many pleasures to wake up to nowadays as there were back in the twenties.
>
> One of the brightest of these was the New York *World*. Whatever stresses the day might hold could be mentally postponed and temporarily forgotten as you turned to Page Opposite.

Years after Swope left the *World,* Gene Fowler asked how he had ever come to concoct this memorable contribution to sheer readability. Swope answered, "It occurred to me that nothing is more interesting than opinion when opinion is interesting, so I devised a method of cleaning off the page opposite the editorial, which became the most important in America . . . and thereon I decided to print opinions, ignoring facts."

Word of Swope's attitude and concept spread swiftly. Other editors, like Lincoln, tended to scoff. "Swope's going high-hat," he said. "He'll ruin the paper."

Many of the better journalists had a different opinion. Shackled by shortsighted editors, whom they often considered only semiliterate, they began to wonder about the possibility of securing berths on the controversial page. Heywood Broun, one of the New York *Tribune*'s ablest journalists, began to brood about it. The more the thought, the more distasteful he found everything about the *Trib,* especially its conservative politics.

When Broun could stand it no longer, he simply called Swope and asked for a job on the new page. Swope asked why he wanted it, when he already had a perfectly good position with the *Trib*. Broun replied that there was more freedom of expression on the *World* than on the *Trib*. That was good enough for Swope, and he invited him over for a meeting.

Swope wanted Broun. The only problem was money. Pulitzer was very happy with the new page, but he had not added one extra cent to the budget to run it. The *World*'s drama critic, Louis V. De Foe, was dying. Although Swope would have liked Broun to devote himself to a column of personal observations and opinions, he could not afford the luxury. He told the reporter that if he also took over for De Foe, he could have the column, and Broun agreed.

Between the two of them, they concocted a name for the new column that summed up its point of view: "It Seems to Me." Broun later recalled that Swope had never told him what to write, only that it should be provocative, controversial, and outspoken. That was fine with Broun, because it was the only kind of column he could write. It would later cause a problem with Ralph Pulitzer.

Some months later, Franklin P. Adams followed Broun from the *Tribune* over to the *World,* bringing with him his popular "Conning Tower" column. He had known Swope for years and had sent him a copy of his 1914 volume of light verse, *By and Large,* inscribed: "For Bayard from Pierce." Shortly after joining the paper, he wrote in Swope's copy of his book *In Other Words:* "To Herbert, who bought this book in 1912, when he loved Literature, this book is inscribed in 1922, when he employed me." That same year, he formally dedicated his new book, *Overset,* "To HERBERT BAYARD SWOPE, without whose friendly aid and counsel every line in this book was written." Over the dedication, he wrote: "With deep love but deep admiration." On the flyleaf of *So There!,* published the following year, he wrote, "To H.B.S. Dear Friend, only too well I know there is nothing serious in *So There!* But deep and serious and true are these lines, with my love to you."

Both Broun and Adams spent the happiest years of their journalistic careers on the *World,* working for Swope. Adams recalled:

> Never had I known such fun in a newspaper office as I had the first few years on the *World.* Whatever office politics there may have been, I was unaffected, for nobody wanted my job, and I didn't want anybody's. . . . Often there were discussions and violent abusive arguments lasting three hours. . . . There were fights—generally by telephone—with my technical boss, Mr. Swope, sir, who never changed a line, in or out, of mine, except once, when he saved me by changing something that had become untrue between the time that I wrote it, at 3 P.M., and 8:30 P.M.

Adams invited contributions from friends and readers, the best of which he would print in his column. Through this device, he brought to the *World* a startling array of talent, including George S. Kaufman, Marc Connelly, Russel Crouse, E. B. White, Edna Ferber, George Oppenheimer, Samuel Hoffenstein, Ring Lardner, John O'Hara, Arthur Kober, Elinor Wylie, Howard Dietz (who signed himself "Freckles"), and Dorothy Parker, who sent in some poems with the comment: "If you can't use these, give them to some poor family."

Among the verses that might have been passed on to some poor family, had they not first appeared in the *World*, were

> Men seldom make passes
> At girls who wear glasses.

and

> Razors pain you;
>   Rivers are damp;
> Acids stain you;
>   Drugs cause cramp.
> Guns aren't lawful;
>   Nooses give;
> Gas smells awful;
>   You might as well live.

and

> Lady, lady, should you meet
> One whose ways are all discreet,
> One who murmurs that his wife
> Is the lodestar of his life,
> One who keeps assuring you
> That he never was untrue,
> Never loved another one . . .
> Lady, lady, better run!

and

> Oh, life is a glorious cycle of song,
>   A medley of extemporanea;
> And love is a thing that can never go wrong;
>   And I am Marie of Roumania.

Swope built his Op Ed team carefully. Occasionally reporters from the other sections of the paper did columns; one would find pieces by John Balderston (the *World* London man), Samuel Spewack (Moscow), William Bolitho, and Clare Sheridan (beautiful sculptor-journalist and cousin of Winston Churchill). In addition to Broun and Adams, the constant team included Deems Taylor (succeeded by Samuel Chotzinoff) on music, Laurence Stallings (succeeded by Harry Hansen and briefly preceded by Robert Benchley) on books, and Quinn Martin on films.

These were Swope's prima donnas, the highest paid and most in-dulged men on the paper. The group was completed when Swope finally got the budget that enabled him to woo Alexander Woollcott away from the *Sun* to serve as drama critic, freeing Broun to devote full time to his column.

Had Swope's career taken a different turn, there is no doubt that he could have been a first-rate novelist or playwright. His stories had both pace and suspense. They manifested his sharp observation of the telling gesture, of the small and revealing idiosyncrasies of dress and speech, all rendered with a flair for melodramatic coloration. This was the sort of writing that he liked, and his stylistic stamp was evident in many of the best stories that appeared during his tenure as executive editor.

It was logical that many of his reporters would go on to distinguished careers as writers of plays, screenplays, and novels. *What Price Glory?*, the first important American antiwar play, was written by book reviewer Laurence Stallings and editorial writer Maxwell Anderson. It has been called the only good thing to come out of the *World*'s odious cafeteria, a restaurant of such low culinary standards that neither Swope nor Cobb would ever set foot in it. Stallings went on to a big career in Hollywood, and Anderson remained in New York to become a prize-winning play-wright, among whose best-known works are *Winterset, Both Your Houses, Mary of Scotland, Knickerbocker Holiday* (including lyrics for the famed "September Song"), *High Tor,* and *Anne of the Thousand Days*. His brilliant sense of theater was often muffled by his penchant for writing fourth-rate blank verse, which ultimately reduced his reputation to its current obscure state.

Dudley Nichols, who became a star reporter under Swope's tutelage, was to write the memorable screenplays for *The Informer, Stagecoach, For Whom the Bell Tolls,* and *The Long Voyage Home.* He also both wrote and directed the film version of Eugene O'Neill's *Mourning Becomes Electra*.

One of Nichols's early introductions to O'Neill in a professional capacity came while he was still on the *World*. Woollcott, who was the drama critic when *Strange Interlude* opened, reviewed the play unfavor-ably in *Vanity Fair* on the basis of a copy of the script slipped to him by the star, Lynn Fontanne. Nevertheless, he expected also to review the production, on the grounds that something that might seem flat on the printed page could come to life onstage, especially with the leading role enacted by one of his favorites.

Swope disagreed with Woollcott. He felt that a man who had already gone on record on a play could not see it without preconceptions. Actually, the critic was already describing it to friends as "the *Abie's Irish Rose* of the intelligentsia."

When Woollcott heard that the assignment was not to be his, he waddled into Swope's office, demanding an explanation. Swope said, "You're already on record against it."

"I'm the first-string drama critic on this paper," Woollcott replied. "And any O'Neill opening is a first-string production."

"That's all very well, Aleck," Swope said martially. "But I'm top sergeant here. And what I say goes."

Woollcott turned and left. It seemed to Swope that he had actually marched out. There was never another office clash between them, but Woollcott was a good hater. He bided his time, knowing that he would eventually have his revenge.

Swope had originally thought of letting Woollcott's assistant, Jeffry Holmesdale (later Lord Amherst), review the play, but, realizing that Woollcott would make the young man's life miserable, he changed his mind at the last minute and gave the assignment to Nichols.

The incident is an example of what Nichols meant when he later said that Swope was a man who "loved nothing better than pushing the strong around and giving a hand to the weak."

James M. Cain was another young reporter whom Swope placed in the editorial department. He later wrote a series of very popular novels of the Dashiell Hammett type, including *The Postman Always Rings Twice, Double Indemnity,* and *Serenade.* He recalled that "ordinarily, Swope's skin seemed made of rhinoceros hide, covered with brass studs, like medieval armor. But he could get thrown off-balance by some little thing in the most astonishing way. . . . He was the least resentful man in the world, being able to take a joke, even one on himself, with cheerfulness almost pathetic. And if caught by surprise, he could be as red in the face as anyone."

Swope sent a young reporter named Sam Spewack to Russia as the *World*'s correspondent. When his articles started coming back, Swope contemplated giving them the collective title *Inside Russia,* an echo of his own book title *Inside the German Empire.* He later thought better of it and opted for *Behind Red Curtains.*

Spewack was a man of fluctuating temperament who was often in trouble with his superiors. Swope saved his job more than once, on the theory that a good reporter was worth more to him than ten editorial bureaucrats. Spewack showed his gratitude by satirizing Swope in a play on which he collaborated with his wife—*Clear All Wires*. Swope was among those who laughed hardest, though not loudest, on opening night.

After the insignificant *Clear All Wires*, the Spewacks went on to write two resounding hits, *Boy Meets Girl* and *Kiss Me Kate*.

Swope introduced another future playwright to the fascination of the theater when he assigned Norman Krasna, who was hardly out of his teens at the time, to cover the vaudeville acts at the Palace. By the time Krasna was twenty, Swope had made him assistant drama and film editor, and he learned his craft on theatrical passes issued to the *World* desk. How well he learned it was proven by a series of pleasant and highly successful light comedies, including *Dear Ruth, John Loves Mary,* and *Sunday in New York*.

There were others who went on to successful careers as writers in other media. Donald Henderson Clarke wrote a series of popular novels that hovered on the lubricious. He later recalled his boss, with a mixture of awe and astonishment: "Swope never thought, I am sure, that he belonged to the *World*. He felt that the *World,* including Ralph Pulitzer, belonged to him. His ambitions were too vast to be limited by personalities or properties. He was a conqueror: an Alexander, Caesar, Genghis Khan, Napoleon."

Pulitzer, Swope's only superior on the paper, viewed his employee's protean activities in much the same way. He wrote a piece of comic verse about Swope that, in light of his position as publisher, was as revealing of the poet as it was of his subject.

> When he enters my room with a crash and a bang,
> Sits down at my desk with a bang and a crash,
> Springs onto his feet as no man ever sprang,
> Hurls open my window 'most out of its sash,
> Bespatters my papers with cigarette ash,
> Flips into my basket his match still aglow,
> Pours forth braggadocio brilliantly brash—
> I wish that he'd stub his toe!
>
> When he wagers ten thousand without a pang,
> And coppers the market without a smash,
> Once explained to Caruso how singers sang,
> And now teaches Jane Cowl how to act with
>   more "pash,"
> When he suddenly makes a society splash
> And he hypnotizes both high and low

And cuts such a naïvely dauntless dash—
I wish that he'd stub his toe!

When this man (as he'd put it) of "Sturm und Drang,"
Whom nothing can faze and nothing abash,
Gives the date of the birth of Li Hung Chang
Or the derivation of sabretache
Or the numbers of millions of U.S. cash
Or the speed of the Mississippi's flow
And is always right, it's enough to fash—
I wish that he'd stub his toe!

L'Envoi

Prince, you who are crowned with the flare and flash
That nothing but genius may bestow,
Can afford to smile at this futile trash:—
I wish that he'd stub his toe!

There were minor writers from the *World* who achieved success in other endeavors, like Louis Weitzenkorn, who dedicated his most popular play, *Five Star Final,* to Swope, "the greatest newspaperman I ever knew." And there were major writers, like William Bolitho, whose *Twelve Against the Gods* has become something of a classic. He dedicated another book, *Italy Under Mussolini,* to Swope: "The type of those newspapermen who are not allowed in Italy under Mussolini."

There were several writers who later found natural homes on the *New Yorker,* a magazine that inherited many of the attitudes as well as much of the talent of the *World.* Among the most congenial of this group was the humorist Frank Sullivan. He was a cub reporter on the *Saratogian,* the Saratoga Springs local paper, when he first saw Swope at the August races. He remembered, "Once you saw him he stood out, you know. Ruddy face and redhead, very big man, rather a handsome man. Prancing up and down the grandstand. I don't know what his assignment was. He was up there playing the horses most of the time. But he was a great reporter. Anybody'll tell you that. And a damn good editor. Almost never go together, those two. But he was both."

When Swope first approached him about coming to work on the *World,* Sullivan was a reporter on the *Evening Sun.* He walked across City Hall Park to meet with Swope, rehearsing a speech in which he would congratulate him for having the wit to snatch him away from the *Sun* and then ask for an advance on his salary. He arrived to find Swope simultaneously dictating to his fiercely loyal secretary, Miss Helen Millar, giving orders to two aides, and shouting advice over the phone to Governor Alfred E. Smith. As Sullivan tells it,

> My speech was not delivered as planned. It was not delivered at all. H.B.S., however, gave me a trenchant address on the ethics of journalism in general, the place of the *World* in particular, my own good fortune in being tapped for that paper, the influence of Stanton in Lincoln's cabinet, the best method for making raised biscuits, the Tacna-Arnica dispute, and the Schick test for scarlet fever.

There was great fraternal feeling among the men who worked on the *World* during the '20s. The feature writers on the Op Ed page were forever writing about each other and about the Swopes. The stories were waggish, teasing, or congratulatory, depending upon the subject or occasion. When a member of the staff needed help with some project, he could often get it from one of his co-workers on the staff.

Laurence Stallings and Maxwell Anderson were having trouble getting a producer for their play *What Price Glory?* The theatrical management of the day felt that nobody would be interested in seeing a war play. They gave it to Woollcott to read, and the critic was so enthusiastic that he decided to do something about getting it on. He took Stallings to lunch at the old Hotel Brevoort, which was then a popular meeting place for those in the theater. The producer Arthur Hopkins was at a table nearby. Deciding to use reach-and-withdraw psychology on him, Woollcott beckoned him over.

"Stallings here has just finished a play that I think has a lot to it. You wouldn't want to read it, of course. Being a producer, you never read plays. Besides, it's a war play." Producers did not then and do not now ignore the opinions of important critics. Hopkins asked for a copy, read it, and the play was produced within a season.

John Balderston, the *World*'s London correspondent, turned a Henry James short story into a play which he called *Berkeley Square*. It was both fantasy and heavy romance, two qualities that did not bode well for theatrical success in the flip '20s. The only chance that the production had was to find a big star for the leading role of Peter Standish.

When Balderston came for a weekend to the Swope country house, he brought the play along for the editor to read. Among the other guests was a young British actor who had achieved some success as Jeanne Eagels' leading man in *Her Cardboard Lover* and in suppport of Alfred Lunt in *Outward Bound*. Theater people were predicting that the right part would make a star of Leslie Howard, but nobody had come up with that part. Swope introduced Balderston to Howard by simply saying, "This is your Peter Standish."

No more had to be said. The play was produced, made Balderston rich, and turned Leslie Howard into a star whose popularity endured until his death in an airplane crash during World War II. Howard's leading lady, Margalo Gilmore, was a peripheral member of the *World* crowd as the "baby" of the Algonquin Round Table and a particular pet of Woollcott, Adams, and Broun.

Sullivan thought that there was not a bad guy on the whole paper and that Swope was the most accessible of editors. Any member of the staff could come to him with a problem, and he would do his best to solve it. His writers came first with him, and he protected them from the onslaughts of management with a fierce paternalism. Occasionally he would be the stern father and reprimand them, but only he was permitted to do so. They were off-limits to Florence White and Ralph Pulitzer. They were "his boys." Some were his boys only by marriage or affection, and never really worked for him. Russel Crouse was an example. He was a columnist on the *Post,* but his first wife, Allison Smith, was Woollcott's assistant on the *World*.

Swope was extremely fond of Crouse and, in Sullivan's words, "practically brought him up," giving him the encouragement he needed to start on what was destined to become one of the most successful writing collaborations in Broadway history. With Howard Lindsey, he was the co-author of *Life with Father, State of the Union, Anything Goes,* and *Call Me Madam.* One of the funniest lines in *State of the Union* came when the wife of the presidential-aspirant hero looked up from a telegram of congratulations that he had received and asked, "Who is Herbert Bayard Swope?" Not only in New York but all over the country it never failed to get an audience reaction.

Swope always referred to Crouse as "one of my boys." The play-wright's widow recently said, "Russel never corrected him, because he was so flattered to be thought of that way."

Guest writers became a part of Swope's plans for the paper from the very beginning. H. G. Wells was one of those who made an appearance during Swope's first year of management. But Swope's greatest passion was reserved for crusades. The causes were often unpopular with the public and worrisome to Pulitzer and White, but he waved their objections aside with an impatient flick of his hand. Once he explained his approach to journalism to Heywood Broun: "What I try to do in my paper is to give the public part of what it wants to have and part of what it ought to have whether it wants it or not."

He was always true to that tenet. The Op Ed page and the guest writers were part of what the public wanted, but the crusades were part of what he felt it ought to have. During that first year, he espoused two noble causes.

The first was general disarmament. The paper kept pounding away at the point until even President Harding was convinced of its desirability, and a nine-power major naval-reduction conference was convened in Washington on November 12, 1921. The *World* could take deserved pride in its part in saving the larger world from the tragedy of an armaments race, until the rise of a menace unforeseeable at the time, Adolf Hitler's Nazi Germany, made rearmament inevitable.

Since the middle of the war, the Ku Klux Klan had been growing in importance and menace. By 1921 it had 500,000 members, with groups in almost every major city and rural district. The bigoted white-supremacist organization took its name from the organization of hooded vigilantes of the Reconstruction era that followed the Civil War. The original vigilantes had directed their activities against the newly freed Negroes. The Klan now broadened its scope to include Jews, Catholics, and alien groups.

The Klan was founded by an itinerant Methodist preacher named William Joseph Simmons. It was chartered in 1916, in Georgia, as a secret fraternal organization. At first, its hooded, white, sheetlike robes were a subject of derision. But by 1921 many people had stopped laughing, as the KKK terrorized helpless minorities throughout the country. The Klan's racial philosophy was the same as the one soon to be espoused by Hitler, and, had it attained his power, the results would have been equally shattering.

Swope obtained material against the group from a former Kleagle (local leader) of the Klan named Henry Fly, who had become alarmed enough by its excesses to want to expose it. His alarm was not so great that he did not demand a goodly sum for his files, which included a membership list.

Rowland Thomas, a part-time novelist, was assigned to do the series. Twenty-one articles ran in the *World* and eighteen other papers, beginning on September 6, 1921. The series started by stating the aims of the pieces in the form of questions that would be answered in the articles:

> What is the Ku Klux Klan?
> How has it grown from a nucleus of thirty-four charter members to a membership of more than 500,000 within five years?

How have its "domains" and "realms" and "Klans" been extended, until they embrace every state in the union but Montana, Utah, and New Hampshire?

What are the possibilities of an order that preaches racial and religious hatred of the Jew and the Roman Catholic, of the Negro and the foreign-born citizen?

What are the possibilities of a secret organization that practices censorship of private conduct behind the midnight anonymity of mask and robe and with the weapons of whips and tar and feathers?

What ought to be done about an order whose members are not initiated but "naturalized," whose oaths bind them in obedience to an "Emperor" chosen for life?

What ought to be done about an organization with such objects, when the salesmen of memberships in it work first among the officers of the court and police departments, following them with the officers on the reserve lists of the military and naval forces?

At the end of months of inquiry throughout the United States and in the performance of what it sincerely believes to be a public service, the *World* this morning begins the publication of a series of articles in which answers to these questions will be offered, set out against the vivid background of as extraordinary a movement as is to be found in recent history.

In their recent books on the *World* of the '20s, Boylan and co-authors Hutchens and Oppenheimer gave opposing opinions of the results of Swope's courageous campaign. The former said, "The series—although it described bigotry, crime, and a wide variety of violence—was a spur to Klan recruiting, for it gave the organization its first truly national publicity. Millions appeared to be ready for the KKK, and the attack in the *World* merely seemed to emphasize the characteristics that attracted them."

The latter stated, "This historic series denouncing bigotry was a major factor leading to the eventual decline of the then-renascent Klan."

There were elements of truth in both statements. If millions flocked to the Klan, it had more to do with elements of native American fascism than with a newspaper series that appeared in only nineteen papers, most of them of a political orientation that would not have attracted would-be Klansmen as readers. If it led to the eventual decline of the Klan, it took a long time doing it, for it was not until the civil-rights movement of the early '60s that the Klan was temporarily forced out of business.

The success of the series was a testimonial to the acumen of the editor who ordered it—with it, Swope brought another Pulitzer Prize to the *World* during his first year of control. He not only sold serial rights to eighteen other papers—he also boosted circulation for his own paper by 60,000 readers.

TEN

A great deal has been and is still being written about the group who met for lunch at the Round Table in the Rose Room of the Hotel Algonquin. The Round Table has become a staple of popular American culture and might indeed be termed the progenitor of "pop" culture. The members included *World* writers Alexander Woollcott, Franklin P. Adams, and Heywood Broun; the future founder of the *New Yorker,* Harold Ross; Dorothy Parker; Edna Ferber; Marc Connelly; George S. Kaufman; Robert Sherwood; and Robert Benchley.

Much of what has become legend about them is entirely illusory. The first illusion is that they were bright young people, "boys and girls," "kids." With the exception of Sherwood, they were all in their thirties and forties in 1922. The truly bright young people were those hollowed by war (again with the exception of Sherwood, none of the Round Tablers actually had seen active duty, the others having spent the war on the staff of the *Stars and Stripes*), a lost generation inventing a lasting literary vocabulary—Hemingway, Dos Passos, Fitzgerald—all of whom were in their twenties in 1921.

The reason that the Round Table members were so often represented as younger than they really were was the quality of their celebrated wit. They excelled at the wisecrack, the essence of college humor, born of the new independence from parental restraint that enabled one to say any audacious thing that came to mind so long as it was funny. And many were genuinely funny in the pseudo-tough, cruel style of college sophomores. The anecdotes have been repeated *ad nauseam* in the many books about the circle. Attribution is often hazy. Whether the book is about Parker or Broun or Woollcott or Kaufman, the best lines are reserved for the leading character. This is not the fault of the respective writers, for the group was not above repeating the best lines and even using them in stories, articles, and plays without giving proper credit. It was only when outsiders did the same thing that the in-group rose in a body to castigate the offender, and their castigation could be formidable.

The representative periodical of the group was the *New Yorker,* which was truly the apotheosis of the college magazine—the Algonquin School of New York University. The profiles had to debunk rather than admire, even if that meant a slight distortion of fact to make a waggish point. The criticism had to be clever, so that the reader came away admiring the critic rather than the evaluation. The stories were often heady exercises in nostalgia, after the fashion of recent adults, confused by their new status, looking back longingly at an innocent childhood. The humorous pieces were generally based on plays on words or the rib-nudging torture of clichés. It was élitist. Anybody with the slightest education could get the point of these send-ups of popular fiction, films, and plays, and feel superior to the poor plebes who took the originals seriously.

The cartoons were among the best features, but they were not concerned with national issues. The battle of the sexes was chronicled from the male-chauvinist point of view. The excellent women cartoonists were not permitted to retaliate—they were relegated to making witty observations on the foibles of upper-middle-class matrons, and their comments were thus in keeping with the magazine's condescension to women. One found Petty maids and Hokinson clubwomen, as well as Arno hookers and Thurber nags. Until fairly recently, nowhere in the magazine was there depicted a woman of the intelligence and tough-mindedness of a Dorothy Parker, Jean Stafford, Mary McCarthy, Lillian Ross, Janet Flanner, or Margaret Case Harriman—even, sadly, in these women's own contributions. This was consistent with the magazine's point of view. Harvard, Yale, and Princeton were "boys' schools."

In later years, the depression and war aged New York. It was no longer a college town, and the *New Yorker* writers moved to the suburbs. The magazine followed them. All that remained of New York was the information that might be of interest to a visitor. Actually, this had a felicitous effect on the quality. The magazine lost some of its parochialism. Fresh air had been let into the stultifying and claustrophobic atmosphere of the Algonquin. One began to find gifted new writers, such as Nabokov, Cheever, O'Hara, Updike, and Capote (although, at his worst, the last-named behaved like a lineal descendant of the Round Table). The sumptuousness of its endless advertisements gave its pages the gloss of a fashion magazine and attracted a faithful female audience. This led to a more intelligent and respectful (for there's nothing like economics to foster respect) analysis of the feminine condition by talented women like Gilliatt, Calisher, Gallant, Warner, Hale, and Taylor.

Harold Ross, founder and guiding force of the magazine, was a brilliant editor, but he behaved very much like a faculty adviser on a student publication, with his skittishness about sex, his insistence upon rewrites, his punctilious blue marks in margins, his sacrifice of style for syntax. A major difference between the editorial policies of Ross and Swope was that Ross always treated his writers like promising undergraduates in need of instruction, and Swope always assumed his were adult professionals capable of independently carrying out their assignments.

In one of its early promotional releases, the *New Yorker* professed to want to be a magazine comparable to the New York *World*. The *World* in the '20s was more than anything a chronicle of the spirit of Swope. The *New Yorker* only half measured up to its intention: the half of the *World* (or Swope) that was concerned with giving the public what it wanted. It was not until years later that the magazine started giving the public what it ought to have whether it wanted it or not.

Swope was never a part of the Round Table. Some say this was because he could not awaken early enough; others say it was because he was essentially a monologist and could not stand the competition. Closer to the truth was the fact that, on the whole, he did not find the Round Tablers serious people. They were witty and hard working; they were socially attractive, good guests; they were pleasant gambling companions; but they were not a part of his inner circle, nor he of theirs.

Their respective attitudes toward the treatment of blacks in American society provide a perfect example of the differences between the adult Swope and the adolescent Round Table. The circle outlooks were all variations on a patronizing and simplistic theme. In not one Kaufman play was there a Negro characterized as anything but a "yas-suh, boss, yuk-yuk, we's house darkies" servant. Connelly's *Green Pastures,* based on Roark Bradford's stories, was essentially an ofay portrait of "nigger heaven" as a fish fry where all the li'l chilluns answered pain with a spiritual under the watchful eye of de Lawd. Edna Ferber's tragic mulatto, Julie, in *Showboat,* was no more than another Mammy sacrificing herself for the blossom of southern-white virtue, Magnolia. Dorothy Parker's *New Yorker* story, "An Arrangement in Black and White," was a bigoted white woman's monologue about meeting a Paul Robeson–like black. It gave nothing of his reactions and told hers in a style that allowed the *New Yorker* readers to think that they knew people like that without ever forcing them to think that they might *be* people like that.

The circle's one good black friend was the not-yet-politicized Paul Robeson. Although there is no record of any of them ever extending to him an invitation to lunch with them in the public restaurant of the Algonquin, they did ask him to play cards in a private room upstairs. The Robeson of the '20s was a star and, more important to them, a celebrity, not above making quotable wisecracks about being "touched by the tar brush." When he did become political and got in trouble for it, not one of his former friends came to his defense. It was Oscar Hammerstein II, who was not a member of the Round Table, who did: "If I were a Rhodes scholar, an all-American athlete, a Broadway and concert star, and on tour I couldn't sleep in good hotels and had to ride in segregated sections of public transportation—I think I might also think that there was something wrong with the system."

Although Swope knew Robeson, the black he chose for a close friend was Walter White, one of the founders of the National Association for the Advancement of Colored People. White helped enormously with the Klan series* and characterized Swope as "an irascible, valuable, impatient, courageous editor."

Swope's attitude toward the condition of the black in American society was also apparent in another way. He was the first editor to insist that the word "Negro" be capitalized in his paper. He commissioned a black journalist, Lester A. Walton (later American minister to Liberia), to write a series on the condition of Negroes who had migrated to the North, and later hired him to write a weekly column in the Sunday *World* on Harlem activities. Not only was Walton the first black columnist to appear in a white New York paper, but he was the only one until well after World War II.

There were some later evidences of social commitment on the part of the Algonquin group, but these came after the members had ceased to

---

*The Klan series was typical of Swope-style crusading, which was generally reserved for national issues. The Round Table's one foray into crusading was of the more easily perceived single-instance variety—the Sacco-Vanzetti case, which was "radical chic," '20s style. More about this later. The traumatic effect of this single instance of social conscience was so pronounced that one of the heirs to the Algonquin attitude, James Thurber of the *New Yorker,* was still using Sacco-Vanzetti as a cause in 1940, in his play about academic freedom, *The Male Animal.* One feels that in performing the same chore, the Swope of 1940 might well have related Nazi Germany to academic freedom.

function as a group. Dorothy Parker indulged in a long and somewhat meretricious espousal of Communism, which was best summed up in her own self-portrait:

> But I, despite expert advice,
> Keep doing things I think are nice,
> And though to good I never come—
> Inseparable my nose and thumb.

Heywood Broun created a brief flurry by running for Congress on the Socialist ticket in 1930, but he found much deeper conviction in his later conversion to Catholicism. Not even the old-line Socialists backed him in his candidacy, finding some grounds for suspicion of his motives in the fact that he had never set foot in Union Square. Broun preferred to remain close to his old haunts, and he set up campaign offices in the Hotel Algonquin. In the '30s, Broun's political views became less pugnacious and more profound. He helped to found the American Newspaper Guild, which has contributed to keeping our press free.

Only Robert E. Sherwood, the young war veteran, gave any enduring impression of awareness. This was obvious as early as 1936, with his anti-fascist play *Idiot's Delight*. It was Swope who indirectly brought about his great role in national affairs by introducing him to Roosevelt's confidential adviser, Harry Hopkins. This led to Sherwood's participation in the Roosevelt administration as special assistant to the Secretary of War, as director of the overseas branch of the Office of War Information, and, most significantly, as one of the most eloquent writers of the president's wartime speeches.

Swope was a natural father image for the Algonquinites. Not only was he in a position to employ them, but he was also a dedicated family man, which was unusual among literary figures. One of their favorite games was Swope-watching, with that combination of awe and mild derision usually reserved for parental figures.

The summer of 1921 was not a particularly outstanding one for Swope-watching. The Swopes summered in a little white rented cottage in Plandome, Long Island, across the bay from the more formidable Great Neck. It was a pleasant, unpretentious residential area, with lanes shaded by tall old trees. The house was distinguished in everybody's memory by an enormous stuffed moose head mounted directly above the second-floor landing.

Swope jokingly called the moose "Frank Adams." He was not alone in seeing the similarity between F.P.A. and the animal. The humorist Irvin S. Cobb was once hunting in Kentucky, and he shot a formidable moose. When the animal fell, its legs crossed and its snout hung down over them. Cobb came over to look at it and shouted, "Good God, I've shot Frank Adams!"

Plandome was not a scene of enormous social gaiety. Swope was working very long hours. The weekends in the country were very much family affairs, devoted almost exclusively to Mimi, Bruce, Margaret, and the two children, Jane and Herbert, Jr., who was called "Ottie" by everybody. It was a name his father had adapted from a very popular series of short stories that Arthur Train had been writing for the *Saturday Evening Post* at the time of the boy's birth. The leading character was a lovable lawyer named Otis Botts. Herbert, Sr., had shortened it to Otts Botts and finally to Ottie. During Margaret's pregnancy, he would greet her with an affectionate pat on the belly and the question, "How's little Ottie doing today?"

An exciting Plandome Sunday excursion consisted of piling the whole group into the Model T station wagon, motoring over to Kiluna Farms, Ralph Pulitzer's place in Manhasset (later purchased by William Paley), to get some fresh eggs, and then driving back with them.

The next summer found them not at Plandome but in Europe, ostensibly to buy the rights to the former Kaiser's memoirs. Swope read the material and found it deadly dull. He told the Kaiser's representative, "There are going to have to be some rewrites."

"But, Herr Swope, nobody rewrites the Kaiser."

"Then he can go peddle his papers somewhere else, because stuff like that isn't going to help peddle mine." The series ultimately ran in the *New York Times,* causing no appreciable rise in circulation.

At the time of their departure, the Swopes were in the midst of moving into a new apartment and a new summer house. Margaret left everything in her mother's hands and then proceeded to fret about it ever after.

In Leipzig, where Swope was busy negotiating with the Kaiser's agents, he had no time for Margaret. She wrote to Mimi on June 7:

> I am here alone in the room writing to you. We arrived here this evening, and I am tired and also unwell, and I suppose the combination makes me so homesick for you and my angels I could weep my eyes out. I do pray you are alright and that everything is going the way you wish it to. Was it much of an agony to move? Did you like the way

I fixed the beds? You might ask Sammy to have the Simmons people attend to the spring-mattress & pillows for the little canopy bed in the front room. Also, when the new pillows come from Simmons, don't put them on the maids' beds—use the old ones on Bruce's bed and put them there or in the front room with Gert's bed in it.

Have the carpets come from Wanamaker's? They are to go in the bedrooms. My old one in my room and the two other ones . . . if they are in good condition and you think well of it they might go on the second floor. When I come back, I'll fill the other rooms out.

Did the carpenters finish the closet in the hall? And what about the screens? I am so anxious to get back and do so many things to the house and enjoy the place. The way I feel now—I never want to leave it or home again. It is so terrifying to me, the frightful distance it is away from you all. When I get blue I am just ready to scream, the agony is so great. I hope you miss me as much.

She gave a short account of friends they had seen and told of planning to return on the same boat as Ambassador and Mrs. Gerard and Neysa McMein, a popular illustrator and auxiliary member of the Algonquin set. She ended:

Herb is working very hard just now, and I am trying to be a bright cheery little bird—so I will make my homesick yelps to you and on paper. Tell Miss Millar [Swope's secretary] to let me know every week how you and the angels are. I must know so I can have a word of cheer once in a while. Tell her to cable it to Lincoln Eyre in Paris, and he will know just where we are. I am missing you and loving you all a million times more than I have ever, and I am just as much of a baby as I was six years ago, when I was here. All of my love and hugs and kisses,

Your own
Pug

She enclosed another letter, dated the next day, in the same envelope.

Well—here I am in Leipzig. It is a dull, small city which has a tiny river running through it. Today I went rowing on it with one of Herbert's nieces, and the boat nearly tipped over twice—but I returned safely and am here in the rooms alone and felt that I must talk to you.

I feel just as though I had been here years—and it looks today as if Herbert will have to be here at least a week longer. I may go on to

Berlin to see Grossie [Swope's mother] and then have him meet me
there. I am not sure, for you know how I loathe being alone, and my
heart has been thumping all day.

She described their accommodations; the down bed covers reminded
her of poverty, and she did not at all like the place.

During the trip, the Swopes met Woollcott in Paris, which gave him an
opportunity to indulge in some vintage Swope-watching. He later wrote
in a letter to Edna Ferber:

> I enclose several items for your entertainment. The letter from
> Deems Taylor (Isn't "living like Swope" a perfect phrase?) will
> amuse you. . . . Speaking of Swopes, I eventually called on them. It
> was high noon at the Ritz. Margaret was in bed, garbed in pink, and
> altogether too beautiful. Herb was receiving correspondents, being
> shaved by an imported *coiffeur,* and describing London hotel prices.
> There were silk stockings and fragments of toast and huge bunches
> of roses in pleasant profusion, but nothing much to do, so Margaret
> and I shot craps while Herb talked.

In spite of Margaret's worries, the move to their new and larger
summer quarters was successfully accomplished in their absence. The
family moved into the new summer house in Great Neck, Long Island,
while their new town residence, a spacious apartment at 135 West 58th
Street, was being renovated.

Like the place at Plandome, the house on East Short Road in Great
Neck was a rental, but the resemblance stopped there. The Great Neck
house was a peaked three-storied edifice that stood impressively on the
top of a hill overlooking Manhasset Bay. A graceful porch ran around it,
embellished by what has since come to be called Victorian gingerbread.
The property, which ran along a series of smaller hills, included a garage
with rooms above it; a gazebo; a small cottage generally occupied, after
their marriages, by one or the other of the Powell brothers; and, edging
the driveway, a broad lawn that was used almost exclusively for croquet.
In those days it was still possible to swim in the bay, and groups with
bulging wicker hampers were often seen crossing the road for beach
picnics. Margaret was the stage manager of idyllic weekends that
adroitly combined an informal simplicity with underpinnings of luxury
that were to become legendary.

Even in those pre-highway days, Great Neck was only forty-five
minutes from Manhattan. After the First World War, it became a favorite

of writers and theater people who wanted a rustic retreat with quick access to the city. The Swope house actually belonged to Lottie Blair Parker, author of *Way Down East,* one of the most durable plays of the '90s, which was still having successful Broadway revivals well after the turn of the century. The children would amuse themselves on rainy days by going up to the attic and rummaging through the old programs, pictures, and posters.

Their immediate neighbors in the country were Ring Lardner and Clifton Webb; the nearby green and golden slopes were peopled by Ed Wynn, Franklin P. Adams, Neysa McMein, and, during various summers, most of the other Algonquinites.

The West 58th Street apartment was composed of two flats, one over the other. The Swopes installed an interior stairway to connect them. The drawing room (or, as it came to be known, the Silver Room) was the first of a series of Maggie's masterpieces. It was papered in alternating dark and light silver squares, all flame and shimmering, flickering glow—a room in which beautiful women looked still more beautiful, a jeweled display case for Swope's eloquence. Here he held forth sometimes too insistently, but never boringly. Its luster so impressed Elinor Wylie that she wrote a short story about it for the *New Yorker.*

As spacious as their quarters might seem, they were necessary for a household that included four Swopes, three Powells, the children's governess, Mae, Margaret's personal maid, Lydia Stephens, a cook, Swope's chauffeur, his valet (who was Mae's cousin, Roy Robinson), a laundress, a kitchen maid, and, for long periods at a time, one or another of what friends maliciously called the resident slaves. The resident slave was that woman friend who was always on tap to act as handmaiden to Margaret Swope. She always needed a confidante to be her go-for and keep her company until Swope returned from the paper, which could be any time from midnight to 5:00 A.M.

Besides free room and board, there were other rewards to compensate the resident slave for a certain loss of freedom. The Swope household was the center of constant activity, a lure to every celebrity of the day, so the resident slave could meet people she might not ordinarily have gotten to know. And Maggie was a fitting idol for any young woman. Her wit was sharp and caustically funny; her taste was flawless; her generosity without bound. In return, she demanded and received, often with an alarming alacrity, just one thing—total possession. The only grounds for expulsion from their Swopian paradise were marriage or an affair with a man of whom Maggie did not approve. She did not approve of many men socially and of fewer still romantically, although, for Swope's sake, she was very adept at hiding this.

Maggie was a woman's woman in the same sense that Swope was a man's man. They were polite with the opposite sex but, except for each other, only truly at home with those of the same sex. Maggie did not really see the justification for any marriage but her own, and, paradoxically, she thought that affairs were fine for men but a waste of time for women. The acolytes rotated with the rise and fall of their romantic affiliations. At one time or another, the role was filled by various more or less prominent women, including the actresses Myra Hampton and Ruth Gordon, the writer Alice Leone Moats, Evie Backer (whose marriage was acceptable because her husband, George, a good friend of Herbert's, had been introduced to her by Maggie), and Ruth Dubonnet.

Mae Fielding recently recalled the period when Ruth Gordon was in unofficial residence at Great Neck:

> There would be thirty coming out to the house, when I was expecting only the family. I would go backstage after seeing her play—to see her. She'd always take me off with her maid, get the chauffeur, and get in the station wagon and go out. I always had places where I could go and get whatever I wanted, whatever day of the week or whatever hour of the night it was. We surely were good customers everywhere.

Miss Gordon herself recollected:

> Whether it was West 58th or Great Neck, it was like Proust's Verdurin circle. What Pearl did, the circle did. Her tailor was Sklar and Wagner; Sklar and Wagner fitted the ladies of the circle. When Swope bought her a new eight-skin sable stole, I bought her *old* one. If Pearl wore a double-breasted black velvet suit with a sable scarf, Bea Kaufman [Mrs. George S.], Peggy Leech [Mrs. Ralph Pulitzer], and I wore one, too. If she said "schlemiel," we did. If she went to Madison Square Garden to see the hockey games, we went. If she got a ruby necklace, we wanted one. Did she serve runny Camembert with the salad? So did we. Beside each Lowestoft place plate she had a small silver dish of pecans. Did we? We did.
>
> If one evening we couldn't show up, for what reason I can't imagine, we gave references or got excused. If the Swopes were going out, we came in later or at the usual time, and Mae served coffee, tea, cocoa, liquor, Ovaltine and sandwiches till Herbert and Pearl got back.
>
> To get in was obligatory; to get out took skill. "Sit down," roared

Herbert, no matter what time anyone stood up to leave. Bedtime was unpredictable. Never before three o'clock. "Sit down," roared Herbert. . . .

The regulars knew how to time things. They were Broun, Ethel Barrymore, Peggy Leech, Gerald Brooks, Charlie Schwartz, Harpo, George and Bea Kaufman, Woollcott. We showed up every night. Where else was better? Where else was as good? At Swopes' you belonged. If you didn't, you didn't get in twice.

Whenever Oscar Levant behaved so outrageously that even the tolerant Maggie could not abide him, she would refuse to have him around. His favorite expression for banishment from the Swopian paradise was "The iron gates are down."

The iron gates descended more or less permanently on Miss Gordon when she became romantically involved with the producer Jed Harris, whom Edna Ferber once described as being "fresh as poison ivy."

Maggie once threw Humphrey Bogart out of the house at three in the morning after catching him playing football in the hall with her son and brother. It took over twenty years for Bogie to be reinstated, but when he was, he eagerly rushed back. Those who were readmitted all did. Bogie told Ottie, "Your ma's finally let me back in. Hell, I've been barred from El Morocco and the Stork Club. Who cared? They're just gin mills. But being barred from the Swopes' is like having a wad burning a hole in your pocket and not being able to sit in on the best game in town."

When Maggie put her mind to it, she knew how to give her girls some memorable evenings. It was no wonder that she played pied piper to a succession of unattached women. She may have demanded total devotion, but that was flattering, since it came from a woman so besieged by some of the world's most famous people.

Maggie first took up with Ruth Dubonnet while Ruth was married to the painter Walter Goldbeck. Between Goldbeck and Dubonnet (as in the apéritif) there was Paul de Vallombrosa, and Ruth was the Countess of Vallombrosa. The Swopes gave a dinner party for the Count and Countess that Ruth Gordon still recalled in detail forty-five years later:

Dinner was elegant and better than anybody else's. No New York table had food like Pearl's. Always just what you wanted, always perfectly served. Mae had trained her flock of handmaidens like Freddie Ashton trained the swans in *Les Sylphides*.

Place cards, small silver dishes with pecans from Vendome, sweet butter from Zabar's on upper Broadway, where Roy took Mimi to choose it. Smoked salmon from Barney Greengrass, where Roy took Pearl's mother Mimi to select it. The blue limousine with Holm was for Pearl and Herbert. The Buick was for Mimi, and Roy was her jehu. He drove her to Fulton Market for the Restigouche salmon in the late Spring. For months with an *r* he drove her to Fulton Market for Chincoteagues. To butcher Tingaud for the roasts and poultry. To Washington market downtown for Jersey corn and early everything.

The Swopes' dinner came from all directions. Bribes and threats and endless phone calls had aided car and chauffeurs and assistant chauffeurs, but when stately, stoic Mae in black taffeta, with real lace-trimmed collar, cuffs, apron and cap, opened the sliding doors between the dining room and the silver drawing room, perfection had taken place.

The best place for Swope-watching was in his office or in one of his homes, so everybody who was anybody in New York at the moment had a chance to play that most popular game. At various times, the apartment was described as "the best all-night restaurant in town"(Kaufman); "the only speak that won't be raided, because it's the mayor's favorite inn" (Broun); "the last resting place of the floating crap game" (Harpo Marx); "the one New York equivalent of a Paris salon" (Noel Coward); and "the silver-leafed shrine of the silver-tongued oracle" (Mencken).

Although enormously interested in the food they served their guests, the Swopes were not really interested in food for themselves. Maggie developed pushing food around her plate into a fine art. While others at her table gorged on smoked salmon or truffled paté and thick, rich soups, she would be happy with a cup of simple consommé. Swope's favorite fare was a sandwich that he invented: Liederkranz cheese, chopped radishes, and lots of pepper, on rye bread. It was odoriferous enough to send others rushing for the Alka Seltzer just from the scent of it. His own cure for indigestion was to send out to Reuben's restaurant on 58th Street for a bologna sandwich with sauerkraut and a beer, often at four or five in the morning, just before he retired. It is no wonder that he suffered from insomnia.

In the summers, the house in Great Neck had a permanent sleep-in population of sixteen family members and servants. There would be about ten more in residence every weekend. As many as forty more would drive out from the city or from other parts of Long Island for Sunday lunch and would remain for dinner. Maggie Swope once looked around at the mob and commented, "For a little out-of-the-way place, we do a helluva drop-in trade."

The Swopes never awakened much before one in the afternoon and then would leisurely breakfast in their rooms, not making an appearance downstairs until three or four. The shank of the evening was generally two or three in the morning, and so most of the guests followed the same schedule as their host and hostess, but breakfast was available either in bed or downstairs on the porch at almost any hour.

The Sunday newspaper order was staggering. Dozens of copies of every journal published would arrive, for Swope read every newspaper from cover to cover and assumed that everybody else did also. They had better, for one of his favorite sports was quizzing them on the contents—and Lord help the "flathead" who flunked. At the age of ten, Herbert, Jr., astonished guests by emulating his father in digesting five newspapers along with his breakfast. Will Rogers once asked Swope how he had acquired his prodigious store of information, and he modestly replied, "I only know what I read in the papers." The remark so impressed Rogers that he used it as part of his monologue in several editions of *The Ziegfeld Follies*.

Swope invitations were casual, as was everything else about their household except the meticulousness with which it was run. They would simply say, "Why not come out for lunch?" A specific time was rarely given, for it always came as a shock to them that other people did not live by their timetable. At nine one evening, it occurred to Swope that he had not seen George Kaufman for some weeks, and he thought it would be pleasant to have him over for dinner. He called and asked, "What are you doing about dinner tonight?"

Kaufman replied, "Digesting it."

First-timers at the Swopes would arrive for lunch at what they considered a logical hour—anywhere from 12:30 to 1:30 P.M. Mae would answer the door and show them out to the porch. A drink and the Sunday papers would arrive, and that would generally be the last they'd see of anybody until after three, when another guest might wander out, murmur something polite, and pass on. Unless it was an immediately recognizable face, there would be no indication of who it was, for another idiosyncrasy of the Swopes was that they seldom made introductions. They simply thought that everybody in their world knew everybody else in it. The exception was when somebody specifically asked to meet somebody else—that would galvanize Swope into immediate action. He loved playing the intermediary—getting people together to their mutual advantage, without thought of any benefit accruing to him except the pleasure of making the arrangements.

Swope had met Ike Levy through Irving Berlin. When Levy's brother-in-law, William Paley, needed to raise money for what would eventually become CBS, Levy sent the young man to Swope for help. Swope arranged an introduction to Adolph Zukor, the head of Paramount Pictures. A deal was arranged to their mutual benefit, whereby Paramount bought into the new CBS. A few years later, Paley again called upon Swope. On that occasion, Swope helped to get together a group of men who backed Paley in buying out Paramount, enabling him to be in complete control of his company. By then, Swope's financial and employment picture had changed, and Maggie urged him to request some sort of finder's fee. He could not bring himself to do it, nor did Paley volunteer the conventional payment. Instead, Swope was offered and accepted a position on the CBS Board of Directors, which, given Swope's fame and broad range of contacts, was more to Paley's advantage than his own.

During the years that followed the golden period of the twenties, Swope was often to be instrumental in making contacts for friends. Although other men were generally paid for such services, Swope seldom asked for anything for himself, and seldom was it offered. Ben Sonnenberg, a public-relations genius who, like all of his profession, often dealt in favors, once told Herbert, Jr.: "If I'd had your father's contacts, I'd be worth 160 million bucks."

There was a good deal of hyperbole in the figure, but the fact remains that Swope did do invaluable turns for a great many people and almost never asked anything in return. To those who were grateful, he was grateful; about those who were not, he was philosophical.

Sunday dinners at the Swopes' were the only times that ever became any sort of ritual. Swope liked everybody to gather for drinks at about nine. The conversation was usually so scintillating that nobody sat down at the table until well after ten. One evening, Ottie was still lounging in his tub at 8:45 P.M. Roy, who called young Swope "Professor," came into the bathroom and said, "You better get yourself out of there. You know your father likes everybody downstairs by nine."

Ottie, who could emulate his mother's mode of expression as well as his father's reading habits, replied, "Roy, you may kiss my ass."

Roy looked at him witheringly: "Professor, you is *all* ass."

Obviously, rapid repartee was practiced downstairs at the Swopes' as well as upstairs. The servants occupied a singular place in the Swope household. Their employers realized very early that the staff made their style of life possible, and they treated them accordingly. Mae arrived in

1919, Roy and Lydia in the early '20s. They were still with Maggie forty years later. People were forever telling the Swopes how lucky they were to keep their help for so long. It had nothing to do with luck and everything to do with having sufficient respect for them to treat them like equals.

Maggie sometimes carried this attitude to quixotic extremes. She could never understand why a servant would want to leave her house, any more than she could understand why a guest should choose to go. Weekenders would often find themselves still in residence on Wednesday, under the influence of Maggie's Lorelei-like enticements. "Stay, stay. Why do you want to go? It's such fun here." And it was. And they did not know why they would want to go. "Where else is it better? Where else is it as good?"

Because she felt that there was no place Roy could go that he would enjoy half so much, he never had any set days off. He would pace himself until he thought it was time to leave. He would then pick himself up and start walking down the drive, never looking back, never heeding Maggie, who would be shouting after him, "Roy, Roy! Why are you going? Come back! Roy, it won't be any fun out there! Roy!"

Roy Robinson originally came to work as a second chauffeur, whose duties were to take Maggie around and to transport the children to and from school. Swope had his own chauffeur, a white man who distinctly disapproved of working with blacks. He finally came to Swope and said, "I don't think it's right for white and colored to be living and working together."

Swope looked him over for a moment and then nodded. "Very well. When are you leaving?"

"I don't mean that I should go."

"I do." From then on, Roy was his chauffeur and eventually his valet. One of the other servants once asked him what he would do if a fire broke out, and he replied, "Save the boss."

Lydia and the others might do for Maggie, but nobody did for Swope except Roy and Mae.

Mae stayed on after his death only because she felt that he would not want her to desert Mrs. Swope. True to Maggie's total lack of differentiation in attitude toward those in her employ and those she called friends, it was her reaction to Mae's desire to marry that broke up the relationship. When Mae, late in her seventies, gave Maggie the news of her impending marriage, Maggie cried, "At your age? Don't be foolish. What do you want to get married for? It's a terrible mistake. You'll regret it. I won't let you do it."

She couldn't stop her. Like Roy, Mae simply turned and left, not looking back, not listening. Unlike Roy, she did not return. The man who became her husband was one she had met indirectly through the Swopes.

The Swopes were going to see the final Jack Dempsey–Gene Tunney fight in Chicago. Dempsey had lost the world heavyweight championship to Tunney the year before in Philadelphia, and there was a lot of speculation over whether he would be able to regain it in the second match. Mae said, "I'd surely like to see that fight."

Swope said, "Would you really?"

"Oh, yes! More than anything."

"Then we'll have to see what we can do." The Swopes were traveling in the private railroad car of Harry Sinclair, the fabulously rich oilman. Swope told his host that it was vital that they bring along Mae to look after Mrs. Swope.

At the fight, Maggie was cheering loudly for Dempsey from the first bell. Swope growled, "What do you think you're doing?"

"What's it look like I'm doing?"

"I've got a big bet on Tunney."

"That's your business. I like Dempsey."

"I liked you better when you were a shy young thing who never opened her mouth." She smiled sweetly and went right on cheering. Even winning his bet didn't soothe him. He went on grumbling all the way back to New York. She finally said, "It's like you always say, Herbie. You made two mistakes. You should never have taught me how to think, and you should never have taught me how to speak."

"If you thought more, you'd speak less."

"Why?" she asked sweetly. "Thinking never stopped you." He went back to his poker game, and she started chatting with Mae about how she would spend *his* winnings, redoing this and that in the already perfect apartment. Mae forbore. She didn't really approve of anybody who talked back to Swope, and that included Mrs. Swope.

Whatever other name Mae bore—for she did have some husbands—to the shopkeepers both in Manhattan and on the north shore of Long Island she was Mae Swope. Not only was there never any question about what she might order and charge, but they would open up on Sundays or the middle of the night especially for her. When Swope would bring

Adams, Broun, Woollcott and half his staff home without telling anybody they were coming, simply assuming, in those pre-freezer days, that a meal would appear, Mae would take out her address book, with its neat entries of both store and home numbers for all the merchants with whom she dealt, make a few calls and, pushing on her hat, grab Roy to take her on the rounds of grocers, butchers and fruitmongers, who would still be blinking sleep from their eyes.

The bills were astronomical, but the Swopes never questioned her about them. Years later, Maggie would point out food stores in Great Neck or Port Washington and say, "He had the nerve to complain because I was a little late in paying. And who paid for his mortgage? Me. Singlehanded." Or, "I put his son through college. Nice kid. Used to deliver the Sunday papers."

F. Scott Fitzgerald and Mae were responsible for changing the way the Sunday dinners were served. Originally they were buffets. People would get plates of food and wander off to find seats on the porch or in the living room. Fitzgerald, followed by a crowd of admirers, would wander farther afield to the gazebo, where the group would ensconce themselves with a couple of bottles of Swope's excellent bootleg whisky (Swope would serve nothing unless it first had been tested at a laboratory to make certain that it was drinkable).

The revelers never brought their dishes back. Sometimes, they would not even bring themselves back, but would curl up in the gazebo or the garden and go to sleep. Fitzgerald was famous for having slept on every lawn from Great Neck to Port Washington.

Mae soon wearied of having to hunt for china and silver all over the grounds. Something had to be done to keep people in one place during those large parties. Without telling anybody, she went to Macy's and ordered ten sets of bridge tables and chairs, charging them to Swope. While everybody was upstairs dressing for the next big dinner party, she had the staff move the dining room table out of the way and put the bridge tables up. Maggie came down to find ten tables for four perfectly set with linen and her lovely china and silver, with fresh garden flowers for centerpieces. Mae waited apprehensively as Maggie inspected the room. She finally turned and said, "Nice restaurant you've got here. How's the service?"

Mae cried jubilantly, "You'll see! You'll see!" The family and their guests of honor sat at one end at the regular dining table. The other guests were scattered throughout the room. The Swope crowd was far too ebullient to observe the segregation into small groups, and conversations were often conducted across tables and, at times, at cross-purposes. They were silent only when Swope, in his stentorian tones, was expounding on some topic that held the entire room entranced. It was the best party they had ever had and became the pattern for all those that followed in Great Neck.

Games were the great pastime at the Swopes'. During the day, a demon form of no-holds-barred croquet was played. It was a far cry from the polite ladies' and children's game that had been in vogue in Victorian times. It was played with heavy mallets, iron wickets, and no bounds. The ball had to be played from wherever it landed. This was particularly exhilarating on the Swope court, which was laid out on the sloping lawn. A ball could easily land in the drain gutter and roll down into the road.

Among the more avid players were Swope, Kaufman, Adams, Woollcott, Ross, and Harpo Marx. These men of no small intellectual endowments were reduced to the level of peevish and ferocious children when engaged in the sport. Fights sometimes occurred that left the participants so angry that they would not speak for months. The croquet court was a marvelous place for Swope-watching, as the following letter from Woollcott to Lilli Bonner illustrates:

> I suppose you want to hear the latest Swope story. Burdened with Gerald Brooks as a croquet partner, he became so violent that Brooks agreed to do only what he was told and thereafter became a mute automaton, a position which Swope enjoyed hugely. Brooks never moved his mallet or approached a ball without being told by Swope: "Now, Brooksy, you go through this wicket. That's fine. Now you shoot down to position. Perfect!" And so on. Finally, before an enthralled audience, Swope said: "Now you hit that ball up here in the road. That's right. Now you put your little foot on *your* ball and drive the other buckety-buckety off into the orchard. Perfect!" It was only then, from the shrieks of the onlookers, that Swope discovered it was his own ball that had been driven off.

The evening games included that form of charades known as The Game, Twenty Questions, Who Am I? and Murder, which probably originated at the Swopes'. Simultaneously there would be backgammon, mah-jongg, rummy, and the inevitable poker—the big game, in which the men played for very large stakes, and the little game, in which the ladies played for smaller stakes, which still were by no means penny-ante.

One night, Adams was concentrating hard on a very big poker pot.

From the other room, he was interrupted by Swope, in another game, shouting triumphantly, "Who was Kleist?"*

An irritated Adams shouted back, "The Chinese Messiah."

The poker games lasted until four or five in the morning and sometimes longer. Although Mae was not the regular cook, she became famous for the hamburgers and fried eggs and onion sandwiches that she would often serve at dawn. Of her own volition, Mae—with perhaps one helper—would stay on call for as long as anybody was still up and might want something.

If the game was not over by eight or nine in the morning, Swope would say, "Somebody close the door. I don't want the kids to know what we're doing." But the kids always knew. When Ottie was barely out of short pants, he was already expert at backgammon, croquet, and poker.

The gentlemen took their poker seriously. Once, Bernard Baruch was in a game with Swope and Arthur Krock. The day had dawned hours before, and even Swope was ready to cash in, but Baruch was losing and insisted that the game go on so that he might have a chance to recoup. Lydia came in and announced, "Mr. Baruch, the president of the United States wants you on the phone."

Suspecting that it might be a ruse dreamed up by Swope and Krock to end the game, Baruch told a startled Lydia, "Tell the president of the United States to go to hell."

It is doubtful that Calvin Coolidge would have been amused, had she relayed the message verbatim.

Similarly, Swope was in the middle of a highly competitive croquet game when he was told that Governor Al Smith wanted to speak to him immediately. He replied, "Tell him to hold his horses. It's my shot."

Swope was generally conceded to be brilliant. Robert E. Sherwood called him "one of the world's greatest talkers," along with Heywood Broun, Booth Tarkington, Will Rogers, Charlie Chaplin, and George Bernard Shaw.

Swope headed Broun's own list of great conversationalists, which he called "the All-American Talking Team." It also included Clarence Darrow, George Jean Nathan, Max Eastman, Irvin S. Cobb, Alfred E. Smith, Alice Roosevelt Longworth, Dorothy Parker, Alexander

---

*The identity of Kleist was one of those obscure facts that were always on call from the depths of Swope's amazingly retentive memory. Heinrich von Kleist, an eighteenth-century dramatist and journalist who killed his mistress and committed suicide, is considered a prototype of existentialists.

Woollcott, Will Rogers, and Floyd Dell. Broun said that he had hesitated to include Swope, because even in such a loquacious line-up, the others wouldn't be able to get a word in once he got started.

On one of his radio broadcasts, Broun recalled a dinner with H. G. Wells, Swope, and six Japanese newspapermen:

> These Oriental journalists were anxious to learn what the great English novelist thought about a number of topics, but they let him get all the way to his demitasse in peace. Then the spokesman for the Japanese began the interrogation. I forget what the question was. I think it had something to do with birth control, but it doesn't matter. Mr. Wells started to answer—and it was going to be at length, I guess—that is, if one can judge by the writing of H. G. Wells. But this time he made a fatal mistake—he paused to clear his throat—erham, like that—and no man can afford to take a chance like that while Swope's around. He's as quick as a Notre Dame halfback to see an opening. H. G. Wells never got started this time. He cleared his throat to no purpose, for the booming voice of my beloved boss cut through the respectful silence of the Japanese journalists, and he spoke up loud and clear, saying, "I think Mr. Wells means to say about as follows." And for the next half hour he held us all—including H. G. Wells—spellbound.

When Ethel Barrymore was invited out for her first weekend at Great Neck, she was warned that she would have trouble finding the Swope place. Miss Barrymore replied, "Nonsense! I'll just go to the edge of town and listen."

Kay Cowdin recently recalled going to parties at his house:

> Herbert was always asking questions. Not to show off that he knew the answers, but because he was really interested in other people's opinions. Some of us would sit there paralyzed with fear. What would happen if he asked us? We'd just make fools of ourselves in front of all these clever people. And then he'd do something so sweet. He'd start another conversation and turn to one of us scared lambs and say, "As you were saying just today . . ." And then he'd attribute some fabulous insight to us. Of course, we'd never protest. We were just too flattered. He was so generous. He had this wonderful way of including everybody, even when he was the only one doing the talking.

As early as the mid-twenties, the Swope household was already famous. George S. Kaufman's second collaboration with Edna Ferber,

The Royal Family, was said to be based upon the antics of the Barrymore family. That was not what they had originally intended. The genesis of the play was described by Scott Meredith in his book *George S. Kaufman and His Friends:*

> The original plan was to do a play which was not about the theatre at all; it was to do a play about a frantic, fantastic household rather like Herbert Bayard Swope's. Swope, it seemed to them, would lend himself rather well to a larger-than-life portrait in play form: they felt they could do quite a lot with a man so bold that he once cut in on the Prince of Wales at a party at Clarence Mackay's house, so regal himself that every member of his household was expected to rise whenever he entered a room, and so well-liked by the celebrity set that big names by the dozens were his house guests every month of the year. . . . The final decision in 1926 was that it was not for the team of Kaufman and Ferber. After much thought, they abandoned the idea on the grounds that, even if they reported things accurately and without exaggeration, it would all seem so incredible and unreal that people would simply not believe it.

One Swope touch that did remain in *The Royal Family* was the very funny business in the opening act in which the servants are kept constantly busy serving endless varieties of breakfast food to all of the other characters in different parts of the house.

Life at the Swopes' was not all roses for the guests. There was the occasional thorny thrust of Margaret's acerbic wit. One night, Peggy Hopkins Joyce was flirting outrageously with Swope, and Maggie cut in with, "I'm sorry. Everyone who comes here has got to have a visible means of support."

On another night, a movie vamp was exercising her well-used seductive charms on the men in the room. Bea Kaufman said resentfully, "She's certainly free with her body."

Maggie replied, "That's probably the only way she can dispose of it."

At one luncheon party, Raoul Fleischmann was swatting the air with his hands. Maggie asked, "What's wrong with you?"

"It's these damned flies."

She drew herself up indignantly. "If there are any flies in this room, they came in on the guests."

A guest at a large party gushed about how thrilled he was to be in a room filled with such illustrious and famous people. He gestured to a pair in a corner and said, "Look at that. Where else could you see Harry Cohn and Harry Hopkins having a terrific conversation?"

Maggie nodded. "Yeah. Harry Common and Harry Preferred."

Despite the barbs, most people remembered Maggie as the perfect hostess. One weekend, Heywood Broun had one of his chronic nervous seizures, which would cause him to get panicky in front of people. In a room full of people having supper, he suddenly rose and stumbled out the door in a daze. Nobody except Maggie sensed that he was ill. She followed him out quietly, walked him up and down, and calmed him until the seizure passed. They returned to their meals as quietly as they had departed, with nobody aware of what had happened.

Her fame as a housekeeper was such that people simply took it for granted that she had anticipated her guests' every wish. One Sunday morning, Frank Sullivan arose early and went to the bathroom across the hall, where he found a bath already drawn. "I marvelled at what an efficient household Mrs. Swope ran, to anticipate her guests' wants so," he said. "I got into the bath and bathed, got out, and on leaving ran into the future Mrs. Pulitzer [Peggy Leech, who was to marry Ralph], who informed me that she had drawn that bath for herself, not for me."

For all the idiosyncrasies, guests found life at the Swopes' idyllic. Noel Coward thought that it was the only household in America where visits could be compared to weekends in an English country house. Raoul Fleischmann paid it what he considered the ultimate compliment. He sighed ecstatically. "When I die, I hope it's at the Swopes'."

ELEVEN

In 1923 there were no gurus, psychic surgeons, or transcendental meditationists, but there was a Frenchman named Émile Coué, who was second only to chicken à la king as the hottest thing on the lecture circuit. His trick was self-mastery through autosuggestion. All over America people were walking around talking to themselves, and what they were constantly repeating was his famous slogan: "Every day, in every way, I am getting better and better."

Swope immediately persuaded Coué to lend his name to a series of articles on his methods, which would be ghosted by a staff reporter on the *World*. The idea was so popular that Swope was able to make a nice profit for the paper by selling the pieces to most of the members of the *World* syndicate.

This was Swope giving the public what it wanted. To give it what he thought it should have whether or not it wanted it, Swope initiated the *World* exposé of the inequities of Florida's system of leasing prisoners to private companies. The investigation grew out of the death of a North Dakota farm boy, Martin Tabert, in a Florida lumber camp. Tabert was no sterling character. He was bumming his way across the country because he did not like the hard work at home, and was caught trying to ride a train in Florida without paying the fare. When he was sentenced to a fine of twenty-five dollars or ninety days in prison, he wired his brother for fifty dollars, claiming that the charge was vagrancy. The brother wired seventy-five dollars to the boy, in care of Sheriff R. C. Jones in Tallahassee. The money was returned by the sheriff, with a terse message that the party was gone.

The family worried about Martin but assumed that he must have found some other way of paying the fine. Not long after, they received a message from the Putnam Lumber Company, informing them that the boy had died of natural causes in their camp and had been given a Christian burial. The Taberts mourned for their son and brother, but, finding solace in the fact that he had been given a proper interment, they investigated no further until they received word from another prisoner that the boy had been brutally beaten by the whip boss, a man named Higgenbotham, and that this had been the true cause of his death. The family then turned the case over to Attorney Norris Nelson of North Dakota.

Nelson came up against a stone wall in his investigation. All he could learn was that, under the peonage system, young Tabert had been leased to the camp. The lumber company explained, "We have all able-bodied men prisoners from Leon County leased for a term of one year. We, of course, have to clothe, feed, and house these prisoners. About once a month the State prison inspector goes through our camp and makes careful inspection. We also furnish a doctor. When Martin was first taken sick, the doctor advised that he would not take his medicine regularly. He first had malaria fever, which terminated in pneumonia. He was sick but a short time, and one of the prisoners was taken off the work to wait on him."

Sheriff Jones justified his actions by writing: "There was some money wired to him here after he was gone, but I could not get it, as it was sent in his name. I therefore returned it."

The lumber company sounded like a charitable institution, and the sheriff like the soul of honesty. But the story told in a letter sent by a fellow prisoner who had befriended Tabert was very different. Martin had been ill, and the whipping boss suspected him of malingering, despite the fact that his condition had been verified by a doctor:

Martin was turned up by Cap Willis for a whipping and [he] reported that Martin was slow in his work and complained of being sick, but that he himself did not think so. The whipping boss was in no mood to use the strap, so he postponed it for two nights. On Friday night he called Martin out of line and by a bonfire and before about eighty-five prisoners he whipped Martin about thirty-five to fifty licks with a four-inch strap five feet long, three-ply leather at the handle, two-ply halfway down. The strap weighs seven and one-half pounds, G. L. Win of Perry, Fla., says. The law of Florida says there shall be but ten licks with the strap for each offense.

Martin begged to be let loose, but his speech was not distinct, and it seemed he was so weak he could not talk plain. The whipping boss put his feet on Martin's neck to keep him from moving out of position as he whipped him. When he let Martin up, Martin started back to get a bottle of medicine that he had dropped out of his pocket, or had been taken out, and the whipping boss drove him back into line with the big strap, hitting him over the head, shoulders and back.

He described Martin's last days, ending with the minutes before his death:

We asked the whipping boss to come in and see him, but he seemed not to want to look upon Martin, we thought because he felt guilty, but ordered some medicine given, and Martin then was too near gone to swallow and was sucking the medicine back and forth in his lungs. He never did have any care, his bed became a stench to sleep by, and he had frothed over his pillow and [there was] no clean one to take its place.

The letter concluded by solving the mystery that had been puzzling the family: why they had not heard from the boy after his first communication.

Martin might have written you for money, but letters were read going in and coming out, and many of them never went, and especially those calling for money to pay out. I had to slip a letter out before I got my money.

Other prisoners also wrote. One simply stated that the boy "was barbarously murdered." Swope went into action. The case described a life far removed from his life of slick Algonquin wits and festive dinner parties. The Florida locale was not the Florida he knew, the lush Palm Beach where that same winter, at just about the time Tabert was dying, Swope had been in a private railroad car playing poker for two days running with Flo Ziegfeld, Harry Sinclair, J. Leonard Replogle, and the millionaire oilman Joshua Cosden. His winnings amounted to almost a half-million dollars. Over $250,000 was still owed to him by Ziegfeld at the time of the producer's death. Tabert had died for $25. Swope never said a word about Ziegfeld. They were both big guys who knew the stakes and the game. Tabert was a little guy in a game he did not understand, for infinitely higher stakes. The feature began:

> The facts which the *World* here reveals about Florida are not those which have to do with the Florida known to the half-million tourists who visit the state each winter.
>
> It is not the Florida of glorious sun and blue skies and of white surf beating lazily on the beaches of Miami and Palm Beach. It is not the Florida which the traveller, looking from the windows of trains gliding northward from Key West, looks at and regrets to leave, a land where the dogwood already is spreading its beauty of white blooms through the forests and jonquils are glowing golden in every dooryard.
>
> It is not the Florida of fruit and flowers, sunshine and contentment, which the whole world thinks of when it hears the name. The last of the winter visitors lounging on the verandas of hotels on the southern coast hears the throbbing dance music of perfect orchestras; he has not heard and may never hear a quite different sound—the scream of a human being under the lash of a convict captain.

The story not only was instrumental in bringing an indictment of first-degree murder against the whip boss, but it also brought about the banning of the lash in Florida prison camps. Not incidentally, the exposé brought the *World* its second Pulitzer Prize in as many years under Swope's direction.

Swope was now firmly entrenched at the paper. With Frank Cobb already suffering from the illness that would end his life within a year, the executive editor felt that he could use his influence to shape the future of the editorial page. To make certain that his own brand of Wilsonian liberalism remained prevalent on the page, he brought over Walter Lippmann from the *New Republic,* which Lippmann had founded but readily relinquished for the more influential *World*.

Swope had first become friendly with Lippmann in Paris, where the latter was one of Wilson's consultants on the peace treaty. By the time he came to the *World*, he already had written two books of political philosophy, *A Preface to Politics* and *Drift and Mastery,* and was completing a third, *Public Opinion*.

Swope realized from the beginning that Lippmann was not a man to compromise. In order to pull the paper out of the financial trouble that the Pulitzers had brought upon it, Swope felt—rightly or wrongly—that one man had to be in control and that he himself was that man. Lippmann would be difficult to control, but he was the best man for the job.

He decided that the only solution was to have somebody else inside the editorial department who might prove a challenge to Lippmann and brought his old friend Arthur Krock up from Kentucky for the job. Lippmann perceived Krock as a threat and refused to have him in his department. At that point, Ralph Pulitzer got into the act. Recognizing Krock's undoubted talents, he offered him a job as his personal assistant, which was the last place Swope wanted to have him situated. It was difficult enough to get through to Pulitzer without having to go through an intermediary. He suggested that Krock be sent to Washington to do a signed column on capital news. Both Lippmann and Pulitzer balked at this, and poor Krock wound up with an obscure job in the circulation department.

One thing that united Krock and Lippmann during those early days of antagonism was resentment of the Op Ed page. Ironically, both ended their distinguished careers as neighbors on the *New York Times* version of the Op Ed page, with Krock writing exactly the kind of signed Washington column that Swope had suggested he do a half-century earlier.

Another Swope innovation was to assign John J. Leary to investigate labor conditions in the West Virginia coal mines. The shocking facts brought to light by his articles resulted in still another Pulitzer Prize. The four prizes won by Pulitzer's own paper were all brought home by Swope. The editorial pages, first under Cobb and then under Lippmann, were never singled out for any awards. This only deepened the schism in the council that daily decided upon the make-up of the paper.

The council was nominally presided over by Ralph Pulitzer, but it quickly became the setting for repeated jousts between Swope and Lippmann. Allene Talmey worked for the *World* as a reporter before becoming an editor of *Vogue*. She described Pulitzer as emerging from these meetings "looking like a pair of pants pressed between the immovable mattress of Lippmann and the springs of Swope."

Swope and Lippmann truly were an irresistible force and an immovable object. In their own ways, both were journalistic geniuses, but those ways were very different. Poor Pulitzer was indeed crushed between them. He had very little talent for the newspaper business and was only in it because he had inherited it from his father, in the legal if not the genetic sense.

Lippmann's attitude toward Swope was always an equivocal one. Often he liked and admired him; sometimes he was exasperated; other times, especially later in life, he was disdainful of what he considered the lack of fulfillment of a great potential. Lippmann, the Harvard-educated political philosopher, could never fully understand Swope, the self-taught pragmatist. Lippmann would never think in terms of giving the public what it wanted but instead would always determine what he insisted was in its own best interests.

Lippmann could remove himself intellectually and discern whole patterns from afar with brilliant, if remote, objectivity. This occasionally led to errors in judgment that could not have been made by a man like Swope, whose very existence depended upon a talent for individual evaluations on a one-to-one basis. As early as 1923, Swope was using the World to warn the people of the potential danger of an obscure rabble rouser in Bavaria named Adolf Hitler. In 1933 Lippmann called Hitler a "truly civilized European." In 1936 Lippmann supported the cool moderation of Alfred M. Landon, while Swope, who felt that the public needed leadership as well as moderation, was for Roosevelt. Swope even went so far as to write to the president, outlining what he felt his image should be, despite the fact that Roosevelt had not really dealt fairly with him in previous associations. In 1952 Swope suggested to his friend Dwight D. Eisenhower that he not accept Richard M. Nixon as a running mate, because there was something devious about him. In 1968 Lippman felt that Nixon had qualities that recommended him for the White House.

Swope's chronic lateness was something about which friends complained throughout his life. His lack of punctuality disturbed his fellow members on the World council, who protested vehemently, often citing the fact that his best friends were equally disturbed by it. Many voiced the suspicion that it was an affectation. Certainly his entrances were sometimes calculated for maximum effect, but that was the public Swope; it was rarely true of the professional Swope.

The council meetings were scheduled for early afternoon, which was convenient for everybody except Swope. Lippmann was responsible for one page. By the time he got to the meeting, he would be fairly certain of what would be on it, could get approval, and could then get it written in time to be home for dinner. Pulitzer was seldom at the paper in the evening. As business manager, White was never there after the book-keepers left at six. Cosgrave, the Sunday editor, had to be there only the one night that the Sunday paper was put to bed. For the *Evening World* people, the council was almost the last task of their business day.

The timetable was very different for the editors and reporters on a morning paper. The very existence of an Algonquin Round Table attests to that. Many of the most prominent members worked on morning papers. That hotel lunch often served as breakfast. They could linger over it, because they did not have to be at work until mid-afternoon.

Swope's desk diaries for those years contain careful notations of his hours. On weekends, when he was not at the office, he noted telephoning in four or five times a day to check on things. On weekdays, he called in at noon or shortly thereafter, arrived about three, and often did not go home until four or five in the morning. A vivid childhood memory of Herbert, Jr., is of running into his father arriving home from work as he started out for school. He recently recalled, "The old man was just getting home from the office. He always smelled of rubber bands."

One afternoon in the spring of 1923, the council was amazed to find Swope waiting for them when they arrived for the meeting on the fourteenth floor of the *World* building. He was in and out of his chair several times, hurriedly ushering the others to their seats. He was so impatient that he could barely contain himself until the meeting got under way. He had an idea to put before them, a glorious idea that would reflect brilliantly on both the paper and the city. He paused and looked around the room. They waited, some with no small degree of anxiety.

Swope announced that he wanted the *World* to start a campaign to have the 1924 Democratic Convention held in New York City. There was immediate protest from the council. It could never come to pass. The paper would look ridiculous when the plan ultimately failed. It was an insanely partisan idea. (To this last, Swope replied, "Let's get the Republicans, too. I don't mind.") He had a reply to every question and doubt. The facts and figures, with which he was so well prepared, rolled forth like a tidal wave, and the others reluctantly consented to "Swope's folly."

The council minutes read tersely: "Agreed success improbable but endorsed campaign." Some were even gleefully looking forward to the sight of the irrepressible Mr. Swope with egg on his face. They did not know their man. When Swope went into action, hurricanes held their breath. It was not that Swope knew everybody in town, although his list of acquaintances was staggering: it was rather that everybody wanted to know Swope. His was a name worth dropping, even if the privilege cost a substantial contribution to the convention.

By the time the selection of a site for the convention was to be made, he had raised what was then considered a formidable sum, $250,000, to bring the convention to Madison Square Garden. A thousand restaurants had signed a pledge not to increase their prices when the delegates arrived. Although liquor was officially banned from the convention hall and the stein was even removed from the hand of the statue of Father Knickerbocker that stood in front of the Hotel Astor, the sponsors knew that banning it would not stop its consumption, and the better speakeasies were inveigled into agreeing not to gouge the city's guests, on the premise that a Tammany Hall–dominated police force would not be likely to raid haunts favored by the visitors. Hotels had promised to be reasonable about rates and to be satisfied with the profits from complete occupancy, down to the last broom closet. When the convention officially opened on June 24, 1924, the city was primed to render services in return for the considerable amount it was to earn. The police had rounded up every pickpocket in the vicinity of the Garden, but could do nothing about that more devious form of filching indulged in by the ticket scalpers, who were getting $100 a seat for gallery locations.

The year was a triumphant one for Swope. Not only had he brought off the convention, but the youthful *Time* magazine had selected him for one of its covers. A smiling, dapper Swope adorned the January 28 cover. Beneath his name was the caption *"Dynamic? No—cyclonic!"*

On June 16, 1924, a week before the convention opened, Hobart College conferred an honorary degree upon Swope and invited him to make the Phi Beta Kappa address on Commencement Day. He called his speech "Journalism: An Instrument of Civilization." In it he quoted Thomas Jefferson:

> The basis of our Government being the opinion of the people, the very first object should be to keep that right. Were it left to me to decide whether we should have a government without newspapers or newspapers without a government, I should not hesitate to prefer the latter.

He called his day "the age of the reporter" and later said:

> There is a growing tendency in America that threatens its civilization. That is the permeation throughout our social strata by a sort of Prussian rule of divine right, whereby laws become sacrosanct and even honest criticism of them becomes sinful. The suppression of liberty cannot go much farther than that. It is the duty of journalism to be a mouthpiece, regardless of its own beliefs, of honest and intelligent oppositional views on any public matter. It must always be in our minds that democracy more than any other organized society depends upon human will, upon individual moral judgment and upon the ability of a member to think and act for himself. If he is not such a person, a collection of his peers cannot make a government that will survive; if he is such a person, he is entitled to be fully informed on all subjects and to be entrusted with full liberty in expression of opinion and in personal habits, within the ordinary limits set by police laws. There is something worse than the conscription of the body, and that is the conscription of the will. The one may save a monarchy; the second will destroy a republic. The tendency toward coercion is most noticeable in a nation when it begins to give itself over more to the prevention of evils than to the protection of rights.

Swope had been brilliant at getting the convention to the city and then getting it off to a good start. Once the Democratic Party took over, it became such a fiasco that it took over fifty years for the Democrats to get the distasteful memory out of their minds and return to the city for another convention. There was a heat wave, which was bad enough in those pre–air-conditioning days, but that was not the major problem. Heat waves also occurred in Kansas City, Chicago, St. Louis, et al., but they made none of these cities an anathema. The party did that all alone, without any aid from weather or locale.

The most controversial issues at the '24 convention were prohibition and the Ku Klux Klan. The leading contender for the nomination was William McAdoo, the patrician son-in-law of President Wilson. He was a liberal on most issues, and one might assume he would have been Swope's logical choice. But the Klan had endorsed him, and McAdoo was against any strong plank condemning it. Even had there been no other considerations, this would have been enough to turn Swope against him.

But there were other considerations, the largest being McAdoo's leading opponent, the progressive Governor Alfred E. Smith of New York State, who was anti-Klan, anti-prohibition (a law which Swope considered both ridiculous and unenforceable), and a close friend of the editor. Swope had known Smith for years and admired him as both a liberal and a man of the people; therefore, he was on the side of the angels. Unfortunately, those angels were Catholics. Smith was devout in his observance of his faith, and this triggered both suspicion and bigotry in the Protestant majority.

McAdoo's peripheral involvement in the Teapot Dome scandal was another discrediting factor in Swope's opinion. The affair had shaken the entire Republican administration. Leases to naval oil reserves at Teapot Dome, Wyoming, had been illegally peddled by Secretary of the Interior Albert B. Fall to a group of oilmen, including Swope's friend Harry Sinclair. (When Sinclair asked that the *World* play down his role in the affair, Swope refused.)

McAdoo had accepted a $100,000 legal retainer from Edward Doheny, another oilman deeply implicated in the reserves-land swindle. Consequently, he could not use the Teapot Dome as political ammunition, for it would rebound upon him. Swope thought that it made absolutely no sense to gag the party on this potentially lethal issue.

There was one incident indirectly linked to the convention in which Swope had allowed personal feelings to modify his journalistic principles. Two years before, Franklin Delano Roosevelt had been stricken with polio. Great attention to this fact in the press could well have meant the end of his career. Mrs. Roosevelt had called Swope to ask him not to make too much of the illness, for her husband's sake, and Swope had buried a small, noncommittal report of the facts amid the advertisements on one of the inside pages of the *World*.

Roosevelt had been chosen to nominate Smith at the convention. He did not want to deliver the speech that had been prepared for him, which referred to the governor as "the Happy Warrior." From his point of view, it was an overstatement of the man's qualities. Smith wore no school ties; he was one of the common men, a rough jewel—a type alien to Roosevelt's background, a type he liked only in the abstract.

Swope intervened. Roosevelt owed him something, and it was to be repaid not to him but to the man they both agreed was the best their party could then offer. The speech was delivered as written, without any of Roosevelt's modifying clauses. It went down in history as the most memorable speech of his pre-presidential years.

It has often been implied that Swope was Baruch's pawn. The events of the '24 convention plainly show that this was not true. Baruch was completely in the McAdoo camp. He later said, "I was unequivocally behind McAdoo. As I wrote to Bryan in March 1924, 'We have a great chance, but that chance will disappear unless we nominate a progressive and a dry'—which described McAdoo exactly."

Swope's colleague and friend Arthur Krock was also a McAdoo man. Baruch enlisted his help in trying to persuade Swope to change camps. Despite his admiration for both men, he would not defect. McAdoo was a dry, although his father-in-law had vetoed prohibition. He would make no stand against the Klan. Even if innocent of direct implication in Teapot Dome, he still had oil on his hands, and, in the slogan popular among Smith boosters, "There ain't no oil on Al."

In the words of the newspaper columnist Frank Kent, the 1924 convention was "the longest, wildest, most turbulent political gathering in the history of the country." Hopelessly deadlocked between McAdoo and Smith, it dragged on for over two weeks in the sweltering heat of Madison Square Garden, where it was considered a delightfully cool respite whenever the thermometer dipped below 100°, which was seldom. Maddening chants of "Oil! Oil! Oil!" constantly greeted McAdoo, while "Booze! Booze! Booze!" was Smith's welcome. In the end, after all of the smoke-filled-backroom bartering, neither was nominated. On July 9, on the record-shattering 103rd ballot, a weary, indifferent, and broke convention nominated a distinguished Wall Street attorney and native of West Virginia, John W. Davis, whose national obscurity was balanced by uncompromising integrity.

It was radio that won the election for Calvin Coolidge more than anything either candidate said or did during the campaign. The New York convention was the first to be broadcast, and, as Baruch noted, "For two weeks, millions tuned in on the clash and clamor."

It was a wild and unruly spectacle that shed no honor or distinction on any of the participants. By contrast, the later Republican convention was well ordered, sensible, united and dull. Radio was a stunning novelty, and voters had not forgotten what they had heard by the time the election rolled around. It sounded as if the choice was between turbulence and order; the people opted for the latter. The incumbent, cool Calvin Coolidge, was still president of the United States. Television had the same effect on both parties' conventions of '68 and '72. In 1976, the Democrats seemed finally to have learned their lesson, with the "love-in" convention held, ironically enough, in New York City.

The conventioneers may have been unhappy with the city, but the merchants were delirious about the conventioneers—and about Swope for having brought them and their purses to town. They expressed their gratitude to the editor in every way except, alas, increased advertising in his paper. In 1926 the party got around to honoring him for his services: he was awarded the first convention badge for "conceiving the idea of obtaining the Democratic National Convention of 1924 for New York." The badge was cut out of silver and appropriately engraved. He was also praised for "the continuous and energetic effort" he had shown as a member of the Executive Committee and for providing for the entertainment of the voters.

There was another honor in 1926. For the first time in its history—and it would be rare in the history of any institution of higher learning—Colgate University conferred honorary degrees on two brothers, Herbert Bayard Swope and Gerard Swope, who was then president of General Electric. The two sons of the poor immigrant watchmaker had traveled a great distance and done it on their own.

By contrast, there were the Pulitzer brothers, Joseph, Ralph, and Herbert. They were also the sons of a Jewish immigrant, but the similarity ended there. No advantage had been denied them, not by virtue of their own hard work, but by the privilege of inheritance; nonetheless, on the whole they achieved no real eminence, no distinction, no reward beyond the wealth with which they had been blessed at birth.

The older Pulitzer's will had divided his fortune eccentrically. Joseph, the oldest son, who ran the St. Louis *Post-Dispatch*, received one tenth of the publishing empire; Ralph, the middle son and Swope's nominal boss at the *World*, got one fifth. One tenth was set aside to reward company executives. The remainder—and largest share—went to the youngest son, Herbert, who was all of fourteen at the time of his father's death.

In 1926, at the age of twenty-nine, after having spent a gilded youth bumming around from one luxurious European resort to another, Herbert Pulitzer decided to make his presence felt at the paper that, after all, belonged more to him than to anybody else. His ignorance of journalism was matched only by his stubborn insistence that his word be law. Swope's idyllic years at the *World* were drawing to a close. His memos in the following years indicate that to Joseph, at the *Post-Dispatch*, he remained a trusted adviser; to Ralph, he was a diplomatically superior but always friendly consultant; while to Herbert, he was the procurer of theater tickets, sporting-event tickets, travel tickets—in other words, a messenger boy rather than a man from whom young Pulitzer could have learned his trade.

Herbert Pulitzer was at the *World* to stay. There was no uncertainty about that. How did the staff regard him? This might be summed up in the bitter words of Franklin P. Adams after the *World* was sold: "Herbert Pulitzer was the shit heard round the *World*."

TWELVE

Ring Lardner, the Swopes' neighbor in Great Neck, complained that the noise of the continual late-hour parties had forced him to rent a hotel room in New York in which to do his writing. It was of course the sort of exaggeration with which one confronted the Swopes' way of life. The parties were always on weekends, and Lardner was often among the guests, frequently making his way home across the field between the houses at 5:00 A.M. More likely, it was his own four high-spirited sons who forced him to seek other writing quarters. Beyond that, there were hotels nearer, cheaper, and quieter than those he sought. The abrasive stimulation of Manhattan and the exile from family were probably what he wanted; the Swopes were the acceptable rationale.

One weekend, Dorothy Parker and Marc Connelly were house guests of the Lardners. It was ten o'clock on Saturday night, and they were comfortably ensconced on the veranda with their after-dinner drinks. A refreshing breeze lifted off the bay and slipped across the lawn, bringing with it the sound of laughter and music from the Swope household.

They smugly noted that those poor people next door were probably just trying to keep their spirits up, while hungrily awaiting a meal that had not yet been served. Suddenly an eerie glow lit up the sky, alarming Mrs. Parker. Her host explained that those were automobile headlights illuminating a croquet game. She took a sip of her drink and said, "Jesus Christ! The heirs of the age."

Mrs. Parker was an infrequent visitor at the Swopes'; she was invited only when Swope insisted upon it, for Margaret did not like her. She wallowed in the two things that the hostess could not abide: alcohol and self-pity.

The gate finally descended permanently for the F. Scott Fitzgeralds. Margaret had tolerated them for some time because of Swope's affection for young writers. Fitzgerald loved to listen to Swope's yarns. Told well and colorfully, they were a great source of material. He used Swope's account of the Becker murder case in *The Great Gatsby,* and many felt that the character of Manheim was based on Swope's old gambling pal, Arnold Rothstein.

Well-run households also fascinated Fitzgerald, probably because he never had one himself. Swope's place in Great Neck and his parties were used as models for the Gatsby house and parties. Later, Fitzgerald was to use what many people considered the Swope counterpart in the South of France, the Gerald Murphy villa, in *Tender Is the Night.* In their respective parts of the world, the Murphys' and the Swopes' establishments were the names to drop in conversation. "What a marvelous time I had last weekend at Swope's place." "Sara Murphy's divine. What fun at their party!"

Margaret and Mrs. Murphy did the dirty work. They cleared away the debris. When people were barred, it was they who did it, as the experiences of the Fitzgeralds in both houses illustrate. It was Zelda Fitzgerald who committed the ultimate offense as far as Margaret was concerned.

Bruce Powell had grown into a charming but rather diffident young man. A few drinks convinced the beautiful Zelda that he had to be brought out of his shell, and that she was the one to do it. At first it was amusing to watch him become shyer as she became bolder. But the fun and games stopped when she tore off all her clothes and chased the terrified adolescent upstairs, where he locked himself in his room while she pounded on the door. That was it for Margaret. Zelda was out. "Not with my brother, sister! Not in my house, Mrs. F.!" Even the lawns were off-limits for the sleeping-it-off drunks.

Bruce stopped telling the story on himself long afterward when his nephew, by then himself an adolescent, asked, "For God's sake, Bruce, why did you run?" Bruce could only blush and stammer something about his youth. Margaret was the reason, as Ottie would learn soon enough.

The insult to the Fitzgeralds was compounded by the *World*'s minority review of the book that has since achieved the status of minor classic. Although unsigned, it dated from the period when Laurence Stallings was doing the reviews and was probably written by him:

F. Scott Fitzgerald's new novel confirms the belief that there should
be a consolidation of reviewers of average books and the selectors of
scenarios. *The Great Gatsby* is another one of the thousands of
modern novels which must be approached with the point of view
of the average tired person toward the movie-around-the-corner, a
deadened intellect, a thankful resigning of the attention, and an
aftermath of wonder that such things are produced.

It was a report with which Swope did not agree. He liked the book and
was pleased with his connection to it, but, in accord with his own
policies, he did nothing to influence his critic. For all the mutual
back-scratching in the Algonquin crowd, even Woollcott called the shots
as he saw them when reviewing the work of Kaufman, Connelly, or
Ferber. In an interview a few years later that appeared in the *World*,
Fitzgerald summed up his opinion of the cultural scene epitomized by
these people:

The best of America drifts to Paris. The American in Paris is the best
American. It is more fun for an intelligent person to live in an
intelligent country. France has the only two things towards which we
drift as we get older—intelligence and good manners.

Coming from the often boorish *enfant terrible* of American letters, it
seemed a dubious judgment. Nevertheless, it was true that, with the
exception of Eugene O'Neill's work, the best American writing was
being done abroad.

As early as 1925, Swope realized the advertising value of radio and
suggested that the *World* take spot advertisements, but there was no
money for the project. There never seemed to be any money. Although
profits were down because of increased expenditures, they still remained
substantial. The problem was that the Pulitzers were not putting a penny
back into the papers. They were greedily siphoning off all the cream to
pay for their extravagant life-styles—luxury cruises abroad, yachts,
houses in Palm Beach, lodges in Bar Harbor, private railroad cars. It was
facetiously suggested that the Pulitzers were only trying to keep up with
the Swopes. The difference, of course, was that Swope lived high at
Swope's expense, and the Pulitzers were living high at the paper's
expense.

With sound investment counsel from men like Baruch, Cosden, and
Sinclair, Swope was amassing a fortune in the stock market. It was a

small one when compared to the financial worth of his advisers, but considerable by any normal measure—on a par with those of his employers. There was no overt reason for him to continue to work for other men, especially men as shortsighted as the Pulitzer brothers. But the need to be a newspaperman came from within, and to satisfy it, he would continue until their idiocies made it impossible for him to remain both in the job and at peace with himself.

One of the classic examples of the Pulitzers' lack of journalistic prescience occurred toward the end of 1925. With the approval of most of the council, they proposed to raise the price of the paper from two cents to three cents. Swope demurred; he was supported only by Arthur Krock, who did not even have a vote on the council. He argued that the *Times* and *Tribune* already exceeded the *World* by fifty to sixty columns of news and pages upon pages of advertising. On what grounds could they possibly justify charging fifty percent more than the competition? If any change was to be made, it should be in the other direction. They should charge only a penny, thereby undercutting the other papers in their class.

The Pulitzers, Lippmann, Cosgrave, and White would not move. A penny meant nothing to men in their position. They argued that people willing to spend two cents for the *World* would certainly spend three. They were wrong. Circulation dropped drastically, and by early 1926 they had lost almost 50,000 readers.

The Pulitzers began to panic. Something had to be done; belts had to be tightened—not theirs, but the paper's. On October 27, 1926, Swope received a memo from Ralph Pulitzer:

> 1927 will have to be a year of strict economy. I hope that this economy will not have to go further than the following order, which must be strictly observed:
>
> The weekly cost for your department for 1927 must not exceed the weekly cost for 1926.
>
> Any increase in salary must be offset by a corresponding simultaneous decrease.
>
> Any contemplated addition to the number or amounts of salaries must be communicated to the Financial Manager, accompanied by definite offsetting retrenchment to be made simultaneously elsewhere.
>
> The time between now and January 1, 1927, should be devoted to making whatever plans or readjustments are necessary to make this order effective.

Swope thought that it was "a damn-fool suggestion." He had gathered one of the most impressive arrays of journalistic talent to be found anywhere in the country. Living costs were going up, and contracts were due for renewal. The men wanted—and in some instances needed—more money. Some had remained as long as they had only out of a sense of personal loyalty to Swope and out of the belief that he would look after their interests. He was not going to disappoint them. The friction mounted. Although he liked Ralph Pulitzer, "his boys" came first. The arguments at the council meetings grew heated and the language rawer. Swope stormed out more than once, pausing only to blush embarrassedly and apologize to the secretary who sat outside the conference room, for it was obvious that she could not help overhearing some of his choicer epithets. She merely found his old-fashioned courtliness charming—colorful language was nothing alien to a woman who worked on a newspaper.

Swope's personal affection for Ralph Pulitzer continued throughout the altercations. Swope always had a gift for departmentalizing his personal and public lives, and men who disappointed him in the former were almost always able to remain close in the latter. In a letter to Ralph dated a few weeks and many fights after the budget memo, Swope wrote:

> Much as I hate to lose the real pleasure I derive from being with you, I will have to on Friday night. I can't get away before Saturday morning—if then. I have a story cooking—one of the biggest the *World* has ever contemplated—and I mean just that; far bigger than the South Carolina lynching exposure, in which I take such a real and, I hope, justifiable pride.*

Swope wrote that because he was expecting somebody with a hot tip sometime between 1:00 A.M. and 8:00 A.M. Saturday (although nothing came of it). He would not be able to join Pulitzer and Margaret would not go alone. He went on:

> Thanks for thinking of me. This may interest you:
> The Paramount Theatre opens tomorrow night. It is the biggest movie house in the world and owned directly by the Famous Players

---

*The month before, on October 8, a masked mob had broken into a jail and lynched three Negroes who had just been acquitted on appeal of murdering a white man. The South Carolina press had played down the incident, but the *World* had taken it up, giving it big coverage and evoking widespread indignation.

people [later Paramount Pictures]. The tickets are not sold but issued only by invitation. Therefore, there is apt to be an interesting hand-picked group of stage and screen celebrities. I have been able to dig up a few tickets, and Margaret and I want to know if you would like to go, coming to our house first for dinner, where you will find the [Neysa] McMeins, Thayers [Peggy Thayer, who later married Harold Talbott, Eisenhower's Secretary of the Air Force] and the Powells— to continue the matriarchal formula.

Herbert Pulitzer soon had another even less inspired idea for solving the woes of the *World*. If the morning paper did not measure up and could not compete with the *Times* and *Trib,* it should be subordinated to the afternoon paper, the *Evening World,* which did not have such formidable adversaries. Evening papers were generally of much less significance, and the *Evening World,* with which Swope had no connection, was about as insignificant as a paper could be.

Swope mastered his temper sufficiently to dash off a terse memo to be delivered by hand to Herbert Pulitzer:

> *Times* running 50-60 columns more than we are. We cannot print the news they print, so we seek to be interesting and featured.
>
> We had a recent exclusive on water-power story, but the *Evening World* didn't even pick it up.
>
> Morning *World* has won three public-service awards; *Evening* has won none. Must be something in that.
>
> We were 404,000 when we went up in price.

After it was sent he obviously concluded that Pulitzer was not clever enough to get his point; an hour later another note was dispatched explaining in greater detail:

> I won Pulitzer Award in 1917.
>
> We won medal for public service in 1922 for K.K.K. exposure.
>
> Leary won prize in 1923 for Labor Conditions in W. Va.
>
> We won the award in 1923 for the Tabert Peonage case.
>
> This year we are offering for the public-service award the S.C. story.
>
> In none of these years did the *Evening World* get an award for reporting or for public service.
>
> Developed sales of *Almanac*.

I brought News Service to $80,000 a year.

Must keep in mind we are not trying to get out a paper in competition with *Times* and *Tribune,* when they average 40-60 columns more news than we do.

We have to get out a paper that is differentiated, that contains news of importance, informativeness and marked by selectivity.

The use of a second and sometimes a third back-up note was one of Swope's more infuriating traits. It was as if he did not trust either his own ability to get through the first time or the recipient's ability to follow through without prodding. Nobody was spared these terse, cold, and not infrequently monarchical memos. They were received by family, publishers, editors, rewrite men, reporters, pets of the Op Ed page. The reactions ranged from irritation to fury; the flappable Mr. Woollcott would throw a fit at the sight of an office boy carrying one.

Conversely, Swope would also send off daily barrages of notes congratulating friends and associates for work well done. "Great story!" "Good show!" "Great race!" "Beautiful party!" No event was so insignificant as to be overlooked. He valued his own opinion and assumed that others did also. In most instances he was right, both in his opinion and in his assumption.

By December 1926, the Pulitzers had realized their mistake in raising the price of the newspaper. They thought that a return to the old price would bring back the lost circulation. Swope doubted this; he had been against the increase, but he thought another change at that point would be equally wrong. He wrote to Ralph Pulitzer, sending copies of the letter to all the members of the council:

You will remember that I went on record as being opposed to the increase from two cents to three cents, especially when we were doing so well, our circulation then being in excess of 404,000. I am opposed now to a decrease, unless its necessity should be proven. Such proof, it seems to me, has more to do with the matter of advertising than of circulation.

He pointed out that advertising had increased at the new rate and that unless it decreased, another change would be a dangerous confession of weakness.

Newspaper reading is largely a matter of habit, but the reading of a specific paper is a habit soon forgotten, if a sense of injury or resentment is provoked.

We have been slipping steadily for more than a year. The slippage, as I see it, is due to the difficulty we have in answering the question of the average reader—why should I, he says, pay 50% more for the *World* than I have to pay for the *Times* or the *Tribune,* especially when the *Times* or the *Tribune* gives me far more reading matter?

We alienated from 75,000 to 100,000 readers by our increase in price. Unquestionably, some of them were fixed *World* readers who miss us and can be won back by a reduction, but I suspect the larger number of those we lost were not very strongly married to us, and they have found themselves arrested and satisfied by the *Times, Tribune* and, at the bottom of the heap, by the *News,* the *Mirror,* the *Graphic.*

We would go to the two-cent level facing a more highly competitive condition than we did two years ago. We have no desire to change the nature of the paper, but, even if we sought such a change, it could only come through coarsening our product, since the particular "class" on which the *Times, Tribune* and the *World* draw is rapidly reaching saturation.

Among these class papers, we were the first to crack, from a circulation standpoint, due solely to our increase in price. For at the moment of increase we were at the peak of our circulation for all time. Our price change gave some help—perhaps 20% of our loss to the *Times* and the *Tribune.* That is now stopped. We have about reached our irreducible minimum, and it is a case of dog eat dog between the other two papers. I suspect the *Times* will be the main sufferer, because it is becoming an increasingly hard paper to read and is trying to become interesting by becoming fakey. It will, in my judgement, gain in the national field more than the city.

I fear, if we were to go to a two-cent base, our increase would by no means equal the figure we had before going up. It will be difficult to regain even 25,000 of our former circulation. We should have to make special efforts over a long period of time before we could pull away any large number of their present readers from the *Tribune* and the *Times.* This will be doubly difficult if we reduce our size, as is to be expected, upon going to two cents. Then the disparity in bulk will be even more noticeable than now, for neither the *Times* nor the *Tribune* will dare to reduce its space, fearing each other as they do.

On the other hand, if we were to stay at three cents, we could have the kudos that comes from taking a courageous and independent position. We could point out that our price is a tribute to our identity and uniqueness. I believe that this attitude could be logically maintained on the present circulation basis, *provided* it did not wreck our advertising. I fail to see any reason why it should, if the circulation can be stabilized around 275,000. The figure can be maintained, I believe, by good promotion and special efforts in circulation, which is still the subject of complaint.

I close with two questions:

(a) Is there no hope of moving the *Times* and *Tribune* to come to our price?

(b) Could a reduction to one cent, with a cut in the size of the paper, yield enough extra advertising revenue to compensate for the deficit in production costs? We might go to 500,000 at that price.

I fear the mistake we made in going up will be doubled in going down. But I hope it is needless for me to add that any action you will take will have my whole support.

Despite Swope's opposition, the price returned to two cents. Some months later, Kyle Crichton wrote an article titled "Sharp Practices in Newspaperdom" in the magazine *Plain Talk*. It was primarily aimed at the disreputable ploys of the tabloids in their efforts to increase circulation. In passing, he noted:

I have lately read that the New York *World* lost 51,000 circulation in 1926. In the same period the *Daily News,* according to *Editor and Publisher,* went ahead by hundreds of thousands. I see by an advertisement in *Printers' Ink* for October 6, 1927, that in the last six months' period the *World* gained 51,787 in circulation. This may have been due to the *World*'s business department offering a button off the breeches of Herbert Bayard Swope with each new subscription, or it may have been the result of the *World*'s reduction of its price from three to two cents, even though the *World*, in my opinion, is as fine and at least as interesting a newspaper as America possesses. I should hate to think of anything happening to it.

Swope was not happy. Few aside from Margaret knew it. The front remained unchanged or, if anything, became still more polished. He was the perfect host, the exuberant sportsman, the hardworking editor, the indefatigable gamester, exuding that unique charm that hovered precariously between boyish gusto and patriarchal urbanity. But within himself he grappled with frustration, a feeling of impotence at his loss of control at the paper. He resented having to expend so much energy placating Herbert Pulitzer. The young man knew nothing about the newspaper business, yet he had a way of turning his wiser associates into lackeys, minions to a vanity that had no basis in reality. Swope looked to the older Pulitzers, Joseph and Ralph, for help, but, by the terms of their father's will, they could do nothing. They were, in fact, more bound than he to their brother's capriciousness.

Bernard Baruch was the only man with whom Swope discussed these inner feelings. He wondered aloud whether the kind of newspaper he was running was possible in the large format of the *World*. The tabloids were making enormous inroads in circulation and were much cheaper to produce. It was true that they were sensation-oriented scandal sheets, but there was no reason not to use the format to publish a literate tabloid newspaper with a liberal orientation. Scandal aside, a major factor contributing to their success was that they were lively and readable. Swope also put out a lively and readable paper. Another factor might well be that they were subway-size. People could read them on public transportation with far greater ease than they could the cumbersome larger-paged newspapers.

Even in rumination, Swope could be very persuasive, and Baruch warmed to the idea. Why not back Swope in starting just such a paper? Swope was overjoyed. He knew that he could make a great success of it. Beyond that, the two men held such parallel views in most matters that any newspaper in which Swope had a commanding voice would necessarily also speak for Baruch.

Margaret cautioned him not to put too much stock in Baruch's promises. He had been disappointed before, in the case of the *Herald;* he could be disappointed again. If he insisted on exploring the possibilities, he ought to do it very discreetly. That was not possible. Although he was the most trustworthy of men in keeping the confidences of friends, discretion in his own affairs seemed to smack too much of subterfuge. There was no reason to be secretive. His belief in Baruch was absolute. If a promise had been made, that promise would be kept. He started his negotiations so publicly that they were reported in the press. Unfortunately, Margaret proved right. Baruch backed away at the last minute, leaving Swope with the onerous job of having to explain things to everybody, including the Pulitzers. The incident did nothing to improve the nearly impossible situation at the *World*.

From the start of his tenure as executive editor of the *World*, Swope had made it a practice to send daily memos to Joseph Pulitzer on items that might be of interest to the other Pulitzer paper, the St. Louis *Post-Dispatch*. So well known was his interest in all of the Pulitzer enterprises that *Variety,* the influential theatrical weekly, called him "the past and present grand master of all 'The World' (New York) besides the St. Louis 'Post-Despatch' [*sic*]."

On September 3, 1926, he sent a memo to Joseph that seemed innocuous enough: "We are starting a Sacco-Vanzetti series on Tuesday next which I think will be interesting for the PD. Regards."

Nicola Sacco and Bartolomeo Vanzetti had been found guilty of armed robbery and murder on July 14, 1921, in Boston. There was a great protest from the combined liberal and radical communities, who claimed that the two had been convicted because they were foreigners and anarchists. The case dragged on with repeated appeals for retrial, which were denied despite new evidence that indicated that the crime had been committed by the Joe Morelli gang. On April 9, 1927, the two men were finally sentenced to death.

Although the *World* was among the papers calling for commutation of sentence and a retrial, Heywood Broun did not feel that Lippmann's dispassionate editorials were sufficient and took it upon himself to use his columns for a more fiery protest.

Public feeling ran so high that Governor Alvin T. Fuller of Massachusetts was forced to appoint an independent investigatory committee, headed by President A. Lawrence Lowell of Harvard University and including President Samuel W. Stratton of the Massachusetts Institute of Technology and Robert Grant, a retired judge of unquestionable integrity. This did not satisfy Broun, who continued to hammer away at Governor Fuller and at the presiding judge, Webster Thayer.

Ralph Pulitzer was disturbed by the polemical nature of Broun's material and told Swope that he had to order his Op Ed page pet to desist. The columnist arrived for a conference at Swope's apartment. The editor was characteristically late, and a poker game among many of Broun's Algonquin buddies was already in progress. Despite their sympathy for Sacco and Vanzetti, they were noticeably cool to him; it was obvious that even his best friends thought that he had gone too far.

When Swope arrived, he took Broun into the study for a private talk. He was leaving the next day, August 2, for Saratoga, where he vacationed each year during the racing season. He made Broun promise to back away from the case in his column.

Broun emerged looking like a chastened little boy. Dwight Taylor, the writer son of Laurette Taylor, was in the poker game. When he addressed Broun, some years his senior, as "sir," the columnist lashed out petulantly, "If you ever call me 'sir' again, I'm going to punch you right in the nose!"

"Sir" was for paternal figures, and Broun had obviously had enough of them for one night. Had the events of the next few days not transpired, he might have kept his promise to Swope and been a good boy. But two days later, the governor, with the concurrence of his investigating committee, refused to exercise his powers of clemency. Sacco and Vanzetti were to be executed on August 23. There would be no reprieves.

On August 5, Broun returned to his outcry against the Massachusetts variety of justice. In the course of the column, he wrote:

> What more can these immigrants from Italy expect? It is not every prisoner who has a President of Harvard University throw on the switch for him. And Robert Grant is not only a former Judge but one of the most popular dinner guests in Boston. If this is a lynching, at least the fish peddler and his friend the factory hand may take unction in their souls that they will die at the hands of men in dinner coats or academic gowns, according to the conventionalities required by the hour of execution.

On August 6, Broun wrote another column, ending with the question: "From now on, I want to know, will the institution of learning which once we called Harvard be known as Hangman's House?"

This prompted a response on the editorial pages of the *New York Times:*

> If we are to measure our condemnation for cowardly bomb throwers, we should not overlook men like MR. HEYWOOD BROUN, who asks in the *World* whether "the institution of learning in Cambridge, which we once called Harvard, will be known as Hangman's House." Such an educated sneer at the president of Harvard for having undertaken a great civic duty shows better than an explosion the wild and irresponsible spirit which is abroad.

That was enough to galvanize Ralph Pulitzer into taking a positive stand. He called in Broun, who argued that he had the right to say anything he wanted under his column's heading, IT SEEMS TO ME, without committing the paper to his opinion. It was, after all, admittedly only his opinion.

Pulitzer told him that he should disabuse himself of that notion:

> A separate entity within an entity is what we call a cancer. Anyhow, we've been over it before. It's the duty of writers to write and editors to edit. After all, in your contract you agreed, if I recall the words

correctly, to "carry out the directions of the party of the first part or its executive editors in the discharge of your duties."

There was only one executive editor, and he was not consulted because he was out of town. Had he been there, the result would undoubtedly have been different. He would have coerced both columnist and publisher into reasonable points of view. There can be no doubt that his influence over both would have been strong enough for that. But he was away, and, strangely, the insult to the Harvard Swope had never been able to attend became a major factor in the outcome of the incident.

It must be noted that in all of his vituperation, Broun never once mentioned the other academic member of the governor's committee, Stratton, nor the institution he presided over, the Massachusetts Institute of Technology. It was Harvard that was at fault—the Harvard that had refused to allow Broun to graduate with his class because he had failed French, the Harvard that had not accorded him a position on the staff of its student publication, the *Crimson*.

Swope aside, the newspapermen involved were all Harvard men true to their alma mater, except for the renegade Broun. It was Broun's attitude toward the college that was the basis of their disavowal, for they all agreed on Sacco-Vanzetti. The *New York Times* had called for a new trial. With Pulitzer's blessings, Lippmann had used the editorial page of the *World* to ask for a commutation of their sentences to life imprisonment, adding, "We do not question and have never questioned the rectitude of the Governor and his advisory committee." No committee that included a president of Harvard would ever be questioned by Lippmann, who had been a classmate of Broun's and who had graduated with a distinguished record.

Broun was not fazed, and he submitted two more columns bemoaning the lack of justice in Massachusetts. The *World* council knew that they had to act quickly, before Swope returned, and on August 11 they resolved to print no more Broun columns dealing with the case. On August 12, Swope in Saratoga and thousands of others in New York City were amazed to read a message from Ralph Pulitzer in place of IT SEEMS TO ME:

REGARDING MR. BROUN

The *World* has always believed in allowing the fullest possible expression of individual opinion to those of its special writers who write under their names. Straining its interpretation of this privilege, the

World allowed Mr. Heywood Broun to write two articles on the Sacco-Vanzetti case, in which he expressed his personal opinion with the utmost extravagance. The *World* then instructed him, now that he had made his position clear, to select other subjects for his next articles. Mr. Broun, however, continued to write on the Sacco-Vanzetti case. The *World,* thereupon exercising its right of final decision as to what it will publish in its columns, has omitted all articles submitted by Mr. Broun.

Swope was immediately on the phone to Pulitzer, thundering in a voice that might well have been heard even without the benefit of mechanical assistance. What right did Pulitzer or anybody else have to make editorial decisions without consulting the executive editor? Broun was the mainstay of his Op Ed page, and Swope wanted an immediate reconciliation.

It was too late. Broun's next column was his resignation:

By now I am willing to admit that I am too violent, too ill-disciplined, too indiscreet to fit pleasantly into the *World*'s philosophy of daily journalism. And since I cannot hit it off with the *World* I would be wise to look for more alluring work. I am still a member of Actors' Equity, the top floor is still well-stocked with early Brouns and I know a card trick. In farewell to the paper I can only say that in its relations to me it was fair, generous and gallant. But that doesn't go for the Sacco-Vanzetti case.

The resignation column was followed by another statement from Pulitzer, which ended with these words:

The *World* still considers Mr. Broun a brilliant member of its staff, albeit taking a witch's sabbatical. It will regard it as a pleasure to print future contribution from him. But it will never abdicate its right to edit them.

Swope returned with the uncomfortable feeling that Lippmann had somehow gained ascendancy over him in the council. He doubted that Pulitzer would have behaved as he did on his own. It was Lippmann and possibly Krock who were responsible, acting out of a disproportionate resentment of "his boys," the spoiled darlings of the Op Ed page. Their fame was galling. In the literary, liberal, upper-middle-class world in which the *World* men moved, people were forever saying, "Did you see

Broun today?" "What did Woollcott think of the play?" "Did you read that Dorothy Parker thing in Adams?" In those days, they also said, "Did you see the editorial in the *World?*" But nobody ever said, "Did you see Lippmann this morning?" He had the often unfair anonymity of the editorial writer whose brilliance goes unsigned. And Krock was not even writing at that point. They were as hungry for fame as the next fellow. They had careers to make. Envy was a natural result.

Swope had to act with a subtlety that left him exhausted. He had no patience for that sort of thing; it took up too much time and energy. What he wanted was the best thing for all concerned. His natural inclination was to get them all together and shout, "Flatheads! Can't you see you need each other?"

He could not do that, for he was dealing with injured sensibilities and vanities. The lawyers were already in the act, which made it still more difficult. Pulitzer's attorneys were insisting that he do nothing until Broun came to him with an apology; otherwise he would compromise his position of authority. Broun had hired Morris Ernst to get him out of his contract, which stated that if he left the *World* he could not work for another newspaper for three years.

The protest over Broun's position on Sacco-Vanzetti was nothing compared to the overwhelming demand from readers that their favorite columnist be reinstated. Pulitzer indicated to Swope, whose close friendship with Broun had not been impaired, that he would not be averse to anything that could be done to get him back on the paper, short of humbling the publisher.

Broun held to his original position. He would not return without guarantees of autonomy. The paper was not necessary to his survival. He was a famous writer and in great demand by the magazines. The *Nation* had already offered to publish a weekly piece. But the *Nation* was not right for him, despite their similar political sympathies. His style was too breezy and facile. His was a quick intelligence that brilliantly skimmed surfaces; it was at odds with a magazine that preferred depth to surfaces, intellect to cleverness. As Dorothy Parker warned him about life at the *Nation,* "You won't be able to hear a thing for the clanking of Phi Beta Kappa keys."

Swope moved adroitly, attempting to conciliate all positions. On Thursday night, September 29, he wrote to Pulitzer: "Broun is coming down to have dinner with us Monday night. He will be in my office about six-thirty. He seemed glad to come."

In addition to the principals, Swope had to contend with their lawyers, who had their own stakes in the controversy. An October 19 memo to Pulitzer stated:

> I had Ernst on my hands for three hours, and Broun's case got no "forarder." In fact, it went back.
>
> Ernst introduced a circuitous piece of legalism, which he tortured into what he called liberalism, about changing the contract. He did what I thought he was going to do. He admitted that he had suggested it to Broun. In no sense of the word, in my opinion, did it answer the demand that Broun made for a formula he could go to his liberal friends with.
>
> Lippmann came into my room while Ernst was here, and so I had him sit in. I am frank to say it left me with a less pleasant opinion of Ernst than I had before. I think he is really seeking to help Broun wriggle off our contract hook. There is nothing further to be done—at least not now. Broun told me he was going to bring in a "formula" within the next day or two. Let's see if he does it.
>
> I don't know whether we are lucky or unlucky, but another one of our staff has scored a hit. Paul Sifton's "The Belt," I am told by Woollcott, is very good.

Negotiations were protracted. Swope began to doubt that a satisfactory conclusion would ever be reached. He began to look around for Broun substitutes who would have a similar reader magnetism. On October 20 he made a suggestion to Pulitzer: "I wish you would be good enough to make it a practice to read from time to time a column in the *Graphic* called 'Your Broadway and Mine,' by Walter Winchell."

In mid-December, a formula was finally worked out that secured Broun's return to the *World*. Swope made a brief statement to the press: "We always have been impressed with the value of Mr. Broun to the *World*. Mr. Broun has learned the value of the *World* to him. We are glad that he is returning."

Broun made his own statement on the situation in an interview in the December 24 issue of *Editor and Publisher*:

> I say, frankly, that I would like to be on the *World* with the privilege of saying anything I please. But I know I have to take a little less. I don't know of any newspaper where absolute freedom is possible. As a matter of fact, when any newspaper gets wedded to a policy, it cannot endure having any of its writers dissent violently from it. The *World* permits a limited dissent. It is more liberal than any paper I know.
>
> I think a newspaper could be run on a policy of printing sharply

divergent opinions. I would like to work on such a paper. But to do that I would have to own it. I would like to own a paper myself, but I haven't the money. The *World* is the paper that comes nearest to fitting my wishes.

I am not sorry about anything I said or wrote during the Sacco and Vanzetti case. If such a situation should arise again, I am willing to discuss it with the executives of the *World*. If they should say to me, "You are a little too strong in expressing this opinion," or if they should object that a phrase such as calling Harvard "Hangman's House" is "too severe," I would be amenable to editing and willing to express the same meaning without being so harsh.

He also said that there would be no subjects from which he would be banned and that he was generally in agreement with the *World*'s editorial policy. He concluded:

I'm glad to return to newspaper work. There is a great advantage in being able to say what you want to say when you feel that way. Sometimes you want to say something on Tuesday that you lose interest in by Saturday. The *World* is the best pulpit I can find.

Although the article included a strong statement of Pulitzer's point of view, the publisher was irrationally irritated by Broun's generally bland comment. Swope once again had to soothe an uncertain ego. He wrote to Pulitzer:

I suppose he wanted to make a little cushion for himself in giving out an interview. On the whole, I think it pretty moderate. I think this is particularly true, since it carries a paragraph relating to your position. Anyway, any return Broun makes to the paper represents a complete capitulation. That's how he regards it, too. He is trying his damnedest to save his face. After all, we are not concerned with what he says elsewhere; we are concerned with what he says in the *World,* and there I think he will be a good soldier.

Swope was both right and wrong. Broun returned to the *World* for exactly four months, during which he was, if anything, too good a soldier. In the words of his biographer, Richard O'Connor:

During that period Broun's columns not only lacked their zest for controversy and their enthusiasm for any issue that might outrage the sensibilities of the comfortable and established but the geniality and easy swing of his work before the possibility of censorship had arisen. Heywood Broun simply couldn't operate in a moral strait-jacket.

Early in May 1928, Broun proved that the *World* was indeed concerned with what he wrote elsewhere, when he wrote a piece for the *Nation* claiming that the *World* was not truly a liberal paper, that Lippmann's editorial page simply vacillated too much.

> It switches front so often. New facts on any given situation may require a complete right-about-face. . . . the *World* on numerous occasions has been able to take two, three, or even four different stands with precisely the same material. So constant were the shifts during the Sacco-Vanzetti case that the paper seemed like an old car going uphill.

He continued that there were issues about which it "has thundered on Thursdays and whispered on Monday mornings."

He concluded with a blistering attack on the *World*'s treatment of an issue that was as difficult to handle then as it is today.

> In the mind of the *World* there is something dirty about birth control. In a quiet way the paper may even approve of the movement, but it is not the sort of thing one likes to talk about in print. Some of the readers would be shocked, and the *World* lives in deadly terror of shocking any reader.

The article was Broun's way of reestablishing his credentials among those left-wingers who had criticized him for returning to the *World*. It was also an act of childish defiance. There were more adult ways of handling the situation, but they would have entailed a confrontation with Swope, and Broun was sadly not up to it. His column did not appear in the May 3 edition of the *World*. It was replaced by a simple announcement: "The *World* has decided to dispense with the services of Heywood Broun. His disloyalty to this newspaper makes any further association impossible."

Conceding that the break was permanent, Swope did what he could to help his old friend. He arranged for the *World* to release him from all provisions of his contract, including the ban on working for another paper. He also permitted him to take the trademark title (which Swope had actually devised with him), IT SEEMS TO ME, for Broun's personal use in any future post. The latter was considered an act of extreme generosity. The more normal procedure was for a paper to retain a valuable title and simply assign another writer to use it.

Broun negotiated a most lucrative contract with Roy Howard, of the Scripps-Howard papers, to appear in the New York *Telegram,* with syndication throughout the chain. His work never regained the dazzling quality displayed during those years that he worked for Swope. It had been the result of an association of two unique talents at the height of their powers.

The luster of Swope's star Op Ed page was doubly dimmed by the loss of another prominent writer during the same month that Broun departed. Alexander Woollcott's contract was up, and he decided not to renew. It was a great blow to the editor who had worked hard to get Pulitzer to agree to all of the critic's terms and even come up with an annual raise of $1,000 despite the paper's unhappy financial condition. Negotiations had been under way for over six months. A memo from Swope to Pulitzer, dated December 30, 1927, indicated his efforts in Woollcott's behalf as well as his esteem for him:

> Woollcott's ideas of a contract include the following points:
> In general outline substantially as now.
> To run for two or three years more.
> He wishes the right of giving three months' notice of resignation but agrees that for the life of the contract he will do no newspaper work of any sort in New York or out of it, should he quit the *World* before his contract expires. This is because he may lecture or go into professorial or pure magazine work.
> I see no objections to these points, and I am sure you and Mr. White will see none. It is by no means certain he will sign again, but I think he is likely to. I myself have seen contracts aggregating $81,000, covering the next two and a half years, most of which he will have to turn down if he remains in daily newspaper work.
> I think it can be safely said that Woollcott is the king of dramatic reviewers in the city, if not in the country, and contributes real value to the paper.

Many factors led to Woollcott's decision to give up his career as drama critic. Preeminent among them was money. Why should he work on a newspaper for $16,000 a year when he could earn more than that in six months? The second was a lust for fame. No matter how good a newspaper critic is—and Woollcott was good when not hampered by excesses of sentimentality and partisanship—his fame is primarily local. Radio, lectures, and magazines offer national acclaim.

The third consideration was certainly the complexity of his relationship with Swope, whom he alternately adored and envied. When they were both young reporters, Swope had scooped him on every story, emerging with a reputation for being the best of his generation. They were both well-known party-givers, but Woollcott was considered an autocratic and eccentric host, while Swope was acclaimed as a charming and thoughtful one.

Although both were marathon talkers, this was one area in which they were not competitive, for Swope preferred facts to gossip, and Woollcott preferred gossip to anything. They were enormously entertaining gentlemen who added flavor to their own and each other's gatherings. Years later, Ben Hecht recalled Woollcott's "boss" as one of the regulars at Woollcott's parties:

> A tall rumbling-voiced chesspiece of a man—the red knight (the red was coloring, not ideology)—added distinction as well as noise to the Woollcott ensemble. Beside him, his trim, dark-haired Maggie stood like a police cordon, for the place teemed with "vampires." A husband in those days walked in danger.

It was Swope's habit to write daily memos to his chief writers, telling them what he thought about their work. If he had something uncomplimentary to say, it was written in a terse, straightforward style without cushioning flattery. Woollcott was one of the great injustice collectors and began to harbor an accelerating resentment, never recalling that he was just as likely to get a note praising his work.

The final indignity was the *Strange Interlude* altercation. That was the end; fathers had all failed Woollcott. His own had actually deserted the family. The story goes that he was in the middle of a poker hand when word came that the senior Woollcott was dead. He took the message, resumed his place, and finished the hand. He then said, "Deal me out. I'll be back in an hour." He went to the morgue, identified his father, arranged for cremation, and returned to his game.

By 1928 Woollcott had attended over two thousand opening nights. One day he decided that was much too many. He looked in his mirror and saw, in his own revealing words, "the harried look of a schoolboy who has too much homework." He was always the pugnacious and rebellious child. In terms of transactional analysis, the game that he played was pushing people until they rejected him and he could prove that he was right in thinking that he was truly unlovable. Reaching that point with Swope would require a great deal more than handing in a resignation, which Swope accepted sadly but without rancor.

A month before the official end of his career as a drama critic, Woollcott brought out a volume of his theatrical essays, *Going to Pieces*. In April 1928 he gave a copy to Swope, inscribing it, "To Herbert Bayard Swope—From his still-ungraduated pupil."

The despair that had begun to set in during the latter part of 1927 persisted into the following year. Swope had a wonderful family and home life; he was one of the most respected and famous men of his generation. The shrewd investment counsel of friends had made him a millionaire several times over. Yet his feeling of futility about his career lingered. He attempted to solve his problems with movement—trying to find in motion the solace that eluded him in repose. November 11 found him addressing the Advertising Club. To these gentlemen, who often attempted to assert influence over the content of newspapers, he said:

> Newspapers should be troubled far more by the question of "Is it true?" than "Is it pretty?" . . . Newspapers have been successful, not because they set out to be successful commercially, but because their commercial success has come to them as a by-product—in no single instance of success has it come to that paper which thought only to cultivate its relations to advertisers and ignore its far more important and developing duty to the public.

January found the Swopes in Palm Beach helping the Irving Berlins celebrate their second wedding anniversary. Mrs. Berlin was the former Ellin Mackay. Her father, Clarence H. Mackay, was president of the Postal Telegraph Company, chairman of the board of the Philharmonic Society, and a pillar of Catholic society. His disapproval of his daughter's marriage to the immigrant Jewish composer of popular songs had filled the gossip columns for months. Mackay had stormed into Swope's apartment to find out what he, a close friend of Berlin, thought Mackay should do about the situation. Swope replied, "Rejoice in your daughter's good fortune. She's married to one of the finest men I know."

On April 19, the Swopes journeyed to Washington for a meeting of the American Society of Newspaper Editors, which began the following morning. Along with William Allen White and David Lawrence, Swope was on the program committee. The theme of the two-day conference was "What I Don't Like about Newspapers," and the attacks were delivered by leaders in other fields, including Clarence Darrow for the legal profession, Governor Albert Ritchie for politics, and Columbia University's president Nicholas Murray Butler for education.

In May the Swopes shared a private railroad car with Charles and Morton Schwartz for the trip to Louisville to see the Kentucky Derby. A tabloid called the *New York Press* reported on his luck that day, saying that he who had

> never allowed the acquisition of a fortune to impair his efficiency as one of America's ablest editors, nor to lead him to high-hat any of his old acquaintances of less prosperous days, was too wise to select any one of the Eastern horses to win the Derby. Once more he put the Midas touch to the mutuel machines and added to his already ample bankroll.*

June 11 found Swope in Kansas City for the Republican National Convention. He carried two sets of tickets, one admitting him to the inner circle of the Republican party as "Asst. Sergeant-at-Arms" and the other admitting him to the Press Platform. He was also armed with guest-privilege cards to the Kansas City Club, the Kansas City Country Club, the University Club, and the Kansas City Athletic Club, as well as with Ernest Hemingway's personal card, inviting him to drop around to see him any time at 6435 Indian Lane, where he would be in residence until July 1.

In Kansas City, he returned to his first love—he acted as special correspondent for the *World*. He was not above using the position to write a little propaganda for the Democratic party and Governor Smith, again his choice for the presidential nomination. With respect to Herbert Hoover's bitterly contested nomination, he quoted Dr. Murray, who was a delegate from New York:

> The Republicans are facing the worst defeat since 1852, when Winfield Scott was beaten, carrying only four states. . . . I was aghast at the depth of feeling among the agrarian elements. They say that they are not for Hoover at the convention and won't vote for him at the

---

*The winner was Reigh Count, owned by Swope's friend John D. Hertz.

polls. I believe them. I am most unhappy at the aspect the convention wears, and I view November with gravest apprehension.

Swope also noted something that should perhaps have been taken more seriously, but this might have been impossible without a hindsight view of the 1929 cataclysm: "Easterners saw in the tumbling prices of securities a Hoover market. To them it reflected a lack of confidence on the part of the public in the candidate."

He concluded his story with a great boost for his man, stated in terms of a pastime at which he was an acknowledged master: "No Republican money can be found to bet that Hoover will carry New York against Smith. On the national scene, the Republicans talk of even money, although a month ago the odds were more than two to one against Smith."

During the convention, Swope stayed at the Kansas City Athletic Club. His fame far exceeded that of most of the campaigners, and he was immediately sought out by George K. Phillips of the Kansas City *Post* for an interview. When asked whether he thought that Smith could be elected president, he replied,

> That brings us up against two imponderables. Al Smith is a Catholic. On the other hand, his history in a way is like that of Lincoln. He is a self-made man of the people, born and reared in the city, whereas Lincoln was rural. Which will weigh most with the voters, his religion or the appeal of his personality and the drama of his career? That is a difficult question to answer. I would say that, were it not for his religion, the odds would be heavily—I say heavily—in favor of Governor Smith's election to the presidency. . . . He has no pride of authorship. Except when principles are involved, he is always ready to accept advice and change his mind. He is one of the few men in politics who have learned the truth that right can be as profitable as expediency.

He also discussed Hoover, saying that in 1920 his paper would have supported him for the nomination by either party, but times had changed. Those qualities that had made Hoover attractive in '20 were no longer the ones that the country most needed in its leader.

Phillips ended his story with:

> Mr. Swope is as interesting as some of the men he discussed. Only the overworked adjective "dynamic" properly describes him. Tall, hefty,

quick of movement, with an energetically husky voice, he has a thoroughly executive temperament. He is a sandy person with reddish hair and pink skin. While being interviewed, he was continually busy unpacking or receiving telephone calls, one from the city desk of the *World* in New York. Obviously, he is the kind of managing editor who "ceaselessly keeps his finger on the news." He is said to have one of the best memories and to be one of the best-informed men in the country. "The possessor of a thoroughly contemporaneous mind" is one way he has been described.

The following week, Swope went to Houston for the Democratic National Convention. The way the Democrats handled the ticket situation offered an interesting sidelight on convention organization. In those days, the Democrats were far better organized than the Republicans. In Kansas City there had been different tickets for each day and different guest cards for each club. In Houston there was only one ticket, good for the entire convention (Swope actually had two—one to the Press Platform and the other to the Speaker's Platform), plus one Democratic National Convention guest card, extending privileges at five different clubs.

After Smith's nomination, Swope wrote a piece for the *World* that echoed the sentiments he had expressed in Kansas City. He concluded: "The questions of rum, Catholicism, and Tammany will all fade into insignificance in face of the fact that he is touched by the divine fire of political genius and human appeal that makes him embody the hopes and aspirations of the man on the street."

Swope proved somewhat less than the inspired seer with this analysis, for it was precisely those three issues that would combine to defeat Smith. In addition to the love letter in the press, Swope sent a private message of congratulations, joining a list of well-wishers including Adolph S. Ochs, Bernard Baruch, Eleanor Roosevelt, Elisabeth Marbury, and Robert Lansing. He ended by saying, "I go into the fight with you, bringing all I have in strength, courage, and determination."

Smith replied, "Thanks for the message, the sincerity of which I deeply appreciate. Your friendship is a valued asset."

After the convention, Swope showed characteristic generosity by writing to a journalistic rival, Kent Cooper, the head of the Associated Press, to congratulate him on a good job:

I thought the Associated Press service on the Republican and Democratic conventions in 1928 was excellent. If it erred at all it erred on the side of too great a volume, but that was a fault shared in all of the big papers, the *World* included. Frequently the American press makes the mistake of assuming that volume is more impressive than clarity—that authority is only to be found in length. . . .

Swope was a part of Smith's inner circle throughout the campaign. He was valued because it was believed that he wanted nothing for himself, not a cabinet post or an ambassadorship, neither of which would have been inconceivable for a man of his gifts. This was a miscalculation. Swope was beginning to think of politics as an alternative to his career at the *World*. Indeed, any alternative was taking on attractive dimensions.

Despite Swope's preoccupation with the exciting Smith campaign, the summer of '28 was intolerable. Ralph Pulitzer had married Margaret Leech, a good friend of the Swopes and a writer who had recently collaborated with Heywood Broun on the first selection of the Literary Guild, *Anthony Comstock, Roundsman of the Lord.* The happy couple went off to Europe for their honeymoon, leaving nobody to stand between Swope and the willful idiocies of Herbert Pulitzer.

It was almost more than he could bear. Although he could not bring himself to break with the *World,* he was definitely receptive to any viable ideas. The *Morning Telegraph* was put on the market for $500,000. A syndicate headed by John Hertz, the president of the Yellow Cab Company of Chicago, decided to buy it. Others in the group included the advertising genius Albert Lasker; Joseph Moore; and Elmer Schlessinger, acting for Thomas Chadbourne. The job of running the paper was offered to Swope. Walter Winchell outlined their plans in a paragraph, ending with a typical Winchell-style pun.

> The paper will offer numerous "names" on its staff, and it will be changed to a snappy theatrical, society, and horse-racing newspaper, appealing to the rich jazzists. . . . M. L. Annenberg [later owner of the Philadelphia *Inquirer* and the father of Nixon's ambassador to England, Walter Annenberg], who made a fortune with his *Racing Form,* saw the possibility of great opposition in the revised *Telly,* so on Friday, in Chicago, he conferred with Moore, Hertz, and Lasker to discuss a proposed merger. . . . That's what you might call making Herbert Bayard Swopee.

Swope rejected the offer. It would only be swapping his present status for a similar one in less distinguished circumstances. He threw himself into the election campaign with still greater vigor, but it was becoming apparent that it was a losing battle.

The sense of futility deepened. He had always known what he

wanted, where he was going, who he was. Suddenly the self-assurance was fading away. He could no longer see a purpose in his life. When his physician suggested that he try psychoanalysis, he reluctantly agreed, and an appointment was made with an eminent man in the field for an afternoon toward the end of September.

Not sure what was expected of him and terribly uncertain about the advisability of the thing, Swope fell back on bravura. Ten minutes late for the appointment, Swope swept into the analyst's office and gestured imperiously to the couch. "Is that where you want me?"

Not waiting for a reply, he stretched out on the divan. "Oh, Doctor, would you mind moving the phone a little closer? I've instructed my secretary to transfer any important calls." He rubbed his hands together enthusiastically. "Now, then, where shall we begin? I was born in St. Louis—" The phone rang, and the doctor answered it. It was Governor Smith for Mr. Swope. For the rest of the hour, it rang incessantly, with Mayor Walker, Bernard Baruch, and George Kaufman all on the wire for Swope. The doctor's incredulity grew with each call. When his time was up, Swope leaped to his feet and shook the doctor's hand energetically. "Thanks, Doc. You don't know how much better I feel." And in a long stride, he was gone.

When the physician called for a diagnosis, the analyst replied, "It's simple. The man has delusions of grandeur." He explained what had happened during their session, and the physician told him that it was not fantasy. Those people did call Swope every day. "Astonishing," the analyst said. "What does he want from me?"

"He's bored."

Swope was essentially a man of action, not given to rumination. He did not often probe beneath the brilliant surface with which he faced his world, for there were areas painfully sensitive to the touch. He returned to the analyst for a few more sessions. Perhaps something did occur during those hours that forced him to turn inward. In a note, he uncharacteristically soliloquized:

> Have poured my life into the paper. Uncertain as to future. Find no assurance of opportunity of improvement. Therefore I am inclined to think it would interfere with happiness. Not of greatest value to paper or paper to me. I am inclined to think inefficiency in business office has interfered with my usefulness, because it dampens my ardor. Worked too hard under handicap of being outdistanced by rivals. Can't make ideas take place of organization. The smart won't always substitute for the solid. . . . Don't want to settle down to another

contract of routine which will make for a drab existence and rob it of all adventure. I have to fight my way through everything I want done. Getting too hard. The paper is slipping fast and I don't want responsibility charged against me.

That last was very meaningful to him. He loved the *World* and knew that the Pulitzers were ruining it. At that point, the paper was much more strongly identified with him than with them, and its failure would be interpreted as his failure.

Margaret used her considerable talents for diversion to try to lift his spirits. He was forty-six, and she vainly dismissed his moodiness as "middle-age crisis." But the language of his introspection was not that of middle age. There was no settling, no complacency, no hint of the smugness with which the self-made millionaire is so often imbued.

The man of action took hold again one afternoon in early October. Herbert, Jr., later recalled his mother describing the swiftness with which Swope made the most important decision of his professional life. They were strolling along Fifth Avenue, discussing nothing of any great consequence, when he came to an abrupt halt and exclaimed, "I know what's the matter with me! I'm tired of being a hired boy!"

He dashed into the Savoy Plaza Hotel and put in a call to Ralph Pulitzer. Within a week he had submitted his formal resignation:

> I am leaving the *World* after many years of pleasant association because there are some things I want to do which I can only do as a free agent and, too, I am a little tired of being a hired man. It is bad to be a hired man too long. One falls into a groove—a groove that deepens and darkens when the future offers little change. All of us want to grow. All of us want to play. And it is hard to play as a hired man. There is always the feeling that it is resented by the boss. The *World* has my respect and affection, though I believe it would be more in keeping with the spirit of the day were it possible for those who make the paper to become part-owners of the property. The system is increasingly used in every enterprise. The *World*'s position is limited because of the will of its founder. At the moment I have nothing to say regarding my plans, but I hope to have an announcement not without interest to make presently.

Ralph Pulitzer wanted him to stay on, at least in an advisory capacity, but Swope felt that the break with the paper had to be complete, if not permanent. What he meant was the paper as it was then constituted;

there was always in his mind the dream of returning as publisher as well as editor if the senior Pulitzer's will could be broken. He even extracted a promise from the brothers that, should it happen, he would be given first refusal. This would eventually lead to more Pulitzer treachery which would directly involve Ralph. Swope should have been less trusting and gotten the agreement in writing.

It was that restless final year that fostered the legend that Swope was an absentee editor, more involved in his own affairs than in those of the paper. It was spread by his detractors, who asked, not without malice, how he could be all over the map and still be running a newspaper. He was taking all of the credit for what was good in the paper without being responsible for any of it. None of the men closest to him professionally ever thought that. To them, he was the *World,* and the *World* was Swope.

John Shevlin, who was his assistant, said that except when he was on official vacation, there was not an issue that was not directly supervised by him. Space, layout, features, series, assignments all were approved by Swope. If anything, he guarded the contents of his paper more zealously than any other editor in the city. There was never a time when Swope did not leave word where he could be reached directly by phone, and he was a telephone enthusiast. He thought nothing of one- or two-hour conversations, which, coupled with his photographic memory, enabled him to see a page as well as those who had it before them could.

His colleagues on the *World* presented him with a scrapbook containing letters attesting to his worth. Their sentiments were epitomized by the words of the most brilliant member of the staff, William Bolitho:

> You reached over to England to give me help, and then you brought me to America; it was the last of a great number of interferences with my fate, which made you the most important influence in the best part of my life. I know you have been the same to innumerable others.

He ended his letter by hoping that he might join Swope again. It was a sentiment shared by almost all of the men who worked for him. Nobody could believe that he was leaving journalism forever. Adolph Ochs of the *New York Times* said:

> I hope we are not to lose you in New York journalism, for you would be sadly missed. Your energy, enterprise and enthusiasm, combined with your uncanny news sense, have ever been inspiriting contributions in making New York newspapers alert and interesting, and

your wholehearted and courageous cooperation in matters of mutual interest to the profession have been useful and constructive.

Walter Lippmann, who shared many of Swope's frustrations with the whims of the Pulitzers—Herbert in particular—wrote most cogently:

> Your decision is, I think, a wise one. It has become increasingly evident to me in the last six or eight months that you had outgrown the possibilities at the office. As I see it you began as the greatest reporter New York has known in this generation. You were also an editor of the most original sort. To have done justice to that side of yourself, you would have had to have complete control of the whole paper and a free hand. That was impossible, given the traditions of the *World*. You would, had you been in complete control, have made something wholly new in journalism. You could only make your kind of newspaper, and the attempt to fit your peculiar and original genius to an old institution could not in the end result in justice to you or to it. I have never seen so clear a case, as it finally developed, of an irreconcilable conflict between a powerful temperament and a settled tradition. The *World* did you no injustice, though your own vitality was too much for it. All that has happened is that in the last five years you have come into full possession of your powers, and for their proper and happy use you need to be your own boss. Had this not happened, the best that was in you would have been thwarted.
>
> You may be certain that you have done an immense service to the *World* and made an enormous contribution to American journalism. What you have done above all, I think, is to take a paper which was running on the inspiration of the past, and improve it with an inspiration suited to the modern age. You did for the *World* in the postwar period what Joseph Pulitzer did for it twenty-five years ago, and your place in the history of the paper, and therefore in the history of American journalism, is secure.

Ralph Pulitzer laid to rest any inference of negligence in a private and unsolicited letter written only for Swope's eyes:

> Now that the very bare announcement of your retirement from the executive editorship of the *World* has been made, I want to try to overcome my damnable inarticulateness enough to give you at least a faint idea of the deep and abiding appreciation I feel for your outstanding contribution toward making the *World* what it is today. Your brilliant intellect, your amazing energy, and your fine courage have been dedicated to the development of the paper. A multitude share my

deep admiration for these qualities. But few know as I do the less obvious virtue of patience which you have so admirably displayed under vexation and difficulties.

If I owed you no other debt of gratitude than for the consistent thoughtfulness with which you have assumed the burdens of so many problems which you might well have unshouldered on me, that debt would be great. But I fully appreciate that you have done infinitely more than that. You have raised the standards of good taste in a paper which retained its fighting spirit, sacrificing neither to the other. You have made a paper which appealed at once to the intellects of the few and the interests of the many.

You have been of ungrudging service to the paper in so many other ways that I cannot attempt to specify them.

For all these things, I want to thank you from the bottom of my heart. In abiding admiration and friendship, I am

                                                                    Yours

The employees tendered him a farewell dinner, at which Lippmann referred to him as "a lucky, fascinating devil." Woollcott made a fool of himself with a speech that barely concealed its vindictiveness under a strained veneer of humor. In an ungracious attempt at self-aggrandizement, he denigrated all of Swope's accomplishments in a manner that would have infuriated the others had it not been for the astonishing way in which the guest of honor took it. James M. Cain recalled that Swope

> sat there, to all outward appearance overcome with delight. If there was any resentment at this waspish, malevolent recital, no hint of it showed on his face. And when at last it was his turn to speak, he did so with the utmost good humor, and to terrific applause. Indeed, amiability under spoofing was one of his most surprising and of course most likable traits.

From his own accounts of the evening to intimates, what Swope was actually thinking as he listened to the rotund little man was closely akin to the final lines of T. S. Eliot's "The Hollow Men":

> This is the way the world ends
> Not with a bang but a whimper.

AFTER THE WORLD

THIRTEEN

The final page of Swope's bulging scrapbook of the '20s is devoted to an unused sheet of stationery on which is imprinted: THE WORLD. NEW YORK. HERBERT BAYARD SWOPE. EXECUTIVE EDITOR. A few pages before that can be found the simple announcement: "Mrs. James Scott Powell has the honor of announcing the marriage of her daughter Margaret Honeyman to Mr. Herbert Bayard Swope. Far Rockaway, Long Island." In the corner, printed in pencil, is the date: 1912.

These two pages frame the golden period of Swope's life. What followed was a long and glorious sunset not without a grandeur of its own. There were those who said that without the platform of a newspaper, Swope would become an obscure figure. Although many were not at all certain what it was that he did, there was not a moment in the thirty remaining years of his life when his was not among the best-known names in the country.

A month before he resigned from the *World,* Swope purchased the Malcolm Sloan estate for $325,000 in cash. Situated at Prospect Point on the tip of Port Washington peninsula in Nassau County, the property consisted of fifteen acres with a thousand feet of frontage on Long Island Sound. The rambling Colonial-style house, designed by Stanford White, sat on a broad terrace above the water and was visible for miles around. The place was called Keewaydin, an Indian name meaning "northwest wind" or, in some dialects, "very wet."

Keewaydin was in the village of Sands Point—only a short drive from Swope's old place in Great Neck, but worlds away in ambience. The new neighbors included the Harrimans, assorted Vanderbilts (including Alfred G.'s mother, Margaret Emerson), the Sanfords, the Morgans, the Guggenheims, the Schiffs, and William Randolph Hearst, who had recently bought the old O. H. P. Belmont estate. The Algonquin crowd predictably had a crack about the move: "Swope thinks he's going social, but he's only going financial."

According to which source one reads, honors for originating the remark are given either to Woollcott or to Edna Ferber. When it was repeated to Swope, it was probably attributed to Miss Ferber, for he did not speak to her again. Years later, she was in the waiting room when he arrived for a medical appointment. He bellowed in a tone that provoked red faces and an instant ruffling of the pages of assorted *National Geographics:* "What's Edna Ferber doing here? She doesn't need a doctor for what ails her! She needs a good lay!"

Swope was actually not the first of the old bunch to remove to the Sands Point area. Two years before, Neysa McMein and her husband, John Baragwanath, had bought a place there. All of the crowd was moving. Broun was in Connecticut. Kaufman would soon be in Bucks County and Woollcott in Vermont. The Swopes' at Great Neck had been a focal point of the group during the years of aspiration; with achievement came dispersal. That was only part of the reason for the end of the Algonquin and all that it implied. Success and age were more decisive factors. Antic capers are more embarrassing than engaging when one is in one's forties or fifties. Adolescent iconoclasm is not so amusing in upper-middle-class members of the establishment.

Within a year, the beginning of the '30s would call for a different kind of iconoclasm. Some of the group continued to write extremely successful, witty and entertaining theater pieces, notably Kaufman's *Of Thee I Sing* and his collaborations with Moss Hart. Dorothy Parker, who had the greatest potential of them all for serious artistry, succumbed to sloth, alcohol, and Hollywood—not necessarily in that order. The creative result of her left-wing politics was more negative and bitter self-pity than angry and constructive criticism. The beginning of World War II marked the group's total artistic eclipse. Except for Sherwood, with *Roosevelt and Hopkins,* not one of them ever again produced a work of even evanescent importance.

The crisis in Swope's life came much earlier. When the futility of his dream of having his own newspaper could no longer be ignored, he set new goals for himself, goals he was largely successful in attaining. His tragedy—although he would have been the first to quarrel with the word—was how few were worthy of him. He was an over achiever at everything required of him, but what was required seldom utilized the full range of his gifts.

Friends waited for him to make his move. Surely the brilliant Swope would soon make the portentous announcement of future plans that he privately hinted to them was on its way. In the meantime, he seemed to be savoring a spontaneous dalliance, a joyous liberation from programmed activity, which left time for endless parties, races, first nights, and games.

The Broadway columnists gave daily progress reports to a readership that considered Swope the peer of stage and movie stars. He appeared regularly in the up-and-coming Winchell, Mark Hellinger, O. O. McIntyre and Cholly Knickerbocker, as well as Adams and Broun. In his *Manhattan Days and Nights,* Herbert Corley observed that Swope's "retirement makes me think of Charles Chapin, who was also executive editor [*sic*] of the *World* at one time and is now in Sing Sing doing life [for shooting his wife]. An old friend called on him:

" 'Are you happy, Charlie?' he asked solicitously.

" 'Well, no,' said Chapin. 'Not happy. But this is better than the *World.*' " (Chapin, who was not *executive* editor, was not on the *World* but on the *Evening World,* which might, in part, explain his unhappiness.)

Swope enjoyed his wealth with boyish relish. Estimates of his fortune ranged from three to fourteen million dollars, and it was probably closer to the top figure than the bottom one. By the time he finished making Keewaydin "habitable" he'd spent nearly one million dollars. Sea walls, tennis court, magnificent lawns, vegetable and flower gardens, greenhouses, a swimming pool beautifully situated on a stretch of lawn between the sun porch and the Sound, and a croquet course that was itself an awesome spectacle were part of the changes wrought in the grounds.

On the interior decorations, Margaret spared no expense in applying the taste and knowledge of design that she had been accumulating during her years with Swope. The finest was barely good enough, and the prodigality with which she spent money to acquire it impressed even Elsie de Wolfe. The interior decorator, who had recently been elevated through marriage to the title of Lady Mendl, was quite a spender herself. Only a few years before, she had turned a slum into elegant Sutton Place by liberally helping herself to the fantastic bankrolls of her two friends Birdie Fair Vanderbilt and Anne Morgan. Impressing Lady Mendl with her way with a dollar was no small feat on Margaret's part.

The Swopes' attitude toward money was one they shared with many other people who had acquired great fortunes during their lifetimes.

Large sums had no reality for them, but small expenditures could cause friction. It was an attitude that the Swope children found very bewildering. They could never understand how their father could put in an *en tout cas* tennis court on one day, without giving a second thought to the enormous expense, and then complain bitterly on the next about the outrageous cost of tennis balls.

While the house was being readied, the Swopes went to Palm Beach to stay with the Thomas Chadbournes. Daughter Jane was brought along for the season. Jane had developed into an extremely pretty teenager, and both Margaret and Marjorie Chadbourne had decided that it was time she developed an interest in boys. The hectic comings and goings at the Swope menage, which her younger brother Ottie adored, only increased Jane's natural reserve. Her great passion—like her father's—was for horses, but in her case the attraction was showing them rather than betting on them. Alfred Vanderbilt recalled going out on a date with her. She was constantly excusing herself to telephone her mother to report on where they were and how long they'd be there. He never asked her out again. Jane did not remember the incident, but, when later reminded of it, she remarked, "My anxiety might have been caused by being with Alfred rather than being away from mother. But that wouldn't occur to him."

The Swopes enjoyed the season in Palm Beach so much that when their stay with the Chadbournes was over, they took a house of their own and invited Heywood Broun down as their guest. Broun had just separated from his wife and was in an extremely depressed state. Swope and Broun's differences at the *World* were immediately forgotten, and Swope was the first on the spot with comfort and aid. Business never interfered with friendship. It was only personal betrayal that was insupportable.

Broun's slovenly attire, for which he was famous among his friends, was a source of great irritation to the fastidious Swope. He had once tried to reform the columnist by taking him to a tailor and having a beautiful suit made for him. Broun was apparently so pleased with his new outfit that he wore it constantly, day in and day out, and it was not long before the suit looked exactly like all of his other clothes.

One morning during the Palm Beach visit, Swope came into Broun's room intent upon a serious conversation. Broun was at the window, holding up a pair of trousers so threadbare that the sunlight shone right through them. He commented, "I guess they'll last through another day."

Swope enjoyed life in Florida so much that he began to question the advisability of going back to New York. His friend William Allen White had made an international reputation by publishing the *Emporia Gazette* in Kansas; there seemed to be no reason why Swope could not do as well in Florida. He made an offer to buy the *Miami Herald* for two million dollars. The paper's publisher, Frank B. Shutts, was both tempted and reluctant. When word of the negotiations was leaked to rival papers by a disgruntled former editor of the *Herald,* Shutts became furious and broke off discussions with the statement, "The *Herald* is not for sale. Someone is talking through his hat."

Meanwhile, back in New York City, Swope's friends were amazed to find that his long-awaited first public statement came in the form of an endorsement for Lucky Strike cigarettes that appeared in all of the New York newspapers and many magazines: "I light up a Lucky whenever I am tempted to eat between meals."

Swope had actually agreed to the endorsement to help one of "his boys," a former *World* ships' news reporter, who was suffering severe reverses and had gone into the business of procuring statements from well-known people for advertisements. He even turned his fee over to the man. Franklin P. Adams could not resist a column on the subject in Swope's old paper.

> It is difficult to shoot a hole in the accuracy of the statement made by Mr. H. B. ("Yes, Mr. Swope, sir") Swope, who had leaped at a bound from journalism to cigaret endorsing. "Whenever I am tempted to eat between meals," his signed statement reads, "I light up a Lucky." Little did the American Tobacco Company know that in Mr. Swope's life there is no such time as between meals. Elementary; he doesn't have any meals. The former—and his bellowing "Tear up the contract!" therefore now makes us only laugh—Executive Editor of the *World* always is five or six hours late for breakfast, luncheon, and dinner, no matter what time they are scheduled for. What he consumes instead of meals—a few steak sandwiches with onions, a few dill pickles and a few apples—cannot be called meals.
>
> Still we congratulate the Dean of Former Executive Editors that his health is now so good that he now lights up a cigaret. The last time we remember seeing Mr. Swope smoke was in 1891, and he did it then, he said, only to get cigaret pictures of Della Fox and Camille D'Arville.

So surprising was this endorsement coming from Swope that *Time* magazine also felt obliged to make an editorial remark: "Observers noticed that the Swopian advertisement was published five columns wide in the *World*'s contemporaries, the *Times* and *Herald Tribune,* but only four columns wide in the no longer Swopian *World.*" The sad truth was that not even Swope could raise the sagging advertising revenue of his old paper.

Radio was beginning to boom as an entertainment and news medium. Swope knew from personal experience that it was beginning to cut into newspaper profits, just as it was taking audiences away from motion pictures, vaudeville, and legitimate theater. Independent stations that could not afford their own news bureaus were opening all over the country. The Federal Radio Commission was setting aside special shortwave intercontinental channels to supply them with news. The newspapers had set up the American Publishers Radio Committee for the express purpose of gaining control of these channels and thereby censoring what news would be transmitted to the stations. Swope knew that the publishers would conspire to keep radio a step behind their papers in quality and timeliness of news. What they did send out would be in a stilted language that would have to be rewritten into the homey conversational terms that the public enjoyed on radio. This would further delay the broadcasts. For the latest news, people would still be dependent on their daily papers. To Swope's way of thinking, this constituted an unfair restraint of competition.

He thought that those bands should be used for a news service geared exclusively to the stations, sending out the news in a style that they could use immediately, without rewrite. This would not displace the newspapers, but it would heighten their quality and force them to do the kind of in-depth stories that he felt were the special sphere of written journalism.

He outlined his ideas for such a service to Charles A. Sloan, the former radio editor of the *World.* Sloan agreed to Swope's proposal that a corporation be set up which Swope would back, with the radio editor acting as president and Swope's secretary, Helen Millar, in the position of treasurer-secretary. Swope did not want his own name associated with the project, lest it be thought that he was acting out of pique at no longer being a part of the newspaper world, to which he had devoted so much of his life.

The company was incorporated as the National Radio Press Association, and it requested twenty shortwave channels for its use. The moment the news was out, protests arose from all directions. The ensuing court actions involved a collective of the major newspaper publishers, plus independent actions by the Associated Press and the Hearst organization. Meanwhile several newly formed smaller companies latched on to Swope's idea.

There was a new note of hesitancy among the stations that had originally expressed interest in subscribing to the NRPA. It became clear that fighting the court actions and restoring confidence would involve a much larger investment than Swope's original outlay of $50,000. And there would still be no guarantee that he would win. He decided that it would be far better to cut his losses and gracefully withdraw.

While the radio press controversy raged, there arose an international incident involving a substantial portion of Swope's financial interests. General Electric Ltd., of Great Britain, announced plans for a large stock issue, available to British investors only, at a price below the current market value. This threatened the interests of the company's American stockholders by cutting into their profits.

The English company had no connection with General Electric of America, the company that had Gerard Swope as its president, beyond the leasing of some patents. When the leases were being negotiated, Gerard saw that the English stocks were going to rise, and he passed the tip on to his brother.

Swope, along with the Baruch brothers and Thomas Chadbourne, bought a large block of the stock. Indeed, American investors owned 60 percent of the outstanding stock, although they had no voice on the board of directors. The board's decision to float an issue excluding them was directly against their interests. It also set a dangerous precedent that could have had disastrous repercussions on all international investments. The Americans immediately organized into a committee to protest the action. They were not alone; the English Stock Exchange and many English investors were also against the issue.

Chadbourne and Swope were commissioned to represent the Americans in negotiations with Sir Hugo Hirst, the Chairman of the Board of General Electric Ltd. British indignation was so high that Hirst was denounced in Parliament as a "superpatriot of German origin," and the company was restrained from any action until after the meeting with the Americans.

The American stockholders were reportedly assessed ten cents a share to cover the expenses of the negotiators. As there were 3,600,000 shares held in the United States, the sum collected amounted to a tidy traveling allowance, sufficient to pay for the best suites both on the *Aquitania* and at Claridge's Hotel in London.

Accompanying the emissaries were Mrs. Chadbourne, her maid, Chadbourne's valet, and most of the Swope household. Swope had decided that the time had come for the family to make what was once known as the Grand Tour. And "grand" was the operative word.

The party included his son and daughter, Mimi, and Bruce Powell's new wife Edna. Mae Fielding was brought along not only so she could minister to their needs but also because Swope thought he owed a trip to the woman he once wrote was "to many, the most popular member of our household."

While at sea, Swope accepted an invitation from the ship's captain to speak at a memorial meeting in honor of Marshal Foch. He recalled for his listeners how impressed he had been with the great general during the Peace Conference. On the platform, he relived his days as a journalist, but the ship's newspaper identified him as "an eminent financier."

This duality, which had begun about a year before he left the *World,* was to plague him for the rest of his life. No matter what else he might accomplish, Swope would always think of himself primarily as a newspaperman; but the public could only think that accumulating a fortune had to be full-time work, and it slowly began to forget his very real journalistic accomplishments.

There were many colleagues who had resented the ease with which he had established himself as a leading reporter, but to Swope's way of thinking, the important thing was not how long one labored at a job but how well one accomplished it.

There was one danger in speed, and that was a tendency to be facile. If it was one of Swope's weaknesses, it was not considered one in his newspaper work, for that very quality was endemic to the job. The first order of business was to get the story in both quickly and accurately. Who, what, where, when, why. Speedy investigation and facile intuition were required to make the front page. In-depth analysis was for the editorial page. The facts appeared as quickly as possible on page one. The editorial writers could take the rest of the week to ponder their meanings. Swope was always a page-one boy, a facts man, deductive rather than hypothetical. His pragmatic philosophy sometimes made him seem officious and dogmatic.

The negotiators were the subject of widespread curiosity in London. The press was suitably impressed by Chadbourne's massive 6-foot-7-inch frame and by Swope's "arresting personality—square-jawed and with a look of grim, bulldog determination." The London

Daily Sketch reminded its readers that the eminent sculptress, Clare Sheridan, had nicknamed Swope "The Human Hurricane." It went on to describe his renown as a host:

> Hollywood, Broadway, Paris and London and Berlin visiting celebrities—all are to be found in the summertime, round Swope's festive board. And the extraordinary thing is that, though the host talks most of the time, it is such good fun that few object. The Swope sustained-talking record stands at four hours—Mary Pickford as listener.

The story suffered some shrinkage in the Atlantic crossing, before it was reported by O. O. McIntyre for the Associated Press in New York:

> Word seeps back that the energetic Herbert Bayard Swope established the non-stop talking record at a London dinner party several weeks ago. His time in sustained talking was recorded at 2 hours and 40 minutes. That's conversation!

Swope had some problems with brother Gerard's contradictory instructions that he clear everything through the American General Electric's London office, while at the same time making it perfectly clear to everybody that there was absolutely no connection between British G.E. and his company, despite the fact that they had the same last name. Well schooled since childhood in evading his older brother's commands, Swope solved the problem by acting as if they did not exist. He neither mentioned Gerard nor checked in at the London office for approval of his actions.

Swope and Chadbourne operated on their own initiative. Chadbourne was the single largest American stockholder in the British company, and, given the size of his own portfolio, Swope was proportionately involved. They felt that their self-interest guided them as well as or better than outside advice.

Hirst, an obdurate man, attempted a delaying tactic. "Very German" was how he was described by Swope in an it-takes-one-to-know-one observation. Eventually, the Americans were able to corner Hirst and hammer home their points. Hirst capitulated, and the new issue was permanently withdrawn. In a jubilant mood, Swope wired Baruch:

WE WIN COMPLETE ABANDONMENT NEW ISSUE.

After the Chadbournes left for home, the Swope party joined forces with John Hertz and his wife, who had arrived in England for the start of the racing season. Hertz, who had made a fortune in Chicago metered cabs, had great social aspirations. In this he was not unlike Robert Scull, a later generation's taxi millionaire. Scull crashed—and cashed—in during the '60s and '70s via a pop-art collection. Hertz's hobby in the '20s and '30s was a racing stable.

While the men pursued their afternoon pleasures at the racetracks, Margaret pursued hers at Christie's and Sotheby's auction rooms, where she started by bidding modestly on a few things to brighten the country house at Sands Point and ended by nearly cornering the market in Regency furniture. The Swopes actually managed to break even. He had a particularly good time winning over $100,000, and she had an equally good time spending it.

In Paris, except for one afternoon when he addressed the American Club, Swope again spent his time at the track, while Margaret switched to Chanel and Lanvin. The financial results were unchanged.

On the Riviera, they were entertained by the Vallombrosas, the Gerald Murphys, and Elsa Maxwell, who mistook Swope's high spirits for affection and thenceforward insisted upon his presence at all of her parties. Miss Maxwell's parties were not actually her own; they were given for wealthy climbers willing to pay a very healthy fee for her expertise and her ability to produce a guest list containing the most socially desirable people.

For the return voyage, the Swopes booked suites on the newest liner afloat, the *Ile de France*. Just two years old, the ship was a floating art-deco palace, a dry American's last touch with bibulous France, complete with a bar that stretched fifty feet, guaranteeing that one need never go thirsty again, at least for the duration of the trip.

There were those who thought that Swope had missed out by allowing Chadbourne to return earlier and get the lion's share of press coverage on the General Electric settlement. Only two papers, the *World* and the *Morning Telegraph,* sent reporters to meet Swope, and they were solely interested in getting his opinion on the lackluster performance at English tracks of the Hertz horse, Reigh Count.

He had been home a week when he went to Louisville as Mayor Walker's guest at the Kentucky Derby. At the last minute, the mayor was forced to stay home for a police parade, and he turned the whole box over to Swope, who made up his own party, including Joseph and Ralph Pulitzer. Seated near them was a publisher named Paul Block. It was not long before these four men were struggling with each other over the final fate of the New York *World*.

That first summer of leisure was passed in quiet pursuit of pleasure. The Swopes finally moved into Keewaydin. It took five underwriters to examine the inventory for insurance. At the end of August the National Radio Press Association finally notified the Federal Radio Commission that it was withdrawing its application for the twenty radio channels, although for several more months Swope continued to evince sporadic interest in acquiring them. It was in August that the Swopes also filled out the information forms for their first appearance in the Social Register.

By September the stock market was behaving so erratically that Baruch advised Swope to get out. He did not see any justification in the national economy for the dangerous high of the market. All Swope could see was how rich he was getting, and he dismissed his friend's warnings as being unduly conservative.

That month, Swope joined a group of friends in founding a new holding company called Manhattan-Dearborn. It was capitalized at $18,750,000 and listed on the Chicago Stock Exchanges. Shares were offered at $53 each. All of the men were self-made millionaires, and all but Swope were Chicagoans. The other members of the board were Hertz; Albert Lasker, the advertising agency genius; William Wrigley, Jr., who built an empire on a national mania for chewing; Charles Pearce, of the Colgate-Palmolive-Peet Company; Herbert L. Stern, head of the Balaban & Katz movie theater chain; and Charles A. McCulloch, whose Parmalee Company grossed millions transporting passengers and luggage to and from Chicago's many railroad stations.

With men of that caliber sharing Swope's optimism, Baruch had to be wrong. The future was limitless; Swope had visions of millions building to hundreds of millions. "Living like Swopes" moved into high gear. Swope registered the racing silks of royal blue and scarlet and set about acquiring a stable. Before he was finished he had spent over one hundred thousand dollars buying racing stock, and an equal sum housing and feeding the horses. Unfortunately he proved a much shrewder judge of other men's horses than of his own and had lost almost the entire outlay by the time he closed the stable door a year later.

The horses that he bought to indulge his daughter's passion for riding and jumping fared much better; King Connaught took a blue ribbon at the Smithtown Hunt Club the same year he was purchased. By the time

Jane switched interests from horses to boys, she had a tackroom filled with ribbons and cups.

The fabulous house parties continued, with Churchills, Roosevelts, and Chadbournes more in evidence than the Woollcotts, Kaufmans, and Brouns of the previous decade. Margaret's incredible notion of what constituted real money was so well known that it affected even her servants. One day a reporter from the *Evening Sun* called with the news that Maggie had won a small prize in the Irish Sweepstakes; he wanted her reaction. Her maid Lydia wanted to know how much was involved before she would consent to disturb her. The sum was five hundred dollars.

It was eleven in the morning, and Lydia replied, "I ain't waking up Mrs. Swope at this hour for no five hundred dollars."

They were regulars at every opening night and would generally come "Swoping" down the aisle to their third-row seats just as the curtain was rising. People would nudge their neighbors, asking the identity of the impressive and elegant couple. "The Swopes. Herbert Bayard Swope." No further explanation was necessary. For many members of the audience, it was the most memorable part of the evening. Producers, playwrights, actors, all would complain about the Swopes' seeming inability to be in their seats earlier, but nobody would dream of not inviting them. Their absence was too often interpreted as a sign that the play was not worth seeing.

Margaret had a style all her own. It was quiet, *soignée*, and timeless. Swope wore clothes splendidly, with a sartorial brilliance that was immediately apparent to even the most uninterested observer, whereas only those who really understood clothes knew how costly Maggie's look was to maintain.

The Prince of Wales's passion for inventing fashions in men's clothes was well publicized at the time. The Associated Press reported that he had startled Londoners by appearing in a double-breasted dinner jacket (what Americans called a tuxedo), a soft shirt with no starch in it, soft cuffs, a soft turned-down collar, a black bow tie and a gray-checked pullover. In a syndicated King Features column, the brilliant Hearst editor Arthur Brisbane felt impelled to reply, "That wouldn't startle anybody in America. Herbert Swope, who is twice as big as the Prince of Wales, and knows him intimately, has worn all of that outfit, with the possible exception of the 'pullover,' for a number of years."

On an October Tuesday in 1929, the party stopped with a crash. Baruch had been right after all. The stock market took a dive. Swope was reputed to have lost five million dollars before the month was out. Harpo Marx was among those who lost almost everything. Swope wired him:

THANK GOD WE'RE STILL ALIVE.

FOURTEEN

Estimates vary on how much Swope actually did lose in the crash. Some said that he was in debt to his brokers for over two million dollars. Others said that he was hit hard, like everybody else, but that he was still a very wealthy man. Nobody knew for certain. Swope was the most public of figures, but in all of his business and financial dealings he was extremely secretive. He kept accounts going at several brokerage houses, and only he knew the extent of his holdings, the contents and value of his portfolio.

That he was an extremely adroit card player stood him in good stead during this period. He played his hand close to the chest, and nobody could tell from the expression on his face what had been dealt to him. One might hazard a guess that he was helped by Baruch and Hertz. However, the help was not in the form of total underwriting but in the form of loans that kept alive those investments that did provide his obviously still considerable income. He surely dipped into capital, but it was apparent that the capital existed for him to dip into. Nobody could live on the level that Swope continued to live on simply through subsidies or loans. The kindness of friends often stretches farther than the kindness of strangers—but not that far.

Swope continued his annual trips to Palm Beach and Saratoga. Not one servant was fired or had a drop in pay. His children continued at expensive private schools. There was no evidence in any of his activities that he had been forced to cut back to meet his obligations.

It was noted by those close to him that he was in a prolonged state of depression. Whether or not the crash had wiped him out, a man who had lost five million dollars overnight surely had more than sufficient cause for dejection. Nevertheless, his standing in the business community was not impaired. He was appointed to the board of directors of Radio-Keith-Orpheum within two months of the crash. David Sarnoff was the chairman of the board and had been a friend since the time when Swope was covering the *Titanic* sinking and Sarnoff was the telegraph operator keeping news of the disaster flowing into the city. Still, Sarnoff was a shrewd businessman, and not even friendship would have motivated him to place a man who was near bankruptcy on his board. It was not long before Swope was also appointed to the boards of Zonite Corporation and North American Aviation. When the latter cut fifteen board members who were no longer considered to be prominent in the financial community, Swope was among those retained.

Swope was placed on these boards strictly on the basis of his own merit and solvency. Neither Baruch nor Hertz nor Swope's brother Gerard was connected with the companies. However, the rumors persisted that he was practically a charity case. Margaret urged him to set the record straight at the time, but he refused to make an issue of it. He did not think it was a matter of sufficient consequence. Let anybody impugn his reputation in journalism, and he would shout the house down. For the rest, let them think what they might. His family was not suffering. His guests were still dazzled by the opulence of his way of life. He could not concern himself with malicious speculations on how it was paid for.

He was forced to recognize that his energies were hopelessly divided between two worlds, but there was no doubt which was dearer to his heart. He said at the time, "I have divided my time between finance and journalism, but my heart still is and always will be with the latter."

There were those who doubted that he ever would be available for serious newspaper work. In July 1930, Philip Schuyler named the "all-American newspaper team" in his column in *Publishers Service*. He had Adolph Ochs as publisher, with Captain Joseph Patterson as his aide. William Randolph Hearst was to be circulation and promotion director. The editorial page would be given over to William Allen White, Walter Lippmann, and Julian S. Mason. He then said, "For managing editor, we wanted Herbert Bayard Swope, but felt we could not drag him from his horses."

Swope maintained his dream of returning to journalism, and specifically to the *World*, but a *World* that he would dominate. He was and always would be a newspaperman. Journalism was the closest thing to a religion that he would ever have. When Hearst made Eleanor Medill Patterson editor-in-chief of the Washington *Herald*, Swope wired her:

Salutations to my sister in GOD. May she discharge well her priestly mission. Score a scoop for Hearst and Brisbane.

That summer Swope turned down an offer from the Democratic party to run for Congress from the 17th District.* The reason given was that he had "previous business commitments." Actually, the reason was twofold.

When he told Margaret about the possibility of his entering the race, she said, "Why do you want to do a thing like that?" She had created a kingdom for him; why should he give that up merely to be a congressman? They had a perfect life together. A good time was had by all. She had no rivals. She was in full possession, and nobody was the worse for it. She made him happy; they fulfilled each other; it was a blissful balance. That he might need more in his life was something she could not countenance, for he was all she would ever need.

But there was something more, and had he been able to attain it, nothing in his life, not even Maggie, would have been strong enough to keep him from it. He wanted the *World,* and there were beginning to be some signs that he might be able to get it. Ralph Pulitzer had turned the paper over completely to his brother Herbert, who had gained the enmity of the entire staff by ruthlessly firing eighteen old-timers just before Christmas. The paper was running at an annual deficit of over one million dollars. It was accepted as fact that the brothers would try to break their father's will before the year was out, and that the paper would then be on the market. Swope was holding himself ready for that eventuality. He had an oral commitment from Ralph.

Had Swope accepted the Democratic offer, he would have been running against his good friend Broun, who was the Socialist party candidate. It was reported in the press that Broun was disappointed that he did not poll 10,000 votes, and that Swope had wagered $15,000 that he would. Swope immediately dispatched a tongue-in-cheek note to Winchell, who was among those who had printed the item:

My friendship for Wayward Broun does not constitute a barrier to my judgment. I did not bet Broun would poll ten thousand. I offered to bet that he would get at least six thousand. As a Democrat who believes in the party system, I could not support Broun. As a friend, I

---

*Thirty-two years later, Swope's son also turned down an offer to run in the 17th District against incumbent Republican congressman John Lindsay.

was interested in the courageous fight he made and the support you gave him. I should like the record altered in your column so I will not be regarded as having been too naïve in my enthusiasm.

An interesting bit of incidental intelligence was that Winchell actually did support Broun, the Socialist candidate. It was that sort of liberal outlook in the '30s and '40s that would place the columnist in the power of Senator Joseph McCarthy during his witch hunt against Communists and Communist sympathizers in the '50s. By threatening to expose Winchell as a sympathizer, which would have caused the immediate termination of his contracts with Hearst and the American Broadcasting Company, McCarthy was able to manipulate the reporter, forcing him to designate many innocent people as Red menaces in his powerful column and radio show. Winchell's cowardice in these circumstances contributed to the waning of his influence in the late '50s.

The *World*'s sad condition was no longer a Park Row secret, but was openly discussed in the press. For the June 25, 1930, issue of the *Nation,* Oswald Garrison Villard wrote an article "What's Wrong with the *World*?" He observed:

The loss of prestige and of news value came largely after the death of Frank I. Cobb in 1923 and during the managing [*sic*] editorship of Herbert Bayard Swope. Here one must write very carefully, for Mr. Swope at his best was one of the most brilliant reporters and newsmen in the entire business. For him as a journalist, it was a pity that he reached the position that he did; there came days when he had other interests and other irons in the fire—and we cannot serve two masters in journalism any more than anywhere else. There came days of entangling alliances, of much absenteeism—often in successful search for good news, of the development of hostile cliques within the office. It is an old problem which confronts the newspaperman of today; shall he have intimate social contacts with those he might at some time have to pillory? Should he, in order "to be in the know," be the friend of men with whom his newspaper may have to disagree?

It was a superficial yet hurtful analysis, and Swope took no comfort in Villard's equally wounding analysis of Lippmann. After praising his growing reputation, abilities, and skill as a writer, Villard added,

Yet the fact remains that editorially the *World* is much weaker [under Lippmann than it had been under Cobb]. There appears to be not only a lack of driving force, but often an inability to take a position and hold it through to its logical end. Too often it charges right up to the breastworks and then slowly retreats or even yields its arms and its entire position.

Neither of the accused had to defend himself, for the next week a response appeared in the form of a letter from William P. Beazell to the editor of the *Nation*:

Sir:

Few, I think, could have read with more interest than I Mr. Villard's "What's Wrong with the *World*?" For twenty years I was a member of the *World*'s editorial organization, and its day managing editor for six and one-half years of the period Mr. Villard had particularly under examination. With less hesitancy, then, than I might feel in discussing a situation with which I was not so intimately acquainted, I make the following suggestion:

Mr. Villard, in saying that "the loss of prestige and of news value [by the *World*] came largely after the death of Frank I. Cobb in 1923 and during the managing editorship of Herbert Bayard Swope," attributes to Mr. Cobb a part in the news organization of the *World* that he never had, and an interest in news, as such, that he never felt. His great gifts and great services in his profession had to do with the discussion and not at all with the gathering or presentation of news. He just wasn't interested subjectively in news, as we had repeated, despairing reason to know.

Mr. Villard has quite as faulty a conception of Mr. Swope's services as of Mr. Cobb's. It is perfectly true that Mr. Swope did not do all of his work in the office, but no one can know better than I how constantly he did work. As for "entangling alliances," three instances come back to me of intimate friendships that ended, and were never renewed, because his professional obligation transcended the personal. As for "hostile cliques within the office," it must be that I am a poorer reporter than I rate myself, for in thirty years of newspaper work I never knew an office where politics played so insignificant a part.

Yet there is really no reason why I should submit my own defense. During the Swope regime, and more than a year after Mr. Cobb died, the *World* reached the peak of its circulation with a daily average of more than 400,000, greater by 100,000 than that of its nearest standard-size competitor. Twice during the Swope regime the Columbia University Gold Medal for Public Service in Journalism was awarded the *World*. Twice during the Swope regime the *World* was cited by Mr. Villard and the *Nation*.

On December 15, 1924, a year after Mr. Cobb died, Mr. Villard called the *World* "the bravest, most outspoken, most liberal New York daily, and the most thoroughly devoted to democratic and American ideals."

On January 5, 1927, three years after Mr. Cobb died, The *Nation*'s Honor Roll listed "the editors of the New York *World* for the crusading devotion to liberal ideals which makes of their daily the finest public servant in the urban press of the North."

Which is the balanced judgement?

The *Nation*'s rather weak rejoinder said:

> Mr. Villard did not forget the *World*'s excellent record nor the number of times it has been cited for its admirable service. It was because of that record that he wrote as he did in alarm lest the *World* be lost to liberalism.

Swope-watching continued, unabated by world or *World* events. In his review of Frank Harris's autobiography, Harry Hansen doubted that anybody could know so many great men or remember so much, and then added, "Yet I believe that active men of affairs like Herbert Bayard Swope cover a great deal more ground and could write much more exciting reminiscences."

The *Graphic* reported "seeing John Faithful Hylan and Herbert Bayard Swope go into a huddle in the Saratoga Club house . . . and remembering how the ex-mayor used to go on tirades against the former executive editor of the *World*."

Frank Sullivan simply gave thanks to "Herbert Bayard Swope for the invention of the spoken word."

Arthur Brisbane mentioned among "some things I've never seen: Herbert Bayard Swope arriving at an opening night on time."

Harry Hansen commented, in his review of the reprint of Francis Hackett's "The Story of the Irish Nation," that one could find in it a prefatory note in which "Hackett pays his own little tribute to the driving genius of Herbert Bayard Swope":

> When I first came to see you just before Christmas [1921] you asked me if I could write a history of Ireland in three days. I said "Not in three days but in three weeks," and on this purely mechanical retort you told me to go ahead for the *World*. You raised only one point: Do men make the epochs or do the epochs make the men? And you flattered and impressed me by inquiring if I agreed with Hegel. Here,

then, is the result, although I had to give it more than the heroic three weeks. I owe you much, for without your superb confidence I should never have had the courage to attempt even this popular story. So let me thank you—and especially for plunging me into the history of Ireland, its "perilous seas," its "faery lands forlorn."

Hansen added: "We wish Swope nothing worse than homesickness when he reads this paragraph."

In January 1931, Swope was the subject of Edwin Alger's radio program "Who's Behind the Name?" on WEAF New York and associated stations of NBC's Red Network throughout the country. In the introduction, Alger said of his subject: "Once upon a time he was a newspaperman, and now he's a financier."

After describing Swope physically and telling anecdotes of his rags-to-riches story, Alger concluded by asking, "Is the baron happy today?" He acknowledged the personal happiness in Swope's home life, but added at the very end of the broadcast: "So far as happiness from money is concerned, I have my doubts. The elements of danger and uncertainty—which money often dispels—were elements upon which Herbert Bayard Swope thrived. The zest they gave him is gone—and I think he regrets it. He's still a newspaperman at heart."

At the time of the broadcast, Swope was surely above all else still a newspaperman. The following month would bring a flurry of activity involving Swope in a series of efforts to gain control of the *World* before it ceased to exist. To trace Swope's involvement in the intrigues connected with the demise of his old paper, one has to go back to a clandestine dinner he had with William Randolph Hearst at Sands Point on December 23, 1929.

Swope knew that the Pulitzers would not be averse to selling the morning *World,* if their father's will prohibiting any sale (no matter how unprofitable the paper might be) could be broken. Swope wanted to make an offer to take it over in partnership with his old friend John Wheeler, of the North American Newspaper Alliance syndicate (NANA). They had been close since their days as reporters on the old *Herald.* The problem was capital; they knew it would take a few million dollars, and Swope could not personally put up so much without endangering his entire financial position.

Hearst had been expressing interest in having Swope join his organization ever since Swope's retirement from the *World.* Swope was reluctant to join the Hearst organization, but having the publisher back him in his own paper was another matter. Rather naïvely, he thought that he could get Hearst both to put up the money and to give him carte blanche to do as he chose with the paper. That was not Hearst's way, and Swope should have seen that, but naïveté seems to have marked all of his dealings in this matter.

Margaret Swope saw things more clearly. She could see that he was setting himself up for disappointment and possible humiliation. She did not understand why he should want to get back into the newspaper business with all of those scoundrels. When Swope went to California—ostensibly for RKO, but actually to continue his negotiations with Hearst—she wired:

PLEASE DON'T SELL YOURSELF AND FREEDOM OF ACTION INTO SLAV-
ERY AGAIN.

Swope was certain that she was wrong, that he could handle Hearst, and he came home with the triumphant announcement that the publisher had authorized him to bid $4,500,000 as a first offer and possibly to go higher in more detailed negotiations. When he placed this offer before the Pulitzers, young Herbert Pulitzer was decidedly cool. Ralph told him that they would have to think it over, that they might not want to sell—or, indeed, be able to sell, unless the will was set aside.

The impression Swope got was that there would be no reason for haste. He could go to Palm Beach as he had planned. All of the Pulitzer brothers intended to be in the resort at one time or another during the season, and they could continue their talks informally in Florida.

Swope had no reason to distrust Ralph, who was his close personal friend as well as his former employer. It was in Palm Beach that he learned how misplaced his trust had been. Ralph had started having talks with Roy Howard, of the Scripps-Howard chain, which included the New York *Telegram*. The subject had first been opened during the previous summer, when Howard and Ralph were returning from Europe on the same ship. When Swope accused him of being a good deal less than honest, Ralph soothed him, dismissing the conversation with Howard as nothing but talk. He reaffirmed his previous promise that Swope would have first crack at buying the papers when and if the family decided to sell. Swope was reassured and again took him at his word.

Things remained unaltered through the summer of '30, except that the *World* began losing more money than ever after Ralph stepped down in favor of Herbert Pulitzer. It was as if they were deliberately attempting to increase their losses in order to have a substantial case for breaking the will, should the matter be brought into the courts.

On October 7 Hearst returned to New York for a party celebrating the official opening of his house at Sands Point. The Swopes were among the guests, who included former president Calvin Coolidge and his wife, Lady Ribblesdale, William Rhinelander Stewart, Vincent Astor, and the Arthur Brisbanes.

The day after the party, there was a meeting of Hearst, Brisbane, and Swope. The publisher withdrew his offer to fund the acquisition of the *World*. He already had one successful newspaper in New York, the *Journal,* edited by Brisbane. What he really wanted to do was turn his mediocre morning paper, the New York *American,* into as big a success. Since his early days in San Francisco, he had always considered himself a morning-newspaper man. He offered Swope the job of editing the *American,* but Swope still had his heart and mind set on the *World*.

By December things were coming to a head. Joseph Pulitzer was traveling east from St. Louis to stand by his brothers in the fight to break the will. When Swope had lunch with Adolph Ochs at the *New York Times* on December 5, it was not the threat of Scripps-Howard that they discussed. A new adversary had entered the field in the shape of Ogden Reid of the *Herald Tribune,* who had let his interest in acquiring the *World* be known to the controlling parties. A *Herald Tribune-World* would be an almost unbeatable rival for Ochs's *Times*. They came up with an alternative plan that day. Ochs would back the employees in acquiring the morning and Sunday Pulitzer papers, and Swope would be given a free hand; he would run them independently of the *Times* and in a spirit of friendly competition.

When Swope and Ochs approached the Pulitzers with the plan, they were quoted the outrageous price of ten million dollars for only the daily and Sunday circulation, excluding staff, equipment, and real estate. Even the name *World* would revert after a few months. Swope and Ochs naturally turned it down, feeling confident that not even Roy Howard would accept those terms.

What Ochs and Swope did not know was that the Pulitzers had already agreed upon terms of a contract with Howard, giving him all three New York papers for five million dollars. They were only using their other offer as a dodge. Any competitive auction of assets, including staff, would have caused serious complications that might have prevented them from breaking the will.

For the first six weeks of 1931, Swope was confident that he would still be given first consideration on any move to sell the *World*. After all, he had Ralph's word on it. Ochs was so certain that nothing would happen that he took off on an extended holiday in Hawaii, which indicates that Swope was not the only newspaperman in New York given to long-distance supervision.

> "Who killed the *World?*"
> "I," said J.P.,
> "With my last will and t.—
> I killed the *World.*"
> Franklin P. Adams

At the end of January, Herbert Pulitzer offered to sell the *World Almanac* to Swope. It was one of the Pulitzer interests that Swope, a fact-o-maniac, had always treasured. Year after year, he sent the new editions as Christmas gifts. He immediately accepted the offer, but before he could act on it, other events intervened.

He should have realized that the situation was coming to a climax. Pulitzer could no more sell the *Almanac* than he could any other parts of the empire, without breaking his father's will. If that was imminent, then the sale of the papers was also imminent. Perhaps it did occur to him. On the evening of February 4, he had dinner with Ralph and Peggy Pulitzer. It is reasonable to assume that at some point he asked about plans for the disposition of the *World* and that Ralph once more allayed any fears he might have had of being barred from participation.

A contract of sale had been signed with Roy Howard on January 31. Ralph's deceitfulness might have been motivated by a pledge to secrecy made by all the brothers. A close personal relationship was of small consequence, especially when it was with a man who might cause complications that could spoil a five-million-dollar deal.

On February 16, the city editor of the *World,* James W. Barrett, found out about the Scripps-Howard contract. Surrogate James A. Foley was to preside over the hearing on ratification on February 24.

Even more shocking to Swope than the Pulitzers' personal perfidy was the thought that there would be no more New York *World*. Howard was definitely planning to merge it with the *Telegram*. Many of "his boys" would be out of work during a severe depression. One of the most brilliant, William Bolitho, had already been dismissed by Herbert

Pulitzer. Franklin P. Adams asked, "Mr. Swope, where have you been buying your apples?"

All of Swope's own plans for buying the *World* were motivated by the desire to reconstitute it as it had been during its last great decade, under his editorship. It might not be too late; there was still a chance right up to the moment of the surrogate's decision. He had a little more than one week. In his calendar, he made notes of his activities during that period "re: *World*."

At two-thirty on February 17, he had a meeting with L. S. Levy, of Chadbourne, Stanchfield, and Levy, about the possibility of getting backing to make his own bid to buy the paper. At four-fifteen he and Wheeler went to see Baruch for the same purpose. He followed this with meetings with W. Averell Harriman and Morton Schwartz. There were pledges from all of them, but there was still not enough to match the Howard offer. Swope was reticent about going back to Hearst: a *World-American* would be no more the *World* than a *World-Telegram*.

His first meeting on the following day was with J. Earle Clauson, who had been one of his assistants on the *World* and had continued working in that capacity for Swope's successor, Ralph Renaud. He asked about the morale of the staff and was told that most of them did not know what was happening, beyond the inevitable rumors that circulated in the office. After a meeting with Wheeler, he was off to see James Forrestal, and from there, to see Baruch, with whom he also dined. He persuaded Baruch to increase his pledge and to get his brothers Herman and Sailing to take a piece of the action.

On February 19, he took Wheeler along for a meeting with his brother Gerard. The older Swope reluctantly agreed to participate but said he would be happier if Herbert would stop trying to beat a dead horse. Herbert had just been made a member of the executive committee which supervised all of RKO's interests. General Electric and RKO were controlled by the same banking syndicate, and Gerard was certain that he could get his brother the job as William LeBaron's successor as head of production. This was a recognition by Gerard of Herbert's ability, not nepotism. Both brothers held stern views against that. But Herbert Swope politely declined the offer. If he wanted that job, he could get it for himself. He wanted the *World*.

After leaving Gerard's office, he went on to a series of talks with Marshall Field, Albert Lasker, Hertz, and Harrison Williams, all "re: *World*."

February 20 found him at the offices of Chadbourne, Stanchfield, and

Colonel Edward R. Bradley, HBS,
and Joseph E. Widener at the 1936
Kentucky Derby at Churchill
Downs.

Swope at Hialeah Race
Course in 1937.

Lorelle Hearst is holding Swope's arm; Janet Stewart is producing a cigarette.

A party given by Averell Harriman on the Hearsts' sixth anniversary, March 29, 1939. (*Center*) William Randolph Hearst, Jr., and Swope. (*Below, left to right*) William Rhinelander Stewart, Bradford Norman, Janet (Mrs. W. R.) Stewart, William Randolph Hearst, Jr., and HBS.

(*Right*) Claudette Colbert and HBS en route to Atlanta for the opening of *Gone with the Wind* in 1939.

(*Left*) John Hay Whitney, Swope, and Mrs. David O. Selznick (Irene Mayer) at the Capitol Theatre in New York, December 19, 1939, for *Gone with the Wind*.

(*Below*) HBS and Mrs. William S. Paley (Dorothy Hirshon) at the Harriman party.

An unusual double-exposed snapshot, taken during a Civil Defense exercise at Sands Point in 1924, shows Harry F. Guggenheim and Swope.

Maggie in Palm Beach in 1940.

Mae Fielding Davis.

Roy Robinson.

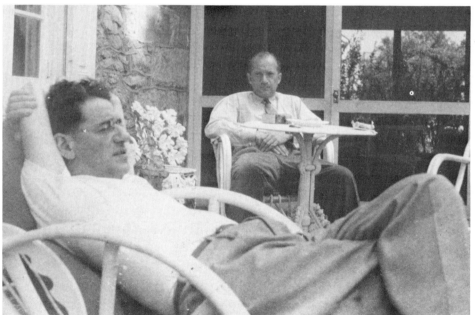

George S. Kaufman, sprawled on his terrace in New Hope, Bucks County, Pennsylvania, in 1944. Peter Vischer, a former member of the *World* sports department who had become publisher of *Horse and Horseman,* looks on.

Aerial view of Keewaydin, Sands Point, Long Island, before the pool was installed on the front lawn. (*Below*) The back porch, looking toward Long Island Sound.

The sun porch.

(*Below*) The entrance hall, where Humphrey Bogart and Ottie once staged a football game. (*Right*) Looking into the dining room.

Swope's dressing table, with photographs of Maggie, HBS, Ottie, and Jane.

General of the Army Dwight D. Eisenhower presents the Medal for Merit to Herbert Bayard Swope in recognition of his exceptionally meritorious conduct in the performance of outstanding services as a consultant to the Secretary of War from 1942 until the end of World War II. The ceremony took place in General Eisenhower's office in the Pentagon, September 8, 1947.

Levy for another meeting with Levy and Mr. Frank, of that firm; a Wall Street man, Austin Clark; and Wheeler. Swope described the conference as "HBS discussion of *World* on his participation." Wheeler recalled it as an absorbing lecture on the newspaper business, with little time left for question and answer.

He proceeded to a meeting with Harriman and Hertz to report on the results of the previous meeting. Along the way he learned that Paul Block, who owned a chain of newspapers that included the Brooklyn *Standard Union,* was going to come forward with an offer that would top Howard's and that might have Hearst money behind it. He put in a long-distance call to Block on the coast. Block was noncommittal. Exactly a month before, when Swope had lunched with him, he had been the reverse, going so far as to suggest that they buy the *World* jointly. Swope also called long distance to William F. Kenny, asking for his participation.

That evening he was on the phone to Gerald Brooks, Hertz, and Sarnoff. More information was needed before he could get the commitments he desired, so he called J. M. Bresnahan, the business manager of the *World,* who agreed to meet with him on the following day. Bresnahan's order from the Pulitzers was to play for time.

The next day, a Saturday, was not the conventional start of a Swope weekend; it was business as usual. In addition to meeting with Bresnahan, he saw Wheeler and spoke to Levy and Frank, who at Chadbourne's urging proposed to issue stock in and manage a new corporation that would buy the *World.* It was amazing to Swope that all of this was finished in time for him to make a luncheon engagement with Sarnoff and Hertz. That evening he dined with Lippmann to discuss the possibility of his coming in with him. There was nobody else he could envision writing his editorials. He finished the night in a poker game with the Thanatopsis Club, a group including Kaufman, Adams, Woollcott, and Broun that had begun meeting for weekly card games in the early days of the Algonquin.

Sunday was telephone day, with calls to Wheeler, who later joined him for dinner, to Bresnahan, and to Levy. Because the twenty-second was a Sunday, Washington's Birthday was celebrated on Monday, but Swope was in his office to continue talks with Bresnahan, Levy, and Wheeler, and to dictate a letter to Roy Howard, putting his position officially on the record. He felt that Howard should either maintain the *World* as a separate entity or open the purchase of the Pulitzer properties to competitive bidding. It was the idle request of a man in search of an honorable conclusion to a situation where honor was in conflict with self-interest.

February 24 was the day Surrogate Foley was to hear the Pulitzers' request. The brothers supposed that it would be a routine matter, for they could easily prove that the *World* was steadily losing money. Their attorneys were very competently presenting their case when Max D. Steuer, a well-known lawyer, strode into the courtroom and approached the bench. Nobody knew why he was there. The spectators began to whisper among themselves, and Foley had to rap for order.

"Your Honor, please," said Steuer, "I represent Paul Block, and he is on his way from the coast to bid on the *World* newspapers."

The courtroom erupted, and it took several minutes to restore order. At length, Steuer proceeded to allege that his client had already submitted a bid far in excess of the Scripps-Howard offer. A contract signed before the surrogate had set aside the will as not a binding one. If Foley decided in favor of the Pulitzers, the bidding had to be reopened.

The hearing went on for hours. Roy Howard warned that a twenty-four-hour delay would wreck the *World* papers. The Pulitzer attorney maintained that because of the delay, circulation and advertising would be lost. The staff would be too demoralized to continue publishing. Nevertheless, Surrogate Foley reserved decision.

The prophets of doom were false. The morning *World* circulation increased 8,000 the next day. Advertising volume went up, and the paper jumped in size from twenty-six to twenty-eight pages. The same was true of the *Evening World*.

Swope did not appear in court that day. He was busy marshaling his forces, conferring with Wheeler, Harriman, Bresnahan, and Baruch. That evening at the *World*, city editor Barrett made a momentous decision. Swope was among the people he notified.

Barrett had decided that the employees would raise the money and buy the papers themselves. He wanted to know whether he could count on Swope's support. Swope answered affirmatively, but not without certain qualifications. He could not pledge his financial backers to a cooperative enterprise without discussing it with them. Most ventures of that sort had been failures. If they went along with him, he would have to be in complete control to protect their investments.

A dinner engagement with the Irving Berlins was postponed, and he spent the night on the phone. He discussed the journalistic possibilities with Lippmann, Krock, Bresnahan, and Wheeler. The pros and cons of the financial side were argued with Harriman, Baruch, and Schwartz. There was also the possibility of reviving the *New York Times* scheme, and he got through to Arthur Hays Sulzberger to find out where his father-in-law, Adolph Ochs, could be reached. Ochs was racing home from Hawaii, and Sulzberger could make no commitments for him. Swope also spoke to Tennant, the editor of the *Evening World*. There would be repercussions the next day in court.

The next day an abnormally large number of reporters represented the *World* in court. Barrett himself was present, along with an attorney named Augustus Rogers. Before the proceedings got under way, a man burst into the courtroom with an armload of copies of the *Evening World,* which were distributed free of charge to everybody in the room. When Herbert Pulitzer read his copy, he turned pale and sent an aide out with instructions to kill the front-page box in all subsequent editions.

It was too late, of course, for everybody, including the surrogate, had read that first edition. In the offending box, there was a statement announcing in boldface type that both the morning *World* and the *Evening World* were showing gains in advertising and circulation. A Pulitzer newspaper was repudiating the Pulitzer contention that the papers were being sold because they were losing money. Tennant had done his job well; even if it was very nearly the last job he would ever do on the *Evening World*.

Before the attorneys for Howard, the Pulitzers, and Block could come forward, Rogers made a motion requesting another postponement, to enable the employees to have a chance to raise the money to buy the papers cooperatively. He pointed out that this was in accord with the wishes of the founder, and that his sons were exaggerating the financial condition of the publication, as the latest edition of their own paper had observed.

The Pulitzer lawyer leaped to his feet to denounce Swope as the man behind this insurrection. When questioned later by the press, Swope would honestly deny that the plan had been his idea. The newspapers were understandably confused and printed still another erroneous rumor concerning Swope. It was said that he was representing Al Smith and Lieutenant-Governor Herbert Lehman, who wanted to buy the *World* in order to use it as a Democratic organ in the city. Swope also denied this; he was acting for himself, and, should they request it, he would also act for the employees, "his boys."

Swope canceled all other business appointments that day in order to concentrate completely on the *World*. He talked with still another possible backer, Robert Dowling of the City Investment Company, as well as with Levy (three times), Baruch, Frank, Bresnahan, and Wheeler. Alex Schlosser, once his assistant, was keeping him informed of reactions down in Park Row. Barrett was relaying accounts of the courtroom activities.

Foley had given still another postponement until the following day. In the meantime, Barrett had called a meeting for that night at the Hotel Astor for the members of the *World* staffs. They were going to raise the money among themselves.

Block was behaving very oddly. Before leaving court, he told Steuer to relay a message to Barrett: "I am authorized by Mr. Block to say that, if his offer is accepted, he will give the employees of the *World* not ten days but thirty days in which to take the paper off his hands at the same price he pays for it. He wants no profit, not even my fee."

What was Block's game? Was he acting for Hearst or independently? Was he merely trying to thwart Howard? Was the offer to Barrett made simply to get the employees to work without any resentment, under the assumption that they would not be able to raise five million once the sale was a fact? Swope saw Block privately and managed to get him to agree to a conference that evening.

While Swope was meeting with Block and Wheeler in his study, 450 *World* staffers were at the Astor. Emotion-charged pledges were coming in from correspondents all over the world, from other publications, from concerned liberals. At the end of the evening, by themselves and on a one-day call, they had managed to raise the phenomenal sum of $1,500,000, half of which came directly from the employees.

Farther uptown, Swope was hammering away at Block, who proved no match for his outburst. Hearst was telephoned to bear witness to the fact that he had no interest in acquiring the *World* per se but every interest in stopping Howard from building a formidable afternoon rival to his *Journal*. That could be done equally well by allowing the *World* Employees Cooperative Association, headed by Barrett, to purchase the paper.

Swope whirled on Block: "You are a Restoration-comedy character!" he fumed. "A 'block' to justice, to allowing the paper to go to its rightful and most interested parties. No matter how the decision goes, the Pulitzers won't let you have it. Withdraw!"

The next afternoon, Alex Schlosser, the acting day city editor, received a bulletin:

SURROGATE'S COURT— WORLD SALE. PAUL BLOCK, OWNER OF THE
BROOKLYN STANDARD UNION AND OTHER NEWSPAPERS THROUGH-
OUT THE COUNTRY, TODAY— THURS.—UNCONDITIONALLY WITH-
DREW THE OFFER MADE FOR THE PURCHASE OF THE WORLDS (MORN-
ING, SUNDAY AND EVENING) THROUGH AN ANNOUNCEMENT MADE
BY HIS ATTORNEY, MAX D. STEUER.

MR. BLOCK BASED HIS WITHDRAWAL ON TWO FACTORS: THAT HE
DID NOT WISH TO OPPOSE THE EFFORTS OF THE EMPLOYEES TO OBTAIN
CONTROL OF THE PAPER AND THAT HE DID NOT WISH TO INTERFERE
WITH THE CONCLUDED DEAL ENTERED INTO BETWEEN THE PULITZER
BROTHERS, OWNERS OF THE WORLDS, AND ROY HOWARD, OF THE
SCRIPPS-HOWARD NEWSPAPER INTERESTS, PUBLISHERS OF THE NEW
YORK TELEGRAM AND OTHER PAPERS.

The surrogate was to announce his decision at eleven that night. Block's statement narrowed the field to the employees, who would carry out the wishes of Joseph Pulitzer that the *World* be continued, and Roy Howard, who would go against them.

Swope was in his office issuing statements to *Time* magazine, the *Evening Post,* and the *New York Times.* He called Block to tell him that he had done the right thing and then spoke to his financial backers, whom he had persuaded to go along with employee management under his direction. He was in a meeting with Owen D. Young, Chairman of the Board of General Electric, when he was interrupted by a call from Roy Howard, asking if his bid would be entered. Swope refused to answer the question. Ten minutes later, there was another call from Howard, asking him to use his influence to get the employees to withdraw their bid and averring that they could work something out between them—businessman to businessman. Swope declined.

That night, the Irving Berlins came to dinner. It had been only two days since they had postponed the meal—it seemed eons. Franklin P. Adams and his wife and Heywood Broun and Ruth Hale (Mrs. Broun) were also there. Now that Block was out of the picture, Swope was certain that Foley would have to decide in favor of the employees. The justice of their case aside, he surely would not recommend throwing 3,000 people out of work during those terrible days. Swope was whistling in the dark. For the first time, it seemed to those gathered that there was a false gaiety to his ebullience, a bluster to his eloquence.

The hour of decision arrived. Swope could not bring himself to make the call and asked whether Adams would mind doing it for him. The columnist left the room. When he returned, there was no need for words:

the outcome was written on his face. Foley had decided that the Pulitzers had the right to sell the paper to whomever they pleased. The brothers had ruled against their employees, insisting that they had to honor the illegal contract with Howard. Their sop to the men, some of whom had been with them for over twenty-five years, was $500,000 set aside to give everybody an extra two weeks' pay as a bonus.

A deathwatch was going on down at the paper. Adams and Broun felt that they had to be a part of it. They asked Swope to come along. He glanced around helplessly, suddenly looking tired and old, the soft evening shirt more wilted than stylish. Margaret leaped in: "I'm sorry. That's impossible. We have guests."

Swope signaled with his hand for them to wait a moment. He wanted to write a few words for them to take to the others. He later jotted down in his diary, "Sent Bulletin to World"—it was his last.

One of the feature stories of that last edition of the *World* was about the murder of a young woman named Vivian Gordon who had been scheduled to give evidence on vice case cover-ups. "This is a real story," Schlosser noted. "The best since the Rosenthal case in 1912." But there was no longer a Swope of the *World* to cover it.

William Randolph Hearst, Jr., had gone to work on the New York *American* in 1928. When the *World* folded, he wanted to bring Swope, the Op Ed page, and the whole *World* feeling over to the *American*. About Swope and the idea, Hearst, Jr., later said, "Pop always admired him. All I can say is that Pop very readily concurred, and I do think he was my ideal."

Swope's desk diary for February 27 carried the following notations:

> Last edition The World dated today.
> Last edition Evening World dated Feb 26/31.
> Session with Coblentz, W. R. Hearst Jr. & Block all day in connection with World & employees & my taking charge of American.
> Sent WRH wire.
> Talked with Hearst on telephone late at night.

E. D. Coblentz was the managing editor of the *American*. As Hearst, Jr., recalled, "Coblentz was ready—'Cobby,' who was Pop's editor from San Francisco and really his close friend—you might say senior editor—was willing to take a back seat if Swope wanted to run the paper."

At first Swope thought, "Why not the spirit of the *World* in the *American?* The *World* by any other name. . . ." Swope's prime concern was the employees. He wanted the freedom to hire and fire and the freedom to dictate a policy for the paper. In the wire to Hearst, he said:

> I BELIEVE ONLY WAY IN WHICH THERE IS REAL CHANCE OF ACCOM-
> PLISHING REAL RESULT ON AMERICAN WHICH SO MANY HAVE TRIED
> TO LIFT AND FAILED IS TO BE GIVEN COMPLETE CHARGE OF PAPER
> SUBJECT OF COURSE TO CERTAIN LIMITATIONS STOP TITLE TO BE
> GIVEN ME AND MANNER IN WHICH IT IS TO BE DISPLAYED IS OF LESSER
> IMPORTANCE THAN FULL POSSESSION OF AUTHORITY WHICH MIGHT
> RARELY BE USED BUT NEVERTHELESS WOULD BE AVAILABLE WHEN
> NEEDED STOP I WOULD BE PERFECTLY WILLING TO RELY UPON YOUR
> PERSONAL ASSURANCES BUT I FEEL IT WOULD BE BETTER TO HAVE
> UNDERSTANDING IN WRITING WHICH I WOULD NOT WISH TO HAVE
> RUN FOR TOO LONG A TIME WITH SALARY SET AT A MINIMUM OF TEN
> THOUSAND DOLLARS A MONTH AND INCREASES IN THE EVENT OF
> CIRCULATION GROWTH.

He described the difficulties inherent in the job and some of the freedoms he would need in order to succeed. The lengthy message ended with an honest appraisal that could not have pleased Hearst, lightened by a touch of humor which was subject to a wrong interpretation:

> WHAT PAPER NEEDS ABOVE ALL ELSE IS NEWS REPORTED WITHOUT
> PREJUDICE AND WITH ACCURACY UNDERSTANDING AND AUTHORITY
> STOP ONE OF THE BIGGEST PRESENT-DAY TROUBLES IS THERE ARE TOO
> MANY AROUND SHOP WHO THINK THEMSELVES LITTLE HEARSTS AND
> TREAT NEWS AS MATTER OF POLICY STOP THAT IS TAINT THAT HAS
> STUNTED AMERICAN STOP ARE YOU COMING EAST SOON STOP ANYWAY
> WE WILL REMAIN FRIENDS WHETHER YOU GO TO WORK FOR ME OR
> NOT.

Hearst's reply contained vague promises but did not give any of the guarantees that Swope had sought. He decided to make one last attempt to find out how far Hearst would allow him to go: in a telephone conversation, he asked what would happen if a Swope-run Hearst paper gave Marion Davies a bad review. Hearst answered that such a thing could never happen in one of his papers.

After the *World* folded, Samuel Chotzinoff remembered Swope's instruction to him when he first joined the paper, replacing Deems Taylor as music critic: "One thing you must always remember—the *World* has no axe to grind, and never can have. If my aunt, cousin, daughter or grandmother should happen to be the person you are reviewing, you must ignore the relationship. Another thing—the *World* has no sacred cows." Frank Sullivan also remembered the "sacred cows" image in Swope's injunction to a new employee.

If Marion Davies was Hearst's "sacred cow," Swope could never be one of his boys. He would have found it as impossible to serve a master and a mistress as it had been to serve two masters.

The moment passed. He would never work for Hearst; he knew that. The restraints were of the sort that he could not abide. As Hearst's own son said much later:

> We thought of imbuing the *American* with some of the *World*'s spirit by getting—trying to inveigle, rather—Herbert Swope to come over. Now, whether he was smart enough to quit ahead, which personally he was, he was a pretty good gambler—and very famous gambler— and a guy who knew the odds. And he quit with a very high name and reputation. There had been that possibility that W. R. Hearst—they were friends of one another—might nevertheless have Swope doing things he didn't want to do—or maybe not let him do things he wanted to do. And if they didn't go well—Pop was accustomed to doing what he wanted to do. I think Swope correctly sized it up and figured he had more to lose than to gain. He might have gotten bigger, had more world renown—I think might have—I think he probably would have certainly. He would have if he had been younger and threw himself in— In any case, he said, "No, thanks." And there was no ill feeling. And I was sorry he didn't do it.

Whether or not Swope was ever sorry is difficult to guess. Hearst senior reached a point when he was sorry. After the demise of the *American* in 1935, when he was forced to merge it with his *Journal* in order to save anything, he wrote to Swope, "If you had been on the paper it would never have happened."

It might have been at Hearst's behest, or it might simply have been the newsmen's opinion of Swope's singular position in the world, but from then on the Hearst press concentrated heavily on Swope as a man of fashion and high society. It rarely took him seriously and did much to contribute to building his reputation as a social lion instead of giving

honest reportage of his serious accomplishments. Such Hearst columnists as Winchell, Elsa Maxwell, Cholly Knickerbocker, Louis Sobol,
Arthur Brisbane, and Dorothy Kilgallen helped to turn the celebrated person Swope was into the celebrity Swope became. Not long
after the Swope rejection, Arthur Brisbane was commenting on the newest men's fashion—"host coats" in which to receive one's guests at
home.

> They allow the eaters and drinkers at the party to pick out the man
> who is paying the bill and prevent mistaking him for the butler. The
> latter advantage is not important, because the butler may usually be
> recognized by his expression of concentrated intelligence, and is
> nearly always sober. . . . Herbert (Bayard) Swope had this "host-
> coat" idea long ago, wearing an evening suit of beautiful claret-
> colored damask. Why, no one knew. In his house there can't be any
> mistake about the host. And the butler has nothing to do with it, for
> Swope's servants are black.

Swope was amused and shrugged the item off. F.P.A. was indignant
and took aim at Brisbane, who was often a guest at the Swopes', by
retorting in his column, "It is in his guests that Mr. Swope makes his
mistakes."

And so it was that friend and foe alike contributed to Swope's being
famous for some of the wrong reasons. It was not that there was no
foundation for what was coming to pass or that Swope did not mightily
add to it by the manner in which he lived; it was rather that there was so
much more to the man, even in those later years, that tended to be
overshadowed by his "star status" in the columns. That sort of renown
reproduces itself like wild and malignant cells and eventually gets out of
control. Those who thrived on column fame, whose antics provided the
livelihoods of the columnists, sought him out. His own enjoyment of the
celebrated, witty, and beautiful gave them easy access. Their press
agents knew that a sure way to get a column break was to send out an
item that such-and-such a client was at the Swopes' place for dinner or a
weekend, whether or not he or she was in fact there. That was the way of
the world (with a small "w") that was enveloping him in the afterglow of
his years on the *World*.

It was not inevitable. Perhaps he should have made some real effort to
resist what was happening, but to have the strength to do that, he would
have had to be possessed of an inner knowledge of who he was. After he
stopped being a newspaperman, Swope was never totally sure of his own

real importance despite the record, and name-in-the-paper fame in some measure may have helped to allay his doubts.

Swope had no real capacity for hatred, no taste for revenge. He even wrote a note of condolence on the *World*'s death to Ralph Pulitzer, to which Pulitzer replied, "When I see you, let's not talk about something I'm going to do my best to forget." Pulitzer would forget, and Swope would forgive.

Within a month of the final edition of the *World,* James Barrett brought out a book that he must have been writing secretly for some time—*The World, the Flesh, and Messrs. Pulitzer.* In it, he placed the blame for the failure of the *World* completely upon the Pulitzer brothers, whose self-interest and greed transcended any sense of duty and decency. His attitude toward Swope was so ambiguous that the *New York Times* reviewer wrote, "He speaks of Herbert Bayard Swope as a super-reporter, one of the best the *World* ever had; but holds he was not exceptional as the executive editor." On the other hand, the *Herald Tribune* reviewer wrote, "To Swope, he gives a credit which some have withheld. Swope was away from the office, he says, but 'whenever he did come into the shop it was like an electric current, so dynamic and stimulating was his attack on the day's work. Swope also manifested a deep interest in the work and personality of every reporter on the staff.' "

Whatever Swope's own assessment of Barrett's attitude might have been, he was at his side the following month when he went to court in an unsuccessful attempt to reverse the surrogate's decision on the sale of the paper. The basis of his case was an obscure codicil in the will stating, in effect, that the newspaper trust could not be broken without the permission of the major editors. Swope gave witness that Barrett was in that category. He noted in his diary on April 10: "2:30 Surrogate's Court. Hearing against World. Had heated talk with Jackson [Pulitzer lawyer] in presence of R. P. [Ralph Pulitzer], Jackson saying report was that I was behind the employees' move. I told him I was not, though justified in being because of rotten deal Pulitzers gave me."

This indirect rebuke was as close as he ever came to reproaching Ralph. There was never any proof that the subject was opened again. In mid-July Pulitzer was toastmaster at a dinner given in Swope's honor by Millicent Hearst. He rose to the occasion with another piece of doggerel:

> Now here's to Herbert Bayard Swope.
> God save the King, God help the Pope,
> And God protect the President

From this demure, retiring gent.
He taught George Rex to put his crown on,
Queen Mary how to put her gown on,
And David Windsor, Prince of Wales,
To fall from horses and for frails;
Explained just how to outmaneuver
Depressions to our Mr. Hoover;
And for the Pontiff, as a pal,
He's written his encyclical.
His lessons finished to Lenin, he
Gave castor oil to Mussolini;
And after multiple attempts he
Coached Tunney how to K.O. Dempsey;
Instructed Lindbergh how to fly,
And taught Münchhausen how to lie,
Trained Washington to tell the truth,
Perfected batting in Babe Ruth.
He fertilized the many ova
Unjustly claimed by Casanova;
And, last and loftiest feat, inspired
The peerless nerve of Herbert Bayard.

During the intervening months, Swope had made two other attempts to get back into journalism. With Harriman's backing, he had pursued a rumor that the *Evening Post* was for sale. It had come to nothing. With Sarnoff's backing, he and Wheeler had tried to get together a list of contributors for a weekly journal, but the times were not right for launching that sort of venture.

He looked around Mrs. Hearst's table. W.R. was on the coast with Marion Davies, but his sons and heirs were there, as were those of Joseph Pulitzer. He felt removed from them. They were a different breed. Had the fathers been there, the gulf would not have existed. They would have understood had he responded to Ralph's toast with a short poem by Franklin P. Adams:

Journalism's a shrew and scold;
    I like her.
She makes you sick, she makes you old;
    I like her.
She's daily trouble, stress and strife;
She's Love and Hate and Death and Life;
She ain't no lady—she's my wife—
    I like her.

FIFTEEN

By the beginning of 1932 Swope had close business relationships with both the National Broadcasting Company and the Columbia Broadcasting System. It would seem logical that one or the other of the radio networks would have asked Swope to head its news department, but the thought apparently never occurred to their respective heads, David Sarnoff and William Paley. They both had other uses for Swope in the Machiavellian patterns of their rivalry.

In the late '20s Swope had helped Paley to negotiate a deal whereby Paramount Pictures bought a 50 percent interest in CBS, giving him the necessary capital to expand. By mid-1931 Paley wanted to buy out Paramount's interest. Paramount was in financial trouble and needed capital itself; accordingly, it was ready to sell. Paley again turned to Swope for help in raising the money.

In the meantime Swope had been placed on the executive board of RKO, which was controlled by NBC's Sarnoff. He did not want to compromise this position, so in April 1931 he asked for Sarnoff's advice on the matter. Sarnoff was very pleased with the radio/motion picture marriage of RKO and NBC, but not so happy with a similar relationship between Paramount and the newly significant CBS. When he advised Swope to go ahead with CBS, dividing the competition was one of his motivations. That he had yet another was apparent from a memo Swope wrote to himself after the meeting: "D. Sarnoff & Columbia deal. I to go into Columbia provided there would be chance to sell it later to RKO & he [Sarnoff] to go with me [as head]."

Although Swope did not know it, what Sarnoff had in mind was gaining control of CBS through the supposedly independent RKO, which was actually a subsidiary of Radio Corporation of America, his parent organization, which also owned both the Blue and Red networks of NBC. It would give him a virtual monopoly on important broadcasting in the United States. Swope gave the terms to Paley, who by accepting them had nothing to lose: he could always refuse later.

Both of these gentlemen were far more adroit businessmen than Swope could ever have hoped to be. He was simply the middleman, and on paper he had nothing, which was exactly what he got when the time came to divide the big profits. In business Swope was ever the gentleman sportsman. He expected everybody to play according to the rules. A handshake was as binding as any legal document. Unfortunately this was seldom the case, and he was constantly being disappointed by men who very well knew the difference between the rules involved in exercising the body and those involved in exercising power.

At the beginning of 1932 the Swopes moved into a sixteen-room, six-bath apartment at 895 Park Avenue. Whatever financial problems he had experienced at the start of the depression were over, and he was once more giving every indication of being a completely carefree man. Although the Democratic Convention was six months away, he looked forward to it with both excitement and pleasure. There was a chance that his man, Alfred Smith, would be the nominee for president and that the party would sweep the boards in November, carrying his good friend to the highest office in the land. The office of United States Senator from New York was an appealing one, and Swope again began to think seriously of a career in politics. But that would have to wait. In the meantime he was occupied with exercising his extraordinary talent for bringing together people who stood to gain by association.

In January he was busy putting together the Paley deal with his usual aplomb, interesting Hertz, Baruch, Harriman, Young, Levy, Lasker, and the National City Bank in providing financing. At the same time, he was having extended conversations with Winston Churchill about doing a weekly radio show from London for CBS. Churchill was never seriously interested, but he toyed with the idea, mostly because he was so enormously entertained by the sound of Swope on the subject.

By February he was involved in talks with Goldwyn about releasing his films through RKO. (He ultimately decided to do this, but not until another decade had passed.) He was also offered the chairmanship of the board of North American Aviation, which he declined, although he did remain a director until six months later, when he resigned in protest against secret manipulations of assets without the approval of the directorate.

Throughout the spring Swope was becoming increasingly upset by the exposure of corruption in the administration of Mayor Walker. He thought that Walker should step down before he became a liability during the presidential campaign. The mayor and Smith were friends; Governor Roosevelt was showing a reluctance to investigate him. It was a potentially dangerous situation.

For himself, there was a personal sadness. Walker and Swope had been pals for years. They had often indulged in the good-natured, almost schoolboy raillery that Swope inspired in many of the men with whom he was close. During the Coolidge administration, Swope had been a speaker at a dinner at which Walker was toastmaster. When he mentioned that he had recently had a twenty-eight-minute conference with the president, Walker interrupted to say that he had spent thirty minutes with Coolidge. Swope refused to be outclassed: "I really spent thirty-one minutes with the President."

Walker retorted: "Yes, Herbie, but you are including the three minutes in which you permitted Mr. Coolidge to get in a word."

Eventually Swope would have to take a stand against "Gentleman Jimmy" and advise Smith that a disavowal was necessary to carry New York State. But not yet, not that spring, when everything still looked so promising. He had lived for exactly a half-century and, without slipping tongue in cheek, could truly say that he'd come a long way from St. Louis. He celebrated the twentieth anniversary of a marriage that was perfect in every way. He could estimate that two-thirds of his life was over, but for the moment the future seemed as bright as the past had been.

That year a new friend came into his life. His friendship with Joseph P. Kennedy was to become almost as close as his relationship with Baruch, but far different in nature. Kennedy was six years younger than Swope; Baruch was twelve years older, two older than Gerard. With Kennedy, there was none of the filial respect that he felt for the older man. Kennedy was a chum, somebody with whom he could gamble, swap yarns and gossip, somebody with whom he could have fun, a quality conspicuously absent from not only his but everyone's relationships with Baruch, who simply wasn't the chum type. Whether it was his youthful career as an amateur boxer or his elder-statesman role of later years, Baruch took it all with an equal degree of seriousness.

Swope and Kennedy were pugnacious redheads scrapping their way to the top—boisterous, energetic, given to boyish enthusiasms. Over the next few years, Kennedy used Swope's office as his own when he was in New York. They conspired to give each other boosts in all sorts of endeavors. Swope was particularly helpful in promoting an intimacy between Kennedy and the leaders of the New York State Democratic party who dominated the national scene during the Roosevelt administration.

Swope had daily telephone conversations with both of his friends. The talks with Baruch tended to be lofty, full of long and objective views

of world affairs. With Kennedy, there was intimacy, a subjective com-
miseration on the frustrations and joys of day-to-day life. It was only to
his close friend Kennedy that Swope would confide his disappointment
in Roosevelt after his election:

> *You* know how earnestly and effectively I worked for FDR, even
> *before* the nomination; I am referring to the two weeks preceding
> Chicago, when we began our talk.
>
> I find myself clutching at the Crown of Martyrdom. I have no
> desire to wear it, but I find my reactions of soreness are much the
> same as yours, though, of course, mine rest on a far lesser basis of
> justification. . . .

Actually, by the time Swope left for the Chicago Democratic Convention on June 22, he was holding his options open. He was outwardly
pledged to Smith but had already given up any hope that his man could
win. At the same time, he had let the New York party leaders, Ed Flynn
and Jim Farley, know that he would not be averse to Roosevelt, remind-
ing them that he had been responsible for getting FDR his first national
job. His real choice, however, was his brother's colleague at General
Electric, Owen D. Young. His desire was for Young to emerge from a
deadlocked convention as the compromise candidate.

The observation car of the Twentieth Century Limited was a particularly lively place that evening. Passengers Swope, Baruch, Lippmann,
Krock, Frank Kent of the Baltimore *Sun,* Clare Boothe Brokaw (later
Clare Boothe Luce), and Mrs. Woodrow Wilson were unified on one
point—a jocular avowal that their real purpose at the convention would
be subversion. Another bond was their antipathy to Roosevelt. Swope
summed up the situation for his brother: "Roosevelt has most of the
delegates but no friends; the others have most of the friends but no
delegates."

Clare Brokaw was in their company not as a delegate or journalist, but
for the purpose of drumming up interest in starting a new political party
in which women would have a greater role. She was being backed
financially in this endeavor by the beautiful Mona (Mrs. Harrison)
Williams, who reputedly had a brain or two beneath her expensive
bonnet. Beyond politics, the two women had in common style, beauty,
intelligence, and money. They were traits that Swope liked in women.
With Janet Newbold Ryan, later Mrs. William Rhinelander Stewart, they
made a triumvirate of Swope's favorite female friends of the period.
Mrs. Stewart led the field in quick wit and beauty, Mrs. Brokaw in talent

and ambition, Mrs. Williams in style and wealth. But all three were endowed with good ears for listening and good minds for asking the kind of questions that Swope adored answering at length.

As Mrs. Brokaw was alighting from the train, Lippmann called after her, "If Roosevelt gets the nomination, you can put me down as a member of your new party."

She later credited Swope and Baruch with having been the first to encourage her to enter politics. She first met Swope while she was still a teenager. She had graduated from finishing school and wanted to go to the Columbia School of Journalism. Her mother had arranged a luncheon party at the old Waldorf Hotel so that Swope and Paul Block could meet the girl and, she hoped, write letters of introduction. Young Miss Boothe was far more impressed by her first meal at the Waldorf than by her companions. Swope did write the letter, but she was too young to be admitted to the university.

Swope was a natural enthusiast and encourager. As he had encouraged Mrs. Luce and Robert E. Sherwood to begin careers in public life, he was also instrumental in starting W. Averell Harriman and Douglas Fairbanks, Jr., in new directions. When Harriman hesitated about accepting what he considered an insignificant job with the NRA, Swope urged him on, saying that a man had to do something for the people, to start somewhere. Harriman reconsidered, and it was the beginning of his distinguished career in public life. A message Swope sent to Winston Churchill with Fairbanks opened the way to the actor's achievements in service to England as well as to his own country. In another vein, when Ring Lardner, Jr., expressed an interest in a career in Hollywood (which led to the mixed blessing of two Academy Awards for writing and unjust persecution by the House Un-American Activities Committee), it was Swope who got him his first job, as a publicist for David O. Selznick.

Mrs. Luce later said, "When Swope spoke, even the chandeliers seemed to vibrate. They were enchanting evenings at Swope's. For the first time, the intellectual Democrats could sniff victory. They were evenings filled with hope and conflict. Invigorating ideas. It was so different from political life today."

When asked about Swope's disappointments and frustrations as he grew older and moved away from the centers of power, she said:

> Herbert loved his life. The search for fame doesn't necessarily make people happy. There is a place in life for a man who could be a real friend, happy in developing the talents of others, bringing people

together. There was nobody quite like Swope. But it required leisure. He enjoyed power, but loved his life more. He made his choice. Those of us who enjoyed him don't regret it. He was so supportive. He had this dear habit of always taking the trouble to write a "memo from HBS," if you did something well. The Swope home was a unique place for talk and deals. A spontaneous coming together of divergent types—actresses and critics. Writers and publishers. He enjoyed inviting people who might be at odds with each other. Not to put them against each other. There was no malice. It was just to get them together. He wanted me to meet Dorothy Parker. We met there. Nothing ever came of it except a spate of apochryphal stories. No truth in them. It was a game people played—inventing supposedly witty things and attributing them to Mrs. Parker.

The most often repeated story, vehemently denied by both women, had them coming to a doorway. Mrs. Luce gestured to Mrs. Parker to go first, saying, "Age before beauty."

Mrs. Parker sailed into the next room, retorting, "Pearls before swine."

It took four ballots to nominate Franklin D. Roosevelt. Although Swope knew Smith's cause was a lost one and he would have settled for the nomination of Owen Young or his old friend from the WLB days, Albert Ritchie, he never gave any outward signs of flagging in his devotion to "the Happy Warrior" and did much to keep the New York delegation for him. The New York balloting on the first vote was 65½ for Smith and 28½ for Roosevelt; on the second it shifted slightly—64½ for Smith and 28½ for Roosevelt; on the third, 63 for Smith and 31 for Roosevelt; a fourth vote was unnecessary, as Roosevelt had the nomination before New York was called. Swope's efforts were so strenuous that he ruefully told a *New York Times* reporter afterwards, "Some people seem to think my name is Herbert *Die-Hard* Swope. That is not true. The New York delegates have no undying hostility to Governor Roosevelt."

All of the important figures at the convention were staying at the Ambassador East Hotel. On the night Smith lost, Mrs. Brokaw naturally expected to find his supporters gathered around him. "I went to his suite and learned one of the cruelest political lessons. Nobody was there except the Governor and his wife, quietly saying their prayers before retiring."

Smith directed her to a room where she might find the others. Swope, Baruch, General Hugh Johnson, Henry A. Wallace, and Admiral

Grayson were there planning Roosevelt's next move with such fervor that one might have thought that they had all been among his most ardent supporters. Swope said, "We must write an acceptance speech for him that will pull the party together."

Swope, Wallace, Baruch, and Johnson immediately grabbed pencils and paper to write their versions of what the candidate should say. Baruch's was immediately discarded, and what emerged as Roosevelt's acceptance speech was actually a stitched-together patchwork of the efforts of Swope, Johnson, and Wallace. Roosevelt, however, was the grand master of the dramatic gesture. He was the first candidate ever to fly to the convention to accept the nomination. The memorable entrance of the polio victim overshadowed any words that had been prepared for him.

After he arrived home, Swope wrote consolingly to Smith that the only thing that stood between the presidency and him was "your religion. That reason, however deplorable, cannot be removed in these days of continued bigotry."

Smith replied, "You hit the nail on the head."

On July 31, Swope was in Boston for the wedding of his nephew, Isaac Swope. He proceeded from there to Hyannisport to spend a week with Joseph Kennedy. It was obvious to the two men that the Roosevelt campaign was not going well in New England. Kennedy thought Smith could turn the tide. If he came out for the candidate in Massachusetts and Connecticut, those states would fall in behind him. Swope wanted to work on persuading Smith immediately, but Kennedy cautioned him to wait for a request from Roosevelt; a favor asked for and granted would strengthen his position.

Swope was skeptical. Immediate action was necessary, so he decided to call his friend Felix Frankfurter at Harvard for another opinion. The future Supreme Court justice also advised caution. These things had to follow protocol. In the meantime, he would suggest to Roosevelt that Swope could be valuable in this situation.

The next move had to be Roosevelt's; Swope could do nothing but wait. For the next month, he kept himself available; he did not even go to Saratoga. He stayed home, attending to his business affairs and keeping a very low political profile. Baruch was in Europe; Kennedy was in Hyannisport; there were no telephone conversations or visits with Smith. Swope waited.

The first break came on August 22, with a message from Herbert H.

Lehman, who was seeking the Democratic nomination for governor at the state convention the following month. Smith, who had brought Lehman into politics, had determined to remain aloof from the convention. He wanted to maintain at least tacit support for James Walker, knowing that the convention would have to demand his removal from office.

Lehman already had Roosevelt on his side, but he needed active support from Smith to counteract the opposition of John F. Curry, the head of the Tammany Hall Democratic political machine. Curry was for Walker, against Roosevelt, and against anybody the presidential candidate might endorse. It was also beginning to look as if Roosevelt would need Smith if he was to carry his own state and New Jersey.

Lehman's approach was to use Swope as an intermediary in order to get some word from Smith. Any opening might lead to a reconciliation between the Smith and Roosevelt forces.

Swope telephoned both Smith and Kennedy. The word from them was to hold still for further developments. These came on August 26, when W. Forbes Morgan, one of Roosevelt's chief advisers, called and asked him to come up to see the governor in Albany the following week. When Swope asked the purpose of the visit, Morgan replied, "Politics. Just politics."

On August 31, Swope noted in his diary, "Left for Albany 1:40. There all afternoon with Governor, going over campaign and my joining it."

Baruch arrived back from Europe on the second of September. He spent the following afternoon with Swope, discussing the "question of Roosevelt policy." In his diary entry for the third, Swope made a special note next to the regular daily notation "telephoned JP Kennedy"; he added, "regarding Gov. Roosevelt."

That weekend the Walker problem had been eliminated by his resignation, leaving Joseph McKee as the new acting mayor. Curry was still insisting that Walker run for the office from which he had just resigned, but Swope felt certain that Smith could be convinced of the folly of supporting that idea.

Swope was now fully committed to the campaign and was relishing every moment of the daily intrigues necessary to maneuver Smith into the Roosevelt camp. Simultaneously, his various business activities were continuing apace. He still maintained his conferences on RKO and CBS. He was part of a complicated series of ploys designed to salvage the debt-ridden New York City subway systems, which were then privately owned companies. There were real-estate deals with Chad-bourne and Hertz, and plans to open a chain of art cinema houses.

His active social life continued at its exhausting pace, with nightly dinner parties, openings, weekend house guests and, of course, the races. He was at Belmont Park's opening day and later at the Futurity classic, after which he made a special note in his diary that he had picked the winner. It deserved special note, for he had two thousand dollars riding on Kerry Patch, who came in at odds of 30 to 1.

But it was politics that was providing him with the most exciting race of all. His Roosevelt contact was Professor Raymond Moley of Colum-bia University, who was a member of the original "brain trust" and one of the candidate's most valued advisers. A close relationship developed between Swope and Moley that would culminate in mutual disillusion-ment with the man responsible for it.

Swope spoke to Smith several times during Wednesday afternoon, September 7. A meeting was set up for that evening with Smith's most trusted supporters. The governor would not be present, but the impor-tance of the conference so impressed the chronically late Swope that he added the word "sharp" after the designated hour for the first time in over a decade of diary entries.

Those present included the woman Smith had called "the brainiest woman I ever knew," Belle Moskowitz; her husband, Dr. Henry Moskowitz; Robert Moses; Judge Joseph Proskauer; and State Supreme Court Justice Bernard Sheintag. Swope recognized that the estimable Mrs. Moskowitz could speak for Smith with more authority than any of the others, so it was to her that he listened most attentively and to her that he addressed his comments. She remains to this day the only female politician ever to attain a position of such importance in the council of an American presidential candidate. Mrs. Moskowitz, who began as a social worker on the Lower East Side, had inspired Smith's programs for social reform for over two decades. Her heart was broken when Smith forever lost his chance to be president, and she died almost exactly two months before Roosevelt's inauguration.

They worked out a plan that Mrs. Moskowitz was certain Smith would accept, no matter how reluctantly. She was no Roosevelt en-thusiast, but she was a practical woman who realized that the party had to win, for only a Democratic administration would enact the sort of social legislation for which she had crusaded throughout her career.

The first step was to frustrate any attempt to nominate Walker. An idea had to be planted in the press that would seem spontaneous, so H. V.

Kaltenborn, of the *Brooklyn Eagle,* was indirectly contacted. On September 9, an editorial appeared in the *Eagle* proposing that Smith be drafted to run for mayor. Swope wrote a letter to the editor endorsing the project, which he read on the phone to governors Smith and Roosevelt, Mrs. Moskowitz, Baruch, and Professor Moley. It was printed on September 11:

> Without attempting to judge the right to vindication that Mr. Walker claims, I believe the *Eagle*'s suggestion of Mr. Smith's nomination would avoid the existing difficulties with respect to city, State, and national tickets.
>
> I should like to see him made the candidate of all the parties so that the compliment might be paid him of a unanimous choice similar to James Monroe's election to the Presidency in 1816 when he was the choice of the Republican and Federalist parties and inaugurated the "Era of Good Feeling" for the ensuing eight years, a period of vital importance to the development of America. I believe Governor Smith could do as much and perhaps more for the city.

The nomination could never be obtained on those terms, as they all knew, but the announcement did serve as public warning to Walker and Curry that the former's candidacy would be opposed even by his friends.

That September Swope was placed on the Democratic party's National Finance Committee. Its goal was to raise $1,500,000 for the campaign, a paltry sum by today's standards. Even more staggering is the entire amount expended by Smith in his drive for the nomination, according to publicly released figures—a total of $9,000. Of that total, $1,500 had been contributed by Swope.

The month also saw Swope named to the Emergency Unemployment Relief Committee, which had the more impressive sum of $75,000,000 as its goal. At least priorities were better that year than they have been in recent years—$1,500,000 to elect politicians and $75,000,000 to help those in need.

Swope gave an interview on September 15 to Walter Trumbull of NANA on the subject of youth. A part of his message was surely meant for his own children: it indicated that his concern for their tomorrow was as great as his simultaneous concern for the imminent election.

> Youth has been indulged and softened by the silken days, peaked in 1929. It has made no assertion of independence, because there was no

need for it. We employ only those virtues we have to. Youth should be a period during which idols are broken and fetishes destroyed. It should be open-minded but at present it is not. The youngsters of today are conservative by training and because of a materialistic philosophy. . . .

The rising generation has had it pretty easy; but the one to follow, the youngsters of tomorrow as differentiated from those of today, those who now are around ten years old, will do better, because they have to do better. The youngsters of twenty-one, still shaped by the last decade, are following a light that has gone out.

Swope's relationships with members of the younger generation were varied. As devoted as he was to his family, he was better at dealing with the children of friends than with his own children. Marti Stevens, the gifted singer and actress, was the daughter of his Sands Point neighbor, the film magnate Nicholas Schenck. The first real encouragement she ever received was from Swope. John Hertz's children remembered that he unfailingly came upstairs for long fatherly visits with them whenever he came to dinner at their parents' home. Douglas Fairbanks, Jr., was always grateful for the affectionate support Swope gave him in both his theatrical and his diplomatic pursuits.

Yet his own children recalled an austerity, a lack of communication. They never doubted Swope's love for them, but they longed for a warmer expression of it. He was the flexible liberal in every area of his life except paternity, where he remained a stern Victorian, withholding from his offspring the affectionate display he craved from all of the father figures in his own life, thereby passing on to them some of his own frustration.

His daughter recalled one afternoon for years afterward. She was reclining on the sofa, when Swope came into the room. He wanted to know why she had not risen, and she replied, "Oh, Daddy, I'm just too beat."

He thundered, "God damn it! No matter how tired you are, you'll get up when your father enters a room!"

It was his way, she explained. He was afraid to let his softness show for fear that he would not be respected, that he would be at the mercy of the love he evinced in every other way.

Ottie never doubted Swope's love; it was manifest in too many silent ways. It was rather the desire for communication and approval that he never felt was forthcoming until after he became an adult. When he came home for school holidays, Swope's first remark to his son was generally, "When are you going back to school?"

Ottie later explained, "I knew he was glad to see me. But you've got to admit, it was a damned awkward way of putting it. We could ask a question on any topic under the sun—and he'd stop whatever he was doing to explain. But he never seemed to have any small talk for us."

Smith left for Albany and the Democratic State Convention on the morning of October 2, accompanied by Swope, Robert Moses, and Henry and Belle Moskowitz. By the time they boarded the train, the word was out that a meeting on September 30 between Lehman and Curry had failed to produce a reconciliation, and that the Tammany leader was gathering forces for a stop-Lehman move. He had already secured the chairmanship of the convention for one of his men, T. Arthur Hendricks. In addition, he was still planning to go ahead with the nomination of Walker for mayor, despite the rumor that Smith might be available for the post.

Smith had made no commitment to work for Lehman's nomination, although he had let it be known that he was in favor of it. Swope argued that it was not enough. Smith had to make a public disavowal of Walker, as well as a statement for Lehman. It was well known that Roosevelt intended to campaign actively for the New York banker. If Lehman got the nomination strictly through the efforts of Roosevelt, Smith was finished as a power in the party. He might as well move to another state.

When Swope presented his arguments to Smith, he was enthusiastically seconded by Mrs. Moskowitz. Smith listened silently to all that they had to say. At length he said quietly, "I'm going to nominate Lehman."

"And Walker?"

He smiled: "We'll attend to Jimmy."

The next step was an endorsement of Roosevelt. Swope knew that would not be so easy to obtain. Despite the fact that Roosevelt had once nominated Smith for the presidency, the two men had never been close. They had not even met since long before the Chicago convention. Smith was too good a party man ever to repudiate Roosevelt, but he was certainly not planning to do anything to help him.

Smith was a man of enormous gifts; he could still be of great importance on the national scene. His position was one of strength, for Roosevelt needed him. It was essential that he offer his services to the candidate. The first step would have to be a well-publicized meeting. Mrs. Moskowitz told Swope that it was up to him to arrange it. He was the only one who was close enough to both of them to do it.

The DeWitt Clinton Hotel was the center of convention activity. Lobbying was as apt a word as one could find for the action, as men gathered amid the potted palms in the cool shadows cast by the marble pillars to swap favors, to whisper those words that could make or break a political reputation. "Can you deliver the Schenectady vote?" "I've got Brooklyn sewed up."

Moments after Swope checked in, he was moving up and down the corridors; in and out of suites; meeting with Farley, Moley, Lehman, Curry. In each inner circle he was welcomed with such ease that one man lacking in that facility commented resentfully, "The trouble with Swope is—he's got an interiority complex."

By the end of the day, he had worked out a deal whereby Smith would nominate Lehman and Roosevelt would second the nomination. Allowing Smith to go first was an adroit political maneuver. While costing nothing, it conferred upon Roosevelt an illusion of graciousness. But Swope knew the man too well to accept such things at face value. He wrote in his diary that night, "My problem will be to keep Roosevelt from stealing the show."

The famous Roosevelt-Smith reconciliation before the press and photographers was an event with respect to which Swope could justly note, "I did this all alone." The two former foes met in the convention hall and shook hands. As the cameras started to click away, Smith said, "You old potato!"

Roosevelt winced involuntarily for just a fraction of a minute, before covering with his enormously winning smile. He did not even like the way Smith pronounced potato. Swope was one of the few who caught the reflex; he may well have wondered about an Irish propensity for using featureless oval shapes as terms of admiration.

Years before, during a weekend at his Great Neck house, another Irishman, F. Scott Fitzgerald, had dropped to his knees before the great actress Laurette Taylor and murmured lovingly, "You egg. You beautiful egg."

The stunned Miss Taylor's reaction was, "I've just seen the doom of the younger generation."

Watching Roosevelt, Swope could easily have felt that he had seen the doom of an older generation of politicians, although he knew that, as far as Roosevelt was concerned, if you endorsed him, you could say patatah while he said potato—you could even say Rusevelt while he said Rosevelt.

By the time they returned to New York, Robert Moses, Swope and Mrs. Moskowitz had prevailed, and Smith had publicly denounced Walker's candidacy. Plans were made for Smith to blaze a trail through the Catholic heart of Southern New England, with Roosevelt following his path. The Democrats were worried about losing the Catholic vote. Disenchantment with the party had become widespread after Smith lost the nomination on religious grounds.

Swope was asked to accompany the former governor on the tour. He withdrew from a conflicting speaking engagement at a meeting of the Port Washington Chamber of Commerce. Considering the religious fence-mending that had to be done in New England, there was a vein of truth in his jocular message to the merchants, "Had to accompany Al Smith to Boston to do God's work."

Swope helped to write the speech Smith made in Boston, which was broadcast all over the New England states. He urged his listeners to vote for Roosevelt and said that there could be "no room for bitterness in Catholic hearts."

F. Raymond Daniell, a reporter for the *New York Times,* asked Swope for his opinion of the speech; with some degree of private self-congratulation, he replied, "No man in America could have made such a speech as that of last night, except Al Smith. The complete disinterestedness and extraordinary candor he brings into politics make him the only man who could have put into words what everyone was thinking about the religious issue."

Swope was also asked to write the speech Roosevelt would be making at a giant rally at the Mineola Fair Grounds in Nassau County, Long Island, on November 5. Swope was invited to ride along with Roosevelt that night in the motorcade that swept through the Bronx and across into Queens on its way to Nassau. In those days the Triborough Bridge had not yet been constructed, and one crossed from the Bronx to Long Island by ferry.

Throughout the trip, the Roosevelt magnetism was as irresistible to the group in his automobile as it was to the crowds lining the pavements; Swope quite understandably felt considerable boyish enthusiasm for his new hero. When the car rolled off the East River Ferry at College Point, a group of children attracted by the sirens raced toward it screaming: "A wedding! A wedding!"

"That's right," shouted Swope. Pointing at Roosevelt, he said, "He's the groom, and he's going to marry Miss Prosperity!"

To Roosevelt's chagrin, Smith's greeting to him had caught the public's fancy—everywhere either of them appeared, there were chants of "Old potato!"

It was evident that Swope had more than proved his worth to the candidate. The *Daily Mirror* carried a three-column photograph of Smith and Roosevelt shaking hands, with Swope looking on like a proud papa. The *Evening Journal* lent credence by publication to a rumor that would become a recurring one throughout the Roosevelt administration: "Long-shot bettors at James A. Farley's Democratic National headquarters here will tell you it's a deep secret that the very tall, distinguished-looking Herbert Bayard Swope, former managing [*sic*] editor of the defunct New York *World,* next March will be an ambassador at an important capital."

SIXTEEN

The Democratic party won a resounding victory at almost all levels. There followed a period of quiescence and rumor before the new administration took office after the beginning of the new year. During the interregnum, Swope served as chairman of a committee sponsoring Al Smith's plans for a revision of the city charter, which would effectively wipe out the corrupt hold of the Tammany political machine. With Roosevelt's support, the changes were enacted, and New York City could look forward to an era of relatively clean government.

In a lighter vein, Swope lent his name and support to the dramatic efforts of two old friends. His former music critic, Samuel Chotzinoff, collaborated with George Backer on a comedy titled *Honeymoon*. It opened to a very tepid critical reception, and in desperation the writers called on Swope for a quote to use in the show's advertisements. He obligingly allowed them to print the wire he'd sent the day after the show opened. From then on, over the show's title in the theatrical pages, there ran this salutation:

> HONEYMOON IS A DAMNED GOOD PIECE OF WORK. IT HAS INTEREST,
> SINCERITY, AND REAL ENTERTAINMENT. CONGRATULATIONS.
> HERBERT BAYARD SWOPE

Despite his enthusiasm, the play managed to limp along for only seventy-three performances at the aptly named Little Theatre.

On New Year's Day 1933, Smith and Swope left for Albany to attend Governor Lehman's inauguration, which would take place on the following day. That evening, Swope called on both Lehman and President-elect Roosevelt. There was general talk of Swope's service in the new administration, but mostly there was the Roosevelt charm, so encompassing that Swope left with a feeling of achievement, although nothing had been offered beyond a few drinks and a dazzling personality. It was not unlike an occasion when Heywood Broun and Morris Ernst went to see the president to solicit his help in the formation of the American Newspaper Guild. When they left, Broun was euphoric, and Ernst asked what he was so happy about. Broun replied that the president had agreed with everything he'd proposed. Ernst asked, "What gave you that idea? All he did was smile."

Just before the inauguration got started, Smith received word that Belle Moskowitz had died. He managed to get through the ceremony and then made plans to return immediately to New York. Swope canceled an invitation to attend Lehman's reception in order to accompany him. John Curry, the Tammany boss whom Smith had opposed, placed his private railroad car at their disposal. Swope remained with the bereaved governor through dinner and a condolence call on Dr. Moskowitz. The funeral was postponed until the fourth, to give Governor Lehman and Mrs. Roosevelt an opportunity to attend.

Smith was a shattered man. He was never again to regain that special liberal perspective that was the result of Mrs. Moskowitz's influence on him. As he drifted further and further to the right, his friendship with Swope gradually diminished.

At the beginning of February, Governor Lehman appointed Swope to the New York State arm of the Reconstruction Finance Corporation, under the chairmanship of Robert Moses. RFC's purpose was to cut through red tape and accelerate the setting up of work projects to alleviate unemployment in the state.

The state appointment did not remove Swope from consideration for the foreign-service appointment. On February 16, the influential German newspaper the *Berliner Tageblatt* stated, "The new appointment of Herbert Bayard Swope as American Ambassador to Berlin is now spoken of as certain in Democratic circles close to the United States Senate."

Swope was hoping that Roosevelt would come up with something else for him. He was lukewarm about the foreign service and would have much preferred something in the cabinet. There were many reasons why he viewed the Berlin post as an unsatisfactory one. He actually could not afford to leave the country for any length of time. To maintain his standard of living, it was necessary that he attend to his business affairs in the states. In addition, the German branch of his family had been keeping him informed of what was happening in that country, and their information indicated that the position would present almost insurmountable personal obstacles. Beyond that, his wife did not want him to accept. She saw no reason for them to give up their extremely pleasant life for a tedious existence in a city she had never liked.

The Reichstag fire on February 27 confirmed his suspicions about the impossibility of his doing an adequate job. Still, he did not withdraw his name from consideration, for fear that it might discourage Roosevelt from considering him for other things. He knew that the president would be briefed on conditions and would himself realize the unsuitability of the appointment. In the meantime, Swope would simply keep all options open.

The inauguration was set for March 4. Swope had Miss Millar paste all of his invitations to the important functions in his scrapbook and then did the most astonishing thing: he left for a vacation in Palm Beach without stopping off at the capital, which, after all, was not out of his way. It was totally uncharacteristic of him deliberately to stay away from such a momentous event, especially one at which he could justly expect to be treated with honor. It was the first of a series of paradoxical decisions he would make throughout the rest of his life. It would be impossible to tell what it was that motivated his more erratic actions—whether it was Margaret's negative attitude toward all pursuits that might alter the order of things, or his own disappointment with Roosevelt, or a post-fifty feeling that time was running out and one might as well opt for small pleasures in the remaining years, or a combination of all these elements. The poker face was turned to life as well as to cards. To all he was simply Swope, unchanged and unchanging, an energetic constant who accepted his seemingly enviable lot without question.

The doubts that he was feeling about Roosevelt were not made evident in his attitude at that time. He wrote to Roosevelt from Palm Beach before the inauguration. After beginning his letter "Dear Frank," he explained, "This is the last time I shall give myself the pleasure of calling you Frank. I do so to please myself (as Al says, there is always a kick in calling the big boss by his first name), and because this is so purely a personal tribute."

Roosevelt, his equal at playing games, replied, "That is one of the nicest letters I have ever received and will be tucked away with my treasures." He went on to say, "I count on you for advice. Do let us know when you are in Washington."

Swope's presence at the inauguration was something even his close friends took for granted. In a poem for the *Saturday Review* entitled "Inauguration Parade," Robert E. Sherwood wrote:

> Another cheer from the crowded stand
> For Oklahoma's Indian Band;
> For Senators McAdoo, Walsh, and Norris,
> Mayor O'Brien, quoting Horace;
> Governors Ritchie, Lehman, Cross;
> Sauce for the gander, apple sauce
> For all the limping ducks that pass;
> Governor Ely, Carter Glass;
> Huey Long with galloping tongue;
> Owen D. and Tammany Young;
> Admiral Grayson, Major Domo;
> Walter Lippman, sapient homo;
> Bishop Cannon, the Methodist Pope;
> Bernard Baruch and Herbert Swope. . . .

By mid-March, the Berlin post had definitely been offered to James M. Cox, and Swope was being considered for Governor General of the Philippines. When Cox refused Germany, Swope was back in the race. It did not matter to him one way or the other, for something else had come up. The *Washington Post* was for sale. He could not afford to buy it alone, and his activities centered upon finding backers, with the same zeal he had used in trying to buy the *World*. But it was a different administration, and all those who had offered to help previously had such high hopes of positions in Washington that a newspaper seemed superfluous. The banker Eugene Meyer beat him out on the purchase and later wrote to him with equanimity, "I am beginning to appreciate how much I have to learn about the newspaper business. . . . I still hope that someday you will talk to me about newspapers as well as banking and politics."

On March 6, Roosevelt took the country off the gold standard. This had a heartening effect on the American economy, although Europe viewed the action with alarm. The Europeans wanted a stabilized world currency, based on gold and a sound dollar, while Roosevelt felt that the way to cure the American depression was artificially to induce inflation. By June the signs of recovery seemed to be bearing out his policy, and he wanted to be left alone to develop it to its ultimate. Unfortunately from his point of view, he was saddled with a commitment made by his predecessor, Herbert Hoover, to a World Economic Conference.

In the area of finance, Roosevelt had what Arthur Schlesinger, Jr., later called "a casualness of mind" that frustrated many of his advisers. It was in this sphere that Hoover proved the internationalist and Roosevelt the provincial. The former believed that the source of the American depression was in Europe and that without full European recovery there could be no sound American recovery. For this reason, he had been one of the sponsors of the Economic Conference in London. The specific problems to be investigated included currency stabilization, the war debt, trade barriers, and international exchange. Roosevelt obviously viewed the whole thing as an onerous legacy that somehow had to be seen through before he could return to his own concerns. Unfortunately he gave no inkling of this either to the Europeans or to the large delegation, headed by Secretary of State Cordell Hull, that he sent abroad. He was so vague in his instructions to his own people that they were fighting among themselves over exactly what their objectives were.

Hull was certain of only one point: Roosevelt was completely against the stabilization of gold. The Europeans felt that most of the other problems could be solved by stabilization. Without it, there was no reason to discuss anything else. The conference was hopelessly deadlocked. The desperate requests for enlightenment that were constantly being sent back to Washington frequently went unanswered for days on end while Roosevelt was off cruising on his yacht. The president was as often criticized for being at sea as Swope was for being at the race track.

It did not take long for the resentment of the American delegation to find sympathetic ears in the press. Walter Lippman, by then ensconced on the *Herald Tribune* version of Swope's Op Ed page, wrote from London:

> Mr. Roosevelt cannot have understood how completely unequipped are his representatives here to deal with the kind of project he has in mind. For one thing, they do not know what is in his mind. For another, there is not among them a single man who understands monetary questions sufficiently to debate them. For another, they have been so frequently repudiated that they are demoralized.

Roosevelt could no longer ignore the situation. Unlike Hull, Assistant Secretary of State Raymond Moley was well versed in international economic realities; the president decided to send him abroad to straighten out the mess. While he was gone, Baruch would unofficially take over his duties at the State Department.

Moley said that he would need an assistant who was familiar with the economic situation, who was skilled in the ways of political by-play, and who could handle the press in a way that would secure favorable comment. Baruch immediately suggested Swope for the job.

Roosevelt was delighted. He had recently appointed the historian William E. Dodd to the Berlin post and still had an outstanding obligation to Swope. This would settle it.

Actually, Swope had disqualified himself for any service in Germany the month before. Fifteen leading Jewish scholars, driven from their positions in Germany by Hitler, had decided to form a "University in Exile." Dr. Alvin Johnson of the New School for Social Research in New York had invited them to use his facilities. Swope was asked by Dr. Johnson to become one of the sponsors, along with retired Justice Oliver Wendell Holmes, Professors John Dewey and Felix Frankfurter, and Connecticut Governor Wilbur Cross. He accepted. Protecting Nazi victims seemed a more worthwhile endeavor to Swope than partying with Nazi officials.

On June 14, Moley and Baruch broached the subject to Swope, who seemed amenable but wanted official notification from Roosevelt for several reasons: without it, he would only be an observer, with no real functions; he was not yet totally sure of Roosevelt's regard for him; and he was damned if he'd travel at his own expense and without a diplomatic passport. On June 16, he received a wire from Roosevelt:

WOULD BE DELIGHTED IF YOU COULD ACCOMPANY RAYMOND MOLEY FOR SHORT VISIT TO LONDON. I AM SENDING HIM SOON AND FEEL YOUR PRESENCE WOULD BE EXCEEDINGLY HELPFUL TO HIM IN MANY WAYS. I SHOULD BE PERSONALLY GRATEFUL TO HAVE YOU DO THIS, HAVING CONFIDENCE AS I DO IN YOUR JUDGMENT AND YOUR WIDE KNOWLEDGE OF INTERNATIONAL AFFAIRS. YOU WOULD BE ABSENT FROM THIS COUNTRY ONLY ABOUT A MONTH.

On June 19, Swope was in Washington for a briefing on objectives with Baruch, Moley, and Roosevelt. The discussion lasted for well over five hours, and the two emissaries departed convinced that they knew Roosevelt's thoughts on the matter. They were to prove sadly mistaken.

Swope started to mend public relations by lunching on June 20 with Arthur Hays Sulzberger of the *Times*. He spent the rest of the day in meetings with Baruch and various leaders of the financial community, including some associates of J. P. Morgan, who—astonishingly—agreed with Roosevelt on the subject of going off the gold standard. He prepared a memo based on his findings for Moley to transmit to Roosevelt. This report, which was meant as a weapon against the country's "sound money" interests, gave convincing arguments against the stabilization of all currencies. Swope never thought it would be made public. In his diary, he headed that busy day "Grievance Day—Tax Assessment." The real grief that was to come of that day's activities stemmed from another source.

Before setting sail with Moley on the S.S. *Manhattan* on June 21, he described his function at the conference as that of "an assistant to an errand boy." His teenaged son was along on the trip to act as unofficial assistant to the assistant.

There were immediate problems within the delegation. Without properly preparing either gentleman, Roosevelt had sent Moley, Hull's assistant, to act as his superior. The only thing upon which everybody agreed was that some sort of statement had to be made that would allow the conference to end without complete loss of face for all of the ministers. Swope enlisted Lippmann to help draft it, and Moley opted for one of the few Englishmen who concurred with Roosevelt's policy, the English economist John Maynard Keynes, whose theories of cheap money and deficit spending were to gain wide acceptance in the capitalist world during the next decades.

The four drafted an innocuous document that accepted the European request for stabilization but did not commit the United States to it. They proudly sent it off to Roosevelt for his approval. To everybody's complete amazement, Roosevelt utterly misunderstood the purpose of the draft. He rejected it out of hand and, in the words of Moley, "torpedoed" the conference with what was called his "bombshell" message. That missive was largely based on Swope's "Grievance Day" memo, which had been written for use in the very different context of domestic politics, against Roosevelt's adversaries at home and not his allies abroad.

Swope later noted, "The only outcome of the mission was a bitter feud between Moley and Secretary Hull, which finally ended in Moley's withdrawal from Washington." There were those who thought Roosevelt's action had far greater consequences, for it also destroyed the

World Disarmament Conference, which had been going on simultaneously in Geneva. Broadus Mitchell commented in his book *The Depression Decade:*

> The decision was probably the most momentous one that Franklin
> Roosevelt made. One may speculate, with cause, whether in defeat-
> ing the world's resolution to stabilize currencies and thereby promote
> trade, President Roosevelt did not contribute heavily to the interna-
> tional economic and political deterioration that led to fresh war. . . .
> Infatuated with the prospect of rising prices at home, did he hastily
> condemn others to frustration, discord, and the appeal to arms? There
> was a lighthearted suddenness in his behavior, which spoke of igno-
> rance or certainly of the little knowledge which is a dangerous thing.

The cataclysmic event that finally lifted this country out of all rem-
nants of a depression was the war, which may have had its roots in the
events of 1933. Nevertheless, Roosevelt used the rest of that decade to
perform the herculean feat of taking control of this country's finances
away from the private few and placing it in the hands of the government,
which, after all, was where it belonged. He preserved capitalism neither
for the mighty minority of financiers nor the disenfranchised minority of
paupers, but for the middle class, in whose hearts he remained deified
forever after. Baruch was wrong when he dismissed Roosevelt's mone-
tary measures as strictly for "a small proportion of the population, the
unemployed, the debtor class—incompetent, unwise people." But the
patrician Baruch was often wrong when his words were not modified by
the interpolations of a Swope.

As for Swope, he told Moley after they returned from London, "You
are one writ with me in sour misfortune's book."

Yet Swope had done a masterful job of presenting his president's
views, and Moley, to the British. Roosevelt's torpedo ended the conference, but neither Moley nor Swope was held responsible.

Some years later, Moley wrote a book about his FDR days, and the
president is alleged to have said: "He's the sort who kisses ass and tells."
His more polite remark, however, was that Moley "bit the hand which
fed him."

Perhaps Margaret was right after all about government assignments:
What did he want to do that for?

Swope made up his mind that he would keep his distance from
Roosevelt. The charm was too much for him; he could not trust himself
to deal with it. It would take a war to make him available for another job

in the Roosevelt government. Seldom did he accede to Roosevelt's importunities that he come down and spend time with him in Washington, but whenever he did, he found himself ensnared by that captivating presence. After one such visit, he informed Lippmann that

> F.D.R.'s charm continues unabated. His ability to make his visitor believe that he alone is essential to the presidential happiness continues. His new-found ability and decisiveness have come to him without corresponding development in character, which must broaden and become more disciplined for the proper control of the qualities he possesses. He is an expedientist but, of course, that is characteristic of every politician. He is sadistic, which probably is a corollary of his physical condition. That attribute makes him the more willing to have around him those who are apt to make mistakes. As between second-rate men, whom he dominates, and the first-rate man who shines independently of him, he is for the lesser type every time.

Consciously or unconsciously, Swope was surely thinking of himself. His thoughts about Roosevelt were scored to a threnody of what could have or should have been—and was not. Roosevelt owed him something, a debt he had incurred long before Swope served in the '32 campaign. Swope had been a sponsor of Roosevelt's career in national politics years before the appearance of Louis Howe, who did not trust Swope, or Farley, who did. He would gladly have submitted to the overwhelming presence, had there been any chance of repayment on a level he considered commensurate with his services and ability. It was simply not enough—in fact, it would actually have been demeaning—to become, as Woollcott had become, "a star boarder at the White House too often called upon to sing for his supper." The Swope arias were reserved for his own house, where he selected the audiences and did not have to share top billing even with a president.

In 1933 there was a three-way race for mayor of New York City. John P. O'Brien was the Democratic nominee, unsupported by Smith, Farley, Swope, and Roosevelt, all of whom came out for Joseph McKee, running on what was called the Recovery party ticket, another name for the New Deal. Another label was also found for the Republican party, which backed Fiorello LaGuardia on the Fusion party ticket.

Swope acted as treasurer of McKee's executive committee. At dinner one night, he upset Bea Kaufman by brandishing a bunch of contribution checks. She was pro-LaGuardia, and he said, "Let's see you do as well for your man."

She reported the incident to Woollcott, who was also for LaGuardia. He said, "Don't you worry, dearie. I'll fix his wagon."

The next day, Woollcott was making a campaign speech at a luncheon party at Town Hall. In the course of it, he said:

> It's too bad, really, that the *World* is not being published now, for I am sure that it would be for Mr. LaGuardia. At least everybody on the *World* at that time is for Mr. LaGuardia now—except Mr. Herbert Bayard Swope. Walter Lippmann, the chief editorial writer of the *World,* who is now the chief editorial writer of the world, is for LaGuardia. Heywood Broun is for LaGuardia. F.P.A. is for LaGuardia. In fact, about the only exception is Mr. Herbert Bayard Swope. Well, as you may know, Mr. Swope was Executive Editor of the *World* in the period before its finish.

He paused just long enough for the listeners to get the implication that Swope was somehow responsible for the paper's demise. He then went on, "It is with particular interest that I watch his connection with this campaign."

Bea Kaufman was shocked that Woollcott had gone that far, as were all of the other gentlemen mentioned in the speech. As for Swope, he was so deeply hurt by the implied falsehood that it was years before he could forgive Woollcott. It was the end of a friendship that had been strained ever since Woollcott himself had deserted the *World.* The critic wrote some conciliatory letters, but to no avail. He had touched on the one area of Swope's life in which he took genuine pride, his record on the *World,* and there could be no return to the way things had been.

The differences between the two men, whom some have mistakenly likened to each other, can be measured in the light of subsequent events. Swope never asked anybody to take sides. Even his son was allowed to remain on good terms with Woollcott without any recriminations. When they met on neutral territory, such as at Thanksgiving parties at the home of Ave Harriman, Swope was unfailingly courteous. Conversely, Woollcott's malicious gibes grew increasingly bitter, until common friends began to accuse him of being a bore with his constant "Swope-swiping."

Margaret Swope was not so forgiving. Not only did she stop speaking to Woollcott, but she refused to have anything to do with Bea Kaufman, who had been one of her best friends. It was Swope who finally brought about a reconciliation by telling his wife how unreasonable she was being. He said, "You can't blame Bea. Woollcott was only using her, the way he uses everybody."

In the McKee campaign, Swope gave an interview that would gladden the heart of any feminist. He recommended a woman mayor as

> . . . one way to curb extravagance in City Hall and guarantee that New Yorkers would get more for their money from the big town's executives. Why not a woman mayor? I wouldn't be afraid of having a woman for President. I don't swallow all the psychologists have to say, when they argue that women are more subjective than men and more inclined to emotionalize a situation than to rationalize it. Emotionalizing a situation is not exclusively a feminine prerogative. To have a good cry about something is not any more emotional than to get drunk.
>
> Even in these days of adjustment and of vast experiments in which we are all participating without being sure about the outcome, I believe women would have as much elasticity as men.
>
> In one characteristic that is valuable in an executive the average woman is way ahead of the average man. That is in her unblushing search for the truth. A woman will dare to say, "I don't know. Tell me about it." But where is the man who does not pretend to know more than he really does know? I think, too, that the average woman is quicker on the uptake than the average man. . . .

Commenting on the charge that women talk too much to be good executives, he said, "I never have met a woman who talks as much as I do."

Despite the fact that the Democratic ticket was split and the LaGuardia forces had dug up spurious anti-Semitic stories about McKee that endangered the Jewish vote, there was a good chance that Swope's man would win if Roosevelt would come out with a strong statement in his favor. The result was summed up by Jim Farley: "The President came through with too little and too late."

In that year, recognition of Russia was imminent. The press again began to circulate rumors of an ambassadorial appointment for Swope. It was as if they, too, could not believe that he would go unrewarded. This time, Swope laughed it off. He said, "Anywhere I was sent, we'd be at war in two weeks if I took Maggie along."

In 1934 Walter Wanger contracted to produce a screenplay by Ben Hecht and Charles MacArthur entitled *The President Vanishes*. The writers had the bright idea of testing Swope for the role of the president, and Wanger went along with it, if for no better reason than the publicity value. To Maggie's horror, Swope agreed to take the test. She called MacArthur and said, "If Herb gets that part, you can do a Western as a sequel. Me Indian. You white man. You get scalped!"

The test was actually an elaborate gag dreamed up by the writers, who were notorious practical jokers. Swope was to deliver a speech extolling the virtues of women, while unbeknownst to him a chorus girl was slowly stripping behind him. To the hilarious delight of the crew, they did thirty takes before he finally caught on. When questioned by the waiting press, he merely said that the test was "not bad," adding, "Other newspapermen have become actors, of course. Heywood Broun became an actor. He was terrible. Alexander Woollcott also became an actor. *He* said he was very good. I'm told William Shakespeare was an actor, too, although I don't recall having seen him."

When Wanger was asked whether the actor had blushed during the test, he replied, "I don't know. It wasn't a color picture."

When the film was finally made—without Swope—its only memorable feature was a good performance by an unknown ingénue named Rosalind Russell, who went on to better things.

Swope's interest in films continued until 1936, when he resigned from the Board of Directors of RKO. Nick Schenck of Loews and Harry Warner had wanted him to resign the year before and replace Will Hays as head of the Motion Picture Producers and Distributors Association, the industry's self-regulating ethics and censorship organization, but Hays refused to be pressured into quitting. Swope did make a visit to the West Coast in 1935, during which he gave a party for the former staff members of the *World* who had found new careers in films. The *Hollywood Reporter* commented:

> The list of graduates of that grand old paper forms today's Hollywood's Who's Who. Dudley Nichols, Abe Jacoby, Norman Krasna, Louis Weitzenkorn, Joseph Jefferson O'Neill, James Cain, Quinn Martin, Wells Root, John Balderston, Patterson MacNutt, Herman Mankiewicz, Morrie Ryskind, Oliver Garrett, Finley Peter Dunne, Jr., Jim McCarthy, Winnie Sheehan, James Gow, Harlan Thompson, Sylvia Lewis, Billie Taussig, and Gertrude Linahan will be Mr. Swope's guests of honor.

They were among the leading screenwriters and studio executives of the day. He listened to them extol the virtues of life in Hollywood. The more they spoke, the more convinced he became that the West Coast was not for him. The hours, the preoccupations, the style, all were at odds with his pleasures and interests. He turned his back on a career in pictures with a comment written to Florence White: "I don't like this thing too well. It's more of a racket than a vocation."

Joseph Kennedy, among others, was directly responsible for his going into public relations as a full-time occupation. Baruch and Swope had been responsible for getting Roosevelt to appoint Kennedy to the chairmanship of the Securities Exchange Commission. Through the years of their close friendship, Swope had guided and advised him, until Kennedy finally reached the position of trust with the president that all of his massive campaign contributions hitherto had been unable to secure.

One of Kennedy's very lucrative ventures was the Somerset distilleries, which were in the business of importing Scotch rather than actually doing the distilling. He offered to take Swope in for an investment of $150,000, the kind of money Swope could lose without thinking twice in a few days of bad luck at the track and cards. Margaret listened with delight as Kennedy outlined his plans for the company. It was obvious that the investment would bring a return of millions. To her absolute horror, her husband pulled one of those mystifying reversals. His back stiffened, and he turned the offer down, on the grounds that he had already given Kennedy more than that amount of free counsel and help; the least he could expect as compensation was to be taken into the business without any cost to him.

After Kennedy departed, Margaret flew into a rage. "If you get so God damned high-handed about giving your advice for nothing, then you ought to start charging for it."

That was exactly what he did. He moved his office into the Squibb Building, at 745 Fifth Avenue, and became what he always called "a publicist." Swope was not one of those public-relations experts who sent out releases or arranged stunts and interviews. He was involved in public *policy:* a company's strategy.

He was his own main asset—his contacts and the people he knew— and so there was no need for a large staff. He could wheel and deal with some of the most important men and companies in the country with no more than a telephone, an assistant, and the ever-faithful secretary, Miss Millar.

The relationship with Kennedy did not end abruptly. Casualness replaced intimacy, and they coasted along at an amiable distance with sufficient points of contact to maintain an acquaintanceship if not a friendship until it all ended irrevocably at the outbreak of World War II.

Kennedy had been appointed ambassador to England in 1937. From the beginning, Swope had not approved of the appointment. He did not believe that it was ethical that a man whose fortune was largely based upon trade with a country (importing large quantities of whisky) should represent his own country there. However, Kennedy had been exceedingly generous during the '36 presidential campaign, and the London post was his choice of reward. It must be added that he wanted this assignment to improve his social position as much as, if not more than, to improve business.

With Swope's help, he had, after years of effort, scaled the essentially gelatinous wall of Palm Beach society. Swope had been among the original members of two of the resort's swankest clubs, The Seminole and The Bath and Tennis. He had resigned from both in the mid-thirties, when their attitude toward minorities became a less intense version of what Hitler was promoting in Germany: they did not want to destroy Jews; they only wanted to pretend they did not exist. "The B & T," as it is quaintly called in "PB," circulated a letter requesting members "to refrain from introducing any guest who is not of the Christian faith."

In resigning, Swope asked, "What would happen if I were to bring my friend the Chinese ambassador to the club?"

Kennedy was a newer member of these clubs than Swope, and he took longer to resign. None of the Kennedys severed relationships until 1960, when it would have proved embarrassing for the family of a presidential candidate to belong to a segregated club. At that point, they began to play golf at the Palm Beach Country Club, known as the "Jewish Club" in PB. Some admired this action. Others simply observed that the Jews had the best golf course in town. Beyond that, the Kennedys were not getting any younger, and the first tee was conveniently across the road from their front door. There were those who might have argued that, in a sense, they still belonged to a segregated club.

At first, Kennedy did improve his social image in England. One of his daughters, Kathleen, even married into the peerage, thereby becoming the Marchioness of Hartington and a daughter-in-law of the Duke of Devonshire. "Kick" was her nickname, and the English adored her, which was more than could be said of their feelings for her father. In a letter from Susan Mary Alsop to Marietta Tree, an English lady was quoted as observing, "Kick is the sensitive Kennedy—I've known them all."

Swope had summed up his own feeling somewhat earlier in a letter to Hugh Wilson, the American ambassador to Germany, congratulating him on a speech he had made which managed to be critical of Hitler's policies without causing international incident: "It is somewhat better, I think, for an Ambassador's efforts to be directed to such subjects as these than to be publicly identified with debutantes and silk knee breeches."

Even had their friendship retained its closeness through the last years of the thirties, the start of World War II would have put a severe strain on it. Swope was ardently anti-Nazi and hoped that the United States would do everything in its power to help the Allied cause. The feeling was intensified after his old friend Winston Churchill became prime minister in May 1940. Kennedy doubted the strength of the British and wanted Roosevelt to intervene in only one way, and that was to make a peace which would leave Hitler securely in power both in Germany and in those countries already conquered. Hitler seemed a necessary evil to Kennedy. The alternative would be a Europe dominated by the Communists, which he found far more intolerable than one dominated by Nazis. It was an attitude that led to the accusation that he was pro-German. Despite his initial popularity, the war made him the most unpopular ambassador this country ever sent to England.

One of Swope's first clients as a professional public-policy consultant was, like Kennedy, in the whisky business. Except for a certain ruthlessness, the similarity ended there between the head of Schenley Industries, Lewis S. Rosenstiel, and the Harvard-educated ambassador. From the beginning, Swope was extremely valuable on a corporate level, but making Rosenstiel socially acceptable was a job that would fitfully occupy Swope for the rest of his life, and one at which he would be largely unsuccessful.

Swope persuaded him to buy a string of horses, which generally makes for automatic acceptance in the sporty set of society. All was going well until Rosenstiel attempted to register a horse under the name of one of his most successful products, Three Feathers. The Jockey Club demurred on the ground that it was a trifle too commercial. One wonders whether the problem was the man's product, his personality, or his methods of persuasion. Some years earlier, the same Jockey Club had approved the names Mars Bars and Forever Yours for two thoroughbreds belonging to Mrs. Ethel V. Mars, whose stable was, not too subtly, named Milky Way Farm. Perhaps the Jockey Club was more familiar with the name of a rye than with those of candy bars.

Rosenstiel's relationships with some of his wives were the kind to delight the gossip press. Until shortly before his death, he was engaged in a seesaw, salacious court battle with one of these mates that created headlines which alternately cast him as a villain and a fool. Their advocates were those masters of the news-making court case, Louis Nizer and Roy Cohn.

Another newsworthy wife was Lee Cohn, the niece of Harry Cohn who it was rumored had cheated her father out of his share in Columbia Pictures. Ms. Cohn had a remarkable marital history. Her first husband was a Las Vegas hotelier and gambler named Kattleman. Her second, Rosenstiel, tough and domineering, was a type not dissimilar from her uncle in those respects. Her third, Walter Annenberg, became American ambassador to England, and she earned the respect and affection of the British when she turned the Embassy into one of the most gracious residences in London. Annenberg's father had founded the *Racing Form* and, at one point, came very close to going into business with Swope as co-owner of the *Morning Telegraph*.

Baruch was another early client, but the formal arrangement lasted for only a few years. Swope's unofficial services to Baruch lasted for his lifetime. It often seemed that Swope was intent upon making of Baruch the man he would have liked to be himself. Margaret Swope once observed that her husband played Pygmalion to Baruch's Galatea. That was only partially true; the roles kept reversing. There was never an important moment in either's life when the other was not called upon for advice.

It was unfortunate that after their first dealings Baruch could never again bring himself to pay Swope for his considerable services. There were many reasons for this, the kindest being that he did not want an employer-employee relationship with his closest friend, the unkindest being that he could not admit that he might need professional help to get recognition. Payment came in the form of inside market tips and, occasionally, stock deals in which Swope would be included.

This worked out badly for Swope, for it allowed people to speculate on the nature of his feelings for Baruch, which some felt were predicated on self-interest. Baruch himself contributed to a tarnishing of Swope's name when, after the latter's death, he allowed it to be tacitly understood that he had carried Swope financially for years. The truth was that had Swope's services been tallied in dollars, it would have become apparent that Baruch was getting a bargain. It might even be said that Swope carried him for years in terms of enhancing his repute.

Of all the positions that Swope held in the thirties, the one he most enjoyed was his appointment in 1934 to the unsalaried position of head of the New York Racing Commission. During his tenure he supervised the easy transfer of track control from the privileged members of the Jockey Club to the public. Serving with him on the commission were the race track architect, John Sloan, and the Jockey Club's own Jock Whitney. Stragely enough, opposition to his democratizing the sport came not from Whitney but from Sloan, who resented what he considered Swope's high-handed way of pushing through reforms, often without stopping for consultation.

Whitney was the youngest member both of the Jockey Club and of the commission. Because he had come of age during a period in which the privileged were becoming less privileged (in their own eyes, they were becoming more *under*privileged each time they were divested of what they considered theirs by divine right), Whitney perceived that Swope was right in his insistence that the only hope for the future of racing was to make it the sport of the common man.

Betting at the track was legalized at about the time that Swope took office. He was an early supporter of the installation of parimutuel machines, claiming from the beginning that they would bring millions in revenue to the state. Mayor LaGuardia was among those opposed to it, but the machines were legalized by public referendum in 1939. The vote for them was overwhelming, a majority of more than 2 to 1.

While Swope was serving as racing commissioner, his civic-minded older brother Gerard was chairman of the New York City Housing Authority. The very day the first parimutuel machine was put in at Jamaica found Mayor LaGuardia laying the cornerstone for a housing project in another part of the area. Without using names, he compared the accomplishments of the two brothers:

> There are two public events in Jamaica today. This is one. The other is at the race track, where the state for the first time is taking an ante from gamblers. This is promise; the other is regret. This is giving something to the people; the other is taking something from the people that they can't afford to lose. I don't believe that the people should be encouraged to spend money needed for food, clothing, and housing. I don't think that gambling is going to be successful in a progressive, enlightened state like New York.

The prudish mayor proved as shortsighted as he was fatuous. A statement that Swope made in another context might serve as reply:

"Certain politicians think that they can get right with God by opposing what they think is sin. But betting is not sin. Mass betting is merely an extension of degree, not a new invention. However, hypocrisy is a dearly loved American virtue."

In relation to the brothers' respective fields of public service at that point in their lives, an observation might be added parenthetically that in no way invalidates the nobler activity of Gerard, but does tend to mitigate aspersions against Herbert. There have been periodic scandals in public housing involving substandard building, bribery, large-scale pilfering, and union corruption, not only during Gerard's administration but ever after. Dating from Swope's ascension to the Racing Commission, there have been almost no instances of corruption at the New York tracks.

Swope was a bettor, a big bettor; he did not stop betting while on the commission, which was the source of a great deal of criticism. It was true that he was in a favored position as far as getting tips on horses was concerned, but the tips were not always good. At the end of a lifetime of betting, he observed, "I think I've just about broken even. It's taken years. But I've had a hell of a lot of fun doing it."

His joy in gambling was both intense and innocent. When concern about his financial condition made him curtail the amounts he bet, his wife grieved for him. She knew that he enjoyed the dangerous thrill of the high stakes more than the thrill of winning, and she cried, "For God's sake, Herb, if you're going to bet, bet high. Cancel the life insurance if you have to. I don't care if we end in the gutter. I can't stand the thought of you placing a five-dollar bet. Not you."

Swope was an early supporter of all forms of legalized gambling. He thought that bookies should be allowed to operate both on and off the track, as they did in England. If they could give better odds than the machines, there was nothing wrong with that; it was free competition, and the bettors got the benefit of it. The important point, to his way of thinking, was that bookmaking should be taken away from organized crime. It should be licensed by law, with books open to inspection, so that the government could receive the same share of the revenue that it got from track betting. And that share was formidable. The hundreds of millions the state has made at the track since Swope's day have built a great many more hospitals, housing projects, and schools than were ever envisioned by the Little Flower's housing authority.

Swope claimed that the greatest force opposing off-track betting was a political group whose motives were sadly suspect. It took over thirty years for the state to come abreast of his opinion, and it was not until after his death that off-track betting was legalized, in another smashing public referendum. His son was one of the early officials of OTB. One of his duties was to attempt to set up closed-circuit telecasts of races. The public would pay admission, as it does at the track, and there would be betting windows set up by OTB. This has not yet come to pass in New York because of opposition from track officials who are afraid it would cut into their gate, although a similar operation is legal in Connecticut, a state with no tracks.

For all Swope's affection for gambling and gamblers, it was during his tenure that innovations at the race tracks made it very nearly impossible for even the most unscrupulous among them to fix races. Horses were given urine and saliva tests to make certain that they had not been doped. Electric-eye cameras were installed so that the results of close finishes could be determined without the physical handicap or self-interest that might becloud the human eye. Judges had to submit to eye tests and jockeys to physical examinations. Electric gates assured a fair start to every race. In short, his commission eliminated the traditional ways of tampering with the fair running of track events.

So praiseworthy was Swope's work at the New York tracks that a movement was started at the beginning of the war to create a national racing authority, with him at its head, to supervise all of the country's tracks. Gas rationing, the inability to secure railroad space for the transportation of the horses, and manpower shortages forced track after track to close, thus putting an end to the project.

During the war, the National Association of State Racing Commissioners decided to hold a series of special races at tracks around the country in order to raise money for Army and Navy Relief. Swope was chairman of the executive committee, and they raised seventeen million dollars, proving his contention that the track provided a welcome release from the daily tensions of life during the crisis.

In 1942 the Republicans won the gubernatorial race, and Thomas E. Dewey was put in office. Normally, jobs like racing commissioner were doled out to party favorites as part of the spoils system. Swope was so effective in the position and so widely identified with it, however, that Dewey thought dispensing with him would be an unpopular move in racing circles, which were a very lucrative source of Republican party contributions. He did appoint two of the party faithful to serve with Swope, and those two had the power to veto many of his excellent ideas. By 1944 he was traveling to Washington several times a day in connection with more important work for the wartime government. It became obvious that keeping the tracks open was a losing cause. That, combined with the frustrations of sporadic combat with his fellow commissioners, brought about his resignation just days before all the tracks, in fact, were forced to close.

SEVENTEEN

In the early thirties, Swope held other important national and state jobs. Governor Lehman named him to serve under Robert Moses on the New York State Park Commission. He was also appointed to the executive council of the New York State arm of the NRA, eventually becoming its chairman. The National Recovery Act had set up state organizations to supervise the allocation of public funds for loans to private industries and to create public works that would relieve unemployment. It was in both capacities that he worked on the planning of the Northern State Parkway, the first of the major highways to link New York City with the more densely populated suburbs of Long Island. It was a project in which he took an almost paternal interest, as his summer home, Keewaydin, was situated in one of the spots that would be serviced by the road, and there were often enough weekend guests to cause a terrific traffic jam on the existing facility.

Some of his personal business was also of great benefit to the public. As a major stockholder in the BMT subway, he was among those who led the way through the maze of red tape blocking its transfer from private to city ownership. There was some movement to name him either police commissioner or head of public transportation at that time, but LaGuardia was not likely to name an old political foe to any commission in his administration.

None of this was sufficiently time-consuming to fill his days and nights, and so he seemed more than ever to be a gentleman of leisure.

> Must be the social climb
> That explains the behavior of all them poor dopes
> Spending money and time
> Entertaining the Whitneys, the Stewarts, the
> Swopes.

So went a bit of light verse popular in a certain sector of New York City. The social world toward which the "poor dopes" were climbing was Café Society, a '30s phenomenon that was an amalgam of renegades from old-guard society, Broadway, and Hollywood. The "in" group had the money, the time, and occasionally the wit to create amusement in a world lamentably short of that quality.

In December 1937, *Fortune* magazine ran an article entitled "The Yankee Doodle Salon" which it explained was "a blending of old socialites and new celebrities called Café Society. But it develops that its most honored members are those seen least frequently in the cafés." It was true that they entertained more at home than out, that their private parties were generally not in public places, but word of them still managed to find its way into the columns. One reason was that when a gala was a benefit, publicity was deemed necessary for the cause (and not incidentally for the largest contributors, who were usually outside the group but wanted identification with those inside—a form, one might surmise, of charity beginning in the newspaper at home). Another reason was the presence of so many theatrical personalities among the guests, all equipped with eager press agents. A third was that the Café Society *doyenne* of "in," Elsa Maxwell, who was the Earl Blackwell of her day, was also the greatest self-publicist of them all.

The metamorphosis of old Café Society into new Jet Set did not begin until 1954, when Mr. Blackwell decided to throw a huge party at the Venice Film Festival. Miss Maxwell was so furious at this poaching on her preserve that she decreed that any who attended it would not be welcome at her parties. Mr. Blackwell had the first of his many social successes. *Sic transit gloria mundi.*

When Café Society was just sweet sixteen, *Fortune* divided it into two groups: "These Are In" and "In and Out." The "ins" were headed by what *Fortune* termed the Regency Council, or the life-givers: in alphabetical order, Mrs. Vincent Astor, Mrs. Margaret Emerson, Miss Elsa Maxwell, Mr. Charles A. Munn, Mr. Condé Nast, Prince Serge Obolensky, Mrs. Charles Shipman Payson, Mr. and Mrs. William Rhinelander Stewart, Mr. and Mrs. Herbert Bayard Swope, Mrs. Harold E. Talbott, Mr. and Mrs. Cornelius Vanderbilt Whitney, Mr. and Mrs. John Hay Whitney, and Mrs. Harrison Williams.

Swope was playing again and doing it remarkably well, letting the fun and games occupy an increasingly large part of his compartmentalized existence. He needed something to absorb those extraordinary energies, and society was the nearest thing at hand.

From the advent of Roosevelt to the American entry into World War II, the Swopes were a social institution—indeed, a phenomenon. Swope's more serious gifts were not forgotten, but they seemed to be dormant, the only sleeping part of his roar through life in New York City and its environs. Stanley Walker, the city editor of the New York *Herald Tribune,* observed him in a 1938 piece for the *Saturday Evening Post* titled "Symphony in Brass":

> More than once, men—that is to say, men who were important to themselves, their wives or their associates—have been under the pleasant delusion that they were running something, say a political convention or a conference, only to discover, to their confusion and chagrin, that the real boss was, or seemed to be, Herbert Bayard Swope. He is as easy to ignore as a cyclone. His gift of gab is a torrential and terrifying thing. He is probably the most charming extrovert in the Western world. His brain is crammed with a million oddments of information, and only a dolt would make a bet with him on an issue concerning facts. He is fifty-six years old now; most of those years have been passed in a furious and highly successful endeavor to impress upon the consciousness of a stupid and lethargic world the fact that there exists, living and breathing and flashing fire, a man named Herbert Bayard Swope. Travelers returning from Europe have been known to report that the first question asked of them by high-placed foreign personages would not be "How are conditions in the United States?" but "How is Herbert Bayard Swope?"

Walker concluded:

> If he doesn't die prematurely of high blood pressure, Swope should remain a first-rate show for at least twenty years. There is some talk that he might run for governor of New York next fall. That sounds like picayune business. He is better at being simply Herbert Bayard Swope, immaculate with yellow gloves and cane, bestowing advice and benedictions upon fledgling reporters, rebuking statesmen, telling Presidents when they have hit upon a good phrase—as when he told Roosevelt to "bear down" on the term "New Deal"—bawling out waiters until they quake in their gizzards, fondling the yellow clippings which embalm his days of grandeur, supervising odd jobs about the estate, being contrite and generous when he learns that he has really wounded someone, beaming at his own feats of memory, laughing at how he outwitted some pretentious fool, making trains wait for him, thinking up rather humorous wisecracks, and finding his seat—always a bit late—in the front row. The show must go on.

About the time span of twenty years, Walker was frighteningly prescient. The story was published on June 4, 1938. Swope died on June 20,
1958. Until that date, he lived quite a bit and quite well; one might
almost say that he lived relentlessly.

Facts were as holy to Swope as pieces of the true Cross were to early
Christian pilgrims. When "Ask Me Another," a popular quiz game and
the forerunner of "Information Please," was published in book form,
the authors' dedication read, "To Herbert Bayard Swope, who might
have dictated the answers to these questions and saved the authors the
trouble of looking them up."

Clyde Roche was a teenager when he heard Swope say something that
remained with him for forty years: "Records stand. Opinions die. An
opinion is an opinion. An office boy's is as good as the Pope's. But when
you sit in judgement, it must be based on a knowledge of the facts."

If fact was Swope's god, fancy was Margaret's: the creation of an
ambience that nobody, Swope least of all, would ever want to leave. It
was the quality of his voice and of what he said that people recalled for
years after, but she was the true Lorelei of Long Island Sound. And
Keewaydin, the Sanford White house perched on a spit of land, has
passed into social legend as an enchanted spot, unforgettable to those
who enjoyed its hospitality; truth, in the form of a fairy tale, is told by the
affluent old to the affluent young about how it was when the best that
money could buy was the best that ever was.*

The entrance was unprepossessing, but beyond a bend, the house
became visible, a gracious white timbered structure, with wings gently
curved to embrace the drive. Beneath twin crystal chandeliers, the
random planking of the entrance hall floor gleamed. There were buffet
consoles with enormous bowls of fresh flowers.

The entrance to the library was directly opposite the front door. It was
a handsome room, used variously for politics and poker. At each end,
there was an enormous fireplace, large enough to contain a man, and the
pale chenille carpeting had such even striations that no drunk could ever
walk one. One of the housemen would start vacuuming at one end of the

---

*Even this year, almost twenty years after Swope's death and ten after Maggie's, the
Swope house was described by the *New York Post,* in a piece about Long Island houses
for sale, as follows: "But if you must have the very best, check out Land's End, the
14-acre Sands Point estate once owned by Herbert Bayard Swope. It will cost you a cool
$2 million—but remember, that includes the English silver and Baccarat crystal."
Land's End is the name given it by its most recent owners.

room, cut a straight path clear across to the other, pick up his machine, return to the end he started from, and begin again.

Beyond the library, a red-brick portico, its overhang supported by four huge pillars, commanded a spectacular view of the Sound and the swimming pool, which ran parallel to the edge of the sea wall. On the portico, people in various stages of dress and undress would gather in the late afternoon for cocktails, while other guests ambled to and from the tennis and croquet courts.

At one side of the front hall was the dining room, with its hand-painted Chinese wallpaper, a large English dining table in the center of the room, and a smaller one by the bay window overlooking the Sound. Normally the family and guests would sit around the large table, while the children sat in the bay. For big parties, the center table was used as a buffet, with tables for four or eight set up around it; Swope would then hold court with his special guests at the window table. There were never any place cards, but Margaret effortlessly directed people to the places that had been assigned them. No one ever felt slighted, as there were always enough fascinating people for some to be at every table. Unlike Elsa Maxwell, who would make up tables of bores at her parties, on the premise that they would never know they were boring if they were together, Margaret never had a sufficient number of bores to make up a table. Al Smith once said, "It beats me how a German gentleman and a Scotch lady can produce so much Irish charm."

The drawing room on the other side of the hall was never actually called a drawing room by the regulars, for Swope insisted that it was for living. It was a pure white room with handsome groupings of gold and white chairs and sofas, artfully arranged to permit general conversation or private talks, depending upon the drift of the party, and to leave ample floor space for "the game." The piano had its curved side to the wall and its straight edge into the room to provide backing for still another conversation group. At one time or another, it responded to the ministrations of George Gershwin, Richard Rodgers, Cole Porter, and Noel Coward. Jule Styne used it to polish the score of *Gentlemen Prefer Blondes,* with Swope's grandson Rusty planted on his knee. When a composer wasn't around, there was always either Oscar Levant or Ralph Strain, the "house pianists" who were there weekend after weekend, to render his works.

Just west of the drawing room was the glass-enclosed sun porch, which was the center of much Swopian activity. It was there that Maggie served a lengthy tea that evolved gracefully into cocktails for latecomers who preferred a stronger drink.

Clyde Roche exclaimed incredulously a lifetime later:

> What! You never heard of Maggie's famous tea? Well, it truly was the best iced tea that ever was, and I'm surprised that nobody— Surely, Janet [Stewart], who knows iced teas as few of us do, would have mentioned it. Well, you've got to ask somebody who's knowledgeable about those things, because it stood alone. People always asked what was the recipe for Maggie's iced tea. And there'd be the most delicious cakes and sandwiches, cookies. But the iced tea was just a triumph. Astonishes me that you would have talked to a lot of people, and no one remarked on that. Well, everyone used to talk about it at the time. By everyone, I mean people who were accustomed to having good food. And it was an integral part of their lives. They would have an enormous number of visitors there at the tea table every afternoon, and it was— The tea itself would go on, I suppose, from a quarter to four to quarter of seven. It was a long, long tea, constantly replenished. The food itself was always marvelous. Did anyone talk about that? The midnight snacks and all that. It wasn't that you could have anything you wanted at any hour of the day or night. It was that you did. I must have heard Ottie do this hundreds of times. It would be two in the morning; they'd ring the bell and he'd say, "Mae, we want some soup." And at two in the morning, there'd be twenty-five people all playing games. And out would come an array of delicious hamburgers, wonderful sausages, all kinds of hot food. And that would be true at two, and it would be equally true at six in the morning. All those people there. All prepared to create anything and called upon to do it, too. Of course, everyone knows how dinner was prepared every night, whether they were going out or not, in case Herbert changed his mind and decided to stay home. Every night, there would be dinner for as many people as were staying in the house, whether they were going out or not. I know it's true, because there were times when Herbert and Maggie were going out, and somebody would say, "I don't feel like going. I think I'll go out somewhere for dinner." And Mae would cry, "Please eat here! It's all cooked. It's all ready. Don't go out." Herbert was a man with strange whims. He might change his mind at the last minute and not go out, and he wanted to eat his dinner. He didn't want anything impromptu. It was always ready.

Mrs. Howard Cullman was one of the legion of people who partook of the wonderful food at the Swopes' home. Wife of one of the heads of

Benson and Hedges Tobacco Company and, in her own right, one of the most discerning theatrical investors of all time, she was also a marvelous hostess who had written a successful book on the subject: *Ninety Thousand Glasses*. She didn't think twice before hiring a cook who listed the Swopes among her references. The woman turned out to be spectacularly untalented, and Peggy Cullman could not understand it. After one particularly disastrous meal, she asked, "Did you prepare this sort of food for the Swopes?"

The woman replied, "I wasn't *the* cook there. I didn't do meals. I was the *second* cook. I did snacks."

In addition to the gardeners and the permanent staff of nine, there was extra help brought in during the time the Swopes stayed at Keewaydin. Including the main house, the apartments over the garage, and the guest cottage, there were thirty-seven rooms, plus more bathrooms than could be found in most small hotels—but then, there were usually more guests than could be found in most small hotels.

Four cars were necessary to keep the family mobile. Swope's personal car bore the stark license-plate designation S, as well as the shield of the New York Racing Commissioner and the state seal. The other cars were numbered HS1, HS2, and HS3.

Swope was not above using his influence to get a police escort when he wanted to travel quickly. An example of this provided the climax to a memorable weekend during which Dorothy Parker was a guest. It was the era of the pilot, when one flyer after another was setting and breaking records. Swope was dressing when he heard on the radio that Howard Hughes was about to land at Floyd Bennett Field on the last leg of his spectacular around-the-world flight. He quickly arranged for a motorcycle escort and then raced downstairs, hustling everybody out, shouting exuberantly, "Hurry up! Come along; come along! We've got to get over to Floyd Bennett to greet Howard!"

Dorothy Parker wound up in the lead car with Swope, Maggie, Ottie, and Bruce. The sirens were screaming; they were going over ninety miles an hour, and Swope was urging, "Faster! Faster!"

A hysterically frightened Dorothy Parker slid to the floor of the car, yelling, "Stop, you madman, stop! Let me out of here before you kill us all!"

Maggie, who generally became apoplectic when a car went over thirty-five, clenched her fists and remained determinedly cool. "Dottie, I don't know what you're getting so excited about. Breaking speed records is in the air. Why fight it?"

The mob was so large that they could not get within three blocks of the field. Swope, as exhilarated as ever, cried, "Turn around! We've got to get home. Dinner's waiting." And off they went at the same speed on the return trip. Back at Keewaydin, Swope swooped off to tell the servants to get dinner on the table, while the others crawled to the bar.

At three in the morning, when they had just begun to regain their composure, Swope burst in upon Ottie, Bruce, and Dottie Parker, crying, "Amy Mollison's landing at Roosevelt Field on her flight from England. What do you say we drive over to meet her?"

Bruce replied wearily, "I wouldn't go to Roosevelt Field to see King Kong with his fly open."

The next weekend, Gerald Brooks came down. When Ottie went out to greet him, Brooks was snickering and fingering his little red mustache as if he had something marvelous to tell but wasn't sure of the reception. After some urging, he said, "Dottie Parker's been telling the most delicious story—but you mustn't repeat it to your parents. She's been telling everybody about the trip to see Hughes. And she ends by saying, 'I wouldn't go back for another weekend with the Swopes to see King Kong with his fly open."

The young man was crushed. Not only had she purloined his uncle's line without giving credit, but it made him doubt all of the marvelous Parker stories he'd ever heard.

There were twenty-four telephone extensions at Keewaydin, connecting variously with one unlisted number, one listed number, and a private line. The phones at Swope's New York residence and the business lines at his office brought the grand total to forty-eight. Somebody once suggested that a switchboard be installed, but Margaret would have none of it. It would have spoiled her fun, for she was as enthralled with eavesdropping as Swope was with speaking. A guest racing from Swope's room to Margaret's would almost inevitably find him speaking on his phone, while she was listening in on hers.

Margaret also had her own cable address. Listed as "sourpuss," it had been a gift from Bea Kaufman. Margaret was delighted with the name, as Bea had known she would be.

Anne Schneider, George and Bea Kaufman's daughter, recalls Maggie as the first adult woman she ever heard use a word in common parlance among the girls at school—"crap." Conversely, Ring Lardner, Jr., recalls that Bea was one of the few women with whom Maggie could communicate in language as colorful as her own.

Ring had reentered the world of the Swopes as Ottie's roommate at

Princeton. One weekend, the boys happened to bring down a rather staid college chum, who never completely recovered from his first conversation with Bea and Maggie. They were discussing the fact that physicians could not find anything wrong with Maggie, the inveterate hypochondriac. At length, she summed up the situation: "All doctors are lying bastards."

Bea heartily concurred: "You're fucking right."

Maggie was also capable of a certain rough tenderness. Just before Ring took off on his first trip abroad, which was to include a stop in Germany, she wrote one of her rare letters to somebody outside her immediate family:

> Ring dear—
> I hope you have a nice trip and see many interesting events take place. I needn't tell you how very fond I am of you even tho' I have voiced my disapproval at times. When you are naughty remember my eagle eye is on you and stop at once. Salute Mr. Hitler nicely and don't wake up in a concentration camp. My love and bon voyage.

As at Great Neck, croquet continued to be the major occupation of the days, which began some time after one in the afternoon, just as they had when Swope was a newspaperman. It was at Sands Point that the Gerald Brooks Memorial Cup was established, an annual championship tournament played mostly at Keewaydin and on the neighboring course at Margaret Emerson's house. Out of malice, the organizers would often schedule Swope for a match at ten in the morning, knowing full well that he never appeared before one. There would be much swearing against the cruelty, and he would threaten to default until they rescheduled him for after one o'clock. He was no longer among the better players. Ottie and Ave Harriman were tops, winning the cup three and two times, respectively.

Margaret Emerson had the best croquet field in the area, but when she left Sands Point for the annual trips to her camp in the Adirondacks, she would pull up all the wickets so that nobody could play in her absence. Her response to complaints was that she was merely letting the grass grow in again.

Emerson was actually her maiden name. Her father, Captain Isaac Emerson, had made millions in Bromo Seltzer, and, four husbands later, she decided his was the best of her names. By her second husband, who went down on the *Lusitania,* she bore a son, Alfred Gwynne Vanderbilt.

Her third husband was Raymond Baker, the director of the mint. That union produced Mimi Baker, who became debutante of the year shortly after Jane Swope turned down a coming-out party with the comment: "Frankly, I'd rather have a new horse." The former wife of the fourth Emerson, Charles Amory, subsequently married Herbert Pulitzer, which seemed to prove that social weddings in the Swope set were rather like merry-go-round rides, with as many brass clinkers as gold rings.

Another much-married friend of Swope, Marjorie Merriweather Post Close Hutton Davies May, also reverted to her maiden name of Post at the end of her life. It was, after all, a very good name, enshrined on boxes of Post Toasties and tins of Postum.

At one point Mrs. Davies, née Post, went to Russia as the wife of Ambassador Joseph E. Davies. There was an old Russian saying: "Comes the revolution, we'll all eat strawberries Romanoff." Mrs. Davies was taking no chances. She took along a tankerful of strawberries and ice cream. This action brought a great deal of public criticism, and Davies asked Swope to help him prepare an ameliorating statement. Roosevelt later advised the ambassador not to use it on the premise that it was much better to let sleeping dogs lie, to which Swope replied, "When you let them lie with wrong thoughts in their heads, they always bark in the same key when they awaken."

Davies wrote a book about his experiences—*Mission to Moscow*—which was sympathetic to the Russians. When they later became our allies and it was necessary to whip up public sympathy for them, Swope suggested to Roosevelt that he use his influence to have a film made of the work. The president persuaded Jack L. Warner to buy the book. In the movie, Mrs. Davies was portrayed by Ann Harding, whose own husband was being criticized in certain circles for alleged pro-German feelings. Ten years later, Miss Harding and all those connected with this picture, which was actually a sympathetic portrait of two quintessential capitalists, came under the fire of Senator Joseph R. McCarthy for having made a pro-Communist propaganda piece.

Promiscuity was not as fashionable in Swope's world as marrying, and marrying, and marrying, *benedictum ad nauseam*. In the most profound sense, the name was more important than the game. It was not that there was an insufficiency of love affairs; it was simply that they were considered more a means than an end. Talk was much looser than morals.

The Swopes were a blissfully happy couple, but there was some talk even about them. There was speculation about Swope and Peggy Talbott, the wife of Harold Talbott, later Secretary of the Air Force. It was true that Mrs. Talbott was often seen alone with Swope, but that was generally at the race track, for Maggie did not share her husband's enthusiasm for the horses. Peggy was pretty and a bit of a coquette, but she was always welcome at the Swope house. According to Anita Loos, she herself was unwelcome merely for having once allegedly lent an apartment to June Walker for a rendezvous with Swope, so it seems doubtful that Peggy would have remained a friend if she had actually had an affair with him.

Marc Connelly claimed that Miss Loos was never a part of their crowd, and that was why she was not welcome. Although the Walker story was never substantiated, after Swope's death Maggie removed a letter from the actress and a carbon of his reply from Swope's files and kept them among her personal papers for the rest of her life. It had been written years after the alleged affair, when Miss Walker was having financial problems. She requested a loan, and Swope sent the money immediately, along with a note wishing her well and implying that he did not want repayment.

Whatever the reason, Maggie was not fond of Miss Loos. Ruth Dubonnet once announced that she was going to take a walk in the zoo with Miss Loos, and Maggie said, "You'd better not go into the monkey house. They won't let her out again."

Maggie could be an extremely flirtatious woman, but there were only a few rumors of extramarital adventures. The first was in the early twenties. It was said that she had seriously contemplated eloping with Allan Ryan, son of Thomas Fortune Ryan. Janet Stewart had been married to Allan's son before she married William Rhinelander Stewart. She confronted her former father-in-law with the story. He neither confirmed nor denied it; he simply said, "I have a letter in my vault from Herbert Bayard Swope, challenging me to a duel."

Later, there was talk of a game of romantic brinksmanship with Joseph Kennedy. Maggie's son observed, "I only know that she went up to Choate with old man Kennedy to see Joe, Jr., play in a football game. She never did that for me. She didn't even like football. As for motoring all the way up to Choate—well—it was extremely unlike her."

Maggie's attitude toward any form of promiscuity was as arbitrary as most of her attitudes. She could seem terribly blasé, as when Swope interrupted her at a card game to say that he'd just had a thrilling conversation with the president. She glanced up with a smile and said, "Isn't that nice, dear? Now, why don't you wipe the lipstick off your face?"

On another occasion, she telephoned Swope at what has been described variously as a Turkish bath and a house of ill repute. He was visiting Hollywood and had gone off to Agua Caliente with Joe Schenck and a group of others. He cried, "How the hell did you find me?"

"Never mind that," she replied. "You just get the hell back here immediately!" Actually, Swope was never very adept at nights out with the boys when girls were included in the party. John Baragwanath, who once described Swope as having "the face of some old Emperor," hosted a party with Sonny Whitney and Harpo Marx at the Hotel Warwick. Swope was among the guests, and no wives were invited. Harpo provided the girls and even agreed to play the piano after dinner for dancing, claiming that he had once played the piano in a whorehouse.

The girls were gorgeous and anonymous—each was introduced as "Miss Benson." Swope's Miss Benson was a pretty little blonde with bee-stung lips and big blue eyes under long curling lashes. She was also very dumb. That she had no conversation did not bother Swope, for he had enough for both of them. Baragwanath was seated nearby and could hear the talk, which was larded with words that were normal to Swope's vocabulary. She sat there with lashes batting in dumb fascination. He finally stopped for a breath, and Miss Benson chirped, "Hey-hey, Big Boy."

Will Stewart, Raoul Fleischmann, and George Abbott were among those present. From then on, whenever Swope started to hold forth with any of them, a falsetto voice would coo: "Hey-hey, Big Boy."

Maggie once summed up her attitude toward Swope and women to Mollie McLean, who was then married to Alfred Vanderbilt and was staying with the Swopes while her own house was being decorated. Swope was away at Jock Whitney's for the Saratoga races. She said, "If he's ever indiscreet on any of these trips, he'd better not dare to make a clean breast of it to me, or I'll rap him over the head with the heel of my shoe!"

Her attitude with Swope was that what she did not know would not hurt her, although that did not stop her from trying to know everything. Her attitude toward her brother Bruce and her son was "I don't know why you can't have your affairs at home. It's much more comfortable here."

One reason for not having affairs at home, her son pointed out, was that she had thrown away the keys to every bedroom at Keewaydin. She patrolled the halls nightly and was likely to peek into the rooms to see that things were all right. Ottie observed, "Knowing that one's mother might stick her head into the room at a crucial moment can be a most inhibiting factor."

Maggie saw no reason not to take keys or to do anything else that might come into her mind at Keewaydin. As far as she was concerned, the house and all who dwelt in it were hers by divine right. One friend recalled, "One night, Herbert was explaining the right of eminent domain. Maggie overheard a few words and got furious. She thought he was talking about her."

Soon after Dr. Alfred Adler, the founder of individual psychiatry and an associate of Sigmund Freud, joined the staff of the Long Island College of Medicine, Swope invited him to Sands Point for dinner. He was seated next to his hostess at dinner, and afterward she took him aside for a private discussion that lasted for two hours. As they rejoined the others, he was saying, "There's nothing wrong with you, my dear Mrs. Swope, except that you wish to run the world . . . but you can't."

Maggie found eternal justification for her nightly forays through the bedroom corridors when she peeked into the room that Ethel Barrymore was occupying one night. Miss Barrymore had fallen asleep with a cigarette still burning in her hand. It had rolled across the blanket, in which there was already a big, smoldering hole. If she had not looked in, the world might have lost one of its greatest actresses, and the Swopes might have been out of a home: the handsome old Sanford White house was built of wood. Any time she was criticized for behaving like a headmistress at a boarding school, she would reply, "Remember Ethel."

One virile young guest answered, "Maggie, when I smolder in bed, it has nothing to do with cigarettes."

The missing key to one door found its way into the coat of arms of Douglas Fairbanks, Jr. When he was made an honorary Commander of the British Empire for his services to England during the war, he was asked to submit a design for a coat of arms. The one he chose depicted a key in one panel, three roses in the next. The roses represented the Fairbanks daughters, and the key belonged to Swope's dressing room–den at Keewaydin.

The Sands Point house was opened for a weekend party over New Year's Eve. Among the guests were the William Rhinelander Stewarts and Mary Lee Hartford. Fairbanks arrived early in the afternoon of New Year's Day, and, naturally, nobody was out of bed yet. Mary Lee was up in the Stewarts' bedroom discussing her unhappiness over the break-up of her marriage to Huntington Hartford. Maggie came in and asked her to go down and talk to Doug until the others appeared.

Fairbanks was a man of great charm as well as one of the best-looking actors of the period. His attentions were flattering and consoling to a girl in Mary Lee's situation on that New Year's Day.

That evening, the older members of the party went out to dinner at Howard Dietz's house, while the young people stayed at home. After dinner, they put on some records and started to dance. On the pretext of avoiding the loud music, Doug managed to draw Mary Lee off into Swope's den, which had been assigned to him, as all of the other bedrooms were already occupied when he arrived. He later admitted that perhaps he was moving in too quickly and agreed to rejoin the others. When he tried to turn the doorknob, the lock snapped closed, and all of his pulling and pounding could not open it. As he was banging on the door, the rest of the party arrived home.

"What's going on in there?" Janet Stewart's resonant contralto boomed through the house, bringing the entire group to the locked door. A key was finally found and the couple emerged, explaining rather sheepishly that they were only having a chat. The next day, the many Swope phones were pressed into service, and it was not long before the story was in general circulation in New York and throughout the north shore of Long Island. If Mary Lee's honor was slightly impaired by the incident, several decades of happy marriage have restored it.

By the standards of the period, the most scandalous activity at Keewaydin was skinny-dipping, a pursuit that was made fashionable by Maggie Swope, who loathed the stricture of any sort of clothing while swimming. She would wrap a large beach towel around herself, go to the edge of the pool and, while slipping into the water under cover of it, divest herself of her "bathing suit." When she emerged, the towel would again be used as a cover. The pile of towels was soon used in a similar manner by guests, except for one giddy Hollywood producer who strolled across the lawn without a stitch on and then was totally confused by Maggie's tirade against his shocking behavior.

A mishap did befall Eleanor "Cookie" Young, daughter of the rail-road tycoon Robert Young and niece of the artist Georgia O'Keefe. When she came out of the water, her front was suitably covered by the towel, but her rear was exposed to the view of two fishermen in the Sound, who were ogling the sight with undisguised relish. When this was pointed out, she looked back at them, turned, and said with a shrug, "Oh, that's all right. I don't know them."

Games continued to be the only source of what might be remotely described as orgiastic revel. Nothing could interfere with Maggie's addiction to canasta and mah-jongg. Not even a natural disaster could deter her. When her car could not get through a flooded road en route to a game, she refused to turn back. She waited for a truck that could make the passage to come by, flagged it down, and persuaded the driver to give her a lift to her destination.

When Robert Moses once walked in on a game she was having with some women he had never met, he expected her to pause for the usual amenities. He was surprised when she looked up only long enough to say, "You know where the bar is," and immediately went back to her move.

He was in good company. A few years earlier Swope had brought Winston Churchill home during one of her sessions. She was only a degree more polite on that occasion. She said, "Herbert, fix a drink for Winston."

If her ability had matched her passion, she would have been one of the biggest winners in her crowd. Alas, it did not, so she contented herself with being a bored loser. In the middle of a mah-jongg game with Janet Stewart and two other women, she picked up a tile, put it on the rack, and then went completely blank for a few minutes. Janet prodded, "Well, Maggie?"

She got up and excused herself. The other women thought she would return in a few minutes. After a half-hour, Janet happened to glance out at the Sound, and there was Maggie floating along in a boat, fishing rod in hand.

The poker games continued to be the late events they had been during Swope's newspaper days. Although Maggie rarely participated in the big games, there were some women, such as Margaret Emerson and Joan Payson, rich enough to qualify. One memorable game started after dinner at Mrs. Payson's house, moved to the Swopes' for breakfast, and ended just in time for everybody to change to go to Millicent Hearst's for lunch. Maggie sighed and said, "Who said play wasn't hard work?"

David O. Selznick had become a part of the Swope set through Jock Whitney, a heavy investor in Selznick's films, most notably *Gone with the Wind*. Accustomed to being at the studio first thing in the morning, Selznick was a habitual early riser. He could often be glimpsed having his orange juice on the sun porch while the game was still going on in the library.

Selznick did occasionally play, when it did not interfere with his sleep. Coming down on a train from Saratoga, he decided to sit in on a game with Baruch and Swope. "I'm not interested in any of your little games," he said grandly. "When I play poker, I like to shoot the works. Give me $10,000 worth of chips."

Baruch stifled a yawn and said boredly, "You're banking, Herb. Go ahead. Throw him a blue one."

For all the high-stake gambling done around her, the one thing that Maggie could not abide was to have somebody hustled into a game he or she could not afford. The writer Terry Lewis was one of Ottie's crowd. When the young people decided to shoot craps one night, she felt that she could not refuse without seeming like an awful spoilsport. She was only a struggling young writer and should not have been pressured into joining a game with the young Swopes, Vanderbilts, and the like. Before she had time to think, she was out $300 that she did not have. She wandered into another room, completely shocked by her own actions and wondering how she would ever pay up. Maggie caught sight of her and asked, "What's wrong with you? You look like death warmed over."

She explained the situation, and Maggie said, "Come on. I'll stake you."

They went back to the game, and, with Maggie at her side, Terry soon recouped her losses. She was about to pick up the dice again, when Maggie pulled her to her feet. "Come on. That's it. You're out of this game."

Terry protested that she was just getting hot, and Maggie muttered, "Pick up your money, and let's go." When they were out of earshot of the others, she added, "No matter what anybody says to you, don't you dare ever let me catch you in a game you can't afford again."

Throughout the '30s the permanent population at Keewaydin kept expanding. There were Herbert and Maggie, Mimi, Ottie, and, after a brief marriage, Bruce was home again. Kenneth Powell, his wife, and their two children were also generally in residence at the cottage.

Jane Swope eloped with a "deb's delight" named Robert Brandt. The Swopes were not at the wedding and never did approve of Brandt, who was neither a "professional man" nor affluent or socially prominent. He was described by various members of the family and friends as good looking, an excellent dancer, an agile athlete. After the wedding, Joe Kennedy lent them his house in Washington, D.C., where they lived until Jane became ill and Maggie insisted she come home to recuperate. She stayed home so long after she was well that Brandt finally asked, "Are you married to me or your family?"

He apparently resolved the question by joining the family as completely as all of the others had. He returned to New York, and Swope got him a job at the advertising agency that handled the race track accounts. After the birth of their son Bayard, the three also took up residence at Sands Point.

Maggie was happy. All of her family was once more with her; the house was suffused with her particular kind of passionate, possessive, all-consuming love. And they were content to have it that way. As much as she could not bear the thought of having any of them get away from her, so much were they content to remain. The remarkable thing about Maggie's love was that it could be so possessive without ever getting sentimental or cloying. Her acerbic tongue was used to sting those she loved as well as those for whom she felt disdain. It was only when she went too far with Swope that she ever apologized. Little notes scrawled in pencil on the backs of envelopes would be left where he would be sure to find them. A typical one: "Darling—I am very sorry; you are right and I was wrong and gabby—Forgive me because I always need your strength and love."

On the occasion of their twenty-fifth wedding anniversary, she wrote more fully and with great passion:

My dearest—only love—

I am just sitting here contemplating the Heaven I have had with you for a quarter of a century. There was a time not so long ago when to think of twenty-five years of my own was hard. Since then you have let me share with you the fleetest, most beautiful years of my life— every day is indelibly engraved in my mind and heart. It seems but yesterday that we went to Old Point Comfort—Bermuda Oaks Bluff—the Azores. I know we got all there was out of them but I am sometimes fearful that we are so careless of the moments we have. To imagine life without you—that is something to strike terror to the soul.

You say I am a cannibalistic mother—I am when I see in them you. Jane with your insistent and never to be diverted strength and Ottie with his world of charm and beauty of soul. I suppose they are mine too—but they only seem you. Even Jane's baby has become you to me.

Your whole domination of my life has been something I can't even be rational about, and if I am inarticulate at moments it is only because I am too full for so inadequate a medium as words: Words to tell you how I adore you—words to voice my gratitude for your boundless gifts of generosity—words to say I am sorry for all my lack of understanding—words to tell you how I loved being your mother's daughter—words to tell you how proud I am of you and how I respect you—words to tell you how I adore my home in the country—words to tell you that you are my sureness of life—love—existence.

I wish I could live my life with you all over again, beginning in Sherrys—but since I can't do that I hope we can be together for at least a hundred years—a day in my heart's hunger for you—my only love—

Mag – Pug

Her passion expressed, practical Maggie reasserted herself for a postscript:

My gift is not finished so you can't have it—today.

One can only wonder what that gift to a man who had so much of everything might have been; it had become a favorite sport of friends to go up to Swope's dressing room just to count the staggering array of suits, shoes, shirts, neckties, socks, and sets of underwear. He was once caught counting them himself, and he explained with a blush, "In a world going to hell, there's something reassuring about three dozen Charvet ties."

Martin Gabel co-produced a little disaster titled *Men of Distinction* that ran for four performances at the 48th Street Theater in 1953. Its most memorable line was in the playbill credits: "Mr. Robert Preston's black tie on loan from the Herbert Bayard Swope Sr. collection."

Swope was famous for helping friends out with their theatrical ventures. His assistance generally took a more substantial form than lending a necktie. He had an acquaintance with Billy Rose, dating back to the time that Rose was stenographer for the WIB. Like the lordly Swope, the diminutive Rose had maintained his friendship with Baruch. The terms of these two friendships with the same man were a study in contrasts. With Rose, Baruch did all the talking, while Rose did the listening and then probably rushed off to take notes in his expert shorthand. With Swope, Baruch did the listening, and the notes that were taken often became parts of speeches that won Baruch a reputation for stirring oratory. Years later, Baruch commented to Maggie, "I don't understand it. I gave Herb many more good tips on the market than I ever gave to Billy. How come Rose is so much richer?"

In addition to what he gleaned from shrewd investing, Rose made a great deal of money as the lyricist for some of the most popular songs of the day, including "Me and My Shadow," "It's Only a Paper Moon," "More than You Know," "Great Day," "Without a Song," and "The Night Is Young and You're So Beautiful." He also wrote an epic called "Does the Spearmint Lose Its Flavor on the Bed Post Overnight?" But he really longed to be another Florenz Ziegfeld. To that end, he even married one of Ziegfeld's greatest stars, Fanny Brice. However, by 1935 he had produced only one success, *Crazy Quilt,* which had been a failure in New York before Rose talked Miss Brice into taking it on a cross-country tour of one-night stands for a solid year. On the strength of her name, it earned a small fortune in the provinces.

If Ziegfeld had become famous for his lavish *Follies,* Rose decided he would do better by mounting a show built around a circus. He commissioned Hecht and MacArthur to write a forgettable book for *Jumbo,* and he got Rodgers and Hart to do a memorable score, which included two of their best songs, "The Most Beautiful Girl in the World" and "Little Girl Blue." He hired Paul Whiteman and his orchestra, Jimmy Durante, and more circus acts than Barnum and Bailey. He did not hire Miss Brice, who was probably the one comedienne in the world who actually could have turned *Jumbo* into a three-ring circus.

Unable to resist any form of publicity, he loudly proclaimed that the Hippodrome was the only theater in New York large enough to hold his spectacle. The result was that when it came time to sign a lease, the owners held him up for $6,000 a week to rent an old barn for which they had hitherto been happy to get $1,000 a week.

He went into rehearsal having spent $35,000 of his own money and needing an additional $200,000 to open the show. An investment of $200,000 in the theater of 1935 was the equivalent of over $2,000,000 in today's theater. This would make it the most expensive production ever. When Rose called Baruch for help, the financier hedged, suggesting he call Swope, who was a good friend of Rodgers, MacArthur, and Hecht.

Swope invited Rose to a dinner party at Sands Point that included David O. Selznick, Jock Whitney, his sister Joan Payson, Ethel and Clyde Roche, and Baruch. Rose stated his case simply, and then, knowing how to listen, he sat back while Swope took over for two hours of brilliant talk on the history of circuses and theater and their logically close relationship. Rose got up to leave early. He had not uttered a syllable for several hours, but as Swope took him to the door he said, "Good night, Billy. You've been enormously entertaining. Enormously."

The host returned, vouching for the talents of the writers and composers of *Jumbo* and offering the opinion that Rose was probably the only showman in the world who could pull it off. Selznick thought that it could make a terrific movie (it was not filmed until 1962 and was a disaster).

Ultimately, Whitney and Mrs. Payson put up nearly $175,000, and

Baruch provided the rest on the condition that Swope look after his interests, claiming that he was really only doing it as a favor to Rose and was not expecting any profit. Swope felt that since he was overseer and Baruch did not expect any profit anyway, any profit there should happen to be should go to him for his time and efforts. Baruch did not agree: if he was doing a favor for Rose and expecting nothing, then Swope should do a favor for him with the same expectations. The argument might have been specious, but Swope loved the theater, and *Jumbo* would provide his closest approach to being a part of it, so he agreed.

Swope was a regular at the rehearsals, which were described with great color by the show press agent, Richard Maney:

> Dress rehearsals, waged day and night for six weeks, drew crowds of the curious despite Rose's efforts to bar intruders. Slumming parties from Harlem and Greenwich Village often dropped into the Hippo-drome around two in the morning to watch an hour's drill. Joan Crawford and Franchot Tone, preceded by native beaters, made it a port of call on their honeymoon. Candid cameramen swooped down on the place like seven-year locusts. There were more gate crashers in the balcony than there were animals in the cellar. Hecht suggested the final ad be headed:
>
> GRAND RE-OPENING BY POPULAR DEMAND!
> "There are thousands of people who think we've opened, gone on tour, and are back for a return engagement," he said.

The Swopes and the Whitneys brought parties of friends every night, along with hampers that Mae packed with champagne and delicacies for midnight picnics at what they began to refer to as "the club." Swope would have been the first to admit that he was no shrinking violet himself, but even he was impressed by "the Manic Midget," a name he coined for Rose. The name was later popularized by Maney, who was continually inventing nicknames for his boss, such as "the Bantam Barnum" and "the Basement Belasco." Watching the producer in action, Swope commented, "I'm willing to wager Rose thinks he won the World War."

The day of the première finally arrived, but the curtain would not have risen without the help of Swope. When the fire department inspector came to check out the Hippodrome, he found enough violations to keep the theater closed for months while they were being corrected. In a panic, Rose sent for Swope, who, reputation for tardiness aside, was there before the fireman had a chance to leave. Rose later described what transpired: "Herbert took that fireman aside and began talking to him, and I don't know what he said, but pretty soon he had the fireman charmed and bedazzled, and we opened that night and played for five months and never heard another complaint."

The reviews were disastrous. Needing a quote for the advertisements, Rose again turned to Swope, who persuaded Al Smith to let them quote him as saying, "I think *Jumbo* is grand. It's as new and as funny to my grandchildren as it is to me, and that's a great test for any entertainment."

A five-month run was insufficient to counteract Rose's inadequacies as a producer, the most substantial being the way he allowed the show to have such a high weekly operating cost that even a sellout would not have brought much profit. *Jumbo* lost $164,000, an unprecedented sum for the time. Before the show opened, Maney had invented a prophetic slogan for Rose: "*Jumbo* will make me or break Whitney."

The atmosphere of the Hippodrome may have provided the inspiration for one of Rose's few theatrical triumphs, which occurred four years later. It was at the old theater that the swimmer Annette Kellerman had made a fortune years before, when she flooded the orchestra pit for her water spectacles. Rose did as well by producing the *Aquacade* at the World's Fair of 1939. That splashy success marked the end of Miss Brice as Mrs. Rose and the start of swimming star Eleanor Holm in the same role.

The Sunday after Swope missed Howard Hughes at Floyd Bennett Field, he was startled to see him on his own home ground. A group was sitting around the swimming pool when suddenly a seaplane swooped down and landed at the foot of the sea wall. Hughes hopped out and clambered ashore. At the time, he was in love with Katharine Hepburn and had been visiting at her home, across the Sound in Connecticut. She was too busy working on a new role to play with him, and he decided literally to drop in on his old friend Swope, at whose home one could always find bright playmates. Hughes's idea of fun and games, as it turned out, was to sit moodily at the edge of the pool and stare off in the direction of Miss Hepburn's house.

Swope greeted the flyer with, "My boy, I've a great opportunity for you to invest in Ollie Garrett's new play, *Waltz in Goosestep*."

Oliver H. P. Garrett was one of Swope's "boys"—having worked as a reporter on the *World*. The producers were having trouble capitalizing his production, and naturally Garrett had turned to his old boss for help.

Whether or not Swope was successful in getting Hughes to invest, the play did get on at the Hudson Theater, where it managed a run of seven performances.

It was this eagerness to help that made his theatrical friends forgive Swope for tardiness on opening nights. The absolution did not come without satire. George Kaufman's first success as the director of a serious play was John Steinbeck's *Of Mice and Men*. One of the running bits of dialogue had the simple-minded Lenny constantly asking his brighter friend, George, to tell him how it would be when they had their own ranch. Kaufman and Hart translated this into a party turn, in which Hart would say, "George, tell me how it's gonna be when our dreams come true."

Kaufman would reply, "Well, Mossie, it's gonna be like this. The curtain is gonna go up on opening night, and Swope will be in his seat."

Enclosed with their tickets to Kaufman's *Fancy Meeting You Again* was a note from the author informing the Swopes of the time of the curtain and adding: "The whole plot is in the first thirty-six seconds. After that the play goes steadily downhill. Will count on your being in your seats." Alas, the critics agreed with Kaufman's assessment of his own work, and the play ran for one week.

Swope might have been late for openings, but he was phenomenally early in requesting tickets. His secretary Kay Gilmore wrote to Kaufman to order seats for *Silk Stockings* on instructions from Swope, who was wintering in Palm Beach. The letter came back with a handwritten message from Kaufman: "This show is 10 months away. No hurry."

On October 6, 1950, Robert E. Sherwood answered his request for opening-night tickets to *Second Threshold* by assuring him that he would have them as soon as they were printed. The play didn't open until January 2, 1951.

Swope actually loathed being late and made countless efforts to reform, but there was always a conversation, a telephone call, a subject in which he would get too engrossed, a point he felt that he had to make—and time would pass without his noticing it. Some people would make adjustments, perhaps inviting the Swopes for 7:30 when they meant to serve dinner at 8:30, but if he found out, he became furious. The subject was too sensitive; he had no sense of humor about it. He would refuse to go, and Maggie would have to make all manner of apologies at the last minute.

One night, he did not arrive at a dinner party until after the soup course. His hostess, Edith Baker, was really rather amused. As he bolted his food, attempting to catch up with the others, she said, "Oh, Swope, you really are, I must say, late indeed. How wonderful!"

Swope exploded, "What do you mean—how wonderful! God damn it, I was tied up! I can't stand being late!"

She looked at him with astonishment. "Can't stand being late? Swopie, I don't believe it. I don't mind being late at all. I'm very often late just on purpose."

He refused to speak to her for the rest of the evening, for the one thing he really could not stand was the thought that anybody might be late on purpose.

Moss Hart and he did not speak for several years because of Swope's sensitivity on the subject. It was the opening night of *White Horse Inn*. Hart, immaculately turned out in white tie and tails, was pacing the cavernous lobby of the Center Theater. He was extremely nervous, for the show was one of his first efforts without the enormous collaborative partnership of George Kaufman, and it was not going well. He wanted to be a success not only for himself but for the beautiful star, Kitty Carlisle, who was eventually to become his wife. The Swopes arrived twenty minutes late, and Hart instinctively looked at his watch. Swope strode up to him and said: "God damn it, Hart, don't ever do that to me. I don't want you ever to make a reference to time, as far as I'm concerned, again!"

He marched into the theater, leaving an apoplectic Hart determined never to speak to him again. It took the efforts of all of their friends finally to reconcile them.

Maggie's lateness was caused partly by Swope and partly by her own nature. After the newspaper years, she stayed up late, not because of Swope, but because sleep was one of the two things that she really feared. The other was thunder. It was more than passive terror; she actively hated them. One friend described it as a "kind of even battle. You could see her, like Beethoven, shaking her fist at the thunderstorm. And I think it was because it was beyond her control, and she couldn't stand that. Anyway, it probably was why her life was so late, too. She didn't want to yield and certainly didn't want to sleep while there was anyone around whom she could influence. Once they were all asleep, then she could sleep. But even then it would be a slow process."

Maggie would revitalize herself by stretching out on the sofa and taking cat naps while a friend massaged her feet. Like Swope, she adored having her feet massaged. As the sun started to rise, Maggie would get up. There would be a flurry of pillow fluffing; glasses would be cleared away, ashtrays emptied. Ethel Roche once asked, "Why do you do it?"

Thinking that she was referring to the clean-up, Maggie replied, "I'd hate to come down to a place looking like a bawdyhouse on the morning after a Shriners' Convention. I don't think Lydia or Roy would like it any better."

Ethel laughed. "I don't mean that; I mean staying up all night."

Maggie paused. "I can't really say why. Every day of my life, I resist sleep. I won't give in to it. I fight it with all of my strength, until it overcomes me."

Everybody knew about Maggie's hours. At about two o'clock one morning, a pregnant neighbor and friend, Lyda Barclay, thought that she was going into labor. Her husband was feeling no pain by that hour, and her mother assured her that it was only indigestion. After about an hour, Lyda decided that it was the baby coming, and she called the only person she knew who would be up and dressed at three in the morning. Maggie and Bruce arrived immediately, complete with a bottle of Scotch. After driving Lyda to the hospital, they sat in the car drinking and listening to reports of the German invasion of Poland. They were still there when the new mother was brought back to her room. When they went up to see her, she was filled with excitement about the birth of her first daughter. Maggie said, "Never mind that shit. Hitler just marched into Poland. There's going to be a war."

EIGHTEEN

Throughout the '30s, Swope had continued to write letters to the president giving observations and advice, sometimes requested but often unsolicited, to which Roosevelt would dutifully reply. Occasionally Roosevelt would take the initiative and write first. Many of these exchanges retained the affectionate and high-spirited schoolboy tone that had characterized their earlier correspondence.

When prohibition was repealed, there was not a politician from the president to the ward heeler who did not take or receive credit for having been responsible. Swope wrote to the *New York Times,* commenting that Frank Cobb deserved credit for having been in the forefront of the battle long before the others. In the course of the letter, he began one sentence, "In the somewhat euhemeristic narrative of those men, women, and circumstance to whom credit should be given . . ." The word stems from Euhemerus, a Greek philosopher of the fourth century B.C., who held that the gods of mythology were deified mortals and that myths were essentially traditional accounts of historical personages and events.

When the *Times* printed his letter, it substituted the word "euphemistic" for "euhemeristic." Swope again took pen in hand, and another letter appeared in the *Times:*

> In a letter which the *Times* printed on Jan. 3, dealing with the honors awarded for prohibition repeal, I used the word "euhemeristic" as qualifying "narrative". . . . But who am I to have my say? A slash of the blue pencil took "euhemeristic" out and wrote in its place "euphemistic," which was not at all what I meant nor does it even remotely resemble the meaning of what I wrote.

The *Times* added a postscript in philological kind: "The error in Mr. Swope's very excellection dictum was due to a composing room blunder."

The exchange did not rest there. Many letters came to the *Times* on the pros and cons of Swope's usage. In that humor-hungry period, editorial writers all over the country took up pens in defense of or offense at Euhemerus and Swope. Roosevelt could not resist getting into the act, and he wrote to Swope:

> Sir:
>
> The Typographical Union has lodged complaint under their code against you for submitting copy to the *New York Times* containing the word "euhemeristic." A hearing will be held by me at your convenience. It is respectfully suggested that a jail sentence can be avoided by you if hereafter you will provide a dictionary of your own copy to all typesetters.
>
> Very truly yours,
>
> P.S.   By the way—what does the darn word mean, anyway?

Whenever Swope felt that the president was losing sight of an important issue, he took it upon himself to remind him of the matter. On those occasions when he felt that Roosevelt might be too sensitive to accept the view of one outside his immediate circle, he used an intermediary—

as when he wrote to Farley in 1935 that the business community's hatred of Roosevelt was becoming irrational and that perhaps something might be done to conciliate the tycoons.

With his broad range of acquaintances, Swope was in an excellent position to know how deep that hatred was. Edward F. Hutton, a Palm Beach pal and head of General Foods (by marriage to Mrs. Post), was urging his industrial colleagues to "gang up in a great business and industrial lobby." William Randolph Hearst ordered his editors to refer to the New Deal in print as the "Raw Deal." Swope was perceptive enough to know that the renegade patrician in the White House would not take kindly to the information, which was why he used Farley. He was right; Roosevelt's position only became more inimical to big business. Had he been more flexible, he might have avoided the humiliating defeats he suffered at the hands of a conservative Congress in the latter part of his second term.

When Swope felt the need to communicate, it did not matter where he was or what he was doing—he sat down to write a letter. Befuddling those critics who claimed there was nothing more important to him than a nag, he would even take pen in hand at Saratoga when the spirit moved him, as it did after one of Alfred Landon's speeches during the '36 presidential campaign. He felt impelled to tell Roosevelt that the Landon speech could not have been more helpful had Roosevelt written it himself. Swope apologized for being "foggy," when actually he was deliberately obscuring another plea for Roosevelt to broaden his appeal by broadening his point of view. Swope said that

> . . . the grand strategy in this battle is to be firm without being ferocious; to be kindly rather than cold; to be hopeful instead of pessimistic; to be human rather than to be economic; to be insistent upon every man having a chance, and above all, to make yourself appear to be the President of *all* the people to whom you are again submitting your candidacy—not merely to the Democrats, but to the Republicans and to anyone else who believes in what you have done, what you have tried to do and what you are going to do.

Roosevelt answered immediately:

> That was a grand letter and I agree with all you say, and, incidentally, I have yet to find your mind "foggy"!
> I saw your boy at Hyde Park and he is grand.
> We are off tonight for the drought region and they tell me the trip

will be hot and dusty, but I really do get a much better picture from seeing things than I do from hearing about them. I expect to be in Washington for about a week after the eleventh of September. Perhaps you will have a chance to run down then. I hope Saratoga was good to you, and wish I could have gone up there for a day of racing.

When the Soviet Union attacked Finland on November 30, 1939, Swope, like most of his friends, was immediately sympathetic to the plight of the gallant little democracy. Sherwood wrote one of his finest plays on the subject, the Pulitzer Prize–winning *There Shall Be No Night*. He worked on it at such a pitch of indignation that it was finished and in production within three months of the attack. The brilliant acting team of Alfred Lunt and Lynn Fontanne dropped all other plans in order to appear in the leading roles.

Such was the intellectual climate of Swope's New York when he communicated with the president within days of the attack, suggesting that Roosevelt forgive the interest on Finland's debt. It would be a gesture of sympathy and friendship of no financial cost to the country, for surely Finland would not be able to pay anyway, under the prevailing circumstances.

Roosevelt replied in a very flippant manner on December 7, 1939, exactly two years to the day before the United States was the subject of an atrocious attack:

> You are a trusting soul in suggesting that I could waive payment on the Finnish debt! I may be a benevolent dictator and all-powerful Santa Claus and though the spirit has moved me at times, I still operate under the laws which the all-wise Congress passes.
>
> For example, when you get conscience-stricken and send me a check for one hundred thousand dollars, which you have forgotten to include in previous tax returns, I would love to say to you, Bayard old dear, I have such a sympathy for your present state of bankruptcy that I hereby remit the check to you. How I wish I could help out you and Finland—brave souls both—but whether we like it or not, Congress and God still live!

Swope responded with a letter redolent of sarcasm, beginning: "Your letter of December 7th was a liberal education in the rights, perquisites, privileges, and appurtenances of a Dictator."

In the summer of 1939, Roosevelt confidentially told Postmaster General Jim Farley that he would not run for a third term. Farley was relieved, for he did not believe in third terms; also, although he did not voice the idea, he thought that, as the loyal chairman of the party, perhaps it was his turn to have a try for the presidency. As late as the spring of 1940, Eleanor Roosevelt believed that her husband did not want to run: "It became clearly evident to me, from little things he said at different times, that he would really like to be in Hyde Park, and that the role of elder statesman appealed to him."

Like many of his friends and colleagues, Swope had mixed feelings about the situation. He did not believe in third terms, especially for so imperious a president. At the same time, he felt that the danger that the new European war might turn into another world war was so great that it was no time to change presidents, despite his qualms about the personality of the man in office. He urged Roosevelt to run that May, but he believed that the president had to make up his mind immediately, one way or the other. Hitler had invaded Scandinavia; the fall of France was imminent; the Dutch and Belgian armies were surrendering in the North. It was no time for Roosevelt to carry on a coy flirtation with the nomination.

On June 28, 1940, an event occurred at the Republican convention in Philadelphia that Arthur Krock called a "political miracle." Wendell Willkie was nominated on the sixth ballot, after trailing Thomas Dewey by over 250 votes on the first ballot. The Democratic convention was to open in Chicago less than three weeks later. Roosevelt still had not announced his candidacy.

Farley was ready to break openly with Roosevelt and make a serious bid. He asked for Swope's support. Swope gave it, believing that if Roosevelt declined to run and Farley got hold of the convention, he would not run himself. Smith and the Catholic issue were still too fresh in everybody's mind. Swope was positive that Farley would support Cordell Hull for the presidency if Farley himself were nominated for the vice-presidency.

By the time the convention opened on July 15, the Roosevelt strategy was clear to Swope. Harry Hopkins, Swope's good friend and Roosevelt's closest adviser, was there unofficially representing the president. He told Swope confidentially that the idea was to have Roosevelt nominated by acclamation without his ever placing himself in official nomination. This would defuse the third-term issue and make it seem that Roosevelt was simply bowing to the inevitability of the people's choice.

Hopkins asked Swope where he stood, and Swope replied that he would not resist acclamation, but, barring that, he would stand by his promise to vote for Farley on the first ballot. Acclamation failed, but when the president was placed in nomination he won easily on the first ballot. Swope's vote was one of the 149 cast against him.

For the second time, he had not been among the initial supporters of the president. Hopkins had warned him that this would not go down well. It did not matter. He neither expected nor desired anything. If there had been no gratitude for bringing Smith around in '32, he knew that he could expect nothing in '40, even if he were to bring Farley back into the fold. He later rationalized to Felix Frankfurter: "I would not have voted for Farley if my vote had been the one that would have made him President of the United States, or even the nominee. I did, however, cast a ballot for him as a symbol of appreciation of his honesty, his hard work, and his loyalty to party and to chief."

After 1942, Roosevelt's relationship with Swope grew ever more distant. The correspondence continued, but when Swope had something important to communicate to the president, he sometimes used indirect channels, as when he wrote a brilliant memo to Hopkins on the subject of providing aid to Russia after the German attack:

> We are opposed to the Communists' formula, and we are opposed to the Nazi formula. In the twenty-seven years since Russia became Communist, our national interest and our way of life have never been seriously threatened by the Soviets. But in the two years of Hitler's mad drive for world enslavement, our very existence, as a free people, has been gravely endangered.
>
> Attempts to divide us have been made by would-be Quislings acting within our borders. They have tried to create racial and religious differences; they have promised peace and quiet through Nazi appeasement.
>
> Now we see what a grim tragedy a Nazi peace treaty is. Now we see again the fate that has overtaken fifteen nations which, relying upon Nazi promises, were destroyed one by one.
>
> We are not for Communism, but we are against all that Hitler stands for. He and his godless Nazis are the pressing threats to a world of peace and justice and security. In his defeat lies our safety.
>
> At this time as ever we must keep in mind that our greatest strength is in unity; our greatest danger in discord.

"To my ⊣̲⊢." Strangely, when Maggie scribbled the address on the back of some pages from Swope's own memo pad, she drew the swastika backward. Certainly the symbol was too painfully familiar in 1939; it must have been that she was extremely overwrought when she wrote the note. One wonders whether she was implying that he was her dictator.

> Darling—Why do you behave so terribly—I was only thinking of you anyway. Your routine approach to our love life is heavy and labored—and your fury is really on a point which has no basis in fact. You know first of all that I adore you—you must know that I honor and respect you above any living soul. I thank my God every minute of every day—for you and your patience—your fine qualities—what you have meant to my existence and everyone's in our very large house—your goodness, your never-ending honesty, and yourself—as a man who has made every other man pale into nonexistence for me. If all this means anything to you—if it puts, as you so often say, ashes of roses—then be sweeter. You are always strong; don't add a weakening bad temper to your mature life. In these dreadful days and in our heavenly home here let's grab all we can of life—love & liberty. Tell me you still care. You are my all—Mag.

Swope was restless, discontented; he felt moribund, stifled by obligations he wanted to be free of. There was a war going on; he wanted to be a part of it, to do his share for a cause in which he believed. She could only interpret this as his wanting to be free of her. When he or anybody else would suggest a way in which he could serve, she would only repeat mechanically, "What do you want to do a thing like that for?"

She was actually begging him not to desert her. Family, friends, a way of life: they were all meaningless when compared to him, for only he had the power to leave her alone and frightened in the sleepless night. He knew, he understood, but this time he would not listen to anything but his own inner voice. He felt the waste of his own accomplishments and time—the promise unfulfilled, plans abandoned, ten years too long at the fair. He was not yet sixty; surely it was not too late. In that menacing period, his gifts might still be gratefully accepted. An image had been projected that denied the seriousness within. He had to free himself of it. Too much family, too much house, too much fun, too much service to others, too much cultivation of the gifts of others. He had to get back to himself, to the self who could still emerge if only he could find the strength to turn away. But there she was, still standing before him, still crying, "What do you want to do a thing like that for?"

She needed him, and he loved her, and it had been so good, this life they had built of their intelligence and passion and adoration of each other. The need—he knew without admitting it—was his as well as hers. Could he leave it, and for what?—the two questions to which he did not have answers. Did that doom him forever to stand beside other men and prompt them to the actions he would take, were it not for this thing they had created, this need, this love?

Averell Harriman recalled him at this period in his life:

> [Swope] was very much the life—the weekend life at Sands Point as far as I was concerned. The conversation was some of the best I ever participated in. He used to talk things over. I didn't necessarily accept his opinions, but they were stimulating. He made you think about things in a different way. He would analyze the situation—the sort of things I ought to be doing—the sort of things the country ought to be doing. . . . I don't know why he didn't settle down and do something. He had such a quick and restless mind. To settle down and be a public relations firm and take on a load of boring accounts would not be something that he would want to do. Maggie was a strong woman. She would always think something he was asked to do was not worth his strength. I think she stopped him from doing some of the things he might have done.

In the spring of 1940 France had not yet fallen, but its collapse seemed imminent. Much of America was still isolationist. Charles Lindbergh, Swope's onetime idol, was traveling through the country, proclaiming "America First." It was not our war. Why should we become involved? He was a national hero, one who commanded attention. With spurious reasoning, he would point out that the only times America had ever been invaded, it had been by England.

All-out support for Great Britain—covering every possibility short of entering the war—was a matter of utmost concern to those Americans whose intellects could pull abreast of their passions. A group of these gentlemen got together to form the Committee to Defend America by Aiding the Allies, with that as its avowed purpose. William Allen White was national chairman, with Clark Eichelberger, formerly of the League of Nations Association, as executive director, and George Field as regional secretary.

The nucleus of the group included many of Swope's friends who were part of the liberal establishment in New York City: George Backer, who was running the New York *Post,* which recently had been purchased by his wife, the former Dolly Schiff; Dr. Frank Kingdon, the crusading columnist and theologian; Hendrik Willem van Loon, the popular historian; and Arthur Goldsmith, who had broken with his partner, Joseph Kennedy, to become an early foe of Americans with pro-German sympathies, among whom many numbered his former colleague.

It was the cause for which Swope had been waiting, one to which he could commit himself wholeheartedly without the threat to Maggie's well-being that would have been engendered by his physical absence. He was elected treasurer, in spite of the skepticism of many of the members, who knew that his attention span was short and he had previously involved himself in causes only to give them up after six months or a year. They were proven wrong, for until the day he died he was completely faithful and available to the organization as it evolved with the changing times.

Within six months of its inception the committee became the focus of national attention when George Field organized the Freedom Rally at Madison Square Garden, where the crowd was so large that 80,000 people had to be turned away. Wendell Willkie was the speaker for the United States, and there was a spokesman for each of the countries that had been conquered by the Germans. Before each speech, the Garden would darken, and a spotlight would pick out the imposing figure of Swope, who would come forward to present the colors of the representative's country and to make a short introduction. It was a majestic ceremony, and many in the audience were moved to tears as the light hit Swope, slowly carrying the flag of the fallen nation toward the center of the stage.

Swope's phenomenal range of contacts was put at the disposal of the organization. Did they need Ethel Barrymore for a rally at the World's Fair, or Tallulah Bankhead at Manhattan Beach, or James Forrestal for a dinner? They would call Swope, and with a ten-minute phone conversation he would have the commitment. When the organization needed a headquarters, Swope got Robert Lehman to give them space in his building on 53rd Street, rent-free.

By 1944 the Committee to Defend America by Aiding the Allies had merged with Fight for Freedom, to form Freedom House. Willkie died in October of that year, and the organization wanted a building on West 40th Street to serve as a headquarters and as a memorial to Willkie. They needed to raise money to make the purchase and perform the necessary renovations. They needed a chairman for the funding committee, and Field again went to Swope, who said, "How about Henry Luce?"

Luce would do just fine. Swope got on his trusty telephone, and within five minutes Luce had agreed. Money did not come in as rapidly as they had anticipated. When it was learned that the building was owned by Lewis Rosenstiel, Field was back in Swope's office, and Swope was back on the phone.

"Lew, I've got this young fellow here, a friend of mine; he's got an interesting deal for you. Freedom House wants to set up a memorial for Willkie. You've got that building on 40th Street. We'd like to have it for that purpose." He put his hand over the phone and asked Field, "How much have you got?" All they had was $150,000. He told Rosenstiel, "I'm told all they have to offer is $150,000."

Rosenstiel hit the roof. He had already turned down an offer of $350,000 for the building. Swope took another ten minutes to describe glowingly what the deal would do for Rosenstiel's public image and how it would actually cost him nothing in his tax bracket. Ultimately, he talked the owner into taking $100,000 in cash and a first mortgage of $50,000. A short time later, he talked him into forgiving $25,000 of that mortgage. Thanks to Swope, Freedom House paid $125,000 for a building now worth approximately $1,000,000.

After the war, the major efforts of Freedom House were directed to fighting all forms of totalitarianism, be they Communist or fascist. Freedom House was also an early supporter of the civil rights movement. In 1948 Swope set up an appointment for a Freedom House group with President Truman and then went to Washington with them. A national council to investigate civil rights legislation was the result of that meeting. At the same time, he recommended the organization to Secretary of War Robert Patterson, who later became president of Freedom House.

Later, Freedom House supported Truman on the Korean action. It also took an anti-Senator McCarthy position long before Eisenhower, or most people in Washington, awakened to the fact that there were sufficient people in the hinterlands who found the Senator offensive to make taking a stand against him a popular cause. During that ugly period in American history, advertisements warning of the dangers represented by Joseph McCarthy were placed in major publications, over the signatures of Swope and the other officials of the organization. Freedom House was one of the few organizations to point out that fighting against Communism should not be done at the expense of American civil liberties.

There was an annual Freedom House Award dinner. Swope worked very hard, arranging for the presence of speakers and recipients. Naturally he saw to it that Baruch was among those honored. In the last years of his life. Swope, who was already an ill man, would develop laryngitis just before the dinner. Speaking of the laryngitis, George Field recalled:

> I think it became psychosomatic in those later years. He certainly was in full possession of his voice in the earlier years. . . . It would happen almost on the day before the event. He would begin to lose his voice. He'd call and say he didn't think he could go through with it. . . . I heard she [Maggie] was trying to discourage him, especially in the last years, the last five years or so of giving that much time to the work at Freedom House. She thought it was helping to undermine his health. She was not too anxious for him to do so much. This was the impression I had. Never fazed him. He continued his activity and interest to the end. . . . It wasn't that he worked so hard. He accomplished more taking it easy than anybody I ever heard of who worked hard. This was the truth. I never in my life experienced this—where you'd walk over to see a man at six o'clock or five, and he'd get on the phone and, in ten minutes, he'd produce what you wanted. Just as easy as that. He'd get on the phone, and I'd have what I wanted. There wasn't a hell of a lot of work attached to it. He just had the command to get what he wanted, and that's what it amounted to.

Freedom House was one of the few things in which Swope strongly believed and to which he stayed faithful despite Maggie's antagonism. She felt that he devoted far too much time and energy to it, with neither financial reward nor personal honor.

During the period between the fall of France and the attack on Pearl Harbor, Swope and Winston Churchill kept up a close correspondence. Swope's letters to the prime minister were filled with the same style of bully-boy vim-and-grit encouragement as were the latter's messages to the British people; Churchill, for his part, used his old American friends as a sounding board for a series of complaints, ideas, and progress reports on English attitudes and morale during that crucial period known as the Battle of Britain.

Averell Harriman was in charge of the American lend-lease program. As part of his duties, he was in touch with British Minister of Information Brendan Bracken. A segment of the American population was still against the concept of lend-lease, and Harriman asked Swope to prepare a memo for Bracken, outlining his ideas on how Bracken could best handle news releases to America to gain maximum support for the English.

In a terse and brilliant paper, Swope put forth concepts combining his experiential knowledge of the needs of the foreign correspondent with his insight into the ways of shaping opinion in his country:

1. The underlying philosophy of British news releases and commentaries should be the unswerving, undying spirit of determination. You know:

   > "Come the world against her—
   > England yet shall stand."

   (That, by the way, is a hell of a good quotation I heard Phillip Snowden use in the House of Lords several years ago. It is from Swinburne.)

2. I do not think policy or expediency should be permitted to affect news releases. The sanctity of a fact should be preserved. There should be no effort made to turn its edge. Interpretation may be added, but that should be on the responsibility of the Ministry.

3. If Britain has a victory, claim it; if Britain sustains a defeat, admit it.

4. I would not attempt to measure the value of a release by its effect on the public mind; first, one cannot be sure what that effect is; and second, one can alienate the reader by attempting to put a ring in his nose. For example:

   > In reporting losses in the Atlantic, I suggest that they should be stated without qualification. With that can be given the comparative figures on the unrestricted U-boat warfare of late '17 and '18. The comparison, by the way, is not bad.

5. Every possible effort should be made to show that Britain is attempting to wage a war of movement, and is not indulging in a "Sitzkrieg"; that she realizes she is on her own and is not waiting for America to pull her chestnuts out of the fire; that she feels herself capable of beating off Hitler and all others who might come against her, and that she is willing to take them all on, if she has to, to preserve her Freedom. (These are answers to the aspersions of the America First Committee.)

6. Do not let the impression gain prevalence that Britain believes she is fighting America's battle. This is her own battle, which may be (as, indeed, it is) the first line of defense for us. But the tendency on the part of some English, and a few Americans, to make it appear that were it not for England's desire to save us she would not be in the fighting is embarrassing.

7. Give us pictures of the air force, of the women, and especially of your leaders. With them should come personality stories— America loves that sort of thing. Give us action pictures of the

R.A.F. Give us action pictures of the American planes—if any are being flown.

8. While pursuing this positive program, don't forget the negative. Attacks on Hitler are always good. Bring out, whenever possible, his perfidy; how many times he has broken his pledged word; his treachery, by which he has tried (and succeeded) in debauching nations.

9. Hess was not used to full extent. It is all very well to talk about the great wall of silence in which he has been buried. Why not tell stories, by indirection, of his having flown with peace overtures; his closeness to Hitler—one away—makes anything he does of great significance. He will not be able to deny the stories, and, besides, the stories would be true in their substance.

10. And if the Army has done away with the Old School Ties and the Col. Blimps, it seems to me the Navy might well break down its specious reputation of being the "silent service." Don't let America think she is doing all the work in the Atlantic.

11. Print all possible pictures of the various English ships. Ships, next to women, have an irresistible appeal to readers.

12. Give us more stuff about the various commanders—we know about Cunningham, but who are the other fellows who are adding new glory to the Nelson tradition?

13. Play up the Irish Catholics in the service. Too bad O'Connor (of the army) was grabbed in Libya just as he was becoming a romantic figure. Play up the Irish, but give emphasis to the Southerners.

14. Make it plain for American consumption that Russia is not a co-equal ally; that she is an associate or, perhaps, an instrument. In America we are not for Stalin; we are against Hitler and any stick is good enough to beat that dog with! . . .

P.S.: One last thought, even though it is supererogatory:
Be brutally frank with the correspondents. Trust them, and if they are unworthy of trust, throw them out. Give background stuff. Help them to get their stories. You will find most of them, although thoroughly honest, are wholly with Britain and America either because they feel that way or because of their environment.

It was this combination of perceptions into the ways of shaping public opinion and the needs of newspapermen, plus an attitude toward military censorship that called for the release of all information that did not directly endanger the lives of combatants (a recurring theme with Swope since his reporting days in World War I), that made a group of influential men around Roosevelt, including Hopkins, Patterson, and Forrestal, think of creating a post for Swope similar to the English Ministry of Information. The military hegemony vetoed the idea. If they were to prepare for war, they could not submit to civilian control over what was told to the people. It was interesting to note that the British armed forces, who were actively engaged in fighting a war, could submit to a civilian Minister of Information, while their American counterparts, who were simply preparing for the eventuality of war, could not put up with one. Ironically, they could not have found a better man than Swope for the post. It might have provided him with his most challenging job since his days on the *World*.

Although Swope believed in maximum dissemination of facts, he was also aware of the exigencies of war. As early as May 1931, he had testified before a joint congressional and cabinet committee known as the War Policies Commission:

> Enlightened and informed public opinion in war is ideal, but the plan is dangerous. Censorship must prevail.
>
> That is a terrifically high cost, but war is never cheap. I oppose war with all my might. But if it comes—however wrong some might hold it to be; however righteous others see it to be—then it should be fought quickly, desperately, and every agency of victory should be utilized. And of these, public opinion, directed, controlled, and disseminated, is the greatest.
>
> Just as other constitutional provisions are ignored in time of war, so, too, must there be an abridgement of free speech, free press, free assembly and even free thought. In no other way can a nation save itself.
>
> Wars are won not by guns, but by spirit; just as raw materials, capital and men are conscripted, so must public opinion be dealt with in time of war. . . .
>
> In time of war the free play of public opinion, with its violent contradictions, its cross-currents, its revelation of truths, must cease. Important as is liberty, life is more important.

That waiting period, during which he saw the inevitability of war and still hated it, became a period of truces in personal animosities. After many years of Swope-sniping, Woollcott wrote to him, "I am writing this on the chance of your sharing my own conviction that the time has come to bury all hatchets—in Hitler's neck."

Swope answered, "I was touched by your letter. The call of the years is hard to resist, so I, too, want the unpleasantness to end. Friends are few and far between and their rarity becomes greater as one grows older."

They met a few times and maintained an amiable relationship for the remainder of Woollcott's life. But it could never be what it once was, for by that time Woollcott was insisting that people take him seriously as a thinker and commentator on world and national affairs. This Swope could not do. Even at the height of their friendship, he had found Woollcott an amusing if waspish companion, an entertaining critic, but not a serious or deep thinker. Nothing had happened in the intervening years to make him alter that opinion.

Maggie brought about an amnesty with Edna Ferber, but the spinsterish writer could never refrain from preaching to him, and the text of the sermon was always based on her personal apocrypha of Swope. In early 1945, during a trip to Europe as a war correspondent, she wrote, "I wish you would go to Europe for a few weeks. Men like you should see this frightful sight and use your fine intelligence and your power and your eloquence to check its spread. And the hell with racing."

She did not seem to have noticed that the race tracks had been closed for the duration the previous year or that Swope's last connection with the sport had been as chairman of the executive committee of the Turf Committee of America, which had raised seventeen million dollars for Army and Navy Relief by holding a series of special races at tracks around the country just before they shut down. He actually had an opportunity to go on a junket to Europe for no greater purpose than looking—he turned it down, because he felt that "no man has the right to go abroad unless he has a specific job to do."

Soon after the United States entered the war, the army's Bureau of Public Relations was placed under the jurisdiction of the civilian Secretary of War, Henry L. Stimson. The Bureau was supervised by General Alexander D. Surles, but he was responsible to the secretary rather than to the chief of staff. Stimson appointed Swope Surles's deputy in July 1942, with the title of Consultant to the Secretary of War.

From the beginning, Surles did not trust him. Surles was a military man used to a rigid chain of command, which he interpreted as meaning that Swope reported directly to him. That was not Swope's interpretation. He thought that Surles was a military hack, and that the consultant to the secretary should deal with the secretary. If he could get no satisfaction there, he planned to go higher, even directly to the president.

The battle of the office was a decisive one. To cut Swope down to size, Surles ordered that he be assigned a small inner office at the Pentagon.

Even in the miles of the Pentagon, there were only a limited number of offices with windows, and the wartime aggregation of army brass had first call on them. Swope enjoyed his close friendships with men like generals George C. Marshall and Dwight D. Eisenhower, but he was overly impressed neither with anybody under their rank nor with the military for the military's sake.

He stormed into Stimson's office and said that the room assigned to him was a deliberate insult to the secretary. Stimson assured him that it was not, that it was only a question of available space. Swope replied, "Every lieutenant colonel has an office with a window. How will it look to the people who come to see me? Important publishers, Senators, Justices, other members of the cabinet. Who comes to see a lieutenant colonel? Other lieutenant colonels!"

Swope got his new office, and Surles kept a polite distance, which led his deputy to suspect, rightly or not, that the general was afraid Swope was after his job.

Swope's goal of consulting with the secretary was not so easily accomplished. The urgencies of time often did not permit this, for the secretary was an extremely busy man and could not make himself available whenever Swope wanted to see him. Beyond that, their schedules were at odds. Stimson was already seventy-five years old and not all that robust; to preserve his strength, he took long naps every afternoon, and afternoons were when Swope was at his best. Swope had to content himself with the undersecretary, Robert P. Patterson. This turned out to be fortunate for both of them. Like many reserved men before him, Patterson was immediately attracted to the exuberant Swope, with his endless outpouring of ideas and opinions on almost every subject. Patterson enjoyed using Swope as a sounding board. As Harriman said, "You did not have to agree with everything Swope said, but it was all worth hearing. It helped to clarify your own thoughts."

Swope served brilliantly as mediator between the army and the nation's press, which was not above criticizing the military even in times of war. Superficially, that was supposed to be his only job; however, he did much more, rushing forth with suggestions that ranged through the entire span of operations of the Department of War. As Stimson pointed out, "Mr. Swope always has a duty of helpfulness, which he performs admirably well in consultation and conference."

Swope and Patterson jointly led a movement to end racial segregation in the services. Owing to their efforts, the army was the first of the service branches to integrate its personnel. Swope also fought doggedly to end censorship of what soldiers were permitted to read. He believed that if a man was risking his life for his country, he had the right to form an opinion on the value of that sacrifice and the right to have access to anything that might help him to formulate that opinion, even the journals of dissent.

Swope generally spent three days a week in Washington, and Maggie often accompanied him. She once boasted that her one wartime service was to ruin the air conditioning at the Hotel Mayflower. In an effort to get proper ventilation, she broke the seals on all the windows. Her justification to the management was, "Just because you pack us in like sardines, you don't have to hermetically seal us, too."

On one of their excursions to the capital, Swope took Maggie down to see his new office on the prestigious side of the Pentagon. He asked the clerk for a pass for his wife. The young man said, "Sorry, sir. But no wives are permitted in the Pentagon building."

Swope demanded imperiously: "Would it make any difference if I told you we were never married?" The clerk was aghast, and Maggie sailed by into the building.

To bolster the roster of writers on the *World-Telegram,* which had sagged badly since the great days of the *World,* Roy Howard hired Eleanor Roosevelt to write a column, MY DAY. It was filled with optimism and observations of gallant behavior during the war. One evening Maggie was complaining so bitterly about the trips to Washington that Moss Hart commented, "I can't wait for Herbert to become President. Then you can write a column and call it MY GOD-DAMNED DAY."

Actually, there was little about which she could feel sanguine. Between the trips to Washington and the wartime shortages of everything from food to help, it was almost impossible to maintain the style of life she had created at Sands Point. Most of the young men she loved were in the armed forces, including both Ottie and Bob Brandt, who were serving in the navy.

Swope was an early admirer of Adlai Stevenson. He contributed financially to all of Stevenson's bids for office, including the Illinois gubernatorial race. One night during the war, Stevenson, who was the Assistant Secretary of the Navy, was seated next to Maggie at dinner. He asked about Ottie. When she told him the branch of the navy in which he was serving—minesweeping—he said, "You must be very proud," and went on to explain that it was the most dangerous branch of the service.

She said, in a voice that rolled down the length of the table, "Comforting bastard, isn't he?"

A few days later, Stevenson wrote a letter to Ottie, saying, "I had dinner with your mother the other night. She's a most formidable lady."

Strangely enough, the only person who did not write to Ottie was Maggie. She later explained that she had not written because she was afraid it would bring him bad luck. It was a strange excuse, and the young man could not help wondering whether it was not at least partially another example of her "out of sight, out of mind" philosophy toward people.

It had often been suggested that the Swopes set up trust funds for their children rather than giving them annual tax-free gifts. Maggie always refused to consider this plan, which was so sensible from every point of view. "No," she said. "If we give them the money now, they might not come to see me again. I don't ever want to have to go to my children. I want them to be with me."

On days when Maggie was not in Washington with Swope and when George S. Kaufman and Cole Porter were busy working on shows, she, Bea Kaufman, and Linda Porter would go to the theater together and to the 21 club afterwards. During the war, it was even more difficult than usual to get a good table at the fashionable restaurant. The three ladies would insist upon having the best table in the room, where, to the chagrin of help and management, they would order only cup after cup of black coffee, tipping commensurately. One waiter shrugged philosophically: "It's better than at dinner. At dinner, Mrs. Swope is a half-hour late for her reservation, insists upon being served immediately so she won't be late for the theater, and then sends the food back because it isn't prepared to her taste."

In July 1945, one month before the end of the war, Swope ended his service with the War Department. Maggie was eager to take up life where they had left off. The boys would all be home from the service soon; it was time to begin again. Swope often said, "My only natural resource is myself." She felt that he had to start using it again to sustain the environment in which they thrived so gloriously.

Swope was beginning to feel his own mortality. He had been very moved by the death of Franklin D. Roosevelt three months before. They had not been close for some time. Swope had not even bothered to attend the '44 convention, which prompted one wag to comment, "It can't be much of a ballgame if Swope's not here to throw out the first vice-president." However, they were the same age and their lives had been intertwined since they had been young men starting out on their careers.

It was indeed time for Swope to start putting his affairs in order. There might not be many years left. Too much of his energy had gone into public service without recompense. He still had an office in the Squibb

Building, staffed only by Helen Millar and one assistant, but that was all he had ever needed. He was indeed his only natural resource (some would have termed it a natural phenomenon), so with the coming of peace he turned his attention back to industrial counseling. He still had CBS and Rosenstiel, to whom he soon added Twentieth Century-Fox, Aluminum Corporation of America, Standard Oil of New Jersey, and the textile complex of Beaunit Mills.

If there was inner tribulation, it did not show on the surface. He was still the *bon vivant,* the first nighter, the magnificent host, the man who could hold forth brilliantly on any subject at such length that people were constantly reminded of the time he was seated beside the actress Mrs. Patrick Campbell. He was interrupted in mid-conversational flight by what sounded like a gurgle coming from the actress. He asked, "What was that?"

She replied, "A word trying to get in edgewise."

Maggie had her own intimation of mortality in October 1945, when Bea Kaufman died suddenly of a cerebral hemorrhage. Bea was younger than she was, only fifty-one, and an irreplaceable friend. They had shared a sense of humor, a point of view, a relationship of equals that could never be duplicated with any of the resident slaves, who changed with the temperature of Maggie's whim. She had known Bea for half a lifetime—Bea had been more consistently close for a longer period than any other friend had ever been. There had been fights and reconciliations, recriminations and defenses, screaming laughter and instant understanding, a ritual of telephone calls and shared confidences.

Bea had been unique among the people Maggie loved. She had never tried to possess her, had never felt the need to, for she had always taken it for granted that Bea would be there should anything go wrong. Who would be there now? She drew the family in closer, making special friends of their friends, and a whole new generation started listening to her irresistible siren song. "What do you want to do that for? Why do anything but be here? Where else is as good? Come to me. Stay, stay."

And they did come repeatedly. They were young, many of them still in their twenties—awed by the opulence, staggered by their own emergence out of obscurity into an atmosphere where dinner might find them seated next to Winston Churchill, Charlie Chaplin, or Henry Luce; Ottie's friends, Bruce's, and Jane's; Bill and Dougie Harbach, Martin Gabel, Arlene Francis, Joan Alexander, Betty Comden, Adolph Green.

Joan Alexander was a struggling young actress when Bruce, who was then a theatrical agent, first brought her out. Swope, the master of the backhanded compliment, said, "Flathead, you've a certain kind of beauty."

Maggie took a shine to her. "Come out. Come every weekend."

"I can't. I've got to look for work."

"Where?"

"NBC."

"Roy and the car will be waiting to drive you."

"I haven't got the right dress—"

"We've got plenty of dresses."

And she did come. And when she married, her first husband came. He, however, made the mistake of borrowing a shirt from Swope and not returning it. Swope neither forgot nor forgave. Swope was generous with everything but his clothes. Then she remarried. When she brought Arthur Stanton out to the sun porch, which was crowded with the likes of Harriman, Alfred Vanderbilt, and Janet Stewart, Joan cried, "Everybody, this is Arthur." So what? They looked up from their games for a moment and went right back to them. Only Swope came forward to shake his hand. "Welcome. Glad to have you here. Welcome."

Betty Comden and Adolph Green were dazzled and delighted. When they met Swope, he knew who they were, what they had done, could discuss their work, commend them for it. "Imagine a man like that taking the trouble!"

For Billy Harbach, son of the lyricist Otto, brought up in a house of music frequented by his father's collaborators Jerome Kern, Rudolf Friml, and Sigmund Romberg, it was "Camelot."

NINETEEN

It was not long before another siren voice called to Swope, and it was irresistible; he went. In 1946 President Truman asked Baruch to serve on the Atomic Energy Commission at the United Nations. At the time, the United States was alone in possessing nuclear weapons, but it obviously would not be long before Russia and the other major powers developed them. The Security Council had established the committee to devise an overall policy that would check the irresponsibility inherent in nationalism. Earlier, Dean Acheson and David Lilienthal had written an American report, which, for their country's own reasons, was deficient as an international document of determent.

Baruch chose as his advisers Ferdinand Eberstadt, a brilliant strategist who had been in charge of industrial priorities at the War Production Board; Fred Searls, one of the world's best mining engineers; John Hancock, an investment banker and a specialist in corporate reorganization; and Swope. It was to be Swope's special duty to handle Baruch's image in the press and to write the words that would give him the sound as well as the appearance of a Solon. Baruch admitted in his memoirs that it was Swope who had taught him how to speak, had turned him from a stammerer into a creature with some reputation for eloquence. "I had a habit of speaking through almost-clenched lips. Herbert Bayard Swope would often say, 'For heaven's sake, open your mouth!' In 1939, I was asked to deliver a short radio tribute on the death of Pope Pius XI. As I talked, Swope stood in front of me making facial gestures to remind me to 'open your mouth.' "

The four associates got on so well that they later commissioned the artist Alois Derso to do a painting of them as Dumas's musketeers, thereby outdoing any Hollywood epic by making Baruch the only d'Artagnan ever to have four musketeers. It was the sort of aggrandizement they knew Bernie would appreciate.

The group, with the exception of Swope, was composed of multimillionaires, so there was no recompense. Although he was concerned about his financial situation, Swope agreed to go along with them, working for no other payment than the greater glory of Baruch.

The commission came up with the Baruch Plan, which called for United Nations inspectors to have the right of unlimited inspection inside countries engaged in producing nuclear arms. It also called for the suspension of veto power in the Security Council, should any of the countries violate the atomic accord. In view of the fact that America was the only country with nuclear weapons and the capacity to build more, it was a generous plan. Had it been accepted, much of the travail that came with the spread of nuclear arms might have been averted.

The Russians were very close to developing their own atomic bomb; in addition, they were extreme xenophobes. The plan was unacceptable to them. The left and right wings in the United States joined, as they so often did, in mutual condemnation. To the right, the plan was unacceptable because it gave away too much. To the left, it was unacceptable because it was too rigid and let American nuclear superiority remain intact. The latter much preferred a plan formulated by the Russians, which called for the United States to destroy its bomb and to share its atomic secrets without any rights of international inspection and without suspension of the veto power, which Russia was then using far more regularly than any other major nation.

Baruch knew that his plan had to be presented with a speech that would be widely quoted; it was the only chance it had for a fair hearing. He naturally turned to Swope, who came through brilliantly with what is still considered an oratorical classic:

> We are here to make a choice between the quick and the dead.
>
> That is our business.
>
> Behind the black portent of the new atomic age lies a hope which, seized upon with faith, can work our salvation. If we fail, then we have damned every man to be the slave of Fear. Let us not deceive ourselves: we must elect World Peace or World Destruction.
>
> Science has torn from nature a secret so vast in its potentialities that our minds cower from the terror it creates. Yet terror is not enough to inhibit the use of the atomic bomb. The terror created by weapons has never stopped man from employing them. For each new weapon a defense has been produced, in time. But now we face a condition in which adequate defense does not exist.
>
> Science, which gave us this dread power, shows that it *can* be made a giant help to humanity, but science does *not* show us how to prevent its baleful use. So we have been appointed to obviate that peril by finding a meeting of the minds and the hearts of our peoples. Only in the will of mankind lies the answer. . . .

Baruch then presented his plan, which also outlined what his country was willing to give up: it would yield all of its knowledge of nuclear power to a World Atomic Authority, provided the proper controls were set up. He concluded with:

> The light at the end of the tunnel is dim, but our path seems to grow brighter as we actually begin our journey. We cannot yet light the way to the end. . . . The way is long and thorny but supremely worth travelling. All of us want to stand erect with our faces to the sun, instead of being forced to burrow into the earth like rats.
>
> The pattern of salvation must be worked out by all for all.

Though the acclaim was general, it did not silence the old adversaries of left and right. Hearst's *Journal-American* announced, "A stunned capital reacted adversely today to the proposal." Henry Wallace made a speech blasting American foreign policy and then released a letter he had written to the president, condemning the Baruch Plan as being condescending to the Russians.

The national controversy gave much-needed aid to the Russians, who began to play a cat-and-mouse game—one day they seemed to agree to the Baruch Plan, only to abstain from voting the next, thus successfully killing it.

The commission resigned in December 1946. The Baruch Plan was neither passed nor rejected, but merely floundered for over a decade, amid supporters and detractors, until some of its major points were taken up by the British "Ban the Bomb" movement, which ultimately succeeded in one purpose of the commission—that of banning use of the bomb in war. It still failed in the broader aim of banning the manufacture and spread of the bomb.

In the first draft of "the quick and the dead" speech, which was delivered in June 1946, Swope had used the phrase "cold war" to describe the state of Russian-American relations. Considered too provocative, it was later deleted. They decided to save it for use in another speech. It was actually first used in a speech Swope wrote for Baruch, which he delivered in April of the following year before the South Carolina legislature. Baruch said, "Let us not be deceived—we are today in the midst of a cold war."

The speech was widely reprinted, and Baruch generously gave Swope credit for it. Walter Lippmann was not so generous—he preempted the term in one of his articles. He wrote, "The cold war will smolder on for generations."

A controversy erupted, with Swope averring that the phrase had first come to him in relation to Hitler in 1939, and Lippmann countering that it was then in common parlance in France and that both had gotten it from the same source.

Swope had always been punctilious about credit for things he did or did not say. When a mild joke that Kaufman had coined in the '20s was credited to him, he wrote such an abject apology that a bemused Kaufman felt compelled to reply, "If you'll meet me at my lawyer's, I'll be happy to deed over to you all rights in and to and against that joke about Lucy Stone. I doubt if this transaction will really stand up in law, because (a) I don't know if I really said it and (b) I don't think it's much of a joke anyway."

The controversy over "cold war" continued, with *The Dictionary of*

New Words in English crediting Lippmann with the phrase, and *American Words* giving it to Swope.

Almost a decade after Swope died, Paul Seabury, professor of political science at the University of California at Berkeley, attempted to clarify the matter for his book *The Rise and Decline of the Cold War.* He wrote to Lippmann about the origin of the phrase and received the following reply:

> I have often been asked that question, and my answer is that I did not invent the phrase "cold war," and neither did Baruch or Swope.
>
> During the 1930's, there were current in Europe two phrases; one, "la guerre blanche," and the other, "la guerre froide," to describe Hitler's methods of undermining governments. When I wrote my book, I wondered whether I should call it the White War or the Cold War, and I decided against the White War because of the confusion with White Russians.
>
> It's a silly thing to claim credit for. The phrase was in public domain for years before any of us used it.

Professor Seabury was not satisfied with Lippmann's explanation and followed it up with his own investigations, by which he learned: "The editors of *Petit Larousse* write me that they first listed the expression 'guerre froide' in 1948. Their archives do not refer to it before the fall of France. The expression 'guerre blanche' is unknown to them. . . . Lippmann might be right, but French lexicographers doubt it."

At about the same time, a biographer of Swope requested an interview with Lippmann. In the course of a discussion with his friend Drew Dudley over whether or not he should grant the interview, Lippmann said testily, "Swope was a vastly overrated man."

Swope would have been the first to be amused. He said in a letter to Laurence Spivack in 1945 that Lippmann meant "much to American thought; he is a guide, philosopher and friend in Life and Politics." Spivack was then editor of the *American Mercury* magazine, which had published, the previous month, a derogatory story about Lippmann written by Fred Rodell.

Swope would probably have tended to dismiss Lippmann as a judge of a man's worth, recalling, with his phenomenal memory, Lippmann's 1932 dismissal of Franklin Delano Roosevelt as "not the dangerous enemy of anything—too eager to please—a pleasant man who, without any important qualifications for the office, would very much like to be President."

TWENTY

The phone started ringing at one in the morning. In most households that would have been cause for alarm; at the Swopes' it was nothing to get upset about; it was not even particularly unusual. Maggie answered it. "Mrs. Swope? This is Maggie—Margaret Hayes. Ottie's at my apartment. He's very ill. I've put him to bed."

"You send him right home."

"I'll do no such thing. He's running a fever of over 103."

"Where do you live? I'll come and get him."

"I wouldn't suggest that. No. That would be a very bad idea." There was a click, and the phone went dead. Maggie Swope was furious; the young woman had dared to hang up on her. She knew her, of course; a beautiful woman, an actress. She was a great friend of George Kaufman, who said she was very gifted. At what? Maggie Swope would have sneered.

The two Maggies were of equal strength and determination. The younger one was true to her word. Maggie Swope did not get into the apartment, nor did Ottie go home until he was completely well. His mother became alarmed. This was no ordinary young woman. She was impervious to charm, and she was impervious to bullying. Maggie began her campaign the moment her son was back on the premises.

"I don't understand what you see in Maggie Hayes," she said. Ottie laughed. To see Maggie was to see what he saw in her.

"She's been married before, you know." Ottie laughed. Divorce was no rarity among the people they knew.

"She's older than you are." Ottie laughed. He knew for a fact that it was not true—and even if it had been, what difference would it have made?

On Maggie Hayes's part, she was not even sure that she wanted him. Kaufman, Hart, all of their common friends had told her that he was mother-ridden, that Maggie Swope would never let go, just as she had never let go of her brother Bruce after his one failure at marriage. Everybody adored Bruce and blamed his sister for being too possessive. Their mother, Mimi, who knew better, did not think it was her daughter's fault. As Maggie Hayes would soon learn, Mimi knew that nobody kept anybody anywhere if that person did not want to stay. All of the people who clung to Maggie Swope were there because they wanted to be there, because there was no place they would rather be. In the final analysis that was also true of her husband. She just made things too damned attractive for any of them to want to escape. With her Scottish asperity, Mimi summed up her son (and many of the others): "The trouble with Bruce is quite simple. He's lazy. And he likes the easy way. Breakfast in bed and all the rest of it. He wants his behind where the easiest seat is—and that's why he's here."

Aside from his mother, there was another obstacle to the romance of Ottie and Maggie Hayes. He was unofficially engaged to Liza Maugham, the daughter of Siri and W. Somerset, whom he had met when Liza came to this country during the Nazi bombing of Britain. Liza was a girl whom Maggie Swope could accept. She was attractive and bright. The family was right, and she was rather unconventional. She might even have elected to live in London while Ottie lived in New York, the two meeting to refresh their relationship during summers at Sands Point. That would have suited his mother perfectly. But Liza had been back in England while Ottie was at sea, and they had not seen each other for over two years.

The love affair between Maggie and Ottie did deepen, and they decided to get married. They refused to elope and tell the family later, as Jane and Bob Brandt had done. The ceremony was to take place in Judge Ferdinand Pecora's living room, and the Swopes were invited.

On the day of the wedding, Swope dressed carefully and came into his wife's room. Maggie was in her dressing gown, talking to Ruth Dubonnet. He said, "Why aren't you dressed?"

"Why should I be dressed?"

"You know damned well why—the wedding."

"I'm not going to any wedding." She turned to Ruth. "Are you going to any wedding?"

"Don't put me in the middle of this."

Swope thundered, "Your son is getting married today! You will get dressed immediately! And you will be there! And, God damn it, you will smile!"

To Ruth's astonishment, Maggie said meekly, "If you say so, Herbie," and did as she was told.

There were now two Herbert Bayard Swopes and two Margaret Swopes. The two Herberts resembled each other physically and in courtliness of manner. The two Margarets resembled each other in impeccable taste and in determination. The identical names were the bane of editors and columnists and led to endless confusion among the

Swope-watchers: "My God, he's in good shape! I remember reading his paper when I was a kid." "She looks older than she does in the movies." "She must be his second wife. She's years younger than he is."

No doubt the junior Swopes added to this confusion when they named their two children Herbert Bayard Swope III and Margaret Tracy Brooks Swope.

By 1947, Mimi Powell was a very ill old woman. Despite the fact that her mother had embraced Christian Science years before, Maggie insisted that she have the best of medical care, with nurses round the clock to administer it. Swope was as concerned as his wife. Mimi had been a part of his life for thirty-five years, closer to him than his own mother, who had died in 1924. She had helped to raise his children and run his house. It was unbearable to contemplate her not being there, and when she died in June, a great sadness descended upon both Swopes.

Maggie looked at her husband closely. He was sixty-five, getting on toward being an old man; she was still in her fifties. Suddenly she realized with terror that she would probably outlive him. What would become of her then? The children now had lives of their own. She had little faith in the army of regulars, did not believe they would remain once Swope was gone, once the party was over. Who would put up with her then? Who would look after her? Her grip slowly tightened on Bruce. He was for her old age.

The old generation was passing away. Bea was gone. Roosevelt was gone. Woollcott was gone. Broun was gone. So many were gone. There were young people coming along, glad to be part of it all, but it was not the same; the quality and fun were going out of it. They could fill the space but never take the place of what had been. And, poor fools, they did not even know the difference. A legend dies slowly, living on long after the reality starts to fade.

Since 1929 there had been periodic financial problems, but Swope had never thought he'd miss a step in the great high-wire act he often performed; now he was worried. Nobody believed it. Legends don't have the same problems as the average guy; a cat can look at a king, but he damned well knows he isn't one.

Things still happened that removed the tarnish, restored the gleam for a while. That year, 1947, General Eisenhower awarded Swope the Medal for Merit, a special citation given only to those few civilians who had "distinguished themselves by exceptionally meritorious conduct in the performance of outstanding public services to the United States during the period of the recent war."

His legend was inescapable. It even followed him into the men's room at 21. One day as Swope was washing his hands, a man approached him, saying that he worked for a newspaper in a small city. He mentioned the name and said, "I just want to tell the boys in the city room that I actually spoke to Swope."

After using the towel, Swope turned to shake the man's hand. He said in that booming, jovial voice, "I'm delighted you spoke to me. Such a pleasure. I well remember . . ." And then he recalled some little-known fact about the stranger's paper. The man left, bursting with pride over a story he might not write, but would certainly repeat over and over again.

People had begun to rise when Swope entered a room. As he grew older and more concerned with himself, he came to expect it as his due and would grow testy if people did not automatically get up. But it was the extraordinary grace that was most memorable. In '47, Abe Burrows was doing a small radio show from Los Angeles. It was before he came east and met Kaufman, before he wrote *Guys and Dolls* and started his illustrious theatrical career. He received a note from Swope, of whom he naturally had heard but whom he did not personally know, congratulating him on the show and forecasting a great future. It was a small but very meaningful gesture, one that Burrows has emulated ever since.

Maggie's legend was also growing, but graciousness—except as a hostess—was not its strongest point. Bennett and Phyllis Cerf were at the theater one night. Phyllis saw Maggie and waved. Maggie did not acknowledge her. Mrs. Cerf was not disturbed; she simply assumed Maggie had not seen her.

At the time, Cerf was publishing a young writer named Truman Capote, with whom Phyllis would lunch about once a week at the Plaza. Difficult as it may be to imagine, Capote was not very secure at the time, and shortly after the Maggie incident, he told Mrs. Cerf about being snubbed deliberately by Cheryl Crawford, one of the greatest theatrical producers of her day and one of the kindest to young new talent. Mrs. Cerf was certain that it had not been done maliciously, and by way of illustration, she told him of the incident with Maggie Swope.

"That bitch Maggie Swope!" he exclaimed instantly, forgetting all about Miss Crawford. He spent the rest of the lunch cheerfully plotting ways of getting back at a woman he had never met. That was unimportant; all that mattered was that she made a lovely, large target.

When he dropped her off at her house, Mrs. Cerf said, "It's been very amusing, Truman. But you must promise not to do any of these things against Maggie."

He said petulantly, "Well—all right—but you're wrong." A few days later, Capote called and said, "Well, your good friend Maggie Swope—you should have heard her talking about you yesterday."

Mrs. Cerf asked, "What did she say, Truman?"

"She said—'I understand Phyllis Cerf has bought a new house in the country. She likes to go around telling people that George Washington slept there. She's so dumb. It's not even colonial.' "

"That's terribly interesting. Maggie's never been to my house in the country."

"Well—I heard her say it."

"No, you didn't, Truman. You did not!" After hanging up, Mrs. Cerf began to worry about Capote's capacity for causing trouble, and she called Maggie to tell her the whole story. Maggie laughed delightedly and said, "Oh, I'd just love to meet the little so and so."

"Perfect! Join us at the Plaza for lunch. I won't tell Truman you're coming. I'll simply say I've a surprise guest who's longing to meet him."

The women were already at the table when Capote came in all atwitter. He looked at Maggie, and it was obvious that he had never seen her before. Mrs. Cerf said, "Truman, I'd like you to meet Maggie Swope."

He turned on his hostess, his eyes so narrow that he resembled a little Chinese doll with bleached blond hair, and spat out, "Oh—you bitch!"

Maggie and the young writer did become friends, but Swope did not like having Capote around the house. He was simply too old to take on another Alexander Woollcott in another tired velvet suit.

Swope had an enlarged heart from a childhood bout of rheumatic fever, but he did not bother too much about it until Maggie, with her concern over all things pertaining to him, got after him, and he was gradually forced to become more and more aware of the infirmities of his body. Maggie had always been a hypochondriac, sending for doctors in the middle of the night to do nothing more than hold her hand and tell her that there was nothing wrong with her. She began to transfer this to Swope. If he had an extra beat, she would immediately assume it was fibrillation. It did not matter what time it was—she would call the doctor and insist that he drive out to Sands Point.

By that time, they had exhausted their original "house doctor," Alvan Barach, and were on to a new one, Dr. Hylan Bickerman, who was younger and stronger. He recalled, "I'd get into the car and drive out. I'd sort of take care of him, which was then no more than sitting around with

HBS, chairman of the New York State Racing Commission, followed by Lieutenant Governor Charles Poletti, at Belmont Park about 1948.

Eddie Arcaro with HBS at Hialeah in 1940. Eddie's horse bears Swope's name and colors.

(*Below*) HBS entertaining two generals, an admiral, jockey Alfred Robertson, and Miss Madeline Carroll at Belmont Park in 1943.

Drawing of Ferdinand Eberstadt, HBS, John M. Hancock, Fred Searls, Jr., and Bernard M. Baruch.

BERNARD M. BARUCH
597 MADISON AVENUE
NEW YORK 22, N.Y.

January 14, 1947.

Mr. Herbert Bayard Swope,
895 Park Avenue,
New York, N.Y.

My dear Herbert:

Never did a man have such devoted and loyal associates in a public undertaking as those who worked with me on the Atomic Energy Commission of the United Nations.

Each did his work superbly. Each did more than his share. The country - the world - owes you a debt of deep gratitude, but none as great as the one I am under. You made possible the success we have achieved - it was you who made me possible.

My grateful thanks.

Sincerely,

BM.

You are the master!

Berme

P.S. - Because of their attestations to the importance of your work, I am attaching copies of letters from the President of the United States, the Secretary of State and General Marshall.

A letter from Baruch to Swope.

Baruch, Swope, and John Hancock at United Nations Atomic Energy Commission session in 1947.

Swope, Baruch, and Trygve Lie, Secretary-General of the United Nations, in 1947.

Eleanor Roosevelt, Swope, and New York *Post* reporter Ted Poston in March 1950. (*Below*) Swope and Henry Ford II at an Anti-Defamation League Joint Defense Appeal dinner at the Waldorf-Astoria, December 13, 1951.

West German Federal Chancellor Konrad Adenauer and HBS, April 16, 1953.
(*Below*) Charles Wilson, Secretary of Defense and former board chairman of General Motors, with HBS in February 1950.

Margaret Hayes Swope in 1957.

HBS and daughter Jane, 1951.

HBS and Marlene Dietrich in July 1948.

A Christmas card from a friend.

(*Below*) Governor's Day at Jones Beach, August 31, 1957: Commissioner and Mrs. Robert Moses, Governor Averell Harriman, HBS, George Backer, Mrs. Clifton Daniel (Margaret Truman), Clifton Daniel, and Mrs. Harriman.

Program of ceremonies for the dedication of the *World* Room at the Columbia University School of Journalism, May 31, 1961.

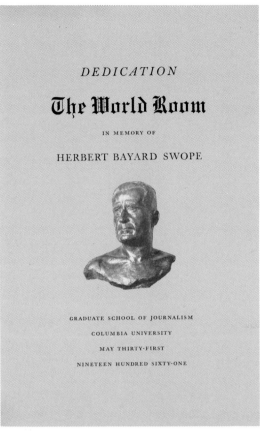

DEDICATION

𝕿𝖍𝖊 𝖂𝖔𝖗𝖑𝖉 𝕽𝖔𝖔𝖒

IN MEMORY OF

HERBERT BAYARD SWOPE

GRADUATE SCHOOL OF JOURNALISM

COLUMBIA UNIVERSITY

MAY THIRTY-FIRST

NINETEEN HUNDRED SIXTY-ONE

(*Below*) Photograph of HBS taken March 11, 1957, with Jenkin Lloyd Jones, president of the American Society of Newspaper Editors (*left*), and William Dwight, president of the American Newspaper Publishers' Association, at a luncheon celebrating the fortieth anniversary of Swope's receipt of the first Pulitzer Prize for reporting. Swope was a Pulitzer Prize juror in 1957.

him. All I had to do was make an appearance, examine him, and reassure her."

The Swope style of living continued very much as it always had, but for Swope the razzle-dazzle was gone. The prodigious feats of memory, the games, the brilliant flights of conversation: it was all sleight of hand, something he did by rote because it was expected of him, a legend in which he was trapped. He wanted out; he wanted to do one more important thing in his life before time ran out.

Nobody really understood; not Maggie, not the family, not his friends, certainly not those who read about him day after day in the newspapers. While he still dreamed of the future, they thought he could rest on his laurels, proud of that supreme accomplishment, the creation of Herbert Bayard Swope, "the most charming extrovert in the Western world." My God, they laughed good-naturedly, what more can he want? He can even collect his social security. But to him the books were not closed; the total had yet to be tallied.

Max Lincoln Schuster, of Simon and Schuster, thought that the time had come for him to sit down and do his memoirs. "What a great book," he enthused. "It's a history of our times. I'd love to publish it."

Swope demurred—memoirs were of the past. "I don't have the time," he said.

His son wanted him to do it, thinking it would be good for him, that it could be an important book. "No, no," he said. "I don't have the time."

"Make the time, God damn it!" Ottie bought him a tape recorder. "Talk into the machine. Tell it as it occurs to you, whenever you have a few minutes to spare."

A few weeks later, Ottie happened to pass his father's study, where he was supposedly working with the recorder. He heard those unmistakable tones: *"This* is Herbert Bayard Swope. This *is* Herbert Bayard Swope. This is *Herbert Bayard Swope."*

My God, Ottie thought, he's doing voice tests! He entered the room. "Pop," he said, "it doesn't matter what you sound like. Only a secretary will hear. Get on with the story."

Swope turned off the machine. He put down the microphone with a sigh. "I can't. Don't you see? It's not finished yet. There isn't enough to tell."

In 1948 Swope broke with Paley and left CBS. Many felt that he did so because his old friend David Sarnoff persuaded him to join NBC and its parent organization, RCA, by making him a more lucrative offer. His son disagreed. The money was not that significantly different. He was on the board at CBS; Sarnoff was not going to put him on the RCA board, and that sort of thing had become increasingly important to Swope as the years passed. He had spent too long working for other men's esteem, and was beginning to guard his own. Ottie felt that he was the reason for the break.

At the time, Ottie was directing prize-winning sports programs for CBS. He quit in a dispute over salary. Without mentioning it to his son, Swope resigned from the CBS board as a gesture of loyalty to his own.

It was so like him. Behind his children's backs, Swope could defend them, put their needs before his own, display pride and love. To their faces he was always the Victorian father, uttering platitudes about duty, honor, position, and behavior. There were never overt displays of the love that he felt so profoundly. It was different with the grandchildren. Both Swope and Maggie were doting, indulgent grandparents; Maggie, in particular, practiced her enticements on the children, but it was a different kind of magic, free of the old possessiveness. It was as if she realized that they were hers not to own, only to love.

On occasion, Swope the lion could still lift up his head and roar throughout the land. One of the things in which he fervently believed was the establishment and maintenance of the State of Israel. He agreed to act as fund raiser for the United Jewish Appeal and managed to get a donation of $100,000 from Baruch. One might think that approaching a fabulously rich Jew for UJA money would be a simple task, but at the time Baruch's attitude toward being identified with Jewish causes was a very strange one. He had refused to appear at a UJA dinner because he did not want to be used as a "bellwether" for the cause.

When funds were badly needed to buy armaments during the Israeli struggle for independence, Swope made an appointment with Baruch for his good friend Dr. Chaim Weizmann. Clare Boothe Luce happened to be waiting in the next room to have lunch with Baruch and overheard the conversation. Weizmann concluded his argument with, "As a Jew, you cannot turn us down."

"I do not think of myself as a Jew," Baruch replied stiffly. "I think of myself as an American."

"Come Armageddon," Weizmann thundered, "you will be counted only as a Jew!"

Most of Swope's Jewish friends were ambivalent about their Jewishness. Janet Stewart recalled being at a dinner party with Robert Lehman, George Backer, Baruch, and some others. It did not occur to her that she was the only gentile at the table until the conversation turned to the question of Jewishness or, more specifically, non-Jewishness. For a good half-hour, they debated about when one stopped being a Jew. Was it when one had a non-Jewish parent, or married a Christian, or formally converted, or simply denied the fact, as August Belmont had done? At length Janet brought the argument to an end by saying, "You are a Jew as long as there's one gentile who thinks you are."

Swope's own musings on the subject were at once more introspective and more profound. When the Jewish Theological Seminary of America was preparing a book about Jewish history and culture, Swope sent a list of questions that reflected his own thoughts on the matter, questions that he hoped the book might answer.

Are the Jews clannish? Do they avoid contractual relationships with others in their community?

Are they more Jewish than they are American? (Does the Jewish interest outweigh the call of the country?)

Have the divisions of Jewry, such as Orthodox, Conservative, Reformed, et al., and the erection of Israel hurt the group?

Has the influence of Jews upon history been recognized?

What other religious or racial body has given the world three such gifts as: 1, Monotheism; 2, The Decalogue; 3, Sabbatarianism? Are these three elements not basic to the present-day civilizations and should they not be more widely emphasized?

In addition to their other difficulties, the Swopes were still struggling with inveterate insomnia. They once spent several weeks at the home of their friends David and Liz Seiferfeld, which was a few blocks away from their own apartment, merely because Swope could sleep uninterruptedly in the bed in the Seiferfeld guest room. It worked for all concerned. The Swopes got in long after their hosts had gone to bed and got up long after they had gone about their business. When they wanted to see them, they made dates in advance, exactly as they would have done had they not been guests in the house.

Swope had taken to prowling the streets at night. He would go for long walks, dropping in at his favorite haunts and staying until closing. The city had changed since he was a young man about town. In those days he would think nothing of strolling through the worst neighborhoods at three or four in the morning. Now Maggie was so fearful of muggers that she sent Roy out to follow him in the car, even if he left at ten in the evening.

One of his favorite stops was Toots Shor's restaurant, a hangout for the kind of crowd Swope enjoyed best: athletes, reporters, politicians, and actors. Toots always tried to keep Swope's regular table reserved for him. If he arrived unexpectedly and it happened to be occupied, Shor would bear down on the people seated at it and shout, "Hey, you bums, you gotta move. Herbert Bayard Swope's here, and this is his table."

When the unmistakable figure entered the room, the reporters gathered at the bar, like Bob Considine and Jimmy Cannon, the great sports columnist, would say, "There's Swope. Let's ask him what he thinks of the fight next week."

"Never mind the fight. I'm a little short of dough. Who's he got in the race tomorrow?"

One evening Shor was sitting with a group of army brass when Swope came in. The generals were certain that the wrong man was about to be appointed Supreme Commander of the Allied Powers in Europe. They felt that the best man for the job was General Lauris Norstad. Shor suggested, "Why don't you talk it over with Swope?"

They invited him over and explained the reasons Norstad should be selected over the other man. Swope said, "It sounds reasonable to me. Let me see what I can do. I'll have to make a few phone calls tomorrow."

The next afternoon, Swope called Shor and said, "Tell your friends not to worry. Norstad's getting the job." And he got it.

On another occasion, a group was holding a dinner for President-elect Dwight D. Eisenhower in the upstairs dining room, and Swope was acting as toastmaster. When they came down after dinner, Swope stopped to talk with some of the gang at the bar. Eisenhower paused at the door and interrupted a conversation to ask, "Where's Herbert? Why isn't he coming with us?"

Shor commented, "I get a lotta guys in my place who claim they know presidents. Swope's one of the few who could claim that presidents know him."

The Barberry Room, presided over by Michael Pearman, was another favored restaurant. Late one evening, Pearman was walking down 52nd Street toward Lexington Avenue to pick up his car, when he saw a solitary figure on the deserted street. It was Swope, who joined him in the stroll to the garage. A few days later, he was amazed to get a note from Swope thanking him for the interesting chat. Restaurateurs generally don't get notes of thanks even from people who have dinner on the house.

Pearman was almost unique among restaurant people in liking the finicky Maggie, despite her irritating habit of sending food back and then not eating what was brought in its place. He found Maggie a wonderfully alert person, always on to the latest vogue, the sort of woman who switched from saying "hep" to "hip" almost as quickly as the kids did.

On the very day that the British-born Pearman was to appear before the Alcoholic Beverage Control Board to get the liquor license required to open Michael's Pub, he received a wire informing him of the death of his mother. He had sixty backers, but nothing seemed important to him except his grief. He was going to chuck the whole thing and fly to the funeral. Maggie heard about it and appeared at his apartment to give him a good talk: "Don't be such a damned fool. Going to the funeral isn't going to help her. She was a sensible woman, and she'd want you to do the sensible thing. Now, you go downtown and get that license."

She was right, of course; it was exactly what his mother would have told him, but he would not have done it without the prodding of a strong and sensible woman. That was Maggie to the end, a lady who could be a no-nonsense broad if the occasion warranted it.

For the Swopes, the year of 1952 was a momentous year. It was the year of their fortieth wedding anniversary, and the Seiferfelds sponsored a sentimental gathering of all the Swopes and their friends. A poem David wrote and had privately printed to mark the event was read aloud by Arlene Francis, Martin Gabel, and Ottie. It was a chronicle of their life together, and Maggie glanced across at Swope with a mixture of the most intense love and fear. He was seventy and beginning to show his years—years, she thought; how many more were there? Fire and ice— that was Maggie at that moment: the cold fear within and the warm love reaching out to him.

Swope's depression was intensified by the death of his secretary, Helen Millar. For over thirty years she had been his right arm, his defender, his guardian, and often his refuge from Maggie's possessiveness, though never in the sexual sense. He turned more and more to his wife for counsel and solace, for he had little heart for the office without Miss Millar's presence. Things piled up. For the first time letters went unanswered. Jock Whitney recommended a young woman who was willing to come in temporarily to help; she had just been released from the women's branch of the armed forces. The temporary assistant, Kathleen Gilmore, stayed on for the rest of his life.

Unlike Miss Millar, Kay got along with Maggie and was soon a weekend guest at Sands Point, as well as a weekday secretary in town.

The enchantment was fading, but there was still enough to entrance the young woman. It was charming to see Marie, the wife of Governor Harriman, fluffing pillows and emptying ashtrays at four in the morning, explaining gaily that she did it because it was the way Maggie liked things.

The arbitrary Maggie grew more conservative with the passing years. She saw no contradiction in respecting the rights of and loving her black servants while still being a bigot; in having liberal, even radical, best friends while, to Drew Pearson's utter amazement, being a McCarthyite. Great causes were Swope's concern, and what had they gotten for him?—certainly not the honors she felt that he deserved. They had failed him when he needed them most, in his old age, and she had bitterly turned against them.

Dr. Bickerman put her in the hospital for an operation for an enlarged ulcer. Maggie in the hospital was not like other people in the hospital; her fastidiousness went with her. Mae and Lydia appeared to redecorate the room with her own things. They took complete charge, down to bringing fresh linen from home every day. Despite the fact that Doctor's Hospital was famous for being the only hospital with a good cook, Maggie's meals were brought from home or the Colony Restaurant. The flowers were not simply put into a hospital vase, but were meticulously arranged under the patient's supervision. The drinks Mae passed around to visitors were served in Maggie's own Baccarat glasses; the hors d'oeuvres were prepared at home and brought in on silver trays; the cocktail napkins were her best Irish linen.

While the hospital staff was being crushed by the weight of Maggie's whims, Swope was having a renaissance. He was positively thriving on being in command again, issuing the orders and seeing that all of her wishes were granted.

When she returned home, the purposefulness that her illness had imposed upon his days was over, and the depression returned. Maggie insisted later that he had suffered a nervous breakdown, but his physician denied it. Dr. Bickerman said:

> It was not an actual breakdown at all. He was only getting a little more hypochondriacal, a little more anxious; it's what we would call an anxiety state—a neurosis. He was still able to function, still able to do all of the things he wanted to do. But he required a little more reassurance. He was a bit more aware of his failings. I think the reason she called it a nervous breakdown was that he became a little irritable with her. He would come to my office. He still had his sense of humor. His reflexes were appropriate. It couldn't be termed a

nervous breakdown. To prove this point, I sent him to a psychiatrist, who concurred with me. He prescribed some tranquilizers. Swope would ask constantly—was this going to hurt his mind—was it going to interfere with his thinking capacity? And I had to reassure him and say, "No, this is simply to relax you and help you sleep."

His faculties were indeed not impaired. He and Farley were able to guarantee delivery of the New York delegates to Adlai Stevenson at the '52 convention—the one that would nominate him as the Democratic candidate for president.

There were still the occasional gratifying moments, one of the more memorable being a testimonial dinner given in his honor by the National Conference of Christians and Jews. He listened to speech after speech extolling his virtues to the sky. When it came time for him to reply, his marvelous sense of timing told him that a one-minute speech would be better than a longer one, and he put the notes he had prepared out of his mind. He rose and said, "You know, after hearing all these speeches, I should be embalmed, because obviously I'm no longer alive. Thank you for the eulogy. All I can say to you tonight is that I cannot give you a formula for success. I can give you one for failure. Try to please everybody."

He sat down to ringing applause. The remark was widely quoted in the press. One morning, he received a check for fifteen dollars in the mail from the *Reader's Digest* for the use of the line in the magazine. It deserved better than that. From his own point of view, it was so heartbreakingly autobiographical. He had tried to please everybody and, although he had succeeded most of the time, all he felt at the moment was a sense of personal failure and utter isolation.

That sense of aloneness was becoming apparent to those who loved him. Each year, he would go to the Silurian's Dinner for old-timers who had been reporters at least thirty-five years before. Swope, of course, would always be invited to sit on the dais. Frank Sullivan and Russel Crouse would go together and sit at a table out front. Sullivan recalled one dinner:

He looked forlorn. There was someone next to him he obviously wasn't interested in, and he was just sitting there staring into space. He shouldn't have been up there. He should have been out front with his boys. That's where he belonged. And Crouse said, "Let's go up and get him to come down here." I forget which one of us went up—he came down like a shot. So after that we three would always have a date to go together. He never wanted to sit on that dais. We'd go together and sit by ourselves. I remember one of the last times—he grabbed my arm and he said, "You know—I'm still a newspaperman at heart. I'd rather be remembered as a good reporter than anything else in the world."

Maggie, Jr., as many called her, and Ottie had followed their careers to Hollywood and were both successful in films, he as a director-producer and she as an actress; Maggie had an Academy nomination for *Blackboard Jungle*. Their two children, Rusty and Tracy, were with them on the Coast, all of which doubtless added to the senior Swopes' loneliness.

On Ottie's visits home, he found things radically changed. His father had become fixated on the cost of things; he now insisted that there never be more than eight guests in the house, when not five years before, thirty or forty had been the norm. He would come into the dining room, and one could see him silently counting. If there were more than eight, the grumbling would begin. More often than not, Maggie, Bruce, and he would have dinner on trays in the library and spend the night watching television. Ottie couldn't stand it. He shouted, "You're worrying yourself sick about the cost of things—and yet you keep ten servants whom you feed and house for this—trays in the library. It's insane."

Swope looked up quizzically. Where would they go, these people who had been with him all these years? This was the only home they knew. He couldn't just pension them off and send them to live out their days in squalid rooms in ghettos. This was where they belonged, and this was where they would remain for as long as he could keep them. The years of devotion meant something. You didn't throw people out like unwanted refuse simply because you were getting old and they were getting old and things were getting rough.

He would go to the races every day and afterward go over to Max Hirsch's cottage at Belmont. Hirsch was one of the great old trainers and had worked for the Schwartz brothers, Rothstein, and Baruch. They were of an age, Swope and Hirsch, and they would sit for hours, Hirsch's dog curled up in Swope's lap, swapping tales about the old days, the good times, and laughing again at stories they had laughed at for years. Then Swope would get up and return to Sands Point, the trays in the library, and the television set that neither spoke nor listened to him, but droned on about a world in which he was becoming a supernumerary.

Bruce was all that remained for Maggie, her hope for the future, but Bruce was beginning to drink too much, to feel that he had to make a break or his life would be over at age forty-nine. That year, 1955, he visited Ottie and Maggie Hayes Swope on the Coast. He talked of staying out there and opening an agency. They encouraged him. The town was booming; he would do well with all the television shows hiring actors by the score. But Bruce knew that it was only talk, that it was already too late, and he returned to that expensive but oh-so-comfortable easy chair. A few months later, he dropped dead of heart failure, and' Maggie Swope's last hope died with him.

The two of them had nothing left to do but grow ill together. Charting their temperatures and exchanging symptoms, most of them psychosomatic, replaced games as a major pastime in the Swope house. In early '57 he began to have certain alarming symptoms that the doctors could not ignore. He was in and out of hospitals for the G.I. series, for every kind of test. They could find nothing, but the pain persisted.

In the autumn of that year, Billy Harbach, who had become a television producer and was living on the West Coast, happened to be in town, and Maggie invited him out to Sands Point. It all looked the same, the perfection of service and appointment; even Maggie was up to the same old tricks. She said heartily, "I don't know why you boys want to work out there, when you could stay here and have fun."

Then Herbert looked out the window at the turning leaves. "Autumn already," he said. "I wonder if there'll be another summer." And Harbach knew that it was not the same, would never again be the same.

The television viewing was largely replaced by a late-blossoming interest in classical music. It was something different in his life. Swope had always loved Broadway theater music and had appreciated the opera more as a social occasion than as a musical performance. Now he would sit for hours, lost in the majestic solemnities of Bach and Schumann. His sister-in-law Phyllis would sometimes come upon him during these rapt moments. Phyllis was a devout Catholic, and he would take her hand and say, "Oh, if I only had your faith—if I only had some faith—I could believe that there was something more—" and the music would close in upon him again.

At the beginning of 1958, he received a call from Mayor Robert F. Wagner, asking whether he would be interested in being New York City's first Commissioner of Human Rights. It was his sort of thing. He had a long history of fighting for the rights of minorities. Wagner recalled,

He would have been a terrific man at that. I got his consent, and we were all set. This problem was really beginning to emerge. It was there. It was latent. But I think he realized it. He was good at sensing these things. He had that great newspaperman's ablity to sense what was happening. He also had that presence to pull people together and get the respect of both sides. It was the first appointment of its type. . . the first independent agency or commission with legal status, a staff, the authority to bring people in for investigation and so on. He had the prestige to get it going. Everybody knew him. Everybody I knew had high regard for him.

It would be better than any medicine, Swope thought; the pain would go away once he had something important to do again. This could be that last great contribution, the thing he had been seeking, and it would be for the city he loved more than any other place on earth.

But it was not the great panacea after all, and the pain did not depart. He knew then that it would never go. It was too late. There was finally no avoiding what it really was, and he asked the doctors to tell nobody. Regretfully, he called Wagner and resigned from the job. He made excuses in the old gruff way: "I'm not a man for commissions or that sort of thing. I like to hunt alone."

Just before entering the hospital, he went to the races for the last time. It was a warm spring afternoon, but the sun did not touch him. He sat huddled in his camel's-hair coat, the sporty snap-brim hat pulled down at a jaunty angle, a pale smile upon his face. And they came by his box, the stream of old friends—Baruch, Jock Whitney, Alfred Vanderbilt, Joan Payson—to say hello, or good luck, or see you soon, or good-by, or whatever it was; the words did not matter: a final greeting or adieu, homage to a unique old man.

Maggie called her son on the Coast and told him that she thought he had better come to New York immediately. Swope was in the hospital again, and she was very worried. He had first entered it in April for what had been described as a hernia operation. Actually it had been an exploratory operation. Suspecting cancer, they took samples from a fairly extensive growth in his stomach to test for malignancy. He was sent home. Two months later he was readmitted for what was called diverticulitis. They removed a very large cancer from his stomach. The operation was a success in that they got all of it, but it was the sort of malignancy that would recur in a year or two. Whether Maggie actually knew the facts would be difficult to say. All that can be ascertained is that she never told anybody, that it was anything but the announced ailments.

Roy was at the airport to meet Ottie, with instructions to bring him to

Sands Point to meet his mother, but Ottie insisted that he be taken directly to the hospital. Something told him to ignore his mother's order.

When he got to Swope's room, Maggie was already there. The doctor had telephoned that she had better come right down. Swope had developed a pulmonary edema, and the prognosis was bad. When Ottie leaned over to look at Swope, his father took his hand weakly and smiled. That was all.

On June 20, 1958, Herbert Bayard Swope died. The doctor later told the family that the operation had been a success, but that pneumonia had set in and his heart could not stand the strain. It was his heart, then, that was the official cause of death.

The funeral services were held at Sands Point. Father George Ford, a close friend and a co-worker at Freedom House, read the Lord's Prayer, risking possible excommunication by officiating at the interment of a non-Catholic. Swope had expressed a wish for a clergyman who was "free from hypocrisy and false religion." The good and liberal priest was as close to that description as anybody the family knew.

Martin Gabel recited W. E. Henley's "Invictus," and the eulogies were given by Robert Moses and Baruch. There were other services. His Freedom House colleagues held a special memorial in the building he was so largely responsible for obtaining for them. The head of Columbia University settled for all time the value of his contribution to the Pulitzer paper. At the university, there is a room called the *World* Room, containing the stained-glass window that had once been in the lobby of the building on Park Row. On May 31, 1961, three years after his death, the room was dedicated as a memorial to Herbert Bayard Swope. Father Ford delivered the invocation; the address was given by Baruch; and John Wheeler was present as chairman of the fund that raised the money to refurbish the room. The contributors ranged across an amazing spectrum of friends of Swope, from Harpo Marx to Cardinal Spellman, including a Supreme Court justice, several ambassadors, a former heavyweight champion of the world, several publishers, the most successful Broadway playwrights, producers and composers of the period, a horse trainer, and the best names in the Social Register.

Racing Commissioner Swope's battles with entrenched interests over bettering the conditions of the track workers and the ordinary fans were inversely commemorated when he was deliberately left out of a mural put up in the clubhouse at Aqueduct after his death. It was a composite portrait of the most prominent people in racing since 1890. When his son pointed this out in a series of calls and letters to trainers, owners, and sportswriters, there was such an uproar from his supporters that he had to be painted into the picture. Even after his death, Swope was a hard man to ignore.

Maggie Swope outlived her husband by nine years. She continued to send out the annual editions of the *World Almanac* as Christmas gifts, just as her husband had done. But mostly she simply withdrew, keeping around her a few of her old servants and Kay Gilmore, who went from being Swope's secretary to being her companion until she died. The temporary office helper spent fifteen years in the service of the Swope family.

For a while Maggie thought of moving down to Sands Point, but the house was too large and filled with ghosts. She sold it in 1962.

The sale of the furnishings was supervised by her daughter-in-law, who did so well for her that Maggie, acerbic to the end, told Ottie, "I have to admit that I admire your wife. I don't always like her—but I admire her."

The younger Maggie's feelings about her mother-in-law might have been expressed in exactly the same words.

She continued to give dinner parties at first, but soon lost interest in them. Without Swope, they were meaningless to her. As her rheumatoid arthritis intensified, she took to her bed, with her television and her telephone. She was not easy to get along with. People would come to see her, and she would not bother to speak to them. The television was more interesting. Except for the faithful few, like Alice Guinzberg, Edna Ferber, Terry Lewis Robinson, and Ralph Strain, they gradually stopped coming by. Many never bothered, once Swope was no longer around. When she thought about it, she was bitter. But most of the time she did not bother to think about it. They never had mattered that much to her. She had never been fooled by the crowd of hangers-on, but had known their worth, down to the last decimal point, from the beginning. Oh, some, some had hurt her, like the actress who had fawned over her when she was an unknown and had never bothered to phone once she became a famous television personality. She reciprocated; the caustic tongue retained its sharpness. But for the most part, they had simply been an audience for Swope—accessories no more important than his velvet dinner jackets and silk shirts—less, for the clothes had worn better.

She was bored, tired of living, and frightened of dying. She didn't even bother to try to possess people. Who was worth having once she'd lost Swope? Her son would bring her a book written by a friend. It would remain on her night table for weeks. "Don't you intend to finish that book?" he would ask.

"I certainly do," she would reply, "once I start it."

He would call every day and tell her she sounded fine; she would answer, "Oh, you fool, don't you know the voice is the last to go?"

Toward the end, the daily visits of her family were almost her only interest. She entered Columbia Presbyterian Medical Center, where she died on November 24, 1967. There was a funeral service at Frank Campbell's. Many who had forgotten she was alive remembered she had died long enough to attend. The eulogy was delivered by David Sarnoff. Everybody agreed that it was the warmest speech he had ever made. It was for Maggie, and so it was for Herbert, too. For they were, after all, inseparable.

At the time of her death, Frank Sullivan was living in Saratoga. Being an invalid himself, he could not get down. He wrote to Ottie:

> When I read about your mother it made me feel like the last guest at the party, who lingers long after the others have gone and can't think of a way to say Good Night. I could write a volume about my own pleasant memories of Maggie and Swope and that wonderful, gay house in Great Neck. For days afterward the memories kept crowding in, all of them fond.

He went on to reminisce at great length, and then closed with:

> She was a girl of uncommon fortitude. She had to be to be married to and keep up with Swope, and to preside over that establishment and cope with us guests.
>
> Well, I said I could write a book about the Swopes, and I seem to have done it, almost. This is not a letter of condolence. At seventy-five, I don't write them anymore, and I doubt that you would welcome any conventional, doleful letter. Consider this a love letter to the memory of two wonderful people whom I'll always cherish. I can't bring myself to believe that I won't see them again, somewhere, somehow.

Of all the many tributes that were paid to Swope before and after his death, the words of Gene Fowler, his old friend from the newspaper days, were the ones he probably would have cherished most:

> Swope, in the opinion of many journalists, was one of the greatest newspapermen of this century. He and I were close friends over the years. We corresponded frequently until just before his death. . . .
>
> In passing, I have to smile at Swope's way of sometimes addressing me as "Young Gene" in his letters. One facet of his enormous

charm was his whimsical manner of regarding old, old friends in terms of the days of the green bay tree. To his mind, the young knights of Park Row still rode out with pomp and circumstance to the tournaments of world news. He refused to admit that the old crusades were forgotten, or that the once stout lances now lay broken in the dust and rubble of the long ago.

Atomic Energy Commr – 267 – Baruch Plan – 269

HBS invented "cold war" for Baruch – 270 – future?

possessive Maggie. Bruce – Ortho – 272 – hard Phu wn. 273

Capote a Woolcott – 272 ⌐ for her old age – 274 – but he

                                                      drew with – 275

HBS leaves CBS – Nov. HBS jr. resig – 278

Maggie – a bigot & McCarthy ite 282

"Try to please everybody" – Sulzberger –283

"Remembered as a good reporter – 284 ⟩

d. June 20, 1958 – 287

Arthur Frances ? – 288

good for Foster – 290

The Department of English

presents

Dr. Anne Hudson

of

The University of Oxford

speaking on

Wednesday, April 19th

at 4 p.m.

First Floor Conference Room
Dietrich Library

BIBLIOGRAPHY

Abbott, George. *Mr. Abbott.* New York: Random House, 1963.

Adams, Franklin P. *The Diary of Our Own Samuel Pepys,* 2 vols. New York: Simon & Schuster, 1935.

————. *By and Large.* New York: Doubleday & Co., 1914.

————. *F.P.A. Book of Quotations.* New York: Funk & Wagnalls, 1952.

————. *Half a Loaf.* New York: Doubleday & Co., 1927.

————. *In Other Words.* New York: Doubleday & Co., 1912.

————. *Nods and Becks.* New York: Whitlesey House, 1944.

————. *Overset.* New York: Doubleday & Co., 1922.

————. *Something Else Again.* New York: Doubleday & Co., 1920.

————. *So Much Velvet.* New York: Doubleday & Co., 1924.

————. *So There!* New York: Doubleday & Co., 1923.

Adams, Samuel Hopkins. *A. Woollcott, His Life and His World.* New York: Reynal & Hitchcock, 1945.

————. *The American Heritage History of the 20's and 30's.* New York: American Heritage Publishing Co., 1970.

American Racehorses of 1936. The Sagamore Press, 1937.

Amory, Cleveland. *The Last Resorts.* New York: Harper & Bros., 1952.

Annals of America, vols. 11–17. Chicago: Encyclopaedia Britannica, Inc., 1968.

Baragwanath, John. *A Good Time Was Had by All.* New York: Appleton-Century-Crofts, Inc., 1962.

Barrett, James W. *The World, the Flesh, and Messrs. Pulitzer.* New York: Vanguard Press, 1931.

————. *Joseph Pulitzer and His World.* New York: Vanguard Press, 1941.

————, ed. *The End of the World.* New York: Harper & Bros., 1931.

Barrymore, Ethel. *Memories.* New York: Harper & Bros., 1955.

Barrymore, John. *Confessions of an Actor.* Indianapolis/New York: Bobbs-Merrill, 1926.

Baruch, Bernard M. *Baruch: My Own Story*. New York: Henry Holt & Co., 1957.

———. *The Public Years*. New York: Holt, Rinehart and Winston, 1960.

Blum, Daniel. *Great Stars of the American Stage*. New York: Greenberg, 1952.

———. *A Pictorial History of the American Theatre*. New York: Crown Publishers, 1969.

Boylan, James. *The World and the 20's*. New York: Dial Press, 1973.

Broun, Heywood. *The Boy Grows Older*. New York: G. P. Putnam, 1922.

———. *Gandle Follows His Nose*. New York: G. P. Putnam, 1926.

———. *It Seems to Me*. New York: Harcourt, Brace, 1935.

———. *Pieces of Hate and Other Enthusiasms*. New York: G. P. Putnam, 1922.

———. *Sitting on the World*. New York: G. P. Putnam, 1924.

Brown, John Mason. *The Worlds of Robert E. Sherwood*. New York: Harper & Row, 1962.

Burns, James MacGregor. *Roosevelt: The Lion and the Fox*. New York: Harcourt, Brace, 1956.

"Cafe Society (The Yankee Doodle Salon)." *Fortune,* December 1937.

Caro, Robert A. *The Power Broker*. New York: Alfred A. Knopf, Inc., 1974.

Case, Frank. *Tales of a Wayward Inn*. New York: Frederick A. Stokes Co., 1938.

Cerf, Bennett. *Try and Stop Me*. New York: Simon & Schuster, 1944.

Coit, Margaret L. *Mr. Baruch*. Boston: Houghton Mifflin, 1957.

Connelly, Marc. *Voices Off Stage*. New York: Holt, Rinehart and Winston, 1968.

Courtney, Marguerite. *Laurette*. New York: Rinehart & Co., 1955.

Coward, Noel. *Present Indicative*. New York: Doubleday & Co., 1937.

Dietz, Howard. *Dancing in the Dark*. New York: Quadrangle, 1975.

Eels, George. *Hedda and Louella*. New York: G. P. Putnam's Sons, 1972.

Eisenstaedt, Alfred. *Witness to Our Time*. New York: Viking Press, 1966.

Elder, Donald. *Ring Lardner*. New York: Doubleday & Co., 1956.

Encyclopaedia Britannica. Chicago: Encyclopaedia Britannica, Inc., 1973.

Ernst, Morris. *The Best Is Yet*. New York: Harper & Bros., 1945.

Farley, James A. *Jim Farley's Story*. New York: McGraw-Hill Book Co., 1948.

Ferber, Edna. *A Kind of Magic*. New York: Doubleday & Co., 1963.

———. *A Peculiar Treasure*. New York: Doubleday & Co., 1960.

Flynn, Edward J. *You're the Boss*. New York: Viking Press, 1947.

Fowler, Gene. *Beau James*. New York: Viking Press, 1947.

———. *Goodnight, Sweet Prince*. New York: Viking Press, 1944.

———. *Skyline*. New York: Viking Press, 1961.

Freidel, Frank Burt, Jr. *Franklin D. Roosevelt: The Ordeal*. Boston: Little, Brown and Co., 1954.

Gelb, Arthur and Barbara. *O'Neill*. New York: Harper & Bros., 1960.

Gerard, James W. *My First Eighty-Three Years in America*. New York: Doubleday & Co., 1951.

Gill, Brendan. *Here at the New Yorker*. New York: Random House, 1975.

Gordon, Ruth. *Myself Among Others*. New York: Atheneum, 1971.

──────. *My Story*. New York: Harper & Row, 1976.

Gottlieb, Polly Rose. *The Nine Lives of Billy Rose*. New York: Crown Publishers, 1968.

Grant, Jane. *Ross, the New Yorker, and Me*. New York: William Morrow & Co.,
1968.

Halliwell, Leslie. *The Filmgoer's Companion*. New York: Avon, 1971.

──────. *The Vicious Circle*. New York: Rinehart & Co., 1951.

Harriman, Margaret Case. *Blessed Are the Debonair*. New York: Rinehart &
Co., 1956.

Hart, Moss. *Act One*. New York: Random House, 1959.

Hayes, Helen. *On Reflection*. New York: M. Evans & Co., 1968.

Hecht, Ben. *Charlie*. New York: Harper & Bros., 1957.

──────. *A Child of the Century*. New York: Simon & Schuster, 1954.

Hohenberg, John. *Foreign Correspondence: The Great Reporters in Their
Time*. New York: Columbia University Press, 1964.

──────. *The Pulitzer Prizes*. New York: Columbia University Press, 1974.

Howard, Leslie Ruth. *A Quite Remarkable Father*. New York; Harcourt,
Brace, 1959.

Hoyt, Edwin P. *Alexander Woollcott: The Man Who Came to Dinner*. New
York: Abelard-Schuman, 1968.

Hutchens, John K., and George Oppenheimer. *The Best in the World*. New
York: Viking Press, 1973.

Kahn, E. J. *The World of Swope*. New York: Simon & Schuster, 1965.

Kaplan, Justin. *Lincoln Steffens*. New York: Simon & Schuster, 1974.

Katcher, Leo. *The Big Bankroll: The Life and Times of Arnold Rothstein*. New
York: Harper & Bros., 1959.

Kaufman, Beatrice, and Joseph Hennessey, eds. *The Letters of Alexander
Woollcott*. New York: Viking Press, 1944.

Kaufman, George S., and Edna Ferber. *The Royal Family*. New York: Doubleday, Doran, 1928.

──────, and Moss Hart. *Six Plays*. New York: The Modern Library, 1958.

Keats, John. *You Might As Well Live*. New York: Simon & Schuster, 1970.

Kirk, Donald. "Herbert Bayard Swope." Master's thesis, Princeton University,
1959.

Kouwenhoven, John. *The Columbia Historical Portrait of New York*. New
York: Doubleday & Co., 1953.

Kramer, Dale. *Heywood Broun: A Biographical Portrait*. Foreword by Herbert
Bayard Swope. New York: A. A. Wynn, 1949.

──────. *Ross and the New Yorker*. New York: Doubleday & Co., 1951.

Krock, Arthur. *Memoirs*. New York: Funk & Wagnalls, 1968.

Lardner, Ring, Jr. *The Lardners*. New York: Harper & Row, 1976.

Lash, Thomas. *Eleanor and Franklin*. New York: W. W. Norton, 1971.

————. *Eleanor: The Years Alone*. New York: W. W. Norton, 1973.

Levant, Oscar. *The Memoirs of an Amnesiac*. New York: G. P. Putnam's Sons, 1965.

————. *A Smattering of Ignorance*. New York: Doubleday, Doran, 1940.

————. *The Unimportance of Being Oscar*. New York: G. P. Putnam's Sons, 1968.

Lewis, Therese. "The World Well Lost." *Town & Country,* March 1938.

Linton, Calvin D., ed. *The Bicentennial Almanac*. New York: Thomas Nelson, 1976.

Loos, Anita. *A Girl Like I*. New York: Viking Press, 1966.

Loth, David. *Swope of G.E.* New York: Simon & Schuster, 1968.

Maney, Richard. *Fanfare*. New York: Harper & Bros., 1957.

Martin, John Bartlow. *Adlai Stevenson of Illinois*. New York: Doubleday & Co., 1976.

Marx, Harpo, with Rowland Barber. *Harpo Speaks!* New York: Bernard Geis, 1961.

Maxtone-Graham, John. *The Only Way to Cross*. New York: Macmillan, 1972.

Maxwell, Elsa. *The Celebrity Circus*. New York: Appleton-Century-Crofts, 1963.

————. *R.S.V.P.: Elsa Maxwell's Own Story*. Boston: Little, Brown & Co., 1954.

Meredith, Scott. *George S. Kaufman and His Friends*. New York: Doubleday & Co., 1974.

Metz, Robert. *CBS: Reflections in a Bloodshot Eye*. Chicago: Playboy Press, 1975.

Mitchell, Broadus. *Depression Decade*. New York: Holt, Rinehart, 1966.

Mizener, Arthur. *The Far Side of Paradise*. Boston: Houghton Mifflin, 1949.

Moley, Raymond. *After Seven Years*. New York: Harper & Bros., 1939.

Morris, Richard B., and Graham W. Irwin. *Harper Encyclopedia of the Modern World*. New York: Harper & Row, 1970.

Murphy, Lawrence, ed. *An Introduction to Journalism*. New York: Thomas Nelson, 1930.

Nicolson, Harold. *Peacemaking: 1919*. Boston: Houghton Mifflin, 1933.

O'Connor, Richard. *Heywood Broun*. New York: G. P. Putnam's Sons, 1975.

Oppenheimer, George. *Frank Sullivan Through the Looking Glass*. New York: Doubleday & Co., 1970.

Parker, Dorothy. *The Portable Dorothy Parker*. New York: Viking Press, 1946.

Perkins, Frances. *The Roosevelt I Knew*. New York: Viking Press, 1946.

Phillips, Cabell. *Decade of Triumph and Trouble*. New York: Macmillan, 1975.

————. *From the Crash to the Blitz*. New York: Macmillan, 1970.

Potter, Jeffrey. *Men, Money, and Magic*. New York: Coward, McCann & Geoghegan, 1976.

Rogers, Cleveland. *Robert Moses: Builder of Democracy*. New York: Henry Holt & Co., 1952.

Roosevelt, Elliot, ed. *FDR: His Personal Letters 1928–1945*, 2 vols. New York: Duell, Sloan & Pierce, 1950.

Rosenbloom, Morris. *Peace Through Strength*. New York: Farrar, Straus and Young, 1953.

Schlesinger, Arthur M., Jr. *The Coming of the New Deal*. Boston: Houghton Mifflin, 1958.

Seitz, Don C. *Joseph Pulitzer: His Life & Letters*. New York: Simon & Schuster, 1924.

Shadegg, Stephen. *Clare Boothe Luce*. New York: Simon & Schuster, 1970.

Shaw, Charles G. *The Low-Down*. New York: Henry Holt & Co., 1928.

Sheridan, Clare. *American Diary*. London: Jonathan Cape, 1922.

———. *In Many Places*. London: Jonathan Cape, 1923.

Sherwood, Robert E. *Roosevelt and Hopkins*. New York: Harper & Bros., 1948.

———. *There Shall Be No Night*. New York: Charles Scribner's Sons, 1940.

Skinner, Cornelia Otis. *Life with Lindsay and Crouse*. Boston: Houghton Mifflin, 1976.

Snyder, Louis L., and Richard B. Morris, eds. *A Treasury of Great Reporting*. Preface by Herbert Bayard Swope. New York: Crown Publishers, 1949.

Sobol, Louis. *The Longest Street*. New York: Crown Publishers, 1968.

Steffens, Lincoln. *The Autobiography of Lincoln Steffens*. New York: Harcourt, Brace, 1931.

Swanberg, W. A. *Citizen Hearst*. New York: Charles Scribner's Sons, 1961.

———. *Luce and His Empire*. New York: Charles Scribner's Sons, 1975.

Swope, Herbert Bayard. "Aim of the New York World." In *Newsmen Speak*, Edmond Coblentz, ed. Berkeley: University of California Press, 1954.

———. *Inside the German Empire*. New York: Century Co., 1917.

———. *Journalism: An Instrument of Civilization*. Phi Beta Kappa address. Geneva, N.Y.: Hobart College, 1924.

Talese, Gay. *The Kingdom and the Power*. New York: World Publishing, 1969.

Talmey, Allene. "First Nighter." *Stage*, January 1935.

Tebel, John. *The Life and Good Times of William Randolph Hearst*. New York: E. P. Dutton, 1952.

Teichmann, Howard. *George S. Kaufman: An Intimate Portrait*. New York: Atheneum, 1972.

———. *Smart Aleck*. New York: William Morrow, 1976.

Thurber, James. *The Years with Ross*. Boston: Little, Brown and Co., 1958.

———, and Elliott Nugent. *The Male Animal*. New York: Samuel French, 1941.

Turnbull, Andrew. *Scott Fitzgerald*. New York: Charles Scribner's Sons, 1975.

Walker, Stanley. "Symphony in Brass." *Saturday Evening Post,* June 4, 1938.

Warner, Emily Smith. *The Happy Warrior: A Biography of My Father.* New York: Doubleday & Co., 1956.

Whalen, Richard J. *The Founding Father.* New York: New American Library, 1964.

Wheeler, John N. *I've Got News for You*. New York: E. P. Dutton, 1961.

Woollcott, Alexander. *Going to Pieces*. New York: G. P. Putnam's Sons, 1928.

————. *The Story of Irving Berlin*. New York: G. P. Putnam's Sons, 1925.

INDEX

297